RELIGION AND CULTURE

Essays in Honor of Paul Tillich

~~~~~~

Edited by

Walter Leibrecht

Essay Index Reprint Series

BOOKS FOR LIBRARIES PRESS

FREEPORT, NEW YORK

Reprinted 1972 by arrangement with
Harper & Row, Publishers, Inc.

Grateful acknowledgment is made to *The Christian Scholar* for permission to reprint "The Spiritual Significance of the United Nations" by Charles Malik, which originally appeared in the issue of March, 1955, Vol. 38, No. 1, pp. 19–30; and to Evangelischer Verlag A. G. Zollikon-Zurich for permission to publish, in English translation, *Wolfgang Amadeus Mozart, 1756–1956*, by Karl Barth.

Frontispiece photograph by Rosemarie Clausen

Library of Congress Cataloging in Publication Data

Leibrecht, Walter, ed.
  Religion and culture.

  (Essay index reprint series)
  Bibliography: p.
  1. Theology--Addresses, essays, lectures. 2. Civilization, Modern--Addresses, essays, lectures. I. Tillich, Paul, 1886-1965. II. Title.
BR50.L38 1972   230   78-167376
ISBN 0-8369-2558-0

PRINTED IN THE UNITED STATES OF AMERICA
BY
NEW WORLD BOOK MANUFACTURING CO., INC.
HALLANDALE, FLORIDA 33009

THIS VOLUME IS PUBLISHED IN HONOR OF

Paul Tillich

PHILOSOPHER AND THEOLOGIAN

Contents

~~~~~~~~~~~~~~~~~~~~~~~~~~~~~~~~~ *Editor's Preface*

There was an enthusiastic response when I wrote, some time ago, to a number of Paul Tillich's friends—and to some of those with whom he has crossed swords in philosophical and theological arguments—telling them about the plan to publish a volume in his honor. Among the many letters which encouraged me in this undertaking were those from Albert Schweitzer, Martin Buber, T. S. Eliot, Jacques Maritain, W. H. Auden and Arnold Toynbee, as well as the distinguished contributors in this volume. Many of Tillich's former and present students, who love and esteem him both as a scholar and as a man, also urged that this plan be carried out. Excellent articles were sent in by exponents of the most varied theological viewpoints; unfortunately, it was impossible to publish them all in this volume, and it was very difficult to make the necessary choices.

This volume as a whole is offered as an expression of deep gratitude and esteem to a great spirit, by those who, with their whole generation, have been inspired and stimulated by his thought.

Let me express here my sincere appreciation to all those who, by contributing, translating, or other effort, have made this volume possible. In particular I would like to express my gratitude to Professor James Luther Adams for his kind advice and help. I gladly acknowledge the valuable aid of Professor Benjamin Nelson of Hofstra College and Harper & Brothers in the critical stages of preparing this work for the press. The nature and diversity of the articles—which express, nonetheless, a common concern—suggest the wide horizons of Tillich's world, geographically as well as intellectually and spiritually. Tillich has bridged with a powerful intellectual effort the distance between the spiritual world of the Continent and that of America—and has reached even to Oriental cultures, where many a philosopher of Asia has acknowledged himself drawn to Tillich's thought and faith. It is true ecumenicity which makes the present volume memorable in its honoring of Paul Tillich.

The Evanston Institute   WALTER LEIBRECHT
For Ecumenical Studies
Evanston, Illinois

ix

A Curriculum Vitae

Paul Tillich was born in 1886 in Starzeddel, Germany, in the province of Brandenburg. He studied at several European universities including the Universities of Berlin, Halle and Breslau from 1904 to 1912, receiving his degree of Doctor of Philosophy in 1911 from the University of Breslau and the Licentiate of Theology from the University of Halle in 1912. In 1914 he joined the army as a war chaplain, serving until 1918. From 1919 to 1924 he was *Privatdozent* of Theology at the University of Berlin, 1924–1925 Professor of Theology at the University of Marburg, 1925–1929 Professor of Theology in Dresden and Leipzig. In 1929 he accepted a call as Professor of Philosophy at the University of Frankfurt.

As an outspoken critic of Nazism he was compelled to leave Germany after the rise of Hitler, and in 1933 he came to America at the invitation of Union Theological Seminary.

From 1933 to 1955 he was Professor of Philosophical Theology at Union Theological Seminary and at Columbia University. He received and accepted the call as University Professor at Harvard in 1954, starting his lecturing there in September, 1955. During several summers since the end of World War II he has returned to Germany to lecture at the Universities of Hamburg and Berlin.

Paul Tillich has received honorary degrees from ten different American universities, as well as special doctoral awards from the Universities of Halle, Berlin and Glasgow. Among other honors he has recently received are the Phi Beta Kappa honorary membership, the *Grosse Verdienstkreuz*—the highest German order—from the President of the West German Republic, the Goethe Medal of the City of Frankfurt in 1956 and the Goethe prize from the City of Hamburg in 1958.

Part I
Introduction: Transition to the Twentieth Century

The Life and Mind of Paul Tillich

BY WALTER LEIBRECHT

When Paul Tillich preaches a sermon, he violates all the rules of homiletics—but the audience is spellbound, carried with compelling force into a stream of thought. The listener has only one option, to become an active partner in thinking through a problem which concerns his own existence. The reason for this is not any particular oratorical technique. It is simply that the speaker stands forth as a man who is himself, with his whole being, at one with his subject. This concentration makes a sermon or speech by Tillich—although it may sometimes be quite involved in its expression—an act of communion. Although his manner is ever disciplined, he penetrates both the mind and the heart of his listener. Speaking from the depths, he incites to new heights.

His ability to bring to clear expression that which others feel only dimly and to make awareness free through the power of right definition amounts to genius. His speech becomes a liberating act, a "shaking of the foundations" which startles, as it summons, the listener to knowledge of self.

One finds in Tillich's sermons both sharp diagnosis of human existence and a vision of the holy, of ultimate reality, God. Both of these elements together make for the radical character of the analysis and make "ultimate concern" the only possible way for man to express the divine.

Tillich is fundamentally concerned about the truth, not primarily the question of epistemological truth but the truth of man's being—that is, the meaning of life. Merciless rational analysis becomes the medium of innermost concern: passion expressed in rationality, driving beyond reason to the depth of reason. It is this truth that is truth of ultimate concern. Such truth cannot be recanted. He did not recant, and therefore was forced to leave the country of his birth.

Paul Tillich has spoken to modern man with a penetration which is perhaps unequaled by any other man of thought. It is the honesty with which he approaches reality and the freshness with which he discusses the per-

3

plexities and joys of our individual and collective lives which make his writings fascinating. Concerned as few have been with eternity, he has never turned a deaf ear to time and his fellow men. The prominence in his thought of the notion of *kairos*, the creative act in the moment of the invasion of the finite by the infinite—about which more must be said presently—illustrates his insistence on speaking to men in the light of changing circumstances which confront them. With candor he has approached every facet of our tangled lives and has been a true guide to the perplexed in our century.

Tillich is not one who counsels the skeptical and insecure modern man to abandon his autonomy, as the root of all his lostness, and to subject himself without questioning to the doctrines and authority of the Church. For him, modern man has no possible way back to medieval "heteronomy," no return behind Kant and the Renaissance. He is convinced that, if doubt is repressed by enforced belief, it will return as fanaticism or as cynicism. Doubt must be accepted. Is it not doubt, he asks, which points to the ultimacy of truth? Would I not violate my participation in truth, my being true, if I force some "truth" upon my doubt? It is the very doubt of modern man that testifies to the intensity of his quest.

Tillich finds that this decisive insight into the predicament of doubt is best expressed in Martin Luther's concept of justification by grace through faith. What Luther said in respect to man's moral works, declares Tillich, namely, that they cannot bring him to God, holds true also in respect to man's intellectual works and sacrifices. They will not bring him to God: only grace will. Just as man is accepted in spite of his unworthiness, so, Tillich concludes, he is also accepted in spite of his doubt. Ultimate reality is already present in the moment of utter separation and doubt.

Here Luther's existential experience of the presence of God's grace in the moment of despair and revolt against God is merged by Tillich with Descartes's passage from doubt to certainty of thought. Descartes's search for epistemological assurance is transformed to new depths by stressing the quest for the truth of being, for the meaning of human existence. The experience of the paradoxical presence of the ultimate in the moment of utter estrangement and doubt leads Tillich to an insight which is fundamental to all his thought, his philosophy, his theology and analysis of culture: namely, that there is no truth without doubt and no doubt without truth; that, consequently, there is no realm of life, even life in its estrangement, which exists without being related to the unconditional, the ultimate. Yes, even the fervent concern of the atheist confesses the ultimate in the very passionate character of its denial.

It has been Tillich's experience, as it was the experience of Luther, Pascal and Kierkegaard, that the way to God, to truth, to ultimate reality, leads through the desert. If we see this clearly we will realize in what sense Tillich can call himself an *ontologist*. "Being" for Tillich is no static substance. In its prime manifestation in man it is the experience of the ultimate, present in the moment of despair, present as the power of being at the moment when our life is threatened by meaninglessness, by non-being. Being is a dynamic concept: the *power* of being. It is known when the ultimate breaks into man's existence. Desperate man, knowing his plight and predicament, reaches out for meaning, for being. He alone really asks the question of being and he alone knows being, as power, as both the abyss and the ground of his own being. To speculate about being per se, from the detached situation of an observer, is impossible. Tillich condemns traditional supernaturalism as objectifying God, as making the ultimate a being among other beings, and therefore no longer witnessing to its ultimacy. Faith in the ultimate is either the expression of "ultimate concern" or it is not faith in God as the power of being.

In this respect we could call Tillich an *existentialist*—though it is a label which only partly fits him. Clearly, he has been influenced by existentialist thought. Indeed, as we have seen, there is no philosophy or theology possible for him without existential participation. "To be or not to be" is the basic question for Tillich the philosopher and for Tillich the theologian. As a matter of fact, his primary concern with this question makes it difficult to classify Tillich as a materialist or idealist, a rationalist or a naturalist—or a supernaturalist. His insistence on the ground of being leads him to break through the lines which keep these "isms" neatly separated. If Tillich is attacked as a naturalist, or as a supernaturalist, idealist or materialist, he is never really hit in the center, but at the periphery, of his thought. The usual line of criticism emerges when someone searches for Tillich's "epistemology" in the attempt to establish his essential position. Since so many university intellectuals, particularly in the United States, are currently preoccupied primarily with the question of how we know things—and incidentally with the question of how to know God—a good deal of the critical exchange with Tillich has been shadowboxing.

For Tillich, the question of being is logically prior to the question of knowledge, even though, ultimately, there is an identity in the structure of being and thought. As he puts it, "depth precedes reason but is manifest through it." This conviction of ultimate identity which marks Tillich's concept of reason has much in common with Heraclitus' concept of the *logos*, but Tillich's concept of reason is in the end more Christian than pre-Socratic, since for him reason serves to reunite the separated. This may make it clear why he rejects the usual concept of reason as too limited to calculating reflection and, therefore, too narrow and inadequate.[1] He offers instead a concept of reason which tends to break the traditional compartments of naturalism and supernaturalism, idealism and materialism. However, we cannot dispense with these terms when we try to characterize certain trends in Tillich's thought, and may use them so long as we are aware of their inadequacy in this context.

With due warning that he is not an anti-rationalist, we can call Tillich an existentialist. Characteristically, he does not begin his thinking by speculating in the clouds; he digs his results out of the earth. He is never satisfied, however, with mere existential analysis; he drives beyond it to that point of identity where the infinite reveals itself in the finite, where the split of subject and object is overcome.[2] We feel this passionate search for the lost identity in the ultimate union of the separated as the driving power behind all Tillich's thought. This stress links Tillich to the fundamental thought of Parmenides, Spinoza and Schelling.

In this respect we may call Tillich an *idealist,* but a modest idealist who does not share Hegel's confidence that, as the great metaphysician, he is accomplishing the union of finite and infinite through and in the power of his own thought. As a Christian, Tillich knows that there is no union without reconciliation of estranged existence to its essence. With his emphasis on the unconditional and ultimate character of the divine, and accordingly his emphasis on the broken line between man and God, Tillich clearly goes beyond idealism and finds himself often akin to Kierkegaard and Barth.[3] This emphasis on man's estrangement from the divine does not lead to a real break with idealism, as it did in the case of these two men. It is Tillich's "idealist" passion for identity, in fact, which has made him especially sensitive to the very element of man's separation. His radical search for unity inevitably leads him to stress the reality of man's fall (and therewith to a break with liberal theology); and his radical understanding of sin and despair as estrangement from essence drives him to the acknowledgment of the final union of the ultimate with that from which it is estranged. Tillich's intellectual power maintains this tension in his thought without breaking it asunder.

To see and follow his intellectual adventure as the struggle of those two opposed concepts is truly dramatic. He succeeds in yoking them in a coincidence of opposites which finds its most powerful expression in his *Systematic Theology.* Here probably is the deepest reason for Tillich's being truly creative in a period for which the end of creative philosophy and theology had been prophesied.

Tillich's point of departure is the German classical philosophy of the early nineteenth century. It is not a matter of chance that Tillich wrote his first two books on Schelling, with whose feeling for life and approach to thought he acknowledges profound affinity. Schelling, the philosopher of romanticism, proclaimed the presence of the infinite in the finite, insisting at the same time that the finite is not absorbed by the infinite, but enhanced, asserted and fulfilled.

Though he prefers to call himself an "ecstatic naturalist," there is quite a bit of the romanticist in Tillich. Let him but speak of a tree and his romantic strain at once becomes apparent. He does not belittle the scientist, but yet avows that the latter can describe only the biological and chemical processes of the tree's growth. He cannot explain what any particular tree is as such, for itself. To see nature in its creative ground requires a poet or a philosopher.

There is more that Tillich shares with the spirit of romanticism. There is his great interest in myth, symbol and sacrament. Like Schelling and Hegel, Tillich interprets the myths and symbols of Christian faith philosophically. Myth for him is neither a primitive type of science nor fantasy; it is the expression of the relationship of man's reason (ecstatic reason) to the power of being. He also shares with the romantics a passion for creativity. His basic criticism of so-called bourgeois capitalism has been that it precluded, for many, the possibility of being creative. A new social order must first of all provide everyone with the opportunity to work creatively, each in his own life in the spirit of artists, among whom Tillich moves freely and has many friends. Creative art, thought and work—as participation in the creative ground and thus expressions of the ultimate—are enterprises of infinite importance. This is the key assumption which underlies Tillich's concern for culture as an expression of religion, and for religion as the ground of culture. In his lecture on "The Theology of Culture" (1919), which made him well known in Europe overnight, he speaks of the artist as the priest of the future Church.

With the romantics Tillich further shares a certain disdain for the bourgeois world of self-sufficiency and easy satisfaction, as well as a lively sympathy with those who protest against this world. Although possessed of a strong sense of duty and self-discipline, Tillich has something of the romantic Bohemian in him: he never wears a conventional hat; he loves his wine, especially shared with his friends. Like the romantics, he has the highest esteem for Greek culture and thought. One of his most splendid lectures was on the pre-Socratic thinkers. Echoes of Hellenism—especially early Greek thought with its deep concern for the question of being, and Plotinus with his vision of the ultimacy of the One, ground and abyss of being—resound in Tillich's thought.

Tillich always emphasizes the primacy of being over thought. It is the givenness of being which limits human reason. He thus affirms the limitation of finite reason. Without falling into the irrationalism and emotionalism of many a romantic thinker, however, he shows the need of "ecstatic reason" to discover the unconditional in the conditional. It is not Schleiermacher's often misunderstood appeal to feeling so much as Plato's *Eros* that reappears in Tillich's "ecstatic reason," for here being is united with its depth, reason is grasped by the ultimate and participates in it. It is the element of *Eros* that gives Tillich's thought its peculiar inner power and tension.

In common with Schleiermacher and Schelling, he holds that the infinite reveals itself in the finite without absorbing the concreteness of the finite. The infinite affirms the finite in its own right, in its true essence. It makes the finite whole, restores it. Like the romantics, Tillich rejects the idea of progress. Then he parts company with the romantics: he has little sympathy for the conservatism which developed out of the romantic philosophers' belief in the immediacy of the divine in *all* periods of history. Once the romantics rejected the idea of progress (their early political hopes had been crushed) they did not see the need to press for social and political transformation. Their faith in the reparative power of the eternal in history finally ended in a doctrine of political restoration. Such romantic conservatism, still the common attitude among the cultured class in Germany, was soon united with the dominant ecclesiastical attitude and tradition in Germany, which saw in man's total sinfulness the need for strong state government and did not expect any significant improvement from political or social change. These two attitudes were merged into one by the strong nationalistic fervor of recent times. It was this conglomeration, this wall of conservatism, against which Tillich early found himself beating his head. His severe criticism of romanticism resulted despite his being himself a romantic at heart.

Tillich is especially influenced by the later writings of Schelling, the Schelling who opposed Hegel's pure essentialism, his system of synthesis. Insisting that being precedes thought and act, Schelling discovers in man's actualization of freedom his original sin, and accordingly develops a doctrine of grace and guilt. Under the influence of these views, Tillich joined the circle of those protesting against the disappearance of the concrete, the individual, the truly historical in Hegel's all-embracing synthesis. Tillich was among those who called Hegel's reconciliation through synthesis a delusion based on the unpardonable separation of pure thought from existence. Hegel, he and his colleagues realized, had overlooked real existence with all its intrinsic struggle and pain. Tillich insisted that thought apart from existence is meaningless and powerless to reconcile.

With this conviction Tillich fought against both the idealism of the Hegelian type and the early Barthian theology, in so far as this theology prided itself on dealing only with a revealed truth totally transcending the secular realm of culture. Certainly Tillich was not alone in opposing Hegel: among the great anti-Hegelians there had been Feuerbach, Marx, Kierkegaard, Nietzsche. Each was quite different from the other, but all pointed to the elemental struggle in concrete reality and agreeing that Hegel's method of driving thesis and antithesis to a higher synthesis had by no means healed the real conflict within existence. The God of pure essence who is infinitely distant as the summit of all values, serenely crowning all the beautiful and good, a God beyond the clouds, was therefore proclaimed dead by Kierkegaard, for whom God had a terrible reality, shaking our existence to its foundations. Like Nietzsche, but in the name of a living God, Kierkegaard protested against the Hegelian god of pure essence. Man before God was in "fear and trembling."[4] Kierkegaard would not speak of God apart from existence, apart from "my" existence.

In quite a different way Karl Marx tried to transform the dynamics of Christian supernatural eschatology by reinterpreting the dynamic power of the inner historical process as a drive to fulfillment within history. The general verdict of this revolt against Hegel was that it is not thought that shapes existence (reality), but existence that shapes thought. This was most radically expressed by Marx in his claim that ideological thought is the defensive rationalization of the interest of the ruling class. Thought is basically the product of a culture, formed by a certain mode of economic production.

Tillich finds some fundamental truth in this observation. He sees the dominating ideas of a historical period as the expressions of the life of the whole rather than of an individual, a whole including not only philosophy, but science, economics and politics as well. The mind has its history. Yet this fundamental discovery does not lead Tillich to the conclusion of many of his contemporaries, that philosophy is destined to be replaced by sociology and psychology. Nor does his assertion of the dependence of thought on existence lead him toward a positivist-materialistic concept of reality in the image of Marx and Feuerbach. Instead, Tillich uncovers a new realism. Thought, he concludes, comes out of existence; but existence will also be shaped by thought, if thought is the true expression of its reality.

Here is the root of his famous principle of *correlation*. Thought which is not "correlated" with reality not only lacks *reality,* it is hardly meaningful.

Conversely, truth which corresponds with and really expresses the situation, and does so in a compelling way at the hour of decision, is more than speculation, it creates freedom for action. It is act. Such is Tillich's new and profound rendering of the Platonic insistence that the ground of being is also the ground of thought.

For Tillich, theology and philosophy are called to actualize themselves in continuous dialogue and encounter with scientists, artists, sociologists, economists, depth psychologists and others intent on expressing and interpreting reality.

If Karl Barth is the theologians' theologian, condemning the mediating function of theology, Tillich stands forth as the theologian for Everyman in the predicament of his existence. He sees his central task as one of mediating between faith and culture. His striving toward the discovery of the ultimate ground in the finite individual is carried out with the fervent Christian motive of reconciling broken man and broken society to their essence. It is his passion for reconciliation that has made Tillich so sensitive to the antagonism of separation and struggle which he finds on all levels of individual and social life. The Christian doctrine of the Fall is accepted by Tillich as a valid symbol signifying man's situation as one of estrangement.

These notions of Tillich's were shared by very few in the years just prior to World War I. Such ideas sounded irrelevant in a society which was successfully improving its standard of living year after year and was dreaming of more glorious times to come. Autonomous modern man had built by his own power a gigantic, technical industrial world. There seemed to be no limits to his power nor to his magic wand of science which he trusted would soon overcome all remnants of evil and darkness in this world. In his hour of triumph modern man was unconcerned about the infinite. The idea of sin and estrangement seemed dismal and remote. Most of the theologians of the period were busy condemning the mystical elements of Christianity as un-Christian remnants of the Middle Ages, finding the essence of Christian religion in solid, practical ethics, the golden rule for modern man. Christianity thus conceived formed an integral part of the cultural pattern of the time, expressed in Europe in the symbol of the state-church. The Church was powerless to stir man out of his presumed self-sufficiency. Christianity no longer presented the ground, but became merely one expression of culture among others and, therefore, all but lost its function as a critic of culture.

Tillich was merciless in his attack on the spirit of placid finitude which he saw expressed in most of the artistic, political, cultural and even ecclesiastical world of the late nineteenth and early twentieth centuries. In his eyes, Western bourgeois society and its civilization were doomed to destruction, not from without but from within. Accordingly, his method became radical analysis, and his words had the sharpness of a surgeon's knife cutting into a cancerous tumor.

World War I came. It broke the nineteenth-century man's world to pieces. His dreams of incessant progress bled to death in the trenches of France. He found that science, his precious instrument for mastering the world, had turned against him and become a means of mass destruction. When Tillich came home from the war the revolution had begun. Was the demand of the hour to mend the broken house of the nineteenth century, to join the ranks of the conservatives and nationalists, as was believed by most educated men and practically all those active in the life of the churches? For Tillich, the world of the past century was ruined beyond repair. The war and the revolution were clear signs that he had been right in predicting that the bourgeois period of history was coming to a catastrophic end and that a totally new period was at hand.

The demand of the hour, as Tillich saw it, was for the intellectual to identify his existence with that of the rebelling proletarian. The ruins of the old world had to fall before a new edifice could be erected. The fact that the masses of the proletariat were admittedly secular and irreligious seemed to Tillich grounds for hope rather than despair. A secular movement such as theirs would be the appropriate instrument for overcoming the smug sentimental religiosity of a self-complacent world and its hypocritical moralism. The radical secular nature of the socialist movement seemed to make it the suitable frame in which the power of the eternal could appear, breaking through in a new and unadulterated way.

Together with some of his friends, Tillich founded a movement for "religious socialism." They wanted to relate socialism to its own depth, interpreting its true meaning to its followers. Although Tillich and his friends anxiously awaited the new that was to come—the expectancy gave an urgent enthusiasm to all their writings—they were from the beginning quite sober about utopian ideas. Soon they found themselves "cautioners" in the socialist movement. They freely expressed their conviction that, without accepting a religious foundation, no planned society could avoid its eventual self-destruction.

Aware of the impossibility of imposing the idea of "theonomy" through a "heteronomous" program, one which would have to be spread by mass propaganda and accepted by the mass, Tillich and his associates refrained from proclaiming any political action program. Members of different parties, from the left as well as from the right, participated in the group. Perhaps they were right in their fear that the concept of theonomy would be deformed into a utopian vision if translated into a political manifesto. In any case, religious socialism as such, in its political aspect at least, proved to be more reconciliation through thought than, as the movement proclaimed, reconciliation in existence. The political will was not forceful enough. The movement could not overcome a lingering hesitation to act politically, although it demanded action. Apparently this reluctance was part of its romantic inheritance. So the field was left to radicals and demagogues. The few men who knew better in the twenties did not try to organize a mass movement or party, which alone might have given historical weight to their concept but which, of course, would have endangered their original purpose of sounding a prophetic cry and a proclamation of theonomy.

Their choice of the word "socialism" for their cause was probably unfortunate. The term meant more to express their solidarity with the general socialist revolutionary temper than to commit them to an actual revolution. Although they asserted the necessity of revolution in the dynamic process of historical development, their socialism had much more in common with certain of the socialist aspects of Fichte and Hegel. Like Hegel, who had taken his ideal from the Greek city-state, Tillich hoped to achieve the unity of the people as a whole in their religious and political life. Tillich's democratic ideal was not merely the mechanical equality of the ballot box, nor did he ever join in any Hegelian glorification of the State. An aristocratic trend, in the best sense of that term, always characterized Tillich and his circle; it expressed itself in their writings in spite of all confessed solidarity with the proletariat.

These men represented the best spiritual and intellectual traditions of the nineteenth century. All strong individuals, their appeal for a new collectivism was not entirely convincing or spontaneous. Rather, it was their response to what they felt was the demand of the hour. Tillich himself uttered his doubts as to whether he would really like to live in the new social order that was to come by necessity. As might be expected, however, this new order which Tillich envisioned was never a "brave new world." Tillich's supreme criterion for right and wrong in a social order was whether it would give its individual members the possibility of creative freedom. The old order was wrong because it excluded millions of the unemployed, and to a considerable extent the proletariat, from actualizing their true selves. So the religious socialists protested against the dehumanizing aspects of the old social order. A true desire for essential manhood and creativity, Tillich believed, would be found among the dehumanized proletarians, who were deprived from actualizing themselves as individuals. This desire must be the true motive of their rebellion. The social order which they might create would have to be one in which *all* men might actualize their true natures.

Tillich and other religious socialists probably understood the needs of the proletarian more deeply than the proletarian did himself. The workers, however, neither understood their language nor accepted their program. The religious socialists failed to present a utopian image of the paradise to come on earth, said nothing of the dictatorship of the proletariat, and vented no hatred against the possessors. When Hitler came and translated the proletarian's dissatisfaction, frustration and misery into a hoarse cry for bread and work, adding the vision of the thousand-year Reich and, soon to come, a car and a radio for everyone, the masses followed him fanatically. Hitler, they felt, had expressed their needs more directly.

Tillich was expelled from his position as university professor immediately after Hitler took power, and forced to leave Germany. A good number of the religious socialists were later put into concentration camps and suffered death. Only the future will tell whether religious socialism as conceived by Tillich and his associates shall ever find its actualization in history. But whatever this answer may be, the final evaluation of this circle will not rest so much on the question of its political effectiveness as on the insight and truth articulated about man's nature and history by Tillich and his friends.

Tillich spoke of the *kairos* of religious socialism. *Kairos* is fulfilled time, the right moment to act according to the inner demand of the *kairos* situation. *Kairos* is the moment when time is invaded by eternity. The *kairoi* in history are all derived from the first *kairos,* the coming of the New Being in Jesus the Christ. An eschatological attitude of an active waiting and demanding was typical of the religious socialists. The character of their message was thoroughly prophetic. For the religious socialists, in their hour of history, the crucial event was the rise of the revolutionary movement. *Kairos* as the break-through of the eternal into the finite means both the divine Yes and the divine No and makes all deification or glorification of political programs, even the socialist one, impossible. It made these men skeptical of all utopianism. *Kairos* as the moment of the eternal breaking into the finite, renewing and fulfilling it, is also the divine Yes. It is the restoring power of being which transforms man and society, which fulfills what is potential in history and in nature. Tillich spoke of a "Gestalt of grace," a structure of grace revealed in the appearance of the unconditional in the conditional. It was his emphasis on the creative possibility of the "Gestalt of grace" in the *kairos* which led him to differ from Barth, with whom he had shared the concept of "radical crisis."

Kairos, eternity in time, was from then on for Tillich the key to a new understanding of time and to a new eschatological interpretation of history. History, for Tillich, knows no static, timeless togetherness of the infinite and the finite; it is a process of moving from one transition to the next, a process of eternal crisis and renewal. Nor is the meaning of a particular period of history ever obvious or intrinsic. It lies rather in the relation of an era to the ultimate that is beyond every point of time—challenging the interpretation of the philosopher and the prophetic theologian. It becomes increasingly clear in Tillich's interpretation of history that he did not intend to construct a super-historical reality, nor any sacred history beyond secular history, but that he was concerned with interpreting actual, concrete history. In describing the *kairos* situation Tillich develops his famous concept of "historical realism," a concept which tries to grasp the power of being in the concrete historical situation, that which is the unconditioned power in every historical act and event. As Tillich says: "Historical realism remains on a comparatively unrealistic level if it does not grasp the depth of reality in which its divine foundation and meaning become visible. Everything before this point has preliminary conditioned reality. Therefore, historical realism has truth to the degree that it reaches the ultimate ground of meaning of a historical situation and through it of being itself."[5]

Just as there is no knowledge of man without self-knowledge, so there is no knowledge of history without a penetrating analysis of our present situation. Tillich shows that the historian must write as a man who is thrown into history. He is summoned to describe the structural necessities of a period, and then to analyze these carefully and derive from analysis the direction for action. Thought leads to action; action follows necessarily out of understanding one's time. Far from being a detached observer of a dead past, the historian is part rational analyst of the period and part prophet, reading the signs of the time which demand action. As such, he strives to realize the meaning and the imperatives of the present moment.

Man is ever under the demand of the hour. Consequently, not only a new interpretation of history but a new doctrine of man rises out of the fire of *kairos:* in the situation of crisis man is confronted with a new creative possibility. Act he must. A decision is necessary. Tillich reflects deeply on the problem of freedom and decision. But the terminology of freedom and decision exists in a strong tension with the terminology of identity, being, participation. However, Tillich again succeeds in forging two seemingly contradictory elements together. In the concrete situation of the *kairos,* man becomes aware of his finitude, of his being "bound into history"; yet he realizes his freedom by understanding his situation and its demand. Freedom and ~~~n finitude become the two poles of the structure of man's being. As

Tillich puts it, *man is finite freedom*. When man knows history in the sense described above, he is free from enslavement to history; he is free to act, to create something new. He is, in Tillich's words, "man transforming the face of the cosmos." Tillich not only overcomes the usual quietism that follows adherence to a system of identity, but also finds in that very identity a new spur to action, without denying the givenness of our own existence and the situation in which we find ourselves. Analysis and action help us transcend and transform the historical situation.

Tillich is too realistic to be seduced into romantic solipsism. Our freedom is never infinite. Existence in its givenness encompasses us and compels our recognition. Here Tillich sharply distinguishes himself from Fichte. If man forgets his finitude and aspires to infinite freedom, he will end in tragic self-destruction. The holocaust is what Tillich sees as the necessary end of all utopian endeavor—and modern history has borne him gruesome witness in truly demonic signs.

The irreducibly tragic element in man's attempts to actualize his yearning for freedom evokes from Tillich pages which have the ring of paradox to some of his readers. Tillich can never, for example, rejoice about freedom in the unreserved, passionate way in which the poet Schiller wrote his hymn of freedom. The self-actualization of man is at the same time tragic, because it estranges man from his original union with being, from his state of "dreaming innocence." Ethical action is not the way to reunion with God. Although Tillich never separates religion and ethics, he sharply distinguishes between them. He makes ethics directly dependent on religion, and therewith finds himself in a position against all those stands of modern theology which, following Ritschl, reduced religion to ethics. This is the point of deepest difference between Tillich and much of the popular theology of many present-day American churches.

This affirmation of the inevitability of estrangement within freedom leads to frequent misunderstanding on the part of Tillich's critics, some of whom have inferred that he would identify finitude with evil. There is in Tillich's thought both the boldness of man's decision to actualize himself and a certain melancholy about the loss of immediate union with being, implied in the very venture of using one's freedom. Sometimes Tillich speaks, like Prometheus, of the infinite value of the creative act; at other times he dwells on the estrangement in the act from original paradisical immediacy. It is characteristic of the depth of Tillich's thought that it can sustain this tension, again and again forging the two opposing aspects together in his analysis of human existence. Thus, sin is man's destiny but is at the same time the act of man's finite freedom.

The idea of the tragic dilemma in the actualization of man's freedom as such is an expression of the Greek background of his thinking. The question remains whether he fully describes the reality of the Biblical God-man encounter, in which the fulfillment of the will of God through the will of man is either the way toward reconciliation with God or the result of the reconciliation. According to Biblical thought, it is man's use of his freedom *against God,* but not man's use of freedom or the very finitude of freedom as such, which estranges him from God. The Biblical writers, even Paul in his interpretation of Adam's fall as the destiny of mankind and of the law as coming "in between" man and God, did not necessarily or universally identify estrangement with man's self-actualization. Tillich's notion that man in his potentiality is good but that man in his actualization is destined to estrange himself from God is the human dilemma which was powerfully expressed in Greek tragedy.

Yet in a way both the Greek and the Christian insights are combined by Tillich in his statement of the fundamental predicaments of human existence. The overpowering feeling of guilt, we might better say "tragic inevitability," often revealed in Tillich's thought and action relates him deeply to Kierkegaard. In the context of systematic theology it expresses itself in the symbolic statement that the Creation and the Fall are one and that there will never be a state of existence without tragedy. All these statements must be brought into relation with what Tillich has to say about the transforming power of the New Being, with which we shall deal later.

Except for a devoted circle of students and colleagues, Tillich was not widely understood when he came to America in 1933. During the years of the war, and during the following years of the cold war with its frustration of the war hopes, a strong general feeling of insecurity and anxiety grew in the nation. There was a good deal of questioning, particularly among the younger generation, and many reflective men and women found in Tillich the probe and solvent of the predicaments for which their spirits yearned. Tillich dared not act as if their anxieties were imaginary. His way was to dig to the roots in the hope of finding a way of regeneration.

In all of the writings in which Tillich analyzes our time, searching for its signs, he seems to emerge as a prophet of both doom and promise. It is the vision of holiness, the ultimacy of the divine, the God beyond, which moves him. He has, in his "Protestant principle," forged a hammer for crushing the idols of modern man: he rejects all attempts to make the conditional into the unconditional, all attempts to give unconditional loyalty to the conditioned. "Theonomy" as divine demand is set by Tillich in opposition to modern man's dizzy staggering between empty "autonomy" and imposed totalitarian "heteronomy." Theonomy is not a divine law "over and against" man, asking for man's subjection; it is not a disguised form of heteronomy. It is "autonomous reason united with its own depth."

Tillich's call to theonomy is his greatest challenge to modern thought. His is a vision of culture in which ultimate concern informs the whole web of life and thought and for which the ultimate unity is an ever-present horizon. With this idea of theonomy, Tillich overcomes the easy deification of culture by liberal theology and yet makes religion relevant to culture in a profound way. He bridges the gap which Barth and the existentialists alike have been able to see but not to overcome. Religion is understood by Tillich as the root of culture, and culture as the efflorescence of religion. Accordingly, Tillich has been successful, as perhaps no other modern writer, in showing the essential relatedness of each cultural expression to its religious ground. The Church has been powerfully called back out of its self-chosen ghetto, out of its disregard for culture, to do its task for the world.

This emphasis has also prepared the ground for a truly ecumenical theology. Tillich has provided in his concept of theonomy a creative possibility for a fruitful encounter of the Protestant and Catholic principles in the present ecumenical discussion. For theonomy includes not only the Protestant principle of protest against human forms of idolatry. The Protestant eschatological prophetism may be united with the priestly sacramentalism on a foundation of the awareness of the holiness of being, and the reconciling force of the New Being. The prophet speaking the word of crisis becomes the priest healing that which is broken, through the power of the New Being, by uniting the separated with its ultimate ground.

Tillich's vision of theonomy has made him an ardent spokesman for a revival of liturgy and a new understanding of the essential importance of the sacramental. In theonomy, both the ultimacy of the divine, as the crisis of the finite, and the appearance of the New Being in history, as the healing and transformation and fulfillment of the finite, are taken seriously. Here is a vision which might help us to overcome the jungle of denominational antagonism and make the Church again a uniting power, reconciling the broken world with God by overcoming its splits and separations, yet doing this from within reality and never by the authoritarian means of ecclesiastical or political heteronomy.

In the moment of crisis and revolution, when the old world was tumbling, Tillich thought he saw the time wide open for the realization of his vision of theonomy through religious socialism. He visualized a dehumanized, dishonored proletariat longing for full manhood as the bearer into reality of this new theonomy. But as it was once with Moses, so it was with Tillich;

when he returned from his mountain with the new law of theonomy, the people were still dancing around the golden calf. The socialists and proletarians had joined in the round dance with the bourgeois, who had managed to save their properties as well as their comfortable mentality through the crisis. His book, *The Religious Situation,* written in 1925, shows Tillich's disappointment. Here he wrote that "a frost has fallen upon all the things of which we have spoken, whether it be the youth movement or the philosophy of life, whether it be expressionism or religious socialism." It was heteronomy and not theonomy which the man of the twenties had chosen, politically as well as theologically. Tillich was by now, as a theologian as well as a political thinker, far from the midstream in Europe. In vain and with increasing despair he raised his voice to warn his contemporaries of the demonic distortions of truth in the growing movement of nazism and of the final destruction to which it must lead. In 1933, at the very height of nationalistic emotion, when people spoke of the "new age" which had come with the appearance of the "leader"—when they spoke of the "demand of the hour" as national socialism—Tillich spoke of an apocalyptic vision in which he saw Berlin in ruins and ashes, with potatoes growing in the famous Tiergarten.

Together with Thomas Mann, Einstein, and many others he had to leave his country. He was forty-seven when he emigrated to the United States, and he had no knowledge of the English language. The fact that he has since become one of the leading spirits of America is a compliment both to the man and his rare intellectual power, as well as to the country ready to receive him as one of her own and to listen to him as a truly great man. The influence of the New World began to show clearly in Tillich's work, which now overcame certain provincial limitations. Indeed, it is his emigration to the new country of his choice which enabled Tillich to be understood everywhere and to speak not only to the few but to the world. After World War I, in the time of revolution, Tillich had become aware of the reality of estrangement and sin on the collective level. The class struggle was the most evident sign of human sinfulness and despair. The dehumanized masses, demanding full acceptance, cried out against injustice. At that time Tillich thought accordingly of salvation in terms of reconciling collective estrangement through religious socialism. But the disappoinment of his hopes led him to look deeper, and to reject the idea of speaking of collective entities as if they were persons, becoming guilty and wanting to be redeemed. It is indeed the class struggle which basically exemplifies social estrangement. But Tillich saw that the antagonism, the separation on the social level, is rooted in man himself. Without ever forgetting the collective dimension of man's life, Tillich now concentrates his analysis on man himself, on his essential estrangement, and it is this new direction which makes Tillich's writings universally heard and valued.

As philosopher, Tillich has asked unceasingly the question of man's being. His existential analysis of its structure has been the center of his philosophic thought. And as theologian, he has concentrated on what being means for us: the New Being in Jesus Christ, as the answer to man's deepest questions. In fact, Tillich became much more a theologian in America after having been primarily occupied with philosophy during his last years in Europe, where he held the chair of philosophy at the University of Frankfurt. Tillich was always both a philosopher and a theologian, but the shift in emphasis after his immigration had its reason in something more than the external factor of his being called to teach at Union Theological Seminary.

Some of the so-called "German Christians" had misused Tillich's terminology of the *kairos* and applied it to the coming of national socialism, speaking of the moment as "the demand of the hour." This bitter experience awoke Tillich's deep indignation, which was expressed in some forceful writings just before he had to leave Germany. Tillich sought to disclose the relationship of *kairos* to *logos:* the *logos* as the criterion of the *kairos* situation. The relationship of the historical *kairoi* to the one *kairos* of the appearance of the Christ was made more clearly explicit; the creative power, the "Gestalt of grace" in the *kairos* situation, understood and defined by Tillich as "the power of the new being," demanded a new Christology. After the more extensive movement of his thought in the twenties, the intensive and more centrally theological activity of the thirties was the logical consequence.

Another, more external, reason doubtless helped to make Tillich's work in America primarily theological. In his last years in Europe, Tillich found himself strongly opposed by the powerful and dominant neo-orthodox theology of Barth, which marked each opponent, particularly if he clung to the concept of "analogy of being," as a *liberal,* a label which in no way fits Tillich. Tillich was clearly never a nineteenth century liberal; indeed, he never sought to eliminate any of the classic Christian doctrines. He remained essentially within his own Lutheran tradition and rejected as absurd the idea of creating or inventing new symbols, as some liberals have tried in our day.

Much confusion on this score is dissipated if we remind ourselves that Tillich has been a *mystical Christian theologian* in the classic sense of the phrase. Traditional crystallized theology is not simply recapitulated in orthodox fashion but becomes instrumental in Tillich's writing for expressing his own encounter with the divine, his ultimate concern. *His is a theology of the spirit*. It is mystical experience, if we do not misconstrue the meaning of this word, which underlies all his theology. Thus Tillich defends his own Christian tradition and its classic doctrines by showing their true and deeper meaning, by interpreting them symbolically. There is no question that this deeper understanding definitely transforms the doctrines from within. In the process of reinterpretation something new appears. Those who look at these often revolutionizing transformations in Tillich's interpretation of the Christian faith are likely to call him a liberal; others, who see only that the material of his interpretation consists mostly of the classical doctrines and the Holy Scriptures, call him conservative and orthodox. Both labels are inadequate. Nevertheless, in the theological circles in Europe he was considered, and by many rejected, as a liberal, which had become a "bad word." Then, when he came to America, he found himself hailed and attacked as neo-orthodox and supernaturalist. He was always named together with Barth, Niebuhr and Brunner. He had not altered the essential content of this thought, but he was speaking on different frontiers. Though he had powerfully asserted his religious concern for culture and social action in Europe, where cultural relativism had spread among the theologians, he found that in the new country he had to warn against and say No to the confidence of an easy confusion of human and divine spirit in much of American theology. Too often religion seemed on the verge of being totally absorbed by ethics, social action and other concerns. Having incessantly demanded action from his quietist brethren in Germany, Tillich found himself speaking out in America against active Martha in favor of contemplative Mary, who, after all, had chosen "the better part." Activism is not religion and sometimes it is the demand of the hour to wait. If American theology has learned one basic lesson from Reinhold Niebuhr, that, despite all, man is a sinner, it has learned another basic lesson from Tillich: God is *ultimate* concern, and confusing Him with other concerns, even the best-intended ones, will mean disaster for theology, culture and politics.

In American theology, which was to so marked a degree the expression of ethical religion (often a tendency toward legalism), crucial theological categories, grace included, had become for many meaningless, either remnants of the past or synonymous with redeeming social action. In this situation Tillich began to work anew, in the hope of reinforcing the sense of grace in American theology.

To do so he had to wrestle with the problem of Christology. In an environment which had become accustomed to the picture of Jesus as a social reformer, as the bringer of a new law, Tillich began to unfold the picture of the Biblical Jesus Christ as the bringer and bearer of the New Being, of grace. The power of the New Being was no abstract theological term, but the redeeming creative power in reality, the new being which appears in the situation of the *kairos*. It is the new which comes out of crisis as the transforming power, the power which restores the individual and the community by overcoming perversion, by overcoming the estrangement of the old. It restores, but is never only a return to the old; it is the power of the "new creation." It reunites the separated elements of existence with their essence, with the totality of being. The New Being is the participation of being itself in existence, and as such in the creative and transforming power. There is no life process which is not determined by the New Being. Therefore, in the New Being lies our confidence that the essential and existential in us are already reconciled. The New Being is the power of healing, the power which makes us whole again. This concept of the New Being means that, for Tillich, history is in its essence the history of salvation (*Heilsgeschichte*): the continuous transforming action of the New Being. The New Being is not, as in Barthian theology, the *Logos,* limited to one particular, unique Christ-event; but, as the power of being, is the essence of all history. *Heilsgeschichte,* the history of salvation, is not a super-historical reality. Nor is it, in the Hegelian sense, the history of "the idea." It is the essence of history as such.

For Tillich, a separation between a holy and a profane history is impossible. The concrete history in which we stand is the continuous conflict between the New Being, as the creative power, and the deformations and perversions of the new, which Tillich calls the "demonic." The presence of the new in our lives is not static but must be described as a breaking into existence, bringing both crisis and reconciliation, bringing the new reality and the contradiction of the new through its being distorted.

It is the Biblical picture of Jesus as the Christ which reveals the reality of the New Being, and therewith the structure of being as such. But it is likewise true to say that only the reality of the New Being can serve as the key for our understanding of the Christ-event. Tillich makes the statement: "My Christology and dogmatics were determined by the interpretation of the cross of Christ as the event of history in which divine judgment over the world becomes concrete and manifest."[6] This is the appearance of the Christ, the New Being, bringing both crisis and renewal. Christ as the bearer of the new reality, the New Being, surrenders his finitude at all points and becomes completely transparent to the mystery here revealed. Since he is able to do this without losing himself, he must first completely possess himself. This means, as Tillich says, that Christ is united with the ground of being. It is this which makes Jesus the Christ, rather than any of his personal, finite characteristics. His personality, his teachings and his acts are not the cause, but the expression, of his being the Christ. Any attempt to make his finite self the object of devotion is rejected by Tillich as idolatry. Only that to which Jesus witnesses is final, neither he himself nor the Church. Tillich expresses this by saying that "Jesus becomes the Christ by sacrificing that which was Jesus in Him to that which was the Christ." This is what makes Jesus Christ final revelation: that he is united with the ground of being through sacrificing himself.

Tillich agrees with Albert Schweitzer on scholarly grounds and, as we have just shown, on religious grounds, in rejecting any attempt to reconstruct through historical research the exact picture of the historical Jesus. Even if such a reconstruction were possible, which is not the case, our faith could not rest on such a structure of historical probability. For Tillich there is no need to go back to every detail of a historical Jesus. Christ is relevant to our faith only as he is pictured in the New Testament, as transparent to the power of the New Being. Only the picture of Jesus Christ in the Bible, which is the result of the New Being, is important for us—Jesus the Christ in whom essence has entered existence, overcoming the estrangement of existence. In this respect Tillich has often been misunderstood as not being really concerned with the Incarnation, with the New Being appearing in history *as individual man.*

But Tillich's Christology has its center in a historic event. It is here that he is basically different from Bultmann.[7] The decisive element in Christianity, as Tillich sees it, over and against all religion in which the New Being is only a hoped-for reality, is just this: "the Logos becomes history, a visible and touchable individuality, gained by a unique moment of time."[8] The certainty of my faith in the reality of the New Being in Jesus as the Christ does not rest, however, on the possibility or impossibility of a scholarly reconstruction of the picture of the historical Jesus. The certainty lies in the Church, where the reunion of man to man is pronounced and realized, and in my personal experience of the power of the New Being as the healing and creative reality of my life.

The "new creation," the New Being, is the summing up of the Christian message for our time and "should be the infinite passion of the Christian." Tillich revives the unique emphasis of Paul's preaching for the present generation. The New Being is the power of salvation which never destroys creation, but transforms the old creation into a new one, actualized through the Spirit who creatively conquers the ambiguities of life.

Tillich's theology of the New Being is powerfully expressed in his volume of sermons, *The New Being* (1955). In a more comprehensive way, this doctrine of the New Being is also developed in his *Systematic Theology,* in which Tillich presents the Christian message of the new creation as the answer to modern man's fundamental questions. Each part of his theological system begins with an extensive existential analysis, systematically penetrating to an understanding of the structures of our existence. Indeed, the uniqueness of Tillich's systematic undertaking lies in the distinctiveness of its existential foundation. As such, his systematic construction is basically different from the *Summa* of Thomas Aquinas or from Hegel's *Phenomenology of Mind*. Tillich's system is open toward the ultimate. It bears witness to the reality of the ultimate's breaking into the finite. Thus, presupposing finiteness, Tillich's system does not claim to be final.

In this systematic effort Tillich correlates philosophy and theology. He shows that one depends on the other, but each remains distinct in its own right. It is the task of philosophy, as Tillich sees it, to penetrate into the structure of existence. Such philosophical analysis will reveal man's fundamental predicament and thereby expose the crucial questions of his existence. Existentialism had the courage to speak of man's anxiety and guilt, and his fear of meaninglessness, as expressions of an existential estrangement, as evidence of a fundamental split in man's nature.

The philosopher who penetrates human nature cannot develop an answer out of existential analysis; as Tillich says, "philosophy cannot answer ultimate or existential questions *qua* philosophy." It is the theologian's task to pay careful attention to the philosopher's analysis and questions, and then to present in his own definitions real answers to man's fundamental questions. Tillich is convinced that if the Christian symbols are rightly understood they will be the true answers to modern man's predicament. He takes great pains to show modern man the meaning of each symbol.[9]

The answer which Tillich the theologian gives to the predicament posed by Tillich the existentialist analyst is the New Being, the salvation of man through the overcoming and healing of the divorce between existence and essence. This implies the Christian confession of faith in the new reality, which has appeared in fullness and power in Jesus the Christ. Particularly in his sermons, where Tillich shows how Jesus the Christ who is called the Saviour makes men whole again, he revives the original and often-forgotten meaning of salvation as healing. His sermons have brought new insight and life to those for whom the Biblical concepts had become dead words. There is a fundamental sense in which Tillich's theology is thoroughly apologetic in its intent; he has achieved a theology of mediation as persuasive in its appeal as that of Schleiermacher.

It is this latter emphasis which has drawn Tillich into vital discussions with men in the healing professions, with physicians and particularly with psychiatrists. Modern depth psychology has uncovered the realities of man's inner life as conditioned by anxiety, fear and the sense of guilt, which are rooted not in the rational but in the unconscious and subconscious dimensions of human existence. Man harbors a profound schism which reveals itself in all his tendencies toward self-destruction. Tillich shows that the findings of existentialism and depth psychology are closely related. The psychiatrists are wrong, Tillich declares, if they expect to deal with these phenomena of human estrangement purely as pathological phenomena, to be treated by professional techniques. In such a common misunderstanding of the ultimate source of healing power Tillich sees the dilemma of modern psychology. The psychiatrist must be called back to an understanding of man's existence as estranged from his true self, from essential manhood. This is the underlying cause of all destruction and disintegration revealed through psychonanalysis.

The psychiatrist or the depth psychologist is no more able to give salvation than is the existentialist. He cannot make man whole again through the exclusive use of scientific methods; only contact with the reality of the New Being can overcome the conflicts of our existence. The psychiatrist can, however, become an instrument of the grace of the New Being if he himself participates in its reality. Then he will see the true cause of human despair and guilt as estrangement. Then he will discover the power of the New Being as the power of love reuniting the separated, repairing the broken and the disintegrated. He will express his awareness by his readiness to accept the patient as he knows himself to be accepted in spite of his being unacceptable, and through this will help his patient to accept himself. Such is the first step toward true integration, the first step toward freedom. Tillich makes it abundantly clear that depth psychologists, existentialist thinkers, and theologians must work together if their common concern is to bear fruit. Tillich's apparent personal success in bringing about this encounter is one of the most promising beginnings in our time.

The power of the New Being, says Tillich, is expressed in love, which overcomes dividedness. If I am driven by love I participate in the power of love. I am open to the healing force of the New Being, which is grace. At such a moment the split in me, the destructive self-hatred, is conquered. Thus Tillich can say that love unites one with oneself, saving the self from despair. True love unites the separated "I" with the "Thou" of one's neighbor, in such a way that both are fulfilled in their individual being and not dissolved by the union. As such, love makes us whole again, and this means it makes us real, by making us each a self-related being, "a being able to resist dissolution into something else." The self-related being is, for Tillich, the most real being. He concludes, therefore, that love is the nature of being, the nature of God Himself. But if we speak of God as being love, then we must see in being an element of "serious otherness," as Tillich calls it, since there is no serious love without such otherness. Love presupposes an otherness within the union of love. Since being is love, it drives toward individualization. It is love which makes being the power of creation, but the essential identity in the ground of being is not disrupted or denied by this element of "serious otherness." For Tillich shows that the very identity of the ultimate ground is possible only through difference.

Here he discovers the ultimate relevance of the Christian concept of *the Trinity:* not an expression of God as static entity, but as love within and therefore love coming out of the identity of the divine ground. The Trinity is being actualized as life (in self-objectivation) and fulfilled through the Spirit, the dynamic unity of abyss and *Logos*. The Spirit unites the divine ground with its self-objectivation. Thus the trinitarian reality is understood by Tillich, as it was by Hegel, in terms of eternal separation of spirit from itself and its eternal return to itself within the divine. The concept of the Trinity is accordingly of central importance for Tillich, since it points symbolically to the motion of love, to the element of otherness yet ultimate identity in the divine ground itself. In this last insight, man realizes that separateness and otherness are ultimately aspects of God's love, aspects of being itself. Despair is conquered in the conviction that God as love embraces otherness. Estrangement is conquered in seeing it as a motion within God's striving toward reunion. Tillich comes close to Hegel again in his deepest insights, penetrating to an essentialist metaphysics in describing the essential structures of being, but follows Boehme and Schelling where he visualizes both otherness and being dynamically united in ultimate reality. It is the awareness of this problem which has led Tillich to venture a new synthesis, witnessing to the final identity in the ultimate ground.[10]

Many of Tillich's most daring statements concerning the structure of being occur in his book *Love, Power and Justice* (1954). His analysis of the ontological reality of love has been criticized by a number of theologians and philosophers as pure speculation, unpermissible for man who lives in existence and from whom the essential, if there is such, is hidden. It has been criticized as dubious metaphysics and questionable natural theology, leading from an existential analysis of love to the conclusion that being itself, or God, is love. Ought Tillich's endeavor not be seen as a poignant instance of faith seeking understanding—*fides quaerens intellectum?* He always presupposes the New Being as having appeared in history. Only as grasped by the power of the New Being, by love, does man know himself as estranged from essence. Only in this relationship, therefore, can he try to say what love, what power, what justice essentially are. Tillich's ontology, which is closely related to the ontological effort of Martin Heidegger, is the backbone of both his existentialist analysis and his existentialist theology. In a way it sets the stage in which the other two stresses merge. For the thinker who has taken the risk of the faith in the New Being, penetration to the essential, as our true being, becomes the ethical demand to move toward our full self-realization. Tillich's book on love is both an initiation into the mysteries of the structure of being, revealed in love, and a statement of profound ethical character and purpose. Here he discusses *libido, eros, philia* and *agape* not as different types of love but as aspects of the one true love. They are all expressions of the power of love as forms of man's self-realization. It is self-realization which is, for Tillich, the criterion in evaluating the utterances of human love. Even the self-sacrifice asked for in Christian *agape* does not conflict with man's self-realization, because in *agape* all self-denial and self-sacrifice are undergone for the sake of love. In this sense, even the individual who dies for others ("namely, for each single one within the many," as Tillich interprets it) dies ultimately for the self-realization of the power of love in himself and in the many. Tillich concludes: "If the individual has infinite value and infinite depth he cannot surrender his meaning. The individual participates in love in the ground of being itself."

One may ask: In making self-realization the ultimate criterion, by defining love as the power of being toward self-realization and the overcoming of self-destruction, does Tillich not inadvertently elevate the *eros* concept over the others? Does he not incorporate the other aspects of love into the *eros* aspect? Is it not Plato's *eros,* which seeks fulfillment through the self-realization of the individual (strengthened through the romantic ideal of the individual personality), which determines the temper and structure of Tillich's thought? His commitment to *eros* accounts for the intuition of being in its rational form, as we find it in Tillich's writings, and for the characteristic inner dynamics of each of his concepts, as well as for the emphasis on the creative act, the dynamic union of the ultimate ground and the self-objectivating form, as the redeeming act of the spirit.

Tillich's theology does not originate in the appreciation of love as God's condescension and forgiveness. The passion of *eros* which underlies the thought makes it mystical as well as rational and drives it beyond all idealism to the transcendent ultimate ground. Is not the domination of the *eros* motive in Tillich's thought and reason why tragedy is conquered by love, but never overcome? We feel the immense intellectual effort and power behind Tillich's attempt to unite the love of Apollo, of Dionysius, and of

Christ. The tensions between Tillich's concepts are evident; here also lies his greatness. He has tried throughout his life to overcome the split between the two great spiritual traditions inherited by the West—Greek thought and Christianity, the two great forces which throughout the history of the Christian West have pressed men to take sides. Tillich stands with those who have sincerely tried to attain an abiding synthesis, in which the split between Greek wisdom and Christian faith is overcome. Augustine, Thomas Aquinas, Erasmus of Rotterdam, Leibniz, Schelling, Schleiermacher and others precede Tillich in this endeavor. For our period, Tillich's attempt is of decisive importance. Through his thought Tillich has tried to bridge the two spiritual worlds. He is one of the few great men in our age who have the courage to venture beyond prophetic criticism and existential analysis and to forge a new synthesis and therewith provide a new possibility for creative action. With a singleness of mind perhaps unique among the true thinkers of our time Tillich devotes his work not only to the pondering but also to the answering of man's ultimate questions.

Part II
Religion and the Dilemmas of Contemporary Existence

~~~~~~ *2*

The Limitations and Dangers
of Psychology

BY ERICH FROMM

The growing popularity of psychology in our days is greeted by many as a promising sign that we are about to approach the realization of the Delphic command "know thyself." Undoubtedly there is some reason for this interpretation. The idea of self-knowledge has its roots in the Greek and Judaeo-Christian tradition; and forms part of the Enlightenment attitude. Men like William James and Freud were deeply rooted in this tradition and they have undoubtedly helped to transmit this positive aspect of psychology to our present era. But this fact must not make one ignore other aspects of the contemporary interest in psychology, which are dangerous and destructive to the spiritual development of man. It is with these aspects that this essay deals.

Psychological knowledge (*Menschenkenntniss*) has assumed a particular function in capitalistic society, a function and a meaning quite different from those implied in "know thyself." Capitalistic society is centered around the market, the commodity market and the labor market, where goods and services are exchanged freely, regardless of traditional standards and without force or fraud. Instead, knowledge of the customer becomes of paramount importance for the seller. While this was true even fifty or a hundred years ago, the knowledge of the customer has increased in significance a hundredfold in recent decades. With the growing concentration of enterprises and capital it becomes all the more important to know in advance the wishes of the customer, and not only to know them but to influence and manipulate them. Capital investments on the scale of modern giant enterprises are not made by hunch, but after thorough investigation and manipulation of the customer.

Beyond this knowledge of the customer ("market psychology") there has arisen a new field of psychology based on the wish to understand and manipulate the worker and the employee. This new field is called "human relations." It is a logical outcome of the changed relationship between capital and labor. Instead of crude exploitation there is co-operation between the giant colossi of enterprise and labor-union bureaucracy, both of which have come to the conclusion that it is in the long run more useful to arrive at compromises than to fight. In addition, however, it has also been found that a satisfied, a "happy," worker works more productively and ensures the smooth operation which is a necessity for the big enterprise of our day. Exploiting the popular interest in psychology and in human relations, the worker and the employee are studied and manipulated by psychologists. What Taylor did for the rationalization of physical work the psychologists do for the mental and emotional aspect of the worker. He is made into a *thing,* treated and manipulated like a thing, and the so-called "human relations" are the most inhuman ones, because they are "reified" and alienated relations.

From the manipulation of the customer and the employee, the interest in psychology has spread to the manipulation of everybody, most clearly expressed in politics. While the idea of democracy was originally centered around the concept of clear thinking and responsible citizens, the practice of democracy becomes more and more influenced by the same methods of manipulation that were first developed in market research and "human relations."

All this is well known and hardly needs fresh proof. I want now to proceed to the discussion of a more subtle and difficult problem which is related to the interest in individual psychology and especially to the great popularity of psychoanalysis. The questions are: *To what extent is psychology* (the knowledge of others and of oneself) *possible? What limitations exist to such knowledge, and what are the dangers if these limitations are not respected?*

Undoubtedly the desire to know our fellow men and ourselves corresponds to a deep need in human beings. Man lives within a social context; he needs to be related to his fellow man, lest he become insane; man is endowed with reason and imagination, his fellow man and he himself are a problem to him, which he cannot help trying to solve, a secret he must try to discover.

The endeavor to understand man by thought is called psychology, "the knowledge of the soul." Psychology, in this sense, attempts to understand the forces underlying man's behavior, the evolution of man's character, and the circumstances determining this evolution. In short, psychology tries to give a rational account of the innermost core of an individual soul. However, complete rational knowledge is possible only of *things;* things can be dissected without being destroyed, they can be manipulated without damage to their very nature, they can be reproduced. *Man is not a thing;* he cannot be dissected without being destroyed, he cannot be manipulated without being harmed, and he cannot be reproduced artificially. While life in its biological aspects is a miracle and a secret, man in his human aspects is even more an unfathomable secret to himself and to his fellow men. We know our fellow man and ourselves, yet we do not know him or ourselves, because we are not things and our fellow man is not a thing. The further we reach into the depth of our being, or someone else's being, the more the goal of full knowledge eludes us. Yet we cannot help desiring to penetrate into the secret of man's soul, into the innermost nucleus that is "he."

What, then, does it mean to say that we know ourselves or that we know another person? Briefly speaking, to know ourselves means to overcome the illusions we have about ourselves; to know our neighbor means to overcome the "parataxic distortions" (transference) we have about him. We all suffer, in varying degrees, from illusions about ourselves. We are enmeshed in fantasies of our omniscience and omnipotence which were experienced as quite real when we were children; we rationalize our bad motivations as being born out of benevolence, duty or necessity; we rationalize our weakness and fear as being in the service of good causes, our unrelatedness as resulting from the unresponsiveness of others. With our fellow men we distort and rationalize just as much, except that usually we do so in the opposite direction. Our lack of love makes him appear as hostile, when he is only shy; our submissiveness transforms him into a dominating ogre, when he only asserts himself; our fear of spontaneity makes him out to be childish, when he is really childlike and spontaneous.

To know more about ourselves means to do away with the many veils which hide us and our neighbor from our view. One veil after another is lifted, one distortion after another dispelled.

Psychology can show us what man is *not*. It cannot tell us what man, each one of us, *is*. The soul of man, the unique core of each individual, can never be grasped and described adequately. It can be "known" only inasmuch as it is not misconceived. The legitimate aim of psychology thus is the *negative,* the removal of distortions and illusions, *not the positive,* the full and complete knowledge of a human being.

There is, however, another path to knowing man's secret; this path is not that of thought, but that of *love.* Love is active penetration of the other person, in which my desire to know is stilled by union. (This is love in the Biblical meaning of DAATH as against AHABA.) In the act of fusion I know you, I know myself, I know everybody—and I "know" nothing. I know in the only way in which knowledge of that which is alive is possible for man—

by the experience of *union,* not by any knowledge our *thought* can give. The only way of full knowledge lies in the *act* of love; this act transcends thought, it transcends words. It is the daring plunge into the essence of another person, or into my own.

Psychological knowledge may be a *condition* for full knowledge in the act of love. I have to know the other person and myself objectively in order to be able to see his reality or, rather, in order to overcome the illusions, the irrationally distorted picture I have of him. If I know a human being as he is or, rather, if I know what he is not, then I may know him in his ultimate essence, in the act of love.

Love is an achievement not easy to attain. How does the man who cannot love try to penetrate the secret of his neighbor? There is one other way, a desperate one, to know the secret: it is that of complete power over another person; the power which makes him do what I want, feel what I want, think what I want; which transforms him into a thing, my thing, my possession. The ultimate degree of this attempt to know lies in the extremes of sadism, in the desire to make a human being suffer, to torture him, to force him to betray his "secret" in his suffering, or eventually to destroy him. In the craving for penetrating man's secret lies an essential motivation for the depth and intensity of cruelty and destructiveness.

This idea has been expressed by the Russian writer Isaac Babel in a very succinct way. He quotes a fellow officer in the Russian civil war, who has just stamped a former master to death, as saying: "With shooting—you only get rid of a chap. . . . With shooting you'll never get at the soul, to where it is in a fellow and how it shows itself. But I don't spare myself, and I've more than once trampled an enemy for over an hour. You see, I want to get to know what life really is, what life's like down our way." [1]

Yet, while sadism and destructiveness are motivated by the desire to force man's secret, this way can never lead to the expected goal. By making my neighbor suffer, the distance between him and me grows to a point where no knowledge is possible any more. Sadism and destructiveness are perverted, hopeless and tragic attempts to know man. [2]

The problem of knowing man is parallel to the theological problem of knowing God. Negative theology postulates that I cannot make any positive statement about God. The only knowledge of God is what He is not. As Maimonides put it, the more I know about what God is *not* the more I know about God. Or, as Meister Eckhart put it: "Meanwhile man cannot know what God is even though he be ever so well aware of what God is not." One consequence of such negative theology lies in mysticism. If I can have no full knowledge of God in thought, if theology is at best negative, the positive knowledge of God can be achieved only in the act of union with God.

Translating this principle to the field of man's soul, we might speak of a "negative psychology," and furthermore say that full knowledge of man by thought is impossible and full "knowledge" can occur only in the act of love. Just as mysticism is a logical consequence of negative theology, love is the logical consequence of negative psychology.

Stating the limitations of psychology is to point to the danger resulting from ignoring these limitations. Modern man is lonely, frightened and hardly capable of love. He wants to be close to his neighbor, and yet he is too unrelated and distant to be able to be close. His marginal bonds to his neighbor are manifold and easily kept up, but a "central relatedness," that from core to core, hardly exists. In search for closeness he craves knowledge; and in search for knowledge he finds psychology. Psychology becomes a substitute for love, for intimacy, for union with others and oneself; it becomes the refuge for the lonely, alienated man, instead of being a step toward the act of union.

This function of psychology as a surrogate becomes apparent in the phenomenon of the popularity of psychoanalysis. Psychoanalysis can be most helpful in undoing the parataxic distortions within ourselves and about our fellow man. It can undo one illusion after another, and thus free the way to the decisive act, which we alone can perform: the "courage to be," the leap, the act of ultimate commitment.

Man, after his physical birth, has to go through a continuous process of birth. Emerging from the mother's womb is the first act of birth; from her breast, the second; from her arm, the third. From here on, the process of birth can stop; the person can develop into a socially adjusted and useful person, and yet remain stillborn in a spiritual sense. If he is to develop into what he potentially is as a human being he must continue to be born, that is, he must continue to dissolve the primary ties of soil and blood. He must proceed from one act of separation to the next. He must give up certainty and defenses, and take the leap into the act of commitment, concern and love.

What happens so often in psychoanalytic treatment is that there is a silent agreement between therapist and patient which consists in the assumption that psychoanalysis is a method by which one can attain happiness and maturity, and yet avoid the leap, the act, the pain of separation. To carry the analogy of the leap a little further, the psychoanalytic situation looks sometimes like that of a man wanting to learn how to swim becoming intensely afraid of the moment when he is called upon to jump into the water and have faith in its carrying power. He stands at the edge of the pool and listens to his teacher explain to him the movements he has to make; that is good and necessary; but if we see him going on talking without cease we begin to suspect that the talking and understanding have become a substitute for the dreaded act. No amount or depth of psychological insight can ever take the place of the act, of the commitment, of the leap. It can lead to it, prepare it, make it possible—and this is the legitimate function of psycholoanalytic work. But it must not try to be a substitute for the responsible act of commitment, an act without which no real change occurs in a human being.

If psychoanalysis is understood in this sense, another condition must be met. The analyst must overcome the alienation from himself and from his fellow man which is prevalent in modern man. As I have indicated before, modern man experiences himself as a *thing*, as an embodiment of energies to be invested profitably on the market. He experiences his fellow man as a thing to be used for profitable exchange. Contemporary psychology, psychiatry and psychoanalysis are involved in this universal process of alienation. The patient is considered as a thing, as the sum of many parts. Some of these parts are defective and need to be fixed, as the parts of an automobile need to be fixed. There is a defect here and a defect there, called symptoms, and the psychiatrist considers it his function to fix these various defects. He does not look at the patient as a global, unique whole, which can be fully understood only in the act of full relatedness and empathy.

For psychoanalysis to fulfill its real possibilities, the analyst must overcome his own alienation, be capable of relating himself to the patient from core to core, and in this relatedness to open the path for the patient's spontaneous experience, and thus for the "understanding" of himself. He must not look on the patient as an object, not even only be a "participant observer," but he must become one with the patient, and at the same time retain his separateness and objectivity, so that he can formulate what he experiences in this act of oneness. The final understanding cannot be expressed fully in words; it is not an "interpretation" which describes the patient as an object with its various defects, and their genesis, but it is a total, intuitive grasp; it takes place first in the analyst and then, if the analysis is to be successful, in the patient. This grasp is sudden, it is an intuitive act which can be prepared by many cerebral insights but can never be replaced by them. If psychoanalysis is to develop in this direction it has still unexhausted possibilities for human transformation and spiritual change. If it remains enmeshed in the socially patterned defect of alienation it may remedy this or that individual defect, but it will become another tool for making man more automatized, and adjusted to an alienated society.

The Individual and Mass Society*

BY KARL JASPERS

Can there still be individuals in mass society? To what extent is it possible for individuals to assert themselves in a collectivized regime? Can the threatened extinction of man be averted?

These questions, which are often and anxiously raised today, demand first a clarification of the relation of the individual and the collective. Man always partakes of both: he is an individual in a whole. Neither the whole— call it what we will, community, society, collective—nor the individual can exist independently of one another. Man is neither reduced to his mere function in a sort of ant-state, a continually recurring whole without history, nor does he walk alone in the world, isolated from society. Without the tradition which the newborn child receives from other men it cannot even become a man. It does not grow like an animal through simple biological inheritance from countless identical generations; it grows through education in the process of group-historical change. In earlier times, people born without hearing and speech were thought feeble-minded. Now that carefully planned instruction in sign language has created for them a substitute for the spoken language, they have proved themselves fully equal to other men. Such is the power of the tradition which makes men truly human.

It is not only the power, it is even more the precariousness, of this very tradition that seems markedly to distinguish human existence from animal existence. The relation of the individual to the collective can never be brought into a perfected, final form. That is why man has history. Through his works, through the ordering of labor in common, he produces something which, by comparison with biologically inherited patterns, is fragile and easy to ruin. The resultant community remains insufficient for him whatever its form, and consequently leaves him dissatisfied. This kind of result is seen most strikingly in modern technology. However man tries, through his inventive gift and his growing control over nature, to transform

* Translated by Harold O. J. Brown.

and transcend nature, he discovers that in the frenzy of activity the environment he has created cannot take on definitive shape.

His technological activity, on which he seizes with typical modern passion, seeking what is better, expanding his power, pushing back the limits of his world beyond all measuring, is for him a frightening development as well. He revolts against it; he wants something permanent. In pretechnological history such permanence was conceived and lived in immense and effective edifices. In the Chinese universe man considered himself to be one with the eternal order of things, with the *Tao;* all irregularity was but a passing disturbance, and human life as a whole was the continual replacement of the eternally identical. In the Platonic world of ideas the permanent configurations and relationships were thought of as a stable firmament above the turmoil of change, which in itself was without purpose or meaning; man could gain a measure of being only by partaking of those ideas. Stoic thought postulated a world reason as the eternally necessary and immutable, which underlay all apparent change. For the Christian Kingdom of God the world was but a place for the soul of man to be tried and to prove itself; the world, the intermediate stage between the Creation and Fall, on the one hand, and the Last Judgment and Resurrection, on the other, itself generated no real development.

All these schemes of life and thoughts now seem a procession of splendid dreams. Today the basic relationship of the individual and the community as a result of the rapid transformation of all human existence in the wake of immense and unforeseen technological domination of nature has become riven and doubtful, in a different and more radical way than ever before.

As a consequence of technology, society itself appears in a new shape. The all-embracing community, which used to move as a unit, has been split asunder. This has become manifest in the opposition of the terms *community* and *society.* Every community, so to speak, with *substance,* which is more than just the collection of its individual members, is historically unique, borne by an unfathomable past which it obeys—a past which is transmitted by oral tradition and by books, by morals, customs, habits, and proprieties, and above all by the family and a common faith. It grows, and cannot be planned; it is preserved, and cannot be made. In contrast, the technological collective we call *society (Gesellschaft)* can disappear overnight; it can be comprehended and made, planned down to the last detail, transposed at will, identically duplicated, and never acquires a remembered past. It can replace every man in it without undergoing any change in itself; it treats the individual only as a means, as a part and function. Its only future is the unfelt, empty future of quantitative increment, of the improvement of its machines, of the replacement of worn-out men and material.

This contradiction is today so stark that it would seem that a *community with substance* and a *technological society* are mutually exclusive. But the contradiction has always existed in the tension between traditional repetition and rational alteration, between thoughtless accommodation to existing patterns and planning, improving thought. We are dealing with a polarity which is distinctive to man. When it is unbalanced, both poles suffer. What is only organically *substantial* in a community is deficient as a reality in the world; it is helpless and powerless against nature. Mere planning, in contrast, indeed gives great power, but tends to extinguish man, for whom this power might be meaningful. Where the man of the organic society feels himself lost in helplessness toward nature, in want and debilitating toil, he enthusiastically clutches at the technological world of the mechanical collective, initially seeing in it only liberation. Where the man of the mechanical collective feels himself ground down, so that he can no longer draw a breath, he longs for the organic community.

In greatly simplified outline, then, we have seen how a double polarity is proper to man: that of the individual versus the collective, and that of the organic community versus planned, technological society.

The *being* of man grows with the fullness of the organic substantiality of his community, of which his creative personality is the representative; he comes to know himself in his reflection of the community. The *power* of man, however, grows with his mastery over nature, won by planning, cooperation, and through the creation of the technological environment. Still, the *being* and the *power* are not mutually exclusive. What *is* is effective in the world only through power, and power has meaning and satisfaction only through being.

In both polarities the tendency today seems to be to sacrifice everything for the sake of a technological apparatus. It is impossible to discuss here the characteristics which distinguish modern technology from earlier technology; we must content ourselves with saying that here something absolutely new in history has arisen, beginning slowly two hundred years ago, gathering speed in the nineteenth century, and developing with frightening velocity in the past eighty years. In this reality lies the reason for the breakup of the polarities of individual and community, and of community and society.

In the extreme case, the community disappears before the machinery, which violates all and breathes a soul into none. Of the rich, living collective in which man once found himself only the activity remains, in which he is a function, interchangeable, and per se expendable. Loss of self and loss of community belong together; at one and the same time, the technical apparatus begets, externally, the inflexible order of labor and, internally—within men—chaos.

This becomes especially clear at the extremes. On the one hand, forced laborers in concentration camps, condemned to murderous exploitation, are depressed to the inhuman existence of mere creatures. On the other hand, people who have been freed by job security and shortened working hours may be distraught, since, having lost their community, they can no longer become *themselves* and therefore can do nothing *with themselves*. Only the collective organization of their free time beckons to save them from their empty freedom. From the business of work they pass over into the business of amusement; such reflections may be fanciful; in reality, to be sure, only the extremes go so far. These perceptions, like everything brought up so far, are only observed phenomena. We are only observing what happens.

But this attitude of scrutiny reaches its limit when we ourselves become the object under examination. We do not know ourselves as we know natural processes, which proceed indifferent to whether we know them or not; by contrast, the way in which we know our existence affects us and shapes what happens to us. We are always *more* than we are aware of in ourselves. This *more* is not a dark background, not some gloomy, unconscious thing; it is our freedom, the brightest element that we ourselves embody, even if objectively we do not perceive it at all. What we do depends on ourselves.

Knowledge of ourselves, if equated with natural, scientific knowledge, tends to drive our actions from some imaginary external source, the knowledge of which supposedly provides the clue to our fate. The outcome of this way of thinking is that we abandon or lose the habit of responsible action. We flee freedom to embrace our imagined destiny.

The result of this kind of knowledge is that we assert, from an imaginary vantage point, our omnipotence or, from within ourselves, our helplessness. Everything, therefore, which is taken to be relevant knowledge, and a few schemes which we have evolved—namely, technology and industry, which devour the State, the family, political freedom, and the individual along with them—everything then serves to supply arguments for despair, to cripple one's own possible initiative, to promote surrender in anticipation of what is apparently inevitable.

But modern myths are offered for our salvation, which claim to transfigure this horror and make it seem splendid.

The new, non-personal man, molded by the concept of technological existence, comes into being. He sees himself as a type, not as an individual, unsurpassable in the skill and sureness of his function; he prides himself on obedience, because he lacks any desire for an existence of his own; he may secretly esteem himself as great and superior to all that is personal, because to be replaceable at will by others intensifies his own self-consciousness. He hates solitude, lives with open doors, and craves no privacy; he is always available, always active, and true to the type; lost indeed if left to himself, but indestructible, because his replacements continually grow up after him. Personality becomes an old-fashioned, ridiculous concept. Being a type gives strength, satisfaction, and the consciousness of perfection.

Other myths arise in the wake of the surrender of self: the best known and most fateful of these are the myth of the continual progress and inexorable necessity of history and the myth of the conviction that the ready and unconditional sacrifice of oneself to the inevitable course of history is the only path to meaningful existence. The individual comes to fancy that he has no value except in the service of history. To resist its demand is to risk elimination of oneself as a sick man. It does not matter greatly whether this course of history is thought of as the economic progress of labor toward the perfected order of the State, at last become enduring; or as the racial evolution to the pure, healthy, perfected race; or as the life of the nation, directed toward an absolute standard of welfare or to the goal of a single, chosen people into which all others will have to transform themselves, or from which others will have to accept rule. These are all false myths, lacking the reality of a transcendence; they are will-o'-the-wisps on the road to the eternal destruction of man. Concealing the truth, they beget transitory realities in totalitarian states, which for all their panoply of power, ultimately fade into nothing.

Those myths hinder what is most necessary for man if he is to realize himself: clear thinking, reasonable experimentation, a responsible direction into the future. People who adhere to those myths ought to horrify us. They do not actually look at us, but merely turn their piercing, if sightless, eyes upon us. They may hardly be said to have a true existence. Something speaks through them, they themselves do not speak. The force of what is unquestioned or the smile of familiarity prevails in all their relations. They offer a fully interchangeable, wholly unreliable comradeship, submitting in terror to what the "line" commands or in conventionality to what everyone seems to do and believe.

This insight into the falsehood of the new myths is readily convincing only in so far as they claim to represent knowledge. Their character, however, as symbols of being, with which being, as true reality, we live, can be grasped or rejected only by the existential decision of the individual. One man will immediately sense that belief in such myths leads him directly into the path of evil. Another will be entranced by them as though they meant his own life to him. Each man must decide whether he will give himself up or will be himself. Here is a question, first, of spiritual intent and then of the powerful struggle for life. The supporters of these myths are ready from the start to resort to force.

Mankind is now divided. On the one side stands that world which inflexibly devours the individual completely in the collective, which subjects everyone to a total plan and offers a myth in the guise of a pseudo science. On the other side stands another world, whose course cannot be predicted and which is neither designed nor managed as a total plan. Its principle is to give the individual freedom for spontaneous development. All depends on the initiative of those rare, perceptive, reliable people who—precisely because political freedom is sought for all—have opportunity for self-development and responsible action.

Although the attitude of the majority may exert powerful pressure on the development of affairs, a few men are still decisive. What an individual often cannot do is to recognize when he is being summoned, when the helm is in his hand. War and peace and the course of events may be largely determined by an individual, but only if he seizes upon what the masses want, when they are told it and see it.

As on the large scale, so also on the small one. Earlier there was an elite of rank; today the real elite is a selection of individuals, no longer determinable by sociological means (that is, by membership in a particular class), who elect themselves. Any man, for example, can take marriage and the family seriously, finding therein faithfulness, responsibility, understanding, the joy of mutuality in living, the security of origins, and the source of justice— all in spite of the statistics about the decline of the family and the descriptions of its desolation. If the Kinsey Report reveals the fact that in the United States 75 per cent of the men want extramarital sexual intercourse and 50 per cent actually practice it, these statistics are neither the expression of what should be nor a determination of what is "natural" for man.

When plebiscites are taken, the majority opinion is not the voice of God, but only a technical function of the momentary climate of opinion, which may be adjusted. The touchstone of democracy is that it is concerned not with majorities alone but with minorities as well. It is not unusual for the best to be in the minority. Mankind's existence has all too often depended on a minority, which through the higher level of its norms and its reality has been a model to others. Men who do and exemplify the right may exercise an influence which is all the more impressive the less it is consciously willed.

For these reasons, in the great trend of the times which is the erosion of the old organic polarities of the individual and the community, of the substantial community and rational society, the great decision is for the individual. In all the ruin there remains the potentiality of man himself. Only the individual, whether in public or in private, can provide the spark for the rebuilding of real community, which may again breathe a soul into the technological world of industry.

It is not true that the individual has disappeared. It is not true that it is necessary for him to be completely lost amidst the most frightful, extreme conditions. We have learned how even in the totalitarian world the individual may put on armor, may prepare himself, even under the most extreme circumstances, from falling prey to delusions, may judge in secret and refuse to place faith in the false gods.

Though the collective be reduced to a giant apparatus of terror, the individual can again be the source of true community. Yet he needs others to be able to remain himself. Nietzsche's words speak to modern man's lostness: truth begins with two. Rival parties have disappeared from the political scene; they have become mere phantoms. The hope for reconstruction rests upon the substantiality from which communities grow. The individual is faced with extraordinary burdens, and it is only in deepest inwardness that the sort of man lives who will bear the future and who now, in being himself, senses the eternity of the True.

Every problem of man stands today in the shadow of the threat of extinction. For now what Jesus and the first Christians mistakenly expected—the immediate end of the world—has become the real prospect of mankind: humanity's self-destruction and the cessation of life upon earth threaten. It looks as though the potentialities of man's technological creations have almost slipped loose from his hands. The present developments of technology are like the first ones when fire was discovered. Only then an uncontrolled blaze destroyed things on a small scale. An atomic blaze would spell total destruction.

It will certainly be important to make treaties and to arrange matters to prevent the most extreme disaster. But all will eventually founder if responsible men do not remain to engender the progress of events; the end is certain to come within decades. Only a newly arising community of "converted" individuals will be able to avert the impending catastrophe of humanity.

~~~~~~ *4*

Biblical Faith and Socialism: a Critical Appraisal

BY REINHOLD NIEBUHR

The historical dynamism of Western civilization, as distinguished from the sleeping-waking cultures of the Orient, is undoubtedly derived from two causes:

One cause is the conquest of nature through the scientific analysis of the laws and processes of nature. This scientific conquest is ultimately derived from Greek science and more generally from the sense of the structure of things in Greek philosophy. Structures were finally revealed to be processes, but even these processes were subject to general "laws."

The other source of our historical dynamism is in the Hebraic attitude toward man's historical existence. The religions of the East exploited the transcendence of man over the historical and temporal process and promised redemption from the contingencies of history by extricating the trans-historical or eternal dimension of the human spirit from the temporal integuments. Buddhism is the classical expression of this impulse toward the eternal. It is probably the only real alternative to Christianity in the field of high religion.

Biblical faith established a much more difficult relation between the temporal and the eternal, which was subject to many corruptions but which laid the foundation for Western man's interest in historical tasks and goals. The God of the prophets was the creator of the world; but He was also the sovereign of history. He demanded justice in the community. The prophets were much more rigorous than the Greek philosophers in indicting the "rulers" and "elders" of Israel because they used their power to oppress the poor and "turn aside the needy at the gate." The philosophers were complacent because they assumed that the reason of the rulers would guarantee their disinterestedness. But the prophets, having a much more adequate view of the unity of the self in body, mind and spirit, assumed the

44

intimate relation between interest and reason and laid the foundation for the idea of an ideological taint in all human pretensions of virtue.

This was an insight into human nature which was unfortunately obscured in centuries of Christian history until Marxism rediscovered it and corrupted it to make it an instrument in the social struggle.

God demanded justice and punished injustice. But justice could not be achieved without setting power against power. The weak would be exploited by the powerful until either the powerful became absolutely good or the weak became powerful. The contrast between the injustices in human history and the divine justice prompted all prophetism into Messianic overtones. The prophets hoped for the day when the Messianic ruler would combine absolute power with an imaginative justice—"He will not judge according to the seeing of the eye or the hearing of the ear but with mercy will he judge the poor." This Messianic vision was at once the great resource and the great snare of the relation of the religious vision of the final good in history to the responsibilities of history. It was the final resource because this vision of the "Reign of God" provided a transcendent criterion for the achievements of history. It was a source of confusion because this reign of perfect justice was ambiguously described partly as a historic possibility and partly as a trans-historical one.

Old Testament prophetism never solved the problem of utopianism, thought it came closer to a solution than modern utopianism or nonutopian piety. The earliest prophets—Isaiah, for instance—were quite clear that the Messianic reign could not be established except in a transfigured nature. "The lion would lie down with the lamb" in the vision of Isaiah, which is to say that the predatory aspects of history, rooted in nature itself, would be transfigured. Davidic Messianism had visions of a transfigured earth as the theater of God's final reign. The later apocalyptic visions of the transcendent Messiah, the "Son of Man," were more unequivocally trans-historical. In all, the vivid and partly undisciplined visions of apocalyptic literature are interesting to any student of the relation of religion to man's social life because they prove how inevitably "man's reach is beyond his grasp"; how the vision of justice which gives meaning to history always transcends the possibilities of history. The ideal justice in the human community, the ideal brotherhood between the peoples of the earth, would not be established until the Messianic age and in that age some of the facts of nature, upon which history is based, would have to be transformed.

This whole strain of Messianism, as well as the eschatological strain in later Christian thought, contains within it all that is creative and confusing in the relation of the religion of the West to the problem of establishing justic within and between the communities. We realize that when the faith of the West falsely identifies the Messianic reign with a historic ecclesiastical institution, as in Catholicism, or when it eliminates the socal dimension from the vision of the ultimate, as in Protestant pietism, or when it regards the ultimate, defined as a kingdom of perfect love, as simply realizable in history, as in Protestant liberalism, the social and political task of the community is either obscured or confused.

The involvement of "prophetic" forms of the Christian faith in socialism in the nineteenth century has some very ironic features because it was an effort to correct some of the worst errors of Christianity as a prophetic faith; and yet it betrayed all of us, who were involved in this effort at correction, into more grievous errors than we tried to correct. This involvement in Marxism and the illusions and subsequent disillusionments are a part of the history of the Christian faith coming to terms with the problem of making life as tolerable as possible, of answering the prayer "Thy kingdom come, on earth as it is in heaven." We must study the episode in Western Christian history more fully to see why it was attempted and why it failed.

The basic clue to the problem, both of Biblical Messianism and eschatology and of the abortive Marxist effort to cure the corruptions of this Messianism in Christian history, lies in the paradox of the relation of the individual and the community. The community is at once the fulfillment and the frustration of the individual. It is the fulfillment in so far as love is the law of life and no individual can fulfill himself within himself. He needs the community for his fulfillment. But the community is also frustration of the individual. This is partly due to the fact that the individual transcends the community and envisages goals and ends which are not immediately relevant to the order of the community. The frustration is partly due to the fact that there is a law in the "members" of the individual which wars against the law that is in his mind, namely, the law of love. This law in his members is the law of self-love or the perpetual and universal tendency of excessive self-regard. This penchant for egotism requires that the order of the community be maintained partly by coercion; and it also results in the fact that the same coercion which preserves order also creates injustice. It creates injustice because the wielders of power in the community always corrupt their function by their interest. That is why Marx was partly right in describing human history as the history of "class struggles."

In short, the community which fulfills the law of love also contradicts that law both by its coercive order and by the injustice which is the concomitant of order and power. This is a permanent ambiguity in man's communal and historic existence. The earlier prophetic Messianism hoped to overcome this ambiguity by the appearance of an ideal king who would combine perfect power with perfect goodness. This is, in a sense, a utopian hope. For no king of such virtue will appear in history. The later, more apocalyptic Messianism did not hope for the fulfillment of human hopes of an ideal brotherhood except at the "end" of history. That is to say, brotherhood and justice can never appear in pure form in history. Brotherhood, beginning with the family and extending to the ethnic community, is established partly by kinship and partly by an organizing authority. Justice is established only by an equilibrium of power, which contains within it the peril of anarchy even as governmental authority bears the peril of tyranny.

The revelation in Christ, with the claim that the crucified one was really the expected Messiah, did not change the apocalyptic hope that the real norm of history would appear only at the end of history, but it eliminated all obscurities about history and emphasized the ambiguities in all human communities. Not a community but only an individual proved to be good enough to establish the final norm of love. But this final norm by which history would be judged ("We must all be manifest before the judgment seat of Christ") cannot maintain itself in history. It is rather the revelation of the eternal love which meets and annuls the sins and ambiguities of history. In this double facet of the Christ event we have the whole logic of the Christian interpretation of history, which approaches the whole historical drama without illusion and without despair. Despair is overcome because there is forgiveness for those who recognize the ambiguity of good and evil in which all historic achievements are involved. Illusion is overcome because the ultimate criterion of history convicts every achievement of man of falling short.

This is the framework of truth in the Christian faith in terms of which Western civilization has approached the problem of man's community and history and been able to exploit all historic possibilities. But it has not been able to do this without becoming ensnared in errors which sometimes obscured and sometimes contradicted the basic truth. The secular revolt against the Christian truth has many roots, but one of the most significant causes of the revolt is its protest against these corruptions.

The most obvious corruption, which dominated Christendom until the dawn of the modern period, was the pretension of the Church that she had realized the eschatological hopes within herself, that her priests were privy to the secrets of the divine, that she could dispense and withhold grace, and that she was the perfect society. These errors were aggravated by the ability of the Church to use its pretensions of sanctity as a source of political power. The "vicar of Christ" became the ghostly inheritor of Caesar's power and dominion, and claimed to hold the keys of heaven and the dominion over the nations. This was a clear repudiation of the truth contained in the Christ event; and it proceeded from a blindness toward the divine mystery which no mortal could understand and toward the divine power which no mortal could manipulate. The Church failed to heed any of the Biblical-prophetic warnings against such pretensions. Much of the secular and sectarian-Christian approach to the problem of community, which bordered on the utopian, was due to reactions against this monstrous claim of a historic institution that it embodied the final good. Unfortunately some of the reactions against this error were equally grievous.

Luther's doctrine of the "two realms," of the "kingdom of heaven" and the "kingdom of the earth," sharply divided so that grace, forgiveness and love were in the one realm, which was at once inner and personal, while the "earthly realm," where "nothing but the law, courts, chains and punishment is known," was a reaction to this papal pretension. Unfortunately it created an ethical dualism almost as grievous as the ascetic dualism against which the Reformation protested. Pure love was relegated to the sphere of personal relations and was made irrelevant to the concern for justice. The "earthly kingdom," or the "kingdom of Caesar," on the other hand, was left bereft of all ideal possibilities of justice, and the community was thus thrown into the outer darkness of pure "order," enforced by power. The coercive function of the State and government were assumed necessary because of this consistent egotism of man.

Political absolutism had its root in the religious pessimism of Luther as in the secular pessimism of Thomas Hobbes. It would be difficult to estimate to what degree this impossible dualism, which made the Christian faith irrelevant to the problems of the community, contributed to the political incompetence of a very gifted nation. Certainly the moral and political inadequacies of the Lutheran faith contributed to the rise of the Marxist heresy on German soil. It is perhaps ironic that Catholicism, freed from its organic connections with medieval feudalism, was better able to come to terms with the problems of justice in an industrial civilization and was therefore able to claim the loyalty of the industrial workers than Lutheran Protestantism, which seemed (until it was awakened from its political slumbers by Hitler) to be completely irrelevant to the political realm and the problem of justice in the community.

But Protestantism not only erred on the side of Lutheran pessimism. If this pessimism and dualism prompted the understandable but mistaken alliance of the morally conscious portion of the Church with Marxism, a similar alliance was formed in Anglo-Saxon nations or perhaps particularly in America as a protest against the irrevelance of a pietistic individualism (which frequently was made grotesquely relevant to politics by becoming translated into social Darwinism) and against the optimism of Christian liberalism, which had absorbed the eschatological motif in the Christian *faith* into the idea of progress and the hope for the perfectibility of man.

It is rather interesting that Continental Christian socialists, reacting against an undue pessimism, and American Christian Marxists, reacting against an undue optimism, found common ground, at least provisionally, in the Marxist apocalypse.

The Continental Christian Marxists, in their reaction to the Lutheran doctrine of the "two realms," forgot what was true in the doctrine. They were blind to the truth of the non-utopian character of the Christian faith. The Marxist creed, a secularized version of Christian sectarianism, strained at the limits of history in seeking the "kingdom of God on earth." The American Christian socialists, on the other hand, reacted against the undue optimism of the liberal creed. They found Marxism "realistic" in contrast to the liberal ideas of a natural harmony of social forces, of the possibility of disinterested intelligence in political life, and of the triumph of justice without the use of force.

It may be somewhat of an enigma why Marxism should appeal as a utopian political religion to Continental Christians and as an anti-utopian faith to American Christians. The enigma may be solved by insight into the fact that Marxism was both utopian and anti-utopian, though it was in its own esteem anti-utopian. It was anti-utopian in its sense of the power realities of the community, in its realistic estimate of the social struggle, in its theory of the "ideological taint" upon all human reason applied to competitive interests, and in its provisional estimate of human motives. It was utopian in its final estimate of human motives, having wrongly derived egotism, the ideological taint, and every form of corruption from the institution of property and having assumed that the abolition of this institution would redeem mankind from every evil.

Significantly both American and Continental Marxists, while accepting the socialist economics and politics, explicitly disavowed the theory of total redemption in Marxism, and with it its ultimate utopianism. But that did not save Christian socialists from involvement in grave Marxist errors. Some of these errors can both be explained and their attractive power to religious temperaments be accounted for by the fact that the errors were due to a "sense of the ultimate," to a religious rather than an empirical approach.

It should be understood that the era in which this Marxist "prophetic" catastrophism seemed particularly plausible, whether for Christians or for secularists, the period of the world-wide depression after the First World War, developed a pattern of history which was deceptively "final" in its import. Socialist governments were in control or partial control in the Weimar Republic of Germany and in Britain. In Britain the Liberal Socialist party of MacDonald was too impotent to overcome unemployment, so that the situation prompted those two devoted disciples of parliamentary socialism, Beatrice and Sidney Webb, to flirt with communism and to publish a ridiculous book, in which the Soviet claims were taken at their face value: *Soviet Civilization.* In Germany the postwar confusion and resentment and mounting unemployment created a hysteria which allowed Hitler and nazism to emerge. The Marxists interpreted fascism as capitalism in the last stages of decay, but even non-Marxists were persuaded that history had reached a climax of evil, which invited "judgment." In America we had both the depression and the beginning of the Rooseveltian "revolution" which was to change the political climate of America.

The temper of catastrophism was very understandable. But it merely proved that there are many periods in history in which history itself seems to be foreshortened and everything seems to be moving toward "the end." One remembers that Luther was in a very eschatological mood at the time of the Reformation. He felt that the evils of the medieval papacy and the triumphs of the Turks proved that the end of history was approaching. Our catastrophism of the 1930's did not anticipate the end of history but merely the end of an era. An era of comparative security indeed ended but not in as unambiguous judgment and redemption as we had imagined.

History proved to be more complex and its processes more multiform than we had imagined. It was, for that matter, more complex in Biblical days than the messianistic prophets imagined.

Was it not confusing that Israel, the righteous nation, was more unmistakably "punished" than the great nations of Babylon and Assyria, whom the prophets had defined as the "rod" and the "ax" of God's wrath? The Biblical experience proves that, while it is possible to discern moral meanings in historical destiny, they are never as simple as religious tempers are prompted to believe either in Biblical or in contemporary periods.

In our own immediate past the sharp distinction between the righteous poor and the unrighteous rich of the Marxist apocalypse proved too simple. The whole class structure of technical society was in fact more complex than Marxism realized; and instead of becoming more simple it became more complex. The "increasing misery" of the poor, which was to provide the revolutionary impetus, did not occur. Instead the poor at first profited relatively from the total increased wealth of a technical civilization. And then they invented instruments of collective power—the trade-unions, for instance—which actually forced the powerful to make a more equitable division of the common social fund. The political power of the State proved not to be so simply the "executive committee" of the "ruling classes." The broadly based political power, the power of universal suffrage, proved in time to be potent enough to force the partial equalization, if not of economic power, then certainly of economic privilege. In short, instead of catastrophe, all the developments of modern history led to the establishment of the "welfare state," whether under socialist or, as in our case, under capitalist auspices. This welfare state provided minimal security for all classes and ended the mood of catastrophism, which seemed such an ultimate and valid principle of historical interpretation.

The economic security of the so-called "free" nations is not as established as the proponents of "free enterprise" would have us believe. Nor has perfect justice been established. But it is now perfectly clear that the "capitalistic" culture which was also a democratic one had more moral and political resources to avoid catastrophe than either the Marxists or their Christian fellow travelers believed. The religious and moral sense of catastrophe as judgment upon injustice was invalidated by a complicated array of historical, economic and political factors. These prevented the injustice from becoming aggravated and from arousing the avenging and rebellious resentments of the industrial workers, who were marked by the Marxist creed for the destiny of acting as the "midwife" of a new order of society. Clearly the religious sense of the problem of the community, whether expressed in traditional Christian terms or in terms of the new secular religion, was too pure; and the sense of the ultimate was too unmediated to do justice to the complex factors in modern history, which only a pragmatic kind of wisdom could appreciate.

We Christian "prophetic" sympathizers with Marxism were as much in error in understanding the positive program of socialism as we were in sharing its catastrophism. For the positive program was utopian, despite the explicit anti-utopianism of the Marxist. It sought to establish the kingdom of perfect brotherhood or of perfect justice on earth. It completely failed to appreciate the possibility of corruption through self-interest in any structure of society. Let us enumerate some of the particular errors in the Marxist hope which led Christian sympathizers astray.

The Marxist creed marked the "poor," more particularly the industrial poor, for a Messianic destiny. This appealed to our sense of justice. It was, in fact, a political version of the religious blessing "Blessed are the poor, for theirs is the kingdom of heaven." The religious blessing of the Scripture undoubtedly refers to the humility and charity of the poor which entitles them to a position in the heavenly kingdom. But if the religious blessing is transmuted into a political one its validity becomes dubious. There is an immediate validity in the Marxist designation of the poor as a Messianic class. The poor are the critics of an unjust civilization. They know its injustices through the evidence of their stomachs and thus acquire greater wisdom than the wise with full stomachs. But if the poor become sufficiently desperate to rebel against a civilization or a social order, their resentments will not generate wisdom, at least not the wisdom of discriminating between what was good and what was evil in the old order. They will burn down the whole of the old house and relish the holocaust.

Fortunately the poor have never become quite that desperate in Western civilization. Therefore the Marxist revolutionary creed was domesticated and became one of the forces of the democratic world. The poor ceased to insist on absolute revolution and, by patient contrivance, finally achieved power, at least sufficient power to balance the power of the rich. When Marxism was thus domesticated in democracy and ceased to be revolutionary it came more and more under the spell of pragmatic wisdom and ceased to find confidence in the historical destiny which would assure victory to any particular cause. Where social injustice was sufficiently grievous, as in the case of the decaying feudal structures of Russia and Asia, the original revolutionary creed of Marxism not only could be maintained but it led to victory. That is the story of bolshevism and its triumph.

But in this case two difficulties with the religious appreciation of a Messianic class emerge. The one difficulty is that when the poor are historically "blessed" they become successful. In that case they cease to be poor and become powerful. They become too powerful in fact. The other difficulty is that the poor are too sharply defined as the industrial poor. They are to have the reins of destiny in their hands. But in the nations in which the Marxist apocalypse seems plausible most of the poor were peasants. They were not propertyless. In fact they loved the property in the soil and were therefore not ripe for the Marxist creed. The industrial poor, having the fanaticism with which the creed endows them, seized the levers of power in the State and used their power to force the poor peasants to conform to the collectivist creed. Many peasants starved and were killed in the resulting "class struggle." The religious appreciation of the poor as the Messianic class was too undiscriminating in defining the poor, in appreciating their virtues, in forgetting that resentment against injustice may turn into an evil fanaticism, and in failing to estimate the effects of success and power upon the poor.

We find, in short, that a too-uncritical religious appreciation of the factors in historical destiny tempted either the orthodox Marxist or the Christian sympathizer to neglect the many modifying factors which enter into the woof and warp of history. A religious passion for justice must be balanced by a pragmatic consideration of all the factors in a historical situation.

But both the catastrophism and the sense of a Messianic destiny for the poor are not as vivid evidences of a too-uncritical religious sense as is the Marxist conception of justice and power. The democratic world has long since learned that the residual egotism of men makes an element of coercion in the community necessary. But the price in justice for the boon of order will be too high if every center of authority is not brought under public scrutiny and control and if every center of power is not balanced by some other center of power. An equilibrium of power is in fact the first prerequisite of justice. The Marxist dream of justice has turned into a nightmare of injustice because the Marxist utopia established a monopoly of power. A series of miscalculations were responsible for this development.

The first miscalculation was derived by the Marxists from the liberal world view. They both equated man's self-regard and his egotism with greed. "Avarice and more avarice," according to Engels, disturbed the primitive innocency of the "Gentile community," that is, primitive society. This analysis of human motives completely obscured the will to power as a dangerous element in every community. Stalin may or may not have been avaricious; but the question is irrelevant. He was active in a system of politics which gave his lust for power unlimited scope.

Secondly, the Marxist creed derived avarice or egotism from a particular social institution: the institution of property. This error was perhaps the most grievous one. It prompted the illusion that the "socialization" of property would radically alter human character. Men would cease to be selfish and would live in complete harmony with one another. This is the very root of the utopian illusions of Marxism. The derivation of the avaricious motive from a particular institution was of course the prime heresy from the Christian point of view. For it made a too-radical distinction between the "sinful" bourgeoisie and the sinless, because propertyless, proletarians. It obscured the universality of sin, which is the cornerstone of any realistic political thought.

Another error was involved in the Marxist conception of the role of property. That error was to obscure the power of the manager as distinguished from the owner. This was an understandable error in the early days of industrialism. But the error contributed to the creation of a social order in which a ruling oligarchy could combine the power of the political leader with the power of the technical manager. It could exercise its power without check or review. Even the trade-union, potent instrument of an equilibrium of power in Western industrial nations, was outlawed in communist states on the theory that the workers, being "owners" of the factories, would not require an advocate of their interests. Thus a cumulation of utopian illusions and wild generalizations, devoid of empirical tests, led to the creation of the awful monopolies of power which have made communist utopia such a hell of injustice.

Since none of us in the camp of Christian socialists had much sympathy with communism, it may seem pointless to analyze the errors which led to the communist tyranny. There were a few Christian "fellow travelers" but no one with any influence in the Christian Church espoused the communist cause. We were, almost without exception, democratic socialists. I have no doubt that communism is really orthodox Marxism; and democratic socialism, whether derived from the revisionism of Bernstein or the admixture of Christian utopianism in the British Labor party, really represented a domestication and revision of orthodox Marxism to fit into the framework of a free society. Thus the idea of the revolution was generally abandoned because in the healthy Western communities the political realities prompted optimism about the achievement of socialist goals through parliamentary methods. But until very lately, that is, until after the Second World War, almost all democratic socialists believed in the nationalization of all basic industries. They did not realize that this step would lead to a greater bureaucratization of the community than was compatible with flexibility in meeting new emergencies; and that even when the bureaucratic power was under democratic control the policy of nationalization would lead to too great centralization of power.

Increasingly, the socialist parties have modified their goals and have sought for a more equal justice by social security measures, by taxation policies, in which political society intervened in economic society where centralization of power led to inordinate privilege, and have used the more equal distribution of political power, universal suffrage, to equalize economic privilege. In short, socialist parties have aimed at the realities which are now usually defined as the welfare state. They have accomplished the same ends as our own capitalist nation has achieved in its welfare measures. Thus the nineteenth-century conception of a class struggle, which even democratic socialists accepted, has been invalidated by the complex realities and social forces of a modern technical society.

The Marxist parties of Europe have been the effective servants of the working classes, though not more so than the ideologically tangled Democratic party of the U.S.A. But even their success in establishing a greater justice in technically advanced communities has not prevented the loss of prestige by European socialism. When the British Labor party was able to defeat the great war hero Churchill, after the war, the event seemed to herald the triumph of Marxism in the whole of the Continent. But even this more modest conception of apparent historical destiny proved to be mistaken. British Labor was defeated after five years in office. Its defeat was accomplished partly by the acceptance by the Tory party of its goals of welfare and partly by the desire of the electorate to evade the rigor of the collectivism which even a modified Marxism proposed. In the whole of Western Europe and America conservatism adopted and absorbed the modified Marxist ends of the workers, and a mixed economy emerged everywhere with an illogical but effective double emphasis upon private initiative and state planning.

In short, Western society had the wisdom, by the process of trial and error which true parliamentary freedom permits through alternating succession of parties in power, to winnow what is true from the chaff of utopian illusions in the Marxist program. Some ironic developments were concomitant to this process. In Germany, for instance, the Socialist party, traditionally or supposedly internationalist, adopted a nationalistic opposition to the modified internationalism of the liberal Catholic party. Thus the old dogma that nationalism was an artifact of capitalism was refuted. In fact every simple theory of historical destiny which Marxism had inherited from Hegelianism was refuted. The forces and the paths of history are much more various, contradictory and complex than either the philosophers or the scientists of the nineteenth century had supposed. There emerged a wise statecraft which directed and beguiled these various forces and traced the different paths in the interest of a broadening justice. The health of Western democracy represents the fruit of the triumph of common sense and empirical wisdom over the dogmas of the right and the left.

We who were Christian Marxists are bound to learn several lessons from this development. In so far as our modified support of the Marxist goals was a reaction to every form of Christian conservatism, defense of the *status quo* or political indifferentism in the name of religious quietism, we may survey our past policies without regret. We tried to express the "prophetic" sense of justice against those who made piety into an instrument of injustice.

But in the light of experience in the past decades we are bound to recognize that it is not easy to avoid the perils of utopianism in countering the errors of otherworldliness and irrelevant eschatologies. For the past and current eschatologies which hope for the fulfillment of the meaning of life and the realization of justice only "in the resurrection" are certainly too otherworldly to be relevant. In that sense Barthianism, initiated by an ex-socialist and pretending to have achieved a sublime transcendence over the vicissitudes of history and a ludicrous irresponsibility toward the ordinary tasks of the political community, must be regarded as a new evidence that it is as easy to fall off one side as the other of the tightrope of eschatological tension which is at the heart of the relation of the Christian faith to the social scene. We regret our flirtation with utopianism but we will not flee into these new formulas of social irresponsibility with which a sophisticated theology seeks to beguile the disillusioned.

But our rejection of an obvious error does not obscure the measure of our own error. That might be simply defined. We tried to rescue that part of the Christian gospel which is expressed in the prayer: "Thy kingdom come, on earth as it is in heaven"; but we could not accomplish this end without falling into two grievous errors: (1) We failed to take seriously enough the central affirmation of the Christian gospel about the universality of the involvement of all men in sin and guilt. Consequently we became involved in a politics which made an absolute distinction between the innocent poor and the guilty rich. We were thus led astray by a genuine religious and ethical impulse into utopian politics; and we fell into error more inevitably because the Marxist politics, with its provisional understanding of the power realities of the community, seemed to be antiutopian. (2) Our sense of historical destiny, particularly of the destiny of judgment upon injustice and of the vindication of the oppressed, was too simple to come to terms with the complex forces of history. God may indeed "cast the mighty from their seats and exalt them of low degree." But in so far as this is done in history it is accomplished by complex processes and by the slow accommodation of the competitive forces in history, which are not fully appreciated either by a simple "prophetic" passion or by a secularized version of that passion.

We cannot dispense with prophetic passion. But now we face the task of accommodating it to a more complicated historical process and of relating it to a more empirical wisdom than either a traditional religious faith or the modern secularized Marxist version of that faith has been able to achieve.

~~~~~~~~~~~~~~~~~~~~~~~~~~~~~~~~~~~~~ Part III

Religion and Creativity

Wolfgang Amadeus Mozart*

BY KARL BARTH

I. MY FAITH IN MOZART

How am I to declare my "faith in Mozart" in a few words? A "declaration of faith" in a person and in his work is a personal matter. Thus I am delighted to have the opportunity of speaking personally. Though I am neither a musician nor a musicologist, I truly can and must express that faith.

My first meeting with great music—when a boy of about five or six years—came when I first met Mozart. I still remember the time when my father struck a few bars from the *Magic Flute* on the piano ("O my Tamino, what happiness . . . !"); I was deeply moved. Since then I have become older, and am finally old. I have heard many more and different compositions of Mozart's music, and he has become more and more a constant of my existence.

I have already been asked whether or not on the basis of my theological thinking I have discovered any other masters in the field of music. I must confess: there is he and nobody else. I must also confess (just as those Indians on the Orinoco whose first meeting with European music has been recently mentioned): it is he and nobody else. I must also confess that, thanks to th priceless invention of the record player, I have listened to Mozart's music the first thing every morning for years and years. Only after this (not to mention reading the newspapers) have I given attention to my *Dogmatik*. I must further confess: If I ever go to heaven I would first of all inquire about Mozart, and only then about Augustine, Thomas, Luther, Calvin, and Schleiermacher. But how am I to explain this? Briefly perhaps in this way: Play, too, belongs to daily bread. I hear Mozart, both the young and the old Mozart, play as nobody else can play. Yet playing is such a high and serious matter that it must be mastered. Mozart's art of playing sounds to me quite different from that of every other person. Beautiful playing pre-

---

* Translated by Walter M. Mosse.

supposes a childlike knowledge of the center of all things—including the knowledge of their beginning and their end. I hear Mozart make music from this center, from this beginning and this end. I hear Mozart's self-imposed limitation because that is just what pleased him. It pleases, encourages and comforts me too whenever I hear him. By this I do not mean to say a single word against anyone else. But this I must say: in this sense I can declare my faith only in Mozart.

II. LETTER OF THANKS TO MOZART

My dear Conductor and Court Composer:

Someone got the curious idea of inviting me and a few others to write a "letter of thanks to Mozart" for his newspaper. At first I shook my head and even looked at the wastebasket. But if there is anything which has to do with you I can say "No" only in the rarest cases. And did you not also write more than one somewhat funny letter during your lifetime? So, why not? They certainly know more there where you dwell now, unimpeded by time and space, about each other and about us than do we ourselves down here. Thus I actually do not doubt that you have known for a long time how grateful I have been to you almost all my life and always will remain. Nevertheless: why shouldn't you read this in black and white?

Two excuses have to be made first. Number one: I am one of those Protestants of whom you are supposed to have said once that we were unable to understand properly the meaning of *Agnus Dei, qui tollis peccata mundi*. Pardon me, probably you are now better informed on that. However, I do not want to bother you with theology. Believe it or not, I actually dreamed of you last week. Here is the dream: I had to *examine* you (why, I don't even understand, myself). I knew that under no circumstances would you be allowed to fail the examination. I asked you about the meaning of "dogmatics" and "dogma," by pointing in the most friendly way to your Masses, which I like especially. But to my great regret I got not the least answer from you!! Don't you think we'd better give this point a blessed rest?

The second excuse is far more complicated. I have learned that you could enjoy only the praise of connoisseurs, even in your childhood. As you know, there are not only musicians but also musicologists on this earth. You yourself were both. I am neither the one nor the other. I play no instrument nor do I have the faintest idea about the theory of harmony, let alone the mysteries of "counterpoint." Those very musicologists disturbed me deeply whose books I tried to decipher when I drew up an address for the recent celebration of your two hundredth birthday. By the way, I cannot help thinking that if I were young and had to start this kind of studying I would clash with a few of your most outstanding theoretical interpreters in the same way that I did with my theological masters forty years ago. But be that as it may, how can I, under these circumstances, thank you as a connoisseur? In other words, how can I make you happy?

To my relief, I have also read that you sometimes made music for hours and hours for very lowly people. This you did only because you somehow had the feeling that they were pleased to listen to you. In this way, with a repeatedly delighted ear and heart I have heard and still hear you play. I myself am so utterly naïve that I cannot tell in which of the thirty-four periods of your life, according to the classification of Wyzewa and Saint-Foix, you are nearest to my heart. Surely, surely, you began to become really great, let's say, about 1785. But I hope I won't hurt your feelings (or will I?) in confessing the following: It has been and always will be impossible for me to listen without deep emotion not only to *Don Giovanni* and to your last symphonies, to the *Magic Flute* and the *Requiem* but no less to the "Haffner" Serenade and the Eleventh Divertimento, etc. Actually, I am deeply moved even by *Bastien and Bastienne!* Consequently, you are interesting and dear to me much earlier than the moment when you can be praised as the "pioneer" of Beethoven!

What I owe you, frankly, is this: whenever I listen to your music I feel led to the threshold of a world which is good and well ordered, in sunshine and thunderstorm, by day and by night. Thus you have repeatedly given me, a human being of the twentieth century, courage (not haughtiness!), tempo (not exaggerated tempo!), purity (not boring purity!) and peace (not complacent peace!). If he really digests your musical dialectics he can be young and become old, he can work and relax, he can be gay and depressed; in short, he can live. You know now, far better than I, that much more is necessary for that purpose than the very best music. But there is music which helps men to this end (*ex post* and only incidentally!) and other music which cannot help toward it. Your music helps. This I have experienced all my life (I am going to be seventy years old and if you were living you would dwell in our midst as a patriarch of two hundred years!). Moreover, I am convinced that our century, which is becoming more and more obscure, especially needs your help. For both these reasons I am grateful to you that you have lived, that you wanted to make and did make pure music in the few decades of your life, and that you still live in your music. Please believe me that many, many ears and hearts, scholarly and unscholarly, just as my own, still like to hear you for ever and ever—not only in the year of your jubilee.

I have only a hazy feeling about the music played there where you now dwell. I once formulated my surmise about that as follows: whether the angels play only Bach in praising God I am not quite sure; I am sure, however, that *en famille* they play Mozart and that then also God the Lord is especially delighted to listen to them. Well, this *alternative* may be wrong. Besides, you know that better than I do, anyhow. I mention this only in order to hint metaphorically at my meaning.

And so, with all my heart,
                              yours,
                                        KARL BARTH

III. WOLFGANG AMADEUS MOZART

The parish register of the cathedral parish of Salzburg for the year 1756 certifies: "Johannes Chrysostomus Wolfgangus Theophilus, legitimate son of the noble Herr Leopold Mozart, court musician, and of Maria Anna Pertlin, his wife, was born at 8 o'clock in the evening of January 27, 1756, and was baptized according to Catholic rite at 10 o'clock in the morning of January 28, 1756." It may be that the first of these four such respectable names of this child, together with the third, will remind us of another Johann Wolfgang who was born in Frankfort seven years before. Perhaps the first name together with the second will remind us of that Church Father Johannes to whom the surname Chrysostomus ("Golden Mouth") was given because of the sweetness of his teaching. However, the last two of these four names have been used and have become generally well known; the fourth of these (Theophilus-Gottlieb) is in the Latinized form, although regularly changed into "Amade" by its bearer.

To begin with, this most extraordinary man to whom a place was to be given in the Zwingli Almanac, was born and baptized, died and received extreme unction as a Catholic. The fact that he became a Freemason in the last decade of his life changed absolutely nothing which he thought he received from the Catholic faith and from it alone (although without much ecclesiastical zeal). On the other hand, he did not like us Protestants ("I do not know whether there is any truth in that") because our religion is too much "in our head." Zwingli would probably have granted to him who lived in the midst of the curious Christian faith of those days one of the special direct accesses to God which he has even provided for sundry heathen. At any rate we must assume that God had a special access to this human being. "He that has ears to hear, let him hear."

Only, nobody should believe that it is easy to perceive with whom and what he has to deal in this matter. Mozart's rich work, together with his short eventful life, involves an account which can in no way be closed entirely; in other words, there is a secret. You must perceive that in order to understand why his music—and in his music his personality as well—is so moving, even in these days.

Whoever has discovered Mozart even a little, and tried thereafter to speak about him, easily slips into a stutter which seems to be extravagant. Think of Sören Kierkegaard; he threatened once that he would "stir up the entire clergy from sexton to consistory" in order to let them acknowledge the superiority of Mozart over all great men—otherwise he would "withdraw from church membership," separate himself from "their belief," and found a sect "which would venerate Mozart not only in the highest way, but exclusively." And hadn't the reserved Goethe previously called him a "miracle" unequaled in music? And didn't it also happen with countless other less famous people that in the unprejudiced comparison of Mozart with various earlier and later masters, expressions such as "incomparable," "perfect," were formed and uttered? Certainly there must be something to that. If only one could say: "For heaven's sake, what! For could it be that you praise Mozart and that you really mean Beethoven or Schubert, the best of whom he anticipated to a great extent in his latest works? Or could you mean one of the style forms of the musically and otherwise extremely fruitful eighteenth century which the Mozart of the early or middle period took over?"

An experiment has recently been ventured and carried through to explain his entire work with reference to the fullness of impulses which he received and amalgamated in his earlier as well as in his later years. (The same experiment was made with the Old and New Testaments!) They have analyzed the influence of the sons of J. S. Bach, and even of father Bach himself, of Handel and Gluck, Joseph and Michael Haydn, and of many, many German, Italian and French composers who are almost forgotten today. Was he "unique" just in the fact that he could not and did not want to be an innovator, a revolutionary, or something extraordinary? Or in the way he wanted to live only in and from the stream of the music of his time? Did his uniqueness consist in the fact that he only could and wanted to make music himself and make it sound unmistakably his own? Was it that he could and wanted to be a master only as a pupil (and yet as such became unparalleled)? Is it not insufficient to consider only the music of *his* time? Is it not rather possible that the original sound (*Urton*) of the early and late Mozart (which cannot be confounded with any other) is identical with the original sound of music as such? Did he find and touch it in its timeless form? Is that why it is so difficult or impossible to define what is typically Mozartian: Lo here, lo there!? Is it for that reason we must turn to helpless superlatives whenever we try to give an account of this man to ourselves or to others?

It has been said that it is a child, even a "divine" child, who speaks in his music to us. The pitiful brevity of his existence could perhaps be the reason for this kind of characterization; perhaps also his undeniable helplessness in all practical matters, as apparent in financial affairs and in the critical eyes of his sister, particularly on the occasion of his marriage. Think in addition of the drolleries in which he indulged in his talk and especially in his letters up to the last days of his life. These, however, come to light most clearly at the time when he really worked hardest. If you want to regard him as a "child" (a conception to which Jacob Burckhardt earnestly took exception), it would be more revealing if only you would remember how this man was a real master of the workmanship of his art. He untiringly refined it; he never burdened his hearers with technics but rather let them participate again and again in his free—let us say—childlike play. The best thing, however, would be to take into account that he was considered able "to laugh and to cry at us in the same breath, just as an innocent child; yet we are not entitled to ask him why." Let us remember too that Mozart never was allowed to be a child in the literal meaning of this word. First at the piano when he was three years old, he played little pieces without any mistake at four; he composed them at five, while at the same time his father taught him Latin, Italian, French, arithmetic and much, much theory of music. At six years of age he started his first concert tour, at seven years his second, which took him to Paris, London, Amsterdam and, on the way back, to Geneva, Lausanne, Bern, Zurich, Winterthur and Schaffhausen. Between the ages of fourteen and seventeen he made three more concert tours to Italy. At this time he continuously composed operas, Masses, symphonies, quartets, etc. And so on, and so on.

A child? No, a real infant prodigy, dressed up with hat and sword, incessantly practicing and performing (Goethe saw him in this way in Frankfort, in 1763). He was admired and favored by the great Maria Theresa, by the kings of England and France (let alone Madame de Pompadour!), examined by experts, made "knight" by Pope Clement XIV, and elected a member by a learned society in Bologna! All that took place under the guidance of his very earnest, skillful father (the son believed the father to come "immediately behind God") who considered the development of the "talent" and the extension of the "fame" of this son to be correct and necessary, for the glory of God. This he did with the full assistance and assent of the lad. It is terrible for Swiss ears to hear: "Wolferl" never had the advantage of a school! He had too much else to do! It may be that these strange juvenile days were the primal causes of the unknown illness of which he died, before he was thirty-six years old. It is also astonishing that he did not become a conceited little rogue; apparently he had no time even for that. At least he never was a child in the usual sense. Rather he was a "child" in that other higher meaning of the word. We must never forget this; otherwise it may happen we may think and say something foolish.

There was a time when we preferred to characterize Mozart's music with words such as "charming" and "gay," and Mozart himself was as a harbinger of an always merry rococo or even as a kind of Phoebus Apollo. The Swiss, Friedrich Theodor Fröhlich, director of music at Aarau, who also died young (1803–1836), has sung of him as a "child of May, with a happy smile on his cheek," walking under an "eternally blue sky." That, however was not and is not Mozart. It is not his life and even less his work. An English contemporary of Mozart was was personally acquainted with him was asked whether Mozart was happy; he answered bluntly: "Never." Don't forget that, whenever you mention the "cheering" character of his music! In this connection the surmise (in reality more than a surmise) should be emphasized that he was enamored often enough but never really loved a woman —with one exception: Dame Music. Add to this the woes which resulted from the cooling down of his affection for his father, from the humiliating situation in the service of the Archbishop Colloredo at Salzburg, the professional disappointments again and again in Vienna, the chronic pecuniary embarrassment in his household, and finally his illness. Mozart often laughed, but certainly not because there was much for him to laugh about. Rather he laughed (and that is something absolutely different) because he was allowed and able to laugh in spite of all.

It is a fairy tale to claim that Mozart was a "child of May"; the only truth in that is that he never knew a doubt, as a gifted Frenchman of this century has said. This is the strangely exciting and appeasing aspect of his music; it comes unmistakably from a height where everything is known and from where the right and left side of existence, happiness and pain, good and evil, life and death have all been perceived in their reality as well as in their limitation. Poor Hans Georg Nägeli (composer of "Most Holy Night")! He wanted to pick a bone with Mozart for these very contrasts which are so characteristic of his works! How could it happen that they misunderstood him so much in just this respect! No, he was no sanguine person, no optimist in his most radiating major keys, in his serenades and divertimenti, and in *Figaro* and in *Così fan tutte!* But he was certainly no melancholiac either, no pessimist, in the small and the great G Minor

Symphonies, in the D Minor Piano Concerto, the "Dissonant" Quartet, and the Overture and the Finale of *Don Giovanni!* His music mirrored real life in its two-sidedness, but in spite of that against the background of God's good creation and therefore, to be sure, always with a right turn, never with a left turn: this is perhaps the meaning of his triumphant "charm." There is no shallowness, but no abyss either, in his music. He takes everything seriously. However, he never lets himself go nor does he allow himself to go beyond proper limits. He only says within limitations how everything is. Thus his music is beautiful, comforting, moving. I do not know of any other music which I could characterize in this way.

Mozart is universal. One admires again and again everything that speaks in his work: heaven and earth, nature and man, comedy and tragedy, passion in all its forms and deepest inner peace, the Virgin Mary and the demons, the High Mass of the Church, the strange solemnity of the Freemasons and the ballroom, the stupid and the clever people, the cowards and the (real or apparent) heroes, the faithful and the unfaithful, the aristocrats and the peasants, Papageno and Sarastro. And he always seems to provide for each in turn not only partially but entirely, rain and sunshine for all alike. If I hear correctly, this is mirrored in the extremely affectionate way (which, however, appears always to be an unintentional necessity) in which Mozart forms and regulates the relation between the human voice or (in the concerti) between the dominating solo instrument and the accompanying (yet, regularly never only accompanying) strings and wind instruments. You cannot listen enough to what happens, lives, and moves in Mozart's orchestra, to what unexpectedly and always is mobilized at the right place and is honored in its special height or depth and timbre. It is as if a small part of the universe is singing. That apparently happens because the man Mozart heard this very universe and let it sing—while he himself was nothing but a mediator! You can certainly call this incomparable.

However, there is also a mystery: so far as we know, Mozart was not at all interested in the rich natural or historical sciences or (with the exception of music) in the arts such as the classical poetry of his time. He was in possession of Goethe's poems; but his relation to the poet became concretely clear only in the composition of "the Violet" song. To my knowledge everything he has written about the literature of his time comprises a few lines about the death of Chr. F. Gellert (he spells it "Gelehrt" in one of his early letters) and a humorous personal description of the poet Wieland whom he casually met in Mannheim in 1777. Even less is there anything that would entitle us to assume that he ever heard the name of his

contemporary Immanuel Kant. Moreover, in all his letters I did not read
a single report which was more than incidental about the impression of
the landscape and architecture of his homeland and the countries he
visited. The way the poet Mörike in his well-known short story lets Mozart
enjoy his "Journey to Prague" is in all probability poetry, not truth. So it
is apparently "love's labor's lost" to try to understand his personality by
referring to Old Salzburg and its environs. Even the political events of his
time (one of which was, after all, the outbreak of the French Revolution)
did not affect and interest him to any great extent. Or may I mention here
the anecdote about how Marie Antoinette, the little six-year-old arch-
duchess and later unhappy queen of France, saved the lad—also aged
six—when he slipped on the polished parqueted floor of the Vienna court?
Then he thanked her by immediately proposing to her! Despite his varied
human and professional relations, it really seems that throughout his whole
life he remained interested only in the things which directly dealt with music.
Question: How did he nevertheless know all these things, as shown so accurately in his music? He knew them just as well as did Goethe with his wide-
open eyes for nature, history and arts. He undoubtedly knew them even more
accurately than thousands and thousands of better-read, "more educated"
(to use the common expression) and more interested connoisseurs of the
world and men of all times. I know of no answer. In spite of his external
seclusion he must have possessed organs which let him perceive universally
that which he could reproduce universally in such an outstanding manner.

Mozart's music, in contrast to that of Bach, has no message and, contrary to that of Beethoven, involves no personal confession. His music does
not give rules, even less does it reveal the composer himself. The attempt
has been made to explain especially his later works in both these ways; but
the results seem to me artificial and not too convincing. Mozart does not
wish to say anything at all; he just sings and sounds. So he does not intrude
a thing upon the hearer, he does not ask decisions or comments of him, he
just lets him alone. You start to enjoy him from the moment you allow him
to act like that. At one time he called death, which he thought of every day,
that true and best friend of men; it is crystal clear in his works that this
was really true for him. But he does not make much of that; he lets us
merely guess it. He does not want to proclaim the praise of God either.
However, he does just that: in the very humbleness in which he is, so to
speak, nothing more than an instrument himself. In this way he lets us hear
what he clearly hears, namely, everything which from God's creation
presses upon him, rises in him, and wants to spring from him.

Here we must also say a word about his church music, to which even

serious experts often have objected. It has been repeatedly called worldly
or even operatic, with the somewhat weak excuse that he followed the
general custom of his time. Only this much is true: his work in this field has
never measured up to the known dogma that the sound (*Ton*) must only
serve, only interpret the word. But is this the only possible dogma for
church music? Besides, Mozart did not obey any such rule in his operas
either. If I hear correctly, his sound in his church and in his other music is
a free mirror of the word given to him. The sound is inspired by the word,
it accompanies and plays round it. The sound corresponds to the word;
and this means indeed that the sound gets and preserves its own life in
relation to the word. However, in Mozart's music this very sound corresponds to this particular word and this very composition to this particular
text and to no other. His music written for the Freemasons could not be used
for the *Requiem*. And, vice versa, he could by no means let the soprano
voice sing in the *Laudamus te* or in the *Et incarnatus est* from the C Minor
Mass the same melody as the page in the *Marriage of Figaro* in the aria:
"Voi che sapete," and so on. This is true even though he has unmistakably
given the same color to each. He hears and respects the word here and
there in its own content and character, yet he adds music, his own music,
here and there—a creature of his own, bound through the word but
sovereign in spite of its bond.

One should ask oneself (and judge according to the circumstances and
without being prejudiced by the general distinction between secular and
sacred music) whether Mozart's music is in this respect appropriate to the
word, even to the church texts. Then one will in all probability more and
more discover that in this connection his music is extremely appropriate to
the very objective statements of church texts—although often in a very
surprising way. Perhaps for that reason Mozart's church music has been
heard and reproduced from a point where God and the world are not identical but from where church and world (these two not confoundable or
exchangeable) are recognizable and recognized in their relative difference
but at the same time in their ultimate homogeneousness, both in the relation
of God to them and in their relation to God.

Finally, there is something we must mention with regret: considering the
brief period of his activity, the number of his extant works is enormous—
but perhaps this is even much less than the number of all that is and
always will be withheld from us. He was, you see, prepossessed all his life
with the habit of improvising. In other words, he played on the piano,
inventing freely, sometimes for hours and hours, both in public concerts as
well as for only a few listeners, without later writing down what he had

created: an entire Mozart world which sounded once and then faded away for ever and ever!

How did he look? Certainly not as he is supposed to have looked according to most of the pictures which have been preserved. All of them depict somewhat the so-called Phoebus Apollo. The unfinished portrait in oil which his brother-in-law, Joseph Lange, painted in 1782 is probably the most accurate likeness, for internal and external reasons. He had blue eyes and a pointed nose of not quite inconsiderable length. He was, according to the word of another Englishman, "an unusually small man, very slender and pale, with an abundance of beautiful blond hair of which he seemed to be proud." By the way, he liked billiards, dancing and—punch. The same Englishman says further: "I have seen him drinking a great amount of this beverage." Certainly not an immediately impressive personality! It was not usually apparent who and what he was. This became visible (and even then perhaps only audible) only when he took a seat at the piano. From that moment on he became the really great Wolfgang Amadeus Mozart. Let's be grateful for being in a position to receive at least a portion of the gigantic reverberation!

IV. THE FREEDOM OF MOZART [1]

Let me begin by quoting some words of the archiepiscopal conductor of Salzburg, Leopold Mozart, the father. He had led his children, the twelve-year-old "Nannerl" and the seven-year-old "Wolferl," on a concert tour through all of Western Europe which had lasted three and a half years. And now, in 1768, the light of the art and technique of the youngsters' playing and composing was to be put on the lampstand in the imperial city of Vienna. The adventure met with difficulties. Referring to these, the father wrote that he was anxious "to proclaim a wonder to the world which God permitted to be born in Salzburg. I owe this action to God Almighty, otherwise I would be the most ungrateful creature . . . It was a great pleasure and a great victory for me to hear a Voltairian say to me in astonishment: "Now at long last, I have seen a miracle in my life, the first one." The Voltairian was the encyclopedist, Friedrich Melchior Grimm, who had heard "Wolferl" in Paris in 1763 and at that time actually declared: "I think this child will turn my head if I hear him more frequently; it becomes understandable to me that it is difficult to guard against madness if you see miracles."

Even Goethe, in his old age, called the whole personality of Mozart a "miracle" which cannot be explained. It would not have been necessary to use the word "miracle" quite so frequently—for a faithful one such as

Father Mozart, for an unfaithful one such as Baron Grimm or even for a man with a name like Goethe. But how many others have used equivalent words about Wolfgang Amadeus Mozart! It strikes me how often—especially other great musicians—in particular Joseph Haydn during Mozart's life time, and later Rossini, Gounod, Busoni, and in our days Arthur Honegger and Ernest Ansermet—go into an almost ecstatic stutter whenever they touch upon their comrade in arts. This is certainly a credit to them! I do not wish to match them, and I want to leave undecided the question which a well-known contemporary recently asked me in a low voice: "Was Mozart perhaps an angel?" I mention all this only as a reminder that the life and works of the man whom we celebrate today apparently have been and still are something singular. What was, and is, this *singular* quality?

The fact that there are two *riddles* in Mozart's personality immediately shows us the way.

The first riddle is this: whoever hears Mozart hears in his music at the same time the music of the entire eighteenth century. Did ever a musician exist who had, in all phases of life's way, such an open ear for the experiments and performances of his older and contemporary, greater and smaller co-musicians? Who also had an ear for the entire world of music in his surroundings, from the church hymn down to the Vienna street ballad of the time? While composing, he was not at all disturbed, but rather animated, if one person sang in the next room, another played the piano downstairs, another the clarinet overhead—and if, on top of it all, there was a bowling game nearby. Moreover, in the very last years of his life he studied Bach and Handel with the earnestness of a beginner. You must prepare for reminiscences and quotations in his works at the most different places. Lowly and great connoisseurs of Mozart to this day have confounded his works with those of other composers. Again and again you may have doubts about certain pieces which were—rightly or wrongly—attributed to him: is it really true that this is *not* his own, or is it perhaps his work *nevertheless?* But the eighteenth century is not simply Mozart, and Mozart is not simply the eighteenth century. There already exists—if only we could define it—a specific Mozartian sound [*Eigenton*] in the piano pieces of the child, which rings throughout all the styles, manners and motifs which he has taken over. What was different, originally strange to him was transformed as he adopted it. In his ears, in his head and mind, and in his hands it became what it had not been before: it became just—Mozart. This man was creative, even and precisely while he was imitating. Verily, he did not only imitate. From the beginning he moved freely within the frame of the rules of the art of his time, and later more and more freely. But he did not revolt against these rules, nor break them. He sought and found his greatness in remaining himself precisely while binding himself to these rules. One must see both his freedom and his restraint, side by side, and seek his singular quality behind this very riddle. Otherwise it is impossible to appreciate the superior confidence with which he moved in his artistic and human environments—and by which he rises as an eagle, even to this day, in the usual environment of the concert halls.

The other riddle is more complicated: Mozart's music sound thoroughly easy, facile and light and for that reason disburdening, easing, relieving. This is true in his famous compositions in a minor key, and when he indulges in the style of the *opera seria,* in his church works until the *Requiem,* in his "Freemason songs," and elsewhere whenever he becomes solemn, melancholy, tragic. He never becomes truly tragic. He plays and never stops playing. The person who does not pulsate and sway while listening to his music, who does not join his play, does not yet hear him properly. However, neither would that person hear him correctly who would regard him (as often happened during the nineteenth century) as a musician of merriment, cheaply acquired and received.

Unflinching industry is the background of Mozart's playing. How much he worked during his short life! He worked (and this was his decisive trait) while something sang and worked in his head, took shape, unfolded and united, during his voyages, in society or simply during a game of billiards. He worked when he committed the result, in all its details, to paper, without stopping as if writing letters, or when he improvised at the piano, for many or a few listeners, or in nocturnal loneliness. Consequently (and this certainly has nothing to do with cheapness!), his music actually never unveils itself without further ceremony and his lightness, although not hidden as such, has something extremely demanding, disquieting and almost inflammatory, even in his very gayest movements. Whoever is not also willing to yield to this cannot and will certainly not be relieved by Mozart. Therefore, it is supposed to be a beautiful task, but one of the most difficult, for the practicing artist to sing, play or conduct Mozart appropriately. Not long ago I read this felicitous statement about Mozart's music: "That which is heavy floats and what is light weighs immensely." Everything considered, is it possible and necessary to say the same thing about any other musician? Certainly, Mozart's singular quality is connected with this inconsistency—or rather with the fact that this does not constitute an inconsistency for him.

Let me now say a word about what I would like to call the great, free *objectivity* with which Mozart traveled life's way. As a *human being* his great experiences were almost always dark and painful, at least beginning with his twentieth year; however, those bright, gay and even funny little experiences continually accompanied or framed, so to speak, the great experiences. In the fever of the night of his death, December 4 to 5, 1791, was he not still absorbed in his *Requiem,* and certainly also in his *Magic Flute,* which was being performed in the theater during these hours? But the *Requiem* is not his personal confession, nor is the *Magic Flute.* The subjective never becomes a theme of his music. He never used music to speak about himself, the situation or his mood. I do not know of any case when we can, with any degree of certainty, explain the character of one of his works from a simultaneous event of his life. Much less can we trace something like a biographical line from the sequence of his works. Mozart's life served his art, not vice versa—unless only in the prosaic way in which it provided him, his wife Constance, and their children with the necessary money (alas, so quickly spent!). If, however, the ever-welcome jobs came in and were executed, then he himself, his wife, his children, or, in earlier times, the unfaithful Aloysia Weber and the angry father, let alone the mean Archbishop Colloredo and his Count Arco, were left far, far behind. He put them aside in order to shape, again and again, a small piece of the sounding universe in which he lived, entirely apart from the great and small experiences of his life. And each time the result was, and still is today, an invitation to the listener, also, to come out a little from the snail shell of his own subjectivity.

Mozart came a long way as an *artist* too, as one can learn from the most comprehensive modern description of his work: in no less than thirty-four periods he touches in in passing and uses so many patterns. To trace this path must be an extremely interesting task for those who are skilled in such matters. But don't be captivated by such meritorious descriptions, for example, not to be induced to listen only to those works of Mozart which seem to come nearer to Beethoven, thus making Beethoven the final criterion for everything. Mozart displays, on his artistic way, so many exceptions to the rule, so many anticipations of later phases and recourses to earlier ones, that it would be unwise not to open oneself to the young Mozart as well as to the late one who was praised as classical. Think of this, for instance: what was *already* possible for him in *Idomeneo* is *still* in the *Magic Flute!* There is also, to this extent, a free Mozartian objectivity. He existed, in this early or that late phase, with the same ears facing the same sounding universe. Here he certainly wanted not to manifest his various technical achievements, but to dedicate himself merely to Dame Music, to whom he was sworn from his early childhood. The *sovereignty* of real *serving* which is perceivable in both these directions may be a genuine token of the singular quality of the man.

For the characterization of his singular quality it now seems appropriate to shift the very idea of *freedom* to the center from still another point of view. Mozart always had something to say, and said it as player and composer. However, you should not complicate or mar the impression of his works by burdening them with doctrines and ideologies which you thinks one has discovered, but which in reality have been read into them. There is no "moral of the story" in Mozart's works, neither a gross nor a sublime one. He has certainly discussed the texts of his operas with the librettists in all detail—but assuredly not for the purpose of achieving a profundity which they would have to create together. Notice what Mozart wrote in 1781 to his father: "In an opera, poetry absolutely has to be the obedient daughter of music." This clearly means that he did not allow Lorenzo da Ponte, much less Emanuel Schikaneder, to offer him any world-shaking themes; nor did he work with the librettists in order to hatch such themes and later transform them into music. What he wanted, and what he discussed, was the most appropriate basis and stimulus for catching and developing his own particular musical themes, motives, dramas and figurations. In their final execution these comprised pure reflections of the modest poetry of those third- or fifth-rate librettists.

In other words, Mozart's *Figaro* has nothing to do with the ideas of the French Revolution and *Don Giovanni* has nothing to do with the myth of the eternal libertine (as Kierkegaard asserted!). Certainly there does not exist a special Mozartian "philosophy of *Così fan tutte*" either, and one should not read too much "humanity-religion" and/or political mysteries into Mozart's *Magic Flute*. The fact is that, whether we like it or not (and it can be seen in his letters), neither the nature surrounding him nor the history, literature, philosophy or politics of his time touched him directly or in a concrete sense. Nor was he moved to represent or proclaim any decisions or dogmas. It is to be feared that he never read much, and he certainly never speculated or taught. There is no Mozartian metaphysics either. He sought and found only his musical possibilities, themes and tasks in the world of nature and spirit. With God, the world, men, himself, heaven and earth, life—and, above all, death—before his eyes, in his ears and in his heart he was an unproblematic person. For that reason he was a free man, in a way which was apparently allowed, ordered and therefore exemplary for him.

This involves the fact that his music was uniquely free from every exaggeration, basic friction and contradiction. The sun shines but does not dazzle the eyes, nor demolish nor scorch. Heaven arches above the earth but does not press upon or crush and swallow it. And so earth remains earth, but without being forced to hold its own against heaven in titanic revolt. In the same way darkness, chaos, death and hell render themselves conspicuous but are not allowed to prevail even for a moment. Mozart makes music, knowing everything from a mysterious center, and thus he knows and keeps the boundaries on the right and on the left, upward and downward. He observes moderation. Again he wrote, in 1781, that "the emotions, strong or not, never should be expressed *ad nauseam* and that music, even in the most horrible situation, never must offend the ears but must please them nevertheless. In other words, music must always remain music." He was (and I quote Grillparzer's beautiful words) the musician "who never did too little, and never did too much, and who always arrived at but never went beyond his goal."

There is no light which does not know the darkness too, no happiness which does not include sorrow; but also inversely, no alarm, no ire, no wailing to the aid of which peace would not come, from near or far. There is no laughter, therefore, without weeping, but no weeping without laughter either. There never was a Mozart of such utter gracefulness that the nineteenth century, after praising him, could grow justly tired of him. But neither did there exist this "demoniac Mozart" whom our century wanted to substitute. The very absence of all demons, the very stopping before the extreme, and precisely the wise confrontation and mixture of the elements (let us say it again) amounts to the freedom in which the true *vox humana* speaks in Mozart's music. In it the entire scale is unmuffled, but at the same time undistorted and uncramped. Whoever correctly hears him, may, as the human being he really is, feel himself understood and called to freedom: as the clever Basilio, the affectionate Cherubino, as Don Giovanni, the hero, or as the coward Leporello, as the gentle Pamina or the raging Queen of the Night, as the all-forgiving Countess, the terribly jealous Electra, the wise Sarastro and the foolish Papageno—all of whom lie hidden in us. Or we may think, as all of us do, of ourselves as persons destined for death, who yet live on and on.

Something at the last, however, must be perceived and mentioned. Mozart's center is not like that of the great theologian Schleiermacher, identical with balance, neutralization and finally indifference. What happened in this center is rather a splendid annulment of balance, a *turn* in the strength of which the light rises and the shadow winks but does not disappear; happiness outdistances sorrow without extinguishing it and the "Yes" rings stronger than the still-existing "No." Notice the *reversal* of the great dark and the little bright experiences in Mozart's life! "The rays of the sun *disperse* the night"—that's what you hear at the end of the *Magic Flute*. The play may or must still proceed or start from the very beginning. But it is a play which in some Height or Depth is winning or has already won. This directs and characterizes it. One will never perceive equilibrium, and for that reason uncertainty or doubt, in Mozart's music. This is true of his operas as well as of his instrumental music, and especially of his church music. Is not each *Kyrie* or *Miserere,* even if it begins at the lowest depth, carried by the trust that the prayer for grace has in fact been answered? *Benedictus qui venit in nomine Domini!* In Mozart's version he has apparently already arrived. *Dona nobis pacem!* This prayer, too, has already been answered in Mozart's music, in spite of everything. For this very reason his church music has to be called truly spiritual music, in spite of all well-known objections. Mozart never lamented, never quarreled. He would have been entitled to do so. Instead, he always executed that comforting turn which is priceless for everyone who hears it. That seems to me, as far as it can be explained at all, to be the secret of his *freedom* and thereby the nucleus of his singular quality, for which we asked at the beginning.

Finally a few words about things which are not closely connected with each other:

I leave one question unanswered: How is it possible that I, an evangelical Christian and theologian, can so proclaim Mozart? How could I do this even though he was such a Catholic and even a Freemason and besides through and through nothing else than just a musician? He who has ears to hear has certainly heard. May I ask all the others, who perhaps shake their heads in astonishment and alarm, to be momentarily contented with the general reference to the fact that the New Testament speaks not only about the kingdom of heaven, but also of the *parables* of the kingdom of heaven?

Briefly a few more sentences about some other points:

Mozart and the other great musicians. Don't be afraid that you will hear something fanatical now, because that would be very little in Mozart's line. Karl Friedrich Zelter, Goethe's musical consultant, once confided with a rude sigh to him: "As if after Mozart nobody else would be entitled to compose, to die or to find rest!" Certainly, nobody could or can be prevented from that. However, it may also be written down that the Prague professor Franz Niemetschek, seven years after Mozart's death, expressed the same idea in a more reticent way: "He who has once taken delight in Mozart's music, will *not easily* be satisfied with the music of another composer."

Mozart and Goethe. It is more than probable that Mozart did not know Goethe's works. He composed the "Song of the Violet" without knowing that he was dealing with this poet. And Goethe, to all appearances contented with the work of his Zelter, ignored Mozart's composition of his text. However, he too spoke about the "incomparability" of Mozart (unfortunately, we do not know in what sense), referred to him in one breath with Raphael and Shakespeare and considered him alone to be capable of setting his *Faust* to music. How would they have got along with each other? It seems to me difficult to compare these two men objectively because the Mozartian center is incompatible with Goethe's concentratedness. If I am not mistaken, the unquestionable unevenness of the two antagonistic aspects of life which characterize Mozart so much, his victorious turn and therefore his "very freedom," have no analogy in Goethe's conception.

Mozart and Basel. One of the Basel newspapers wrote this winter that Basel cannot be called a Mozart city. Well, Basel is not Salzburg or Prague or Vienna; Basel is just Basel. It may be that Bach and Beethoven are in general more highly valued here than Mozart. I cannot get away from a monstrous historical fact: when the Mozart family, on returning from their great concert tour in the fall of 1766, traversed Switzerland in haste, Mozart's father inconceivably preferred the itinerary through Zurich instead of through Basel in order to let his infant prodigies play there instead of before us. That happened, thank heaven, long, long ago. And if there live today a few hundred good people who continuously have an especially open ear for Mozart, that would be enough to make Basel, albeit on the quiet, a "Mozart city."

Finally: *Mozart and the great painters.* Goethe and, later on, others have drawn a parallel between Mozart's music and the paintings of Raphael. If a parallel may be drawn, I dare say it would be more appropriate to think of Sandro Botticelli's paintings, with their diversified but always quietly undulating and at the same time so admirably perspicuous treatment of outline, with their unmistakable relations and limitations and, especially, with their impenetrable knowledge, the questioning and answering of human eyes. In the same way that these eyes seem to *see,* Wolfgang Amadeus Mozart may have *heard* in his great freedom and may have been able then to play in the same great freedom which was given to him.

But now it is high time to hear Mozart himself again at the end of this festival![2]

~~~~~~~~~~~~~~~~~~~~~~~~~~~~~~~~ *6*

Christian Presuppositions for a Creative Culture

BY NELS F. S. FERRÉ

I

Every culture is a venture of faith. It is, as Tillich tells us, a response to the unconditional. There are three live options eligible to faith: the *supra*natural (Tillich's term), the *supernatural,* or the *natural.* Which shall faith choose? The thesis of this essay is that, in the Christian view, supernaturalism alone provides the conditions for a creative culture.

*Supra*naturalism denotes a realm which is beyond and essentially different from nature. No inner necessity yokes the two realms. The supranatural is related and manifested to the natural in a purely arbitrary and extreme fashion. The supranatural, therefore, neither affords a relevant social science nor exhibits inherent power for social change.

The *natural,* by contrast, denotes the world we know. However, mere description of it does not spell improvement any more than scientific statistics work salvation. If certain selective strands of social behavior are elevated as standards for human conduct, no added power is made available for social advance and no certainty is given that any forward movement will last. Unmitigated naturalism generates mere social realism.

Are there, then, Christian presuppositions for a creative culture that will be neither arbitrary and external nor impotent and fugitive? Do our hopes for culture rest on Christ?

*Super*naturalism, in contrast to supranaturalism and naturalism, has a truly chromatic relation to the world. Being is expressed in but not exhausted by existence. Our Christian faith postulates an event in active history wherein what is greater than this world comprehensively fulfills what is of this world. The confrontation of the world by the very principle of creativity at one and the same time establishes the needed tension within the everyday and discloses the power which works for change. Christ, who is *Agape,* is this event.

Agape—God—is outgoing and inclusive Love. He is not derived from, nor explained by, our ordinary world and yet is alone able to assure it ultimate meaning and salvation. Three sorts of demonstration would be needed to vindicate and illustrate these views:

1. A *historical* study showing that, whatever may be the relation of the historic Jesus to the historic and contemporary community, in Jesus Christ as a total historical event, *Agape* became known and proclaimed as fulfillment and realization.

2. A perceptive *social* analysis exhibiting the relevance of *Agape* as decisive meaning and power for fulfillment in both personal and social life.

3. Lastly, a *metaphysical* analysis to prove that the supreme option for faith is an event which (a) is inclusively related as fulfillment to all that we know and (2) points with power to the full potential for man, history, and nature. Faith's imperative choice and, fortunately, its goal is the Ground of Being.

While the Christ-event, having taken place in this world, is not known in some arbitrary system joined to this world and yet is also more than this world, it is still a definitive and exhaustless pattern for creative culture. *Agape* is never a mere principle; it is always a personal reality. Beyond being a pattern, it is a way of life, involving concern for each and all, without stunting imitation or dependent identification.

Being creatively for all without discrimination, *Agape* constitutes the standard for total or open community, allows no confinement to "in-groups." This Christian presupposition encourages a vital cultural pluralism which does not, however, set its members over-against and in conflict with each other. It provides a drive to creative fulfillment which enhances the kind of striving, in both persons and groups, which makes life adventure and gives it zest.

At the same time *Agape* is for each and every one *as a person.* No one becomes a means, but everyone is fully an end in himself. *Agape* implies not selflessness, but *self-fullness,* the fulfillment of the self in creative and co-operative concern for and service of the community. Even as the total community, if *agapaic,* offers unstinted concern for each person and for every group within it, so each person and group has a spontaneous responsibility and craving for the good of the community as a whole.

Moreover, if *Agape* be truly practiced, neither the entire community nor any person or group can then substitute attitude for action, or good intention for significant inquiry and conduct. *Agape* is concrete concern for the good of all and each, requiring complete enactment in deed. In *Agape,* attitude and act go inseparably together to maximum realization. Action within the austerity of *Agape,* moreover, demands study of the concrete situation of the person or community to be helped, in search of particular need. Such study opens action to influences of both the past and the contemporary world, preventing all invidiousness of application. As a standard, *Agape* is concerned with the fiulfillment of the past, with choice and the implementation of choice in the present, and with the fullest possible creative realization of the future. *Agape* is thus both an open and a definitive standard, eliciting attitude, inquiry, and act.

It is a capital mistake to reduce the Christ-event either to the Cross or to the historic Jesus. *Agape* involves God's own self-identification with the world that began far back with Creation but culminated in life and death for Jesus as the Christ. Although always centered beyond this world, *Agape* is insistently for this world, releasing to it creative life. In the total Christ-event, God has identified Himself with the world, in the world, for the world. The Christ-event, moreover, is continued in history through the inclusive, outgoing, and open community by which the Church is defined and appraised. In this community the power of ultimate Reality is available for effective social change, a leaven for the whole lump of society. Such power is the secret of the "saints who change the world."

Such power ultimately comes, directly or indirectly, from the Holy Spirit, who is the Spirit of love and truth. The Holy Spirit is the power for genuineness of persons and of community. He is the final dynamic and standard for integrity and the truly open society, for to be genuine is to accept the true self and the true community. Both are prepared for us by God and can be had effectively only as we come to know the open secret of Christ, as we accept the objective community that came through God's Christ-deed, and as we live in the present power of the Holy Spirit.

Christ, the Church, and the Holy Spirit are presuppositions for the maximum creative culture, not as statements of dogma nor as standards for pious "in-groups," but as the disclosures and bearers of reality. Theirs is the power by which we may become genuine and learn to share the creative freedom that comes from self-acceptance and community-acceptance within the outgoing and inclusive Love who God is. In or out of the Church, society attains its aim in proportion as it embodies God's will for creative truth. Culture is the fruit of faith, in accordance with the strength of its leaven or the way in which its past has been leavened by genuine believers.

The chief sign and symbol of the power not of this world is the Resurrection. The Son of God, God's fulfilling identification with a true man, could not be held fast by death. The death of the human was the climactic transformation of the human within its superorganic union with God. The historic became superhistoric. With Christ there began a new power for history: a new community. This new community, the community of the Resurrection, is, however, maintained only by its constant empowerment and guidance by the Holy Spirit—God's contemporary identification with His people through the Church for the world. Unless the Church be a community of concern for the world in all its needs, the Church is not the community of Christ.

II

The first Christian presupposition for a creative culture, then, is supernaturalism. Christian supernaturalism in turn involves faith in a personal God—the second presupposition. God is not a spiritual Personality, but a personal Spirit. He is the Ground of Being, not as the ontological basis of an impersonal order, however much structured for human good, but as One who by His very nature *purposes* the total as well as the individual good. He first purposed it for us in creating this cosmic order. He continues to purpose it in controlling the conditions for nations and persons. He is, as J. B. Pratt put it, a "Determiner of Destiny." Though nations rise and fall and mighty empires crumble, though human life itself vanish from the earth, we are assured that beyond evanescence and tragedy there is a total pattern in which nothing "walks with aimless feet." The great ages of faith, on the whole, have been the creative ages. The human spirit becomes most free to dare when it knows that man does not decide the final issue.

Man can know the existence of such control of the total world for the total good only when he understands and accepts the fact that God is *Agape*. Being *Agape*, God creates, purposes, and fulfills his intentions simply because it is His nature to do so. He purposed an order in Creation, it is claimed, wherein gradually the human spirit would be reared to be free and to be fulfilled in fellowship with God and man. The total orders of nature and of history exhibit the patient ways of God in achieving His eternal Purpose. Both orders, when finally seen in the full light of God in Christ as *Agape*, presuppose that eventually God Himself would come to fulfill, through the declaration and embodiment of His own Love, the work He had begun in nature and history.

On this point, Luther's words went quite contrary to Christian supernaturalism, as here interpreted, when he claimed that God did not need to come and be made Man, except that it was needful and profitable for us. On the contrary, the need of Love to come to those loved and to do everything possible for them is Its perfection.

Such a personal God establishes an order of providence in which man may participate. He has made a world where freedom matters. God's action is like that of the wise parent who steps aside—accepts a passive role—wherever children need to assume responsibility in order to grow. For this reason nature and history are open to man's creative contributions, even though God has never released the total outcome from His hands. Such generosity on the part of God is the presupposition for the general order of providence, which is, evidently, thus a further presupposition for a creative culture.

Regarding providence, another Reformer has faltered. Calvin made the will of God ultimate: God was sovereign and nothing could be rightly taught contrary to this fact. The sovereignty of God was thought of in terms of power. Therefore, God could not permit what He did not will. Man's free will was a contradiction of ultimates. So strange is religious truth, however, that this very Calvinist stress has led peculiarly to the enhancement of psychological responsibility before God and to an insistence on cultural seriousness that is hard to equal in the history of society. This one fact, in truth, witnesses that both life and history are under an ultimate Purpose! Calvin could have underscored God's control, however, as we shall see shortly, while still maintaining that God's sovereign purpose includes responsible freedom.

Modern man does not relish Calvin's faith. Instead, he glorifies responsible freedom. We cannot escape freedom, says Sartre, nor dare we forget that freedom entails social involvement. Such responsibility, apart from any sustaining ultimate order, however, becomes a tragic burden, and a source of despair to modern man. This should occasion no surprise. The sense of meaningless freedom is surely less conducive to the highest possible creative culture than the sense of determinism. Only the Christian order of general providence integrates and fulfills what is true in the stresses of both Calvin and Sartre.

Yet a conviction neither of purpose nor of participation in its embodiment is enough. Man's life is too short, too powerless, and too shut-in for these to suffice. Man needs to do more than work with God. He needs to rest in God and to see God's fulfilling action beyond his own achievement. He needs, therefore, to know the reality of *special* as well as of *general* providence; he needs to know of an order wherein he can commune with

God, repose in Him, and find concrete help from Him. He needs to pray! Prayer is communion with God, the resting of man's spirit in God's Spirit. Man's work with God becomes significant and effective mostly when it is a great prayer of thanksgiving and of companionship with God. Although God, on His side, needs man's participation because He ordains man to be free, and although He needs man to care, to create, to help others, to learn to build and to be built himself through such learning, man finds, on his side, that all human works are, in the end, puny beside the wonders of God that come for man's praying. When we are ready to receive for ourselves and for others what God has purposed, and when we express such readiness by communicating with God in prayer, God Himself enters history as the mighty champion of our common and individual good. Only thus can the power of lives like those of Jesus and of St. Francis be explained. God Himself came into history as power for good, behind, yet fulfilling, the mere presence of man.

A caution must be added. False prayer becomes a substitute for social responsibility. An overwhelming proportion of our prayers, it seems, are of this kind. True prayer, however, is the occasion for social participation. To participate with God in prayer is to learn of His purpose and also to enter into the kind of participation with men through which God works out His purpose. Although the primary reality of prayer is not social fruitfulness, but communion with God, no prayer is right or real that does not result in the kind of attitudes and commitments which promote open communication and creative community.

III

The third Christian presupposition for a creative culture—in addition to supernaturalism and faith in a personal God—is *life everlasting*. Supernaturalism, centered in the God who is the personal Spirit of *Agape,* cannot believe less. Life everlasting is an intrinsic involvement of the Christian God seen through the Christ-event. Life everlasting alone gives full and final meaning to history.

History has meaning as a whole only eschatologically. For purpose to be full and final, it must somehow gather up all of history in one great consummation. What we know of life "here below" is a matter of partial fulfillment, of broken patterns and final defeats. Such history neither solves nor settles issues. Unless there is a final event concluding and consummating our human history for all who live, have lived and shall live, then for the dead all things become as though they had never been. Nor is there any ultimate consummation of life on earth. Therefore, there can be no complete fulfillment of history apart from its being gathered up within the eternal purpose of God, and there fulfilled for all.

History is fulfilled within the Christian reality only in so far as it offers more than organismic wholeness. There can be total and purposive involvements of parts, as in a sick body, without there being total health. The imperfect organism requires healing and growth. Similarly, although the universe displays organic relations in the sense of mutual interaction and interdependence of parts—for otherwise the universe would have no real unity—our world is not well. The Christian faith goes basically beyond organismic wholeness, such as that proclaimed, for example, by Alfred North Whitehead, revealing instead a Planning beyond planning. Our world is one of organismic interaction of parts and persons, for freedom is real and serious; but beyond our planning lies the final planning of God. The meaning of history is not exhausted by our relations and its course is never finished by our last acts.

History for us has upper and lower limits, but it has no forward limit. God is always in front of history with endless possibilities at His disposal. History has a ceiling, for its purpose is to teach men responsibility, initiative, freedom, and personal reality through fellowship. History is not heaven. If our problems could be solved in history, history would become heaven and thereby be destroyed as history. History is ambiguity, problem, and suffering. All our victories and satisfactions are mottled, either partially or sooner or later. But neither is history hell. Just as history has a ceiling, so it has a floor. History knows collapse and extinction of civilizations as well as their rise and growth. Even our whole earth might be destroyed by human ingenuity and moral death. But God is the keeper of history above and below. His direction is forward. He stands in front of all historic choices with the resources of eternity, and all limits are contained within His limitless grace.

History is also the arena for the overcoming of evil. On the level of experience, evil can only be mitigated by the gathering up of meaning and making it effective within the transmutation of life. God's forgiveness of sin and His redemptive activity reach to the uttermost—above, below and beyond history. The Cross is the clue to the meaning of evil—the identification of the innocent with the guilty. The Resurrection is the key to the *solution* of evil—its conquest, transformation, and elimination by victorious Love.

Moral evil owes its existence to man's need to learn freedom through over-againstness. Sin is man's faithlessness and rebellion, his selfishness and self-perversion that are as real and as horrible as depicted by the Cross-light of God's love in Christ. But God foresaw and willed our kind of world not causing sin—which is the act of man's freedom—but preparing for the use and cure of sin by the eternal purpose which He purposed in Christ before the Creation: namely, to reconcile all men to Himself through grace, the grace symbolized and summarized by the Cross. Thus evil does not exist as a constant contrast to good, but as the occasion for learning and holding fast to the love of God. Natural evil begins to acquire context for its solution only within the central meaning of the gospel.[2] And upon the dependable truth of God as *Agape,* the Sovereign Lord who is ultimately saving Love, depends the full and final meaning of history. History flowers in creative culture most readily when it is understood as the carrier of a total meaning, a final fulfillment within right relations to God through His own mighty acts and saving deeds.

History is fulfilled only by eternity. The Resurrection is both a power and a promise. The Christ-event covers all of life within one whole community consummated at the end of human time. Within its boundless reality and richness all generations meet and assist each other across time, in life here and beyond, in ways that are not now for us to know. It is sufficient that we can trust God and fulfill the invitation to creative culture.

However clear is the central light of God in Christ, eternity must be mystery. Kierkegaard knew that the gospel, while in itself crystal clear and complete certainty, is at the same time paradox to sinful creatures of time. In one sense God is hidden from men in history, for they must be free from God if they are to carry real cultural responsibility; in another sense God has taken away the veil and put His light in the face of Jesus Christ, for men must see and trust beyond their knowing. History involves freedom from God, freedom with God, and freedom in God. God gives us revelation for a dependable direction, the direction of the open and inclusive community of concern. Yet He gives us also an unknown way to walk for the sake of adventure in creative culture.

In sum: There are *three* Christian presuppositions for a creative culture:

1. A world of reality beyond all culture, affording a pattern for explaining the origin of human history, offering power for social change, and providing a standard for social conduct.

2. God, who is the personal Spirit of *Agape,* creating the conditions for responsible freedom through the order of general providence, and for personal trust and the effectiveness of prayer through special providence.

3. Life everlasting as a permanently dependable direction for life and culture creatively walking in the way.

The Christian faith gives full hope to all, creatively in search of full sight. The Christian faith is therefore measured by the genuineness of its love, which is never confinable to personal relations but must reach realistically and redemptively into every realm of culture and social relations. The sign of man's redemption is that he has been set free and is at work within a concrete community of concern, under God, for all men in all their conditions.

~~~~~~ Part IV
Religion and Language:
Myth, Symbol and Belief

7

The Modern Diogenes:
A Kierkegaardian Crotchet

BY STANLEY ROMAINE HOPPER

Bevor man den Menschen sucht, muss man die
Laterne gefunden haben.
—Nietzsche, *Menschliches, Allzumenschliches*, II, 7

When it comes to man's plight in the "modern world" one hardly knows whether to begin with Nietzsche or with Kierkegaard. Nietzsche's aphorism given in the original in the above legend has the advantage of being terse and to the point: "Before one seeks for men, one must have found the Lantern." It takes hold at once. It elicits an immediate and intuitive consent. It adheres to the mind like a burr, and once its aphoristic hook has caught in the subconscious it works there secretly, stirring the self into a disturbing sense that there is something more here than was at first perceived.

With Kierkegaard it is different. We know beforehand that every stylistic blandishment is an invitation to his particular kind of rhetorical arabesque; and if we follow, as we invariably do, we soon learn that he is the Piper piping us out of our habitual Hamelins toward some unforeseen mountain of decision where, like as not, a cavern will open and swallow us. For

> . . . lo, as they reached the mountain-side,
> A wondrous portal opened wide,
> As if a cavern was suddenly hollowed;
> And the Piper advanced and the children followed.[1]

The following passage from Kierkegaard is longer than Nietzsche's, and looks to be quite innocent; but it is really a wonderful little puzzle that has somehow escaped the notice of the many scholars and theologians who have hastened in recent years to write books about him. It occurs in what he calls a "confession of faith." He writes, simply, that "if a man is to be a Christian, it is doubtless requisite for him to believe something *definite;* but it is just as certainly requisite for him to be *quite definite* that 'he' believes. In the same degree that thou dost direct attention exclusively to the definite things a man must believe, in that same degree dost thou get away from faith."[2]

It is the latter part—about definite beliefs and faith—that contains the conundrum, and which relates it eventually to Nietzsche's problem: for the one (Kierkegaard's) has to do with theology and faith and the other (Nietzsche's) has to do with our search for truth; and the place where they meet is in the problem of the Self, particularly as we know this problem today.

This coinciding will not be apparent at first (which would spoil the conundrum); and since they are both "thoughts which wound from behind," we shall do well to begin as they begin, complying with Kierkegaard's strategy as though completely taken in by it, and then rescuing ourselves at the appropriate moment by way of Nietzsche's lantern. For Nietzsche's aphorism deletes its author quite easily. It rises into the autonomy of its own paradox, and presides there, like a Presence, over our dialectical twistings and turnings; whereas Kierkegaard, though he never explored the city of Athens "looking for a man," was nonetheless a gadfly not unlike Diogenes, the "Socrates gone mad," haunting the streets of Copenhagen searching for a genuine Christian. And this is not far from the subject of our inquiry either, for it is doubtless true that he who would search for men, or for truth, or for a Christian, must first have found the Lantern.

I

We begin, then, with Kierkegaard.

We shall not be surprised to find that his little paradox opens directly into the heart of his total problem—the problem of faith itself, and of the Self in relation to reality. Were we also writing a book about Kierkegaard we should be delighted to follow this unfolding line by line into the heart of his argument; but we must be content with a few indications only, and with these as illustrating a problem of our own—the problem of theology and faith in our present culture.

When Kierkegaard says that in the degree that we direct attention exclusively to the definite things a man must believe we are in the same degree getting away from faith he is pointing to one of the sharpest dilemmas confronting the contemporary theologian. It is not merely that "Christianity is not a doctrine but an existential communication," as he argued in the *Concluding Unscientific Postscript,* or that Christianity is "the precise opposite of speculation" and our task is to learn how "to exist in it, and not to waste time by trying to understand it speculatively."[3] *Dogmatic* theology can direct attention *systematically* to the definite things a man must believe and may do so, at least hypothetically, without doing it *speculatively*. We come nearer to the point in another of Kierkegaard's remarks, namely, that "in relation to an existential communication, existing in it is the maximum of attainment, and understanding it is merely an evasion of the task."[4] Here, again, one may engage in the constructive task of theological definition of doctrine without aiming at "understanding" in any analytical sense; moreover, the term "understanding" is so manifold that the point is far from precise. Does not Kierkegaard himself *understand* that he must always "reason from existence, not toward existence," and that the Reason always "seeks a collision" with that which thought cannot think, with the Unknown, and that it calls this Unknown "God"?[5]

But his term "evasion" is useful. It is quite possible to talk about the things it is necessary for one to believe in such a way as to avoid the issue of faith. It is quite possible for the theologian to enumerate the doctrines and to proclaim their authority in such a way as to deprive his time of its *encounter with itself* in faith. This is the problem: despite the fact—and perhaps even because of it—that we have witnessed in the past thirty years the most vigorous resuscitation of theological consciousness since the time of the Reformation, Kierkegaard is already there to remind us that this extraordinary activity may have applied itself so assiduously to the definite things a man must believe if he is to be a Christian that the very effort has constituted a primary factor standing in the way of a recovery of faith in our time.

We must add immediately that an observation of this kind must not be proposed superficially. Michelet's remark that "theology is the art of befuddling oneself methodically" has no relevance here, since it belongs to an era of overconfidence and levity. Nor has our observation anything to do with the easy optimisms and pessimisms of the preceding decades, nor with either the pietisms or the skepticisms stemming from the same: the dreams of the one and the melancholias of the other have long since shattered on our epoch's agonies. We are dimensions deeper than all of that, else the question could not even arise. The dilemma of the theologian arises from the uneasy realization that in directing his energies and attention upon the definite things a man must believe, and by supporting them by appeals to authority (whether of "revelation" or the "Word" or "tradition" or the "Church"), he may unwittingly have been masking the time's consciousness rationalistically from the abysses of uncertainty which everywhere open beneath it. Which means that, while theology's claims might be "true" within its own context, the context itself has failed to reach into the derelict inwardness of the aeon's despair: hence it brings with it no healing and is powerless to reconcile, and by both obscuring the cause and obstructing the cure it becomes an accomplice in further alienating man from himself.

It is to Kierkegaard's credit that he saw this. He turned from the "objective" problem to the time's subjective concern, as though he saw almost intuitively that the forms and symbols of the culture had become but husks of former meanings and therefore no longer opened into life but imposed the burden of their emptiness upon the people. His was an age which, while it had left everything standing, had none the less emptied many things of their significance. So Kierkegaard did what the other earnest seekers of the age have done: he turned inward to see whether some foothold for meaning might be found by way of self-knowledge and faith.

What he discovered about faith was disconcerting: disconcerting, that is, to all but those who have made the same discovery. It was that faith is not faith in any object, nor in a doctrine, nor in "definite things a man must believe"—"for in fact He who is the object of faith is considerably nearer to a man than the distance of eighteen hundred years suggests, mediated by the traditions . . ."[6] Just how near is this "He" of our faith? Kierkegaard more than once suggests that the quickest way to find out is in moments of mortal danger, for "in mortal danger one becomes infinitely sharp of hearing, and what one must hear is *infinitely near.*"[7] But how near is the infinitely near? This will be learned by the man who has so far discovered the depth of his need as to become the man who is *"truly concerned."*[8] He it is who learns that

the need brings with it the nutriment, [that] *the thing sought is in the seeking which seeks it;* faith, in the concern at not having faith; love, in the concern at not loving. The need brings with it the nutriment, not *by itself,* as though it produced the nutriment, but *by virtue of God's ordinance* which joins together the need and the nutriment.[9]

It is this which effects that "inward transformation of the whole mind"[10] which characterizes the man of faith.

Now, Kierkegaard proffers his insights not as a principle but rather as a testimony or witness to a fact of experience. It turns out *existentially* that the thing sought is in the seeking which seeks it: the secret of faith is the secret of seeking, and through the seeking of making a discovery—the discovery that the finding is experienced paradoxically as *being found;* or, more paradoxically, of returning to where we have always been—

You will come to a great city that has expected your return for years.[11]

Pascal, in his devotional poem entitled *The Mystery of Jesus,* put it a little differently. For him, it is Jesus himself who speaks to him inwardly, saying

Console yourself! Thou wouldst not be seeking me hadst thou not already found me.[12]

It is in such passages, Sainte-Beuve remarked, "that Pascal has more hold upon us today than any writer of his time."[13] But in spite of this opinion, the analogous witness of Hölderlin is probably nearer to us, for the simple reason that he is more God-forsaken and not sustained in like degree by any adequate Christ symbol. Nevertheless, he also knows that

That which thou seekest is near, and already coming to meet thee.[14]

And obviously Lessing's choice of the eternal pursuit of the truth over the truth itself (reserved to God alone) will be seen to be relevant here. Let us remain, however, with Kierkegaard.

His proposition that the thing sought is in the seeking which seeks it is preceded by two *Discourses,* the one entitled "Man's Need of God Constitutes His Highest Perfection" (1844) and the other "What It Means to Seek God" (1845),[15] and these in turn are flanked at one end by his great explorations of the problem of self-knowledge in Plato's *Meno* (in the *Philosophical Fragments,* 1844) and his definition of the Self as Spirit (in *Sickness Unto Death,* 1849) at the other.

Since a detailed examination of this elaborate argument is out of the question here, let us note simply that in postulating man's need of God as his deepest need Kierkegaard makes a distinction between a man's "first self" and a "deeper self" and evokes a dialogue between these two: such a dialogue, indeed, as suggests anticipations of the distinction between the Conscious and the Unconscious as disclosed in modern depth psychology; and such a dialogue also as permits him to distinguish between a "sickness unto death" and a "sickness unto life." In the discourse on what it means to seek God he distinguishes between a "first wonder" and a "second wonder."

It is out of this dialogue between selves that man comes to recognize his need of God. The "first self" is a self which founds itself upon its prudential self-knowledge. It is enamored with the external world and with its own competence to deploy that world in terms of its wishes, dreams, projections and desires. During this phase, as Kierkegaard says, "the real self seems so distant . . . that the entire world appears to him to be nearer than his self."[16] This statement describes very accurately the attitude of our modern utilitarian man, who has his existence, as it were, outside himself, with his "understanding" (rational, logical, positivistic, empirical, practical, and, because of all this, unwittingly magical) outside the immediacy of his own being. But the "deeper self" disturbs this dream. It begins to whisper that

> . . . the world, which seems
> To lie before us like a land of dreams,
> So various, so beautiful, so new,
> Hath really neither joy, nor love, nor light,
> Nor certitude, nor peace, nor help for pain . . .[17]

This is a painful moment for the self which does not know that this is the beginning of a deeper self-knowledge. Such a man will experience the insight as "an anxiety-breeding deception," for "instead of being a master of his fate he becomes a needy petitioner; instead of being able to do everything he can do nothing at all."[18] He reaches the point where he must either "slay the deeper self, plunge it into oblivion, when all is lost! or he must admit that the deeper self is right."

This is indeed a painful state: the first self sits there and gazes at the alluring fruits displayed all about it, and it is so clear that it needs only to grasp the means at hand to achieve a complete success, as everyone must admit. But the deeper self sits there thoughtful and serious, like a physician at the bedside of the sick. But it also wears an air of translucent gentleness, because it knows that this sickness is not unto death but unto life.[19]

So, when the first self yields, the two are reconciled, and the Self emerges as having met the first condition of true self-knowledge. It is now in a position to discover, since trials and dangers and conflicts will still come, that it is no imperfection to be in need: that, as a matter of inward fact, it is precisely in the recognition of the *fundamental* need that the highest perfection of the true Self lies, for the Self discovers that *of itself* it can do nothing—either outwardly or inwardly. And at precisely this point it comes to know God.

Then God is with him, coming more quickly than the light that penetrates the darkness, swifter than the thought that dispels the fog; present as promptly as only He can be, *who was already there.*[20]

Equally impressive is Kierkegaard's argument from "wonder," developed in parallel form. It rightly comes *after* the foregoing disclosure of man's need for God, the God who is already there; for the moment we are aware of the need we become seekers for the place where God is—our highest good. We do not know at first where or what this unknown good is, but where it "shows itself, there wonder is present, and wonder is the sense of the immediate consciousness of God, and the beginning of all deeper understanding."[21]

The first wonder, however, is the naïve and ambiguous wonder (containing both fear and ecstasy) which we experience when first we are overwhelmed with the incredible miracle of things. This is Kant's wonder at "the starry heavens above," and Augustine's paean to the beauty and utility of the creation,[22] and Byron's apostrophe to the ocean, and Christopher Fry's astonishment at the intrinsic miracle of the commonplace.

> Nothing can be seen
> In the thistle-down, but the rough-head thistle comes.
> Rest in that riddle. I can pass to you
> Generations of roses in this wrinkled berry.
> There: now you hold in your hand a race
> Of summer gardens, it lies under centuries
> Of petals. What is not, you have in your palm.
> Rest in the riddle, rest; why not?[23]

But we do not rest in the riddle, though the highest expression of this wonder is "that God is the inexplicable whole of existence, as sensed by the imagination . . ."[24] There is that in the "infinite spaces" which frightens us, as Pascal confessed. We are intimidated by the sense of "an enormous being which is when it has been, which is and yet is not" and which bends over us as a kind of fate imposing intimations of death and awful indifference to our seeking: and alas! our seeking passes over into striving, as we set out to secure ourselves by our own powers against the magnificent mutations of an alien world. So "the enchantment is over, the wonder forgotten. . . . It happened once to every man when he took leave of his youth, that life stood still and he perished."[25] "One learns wonder from a child and fear from a man."[26]

A second wonder is possible when the first wonder has been lost through striving and being driven upon despair. It is possible that such a man may be brought to discover that *he already has* what he has so assiduously been seeking, that "the thing sought is given, that it is in the possession of him who stands there and loses it in his misunderstanding: this arouses the whole wonder of man."[27] Now comes the decisive passage:

And so it is with this second wonder, it changes the seeker, and by this change he comes to seek something different, indeed the very opposite; for now seeking means the seeker is himself changed. He no longer looks for the place where the thing sought is concealed, for this is exactly within him; nor does he look for the place where God is, he does not strive there, for God is with him, very near him, near him everywhere, omnipresent in every moment, but he shall be changed so that he may in truth become the place where God dwells . . . was it not a fearful thing, my reader, that the object of your seeking was so near you, that you did not seek God, but God sought you?[28]

II

Now, it has been necessary to put the reader in possession of this argument, rather hastily sketched, in order to place ourselves in position to make several observations—on Kierkegaard, on ourselves, and on the task of theology in our time.

First of all, we see through Kierkegaard how this recognition of man's need of God, and the existential paradox of finding through right seeking, leads to a solution to the problem of self-knowledge first propounded in the *Philosophical Fragments*. This was the "pugnacious proposition" of Plato's *Meno:* "one cannot seek for what he knows, and it seems equally impossible for him to seek for what he does not know. For what a man knows he cannot seek, since he knows it; and what he does not know he cannot seek, since he does not even know for what to seek."[29] Socrates resolves this difficulty by arguing that we have been in possession of the truth all along, but have forgotten it through mistaking the "outside" world of appearance for the real; so he has but to cross-question us out of our supposed fixed knowledge, or opinion, back into ourselves where we shall "recollect" the true world of noetic essences, forms and ideas. Kierkegaard objects to this view on the ground that it underestimates the nature of our defection, regarding that as *ignorance* which ought to be regarded as *error* or sin, and conceiving the Teacher as one who is merely the occasion of my recalling the knowledge of the Truth of which I am antecedently the possessor, whereas when I realize the real nature of my error I will realize too that my *condition* has changed and I must find a Teacher who can also restore the condition and "give the learner the Truth."[30] Such a Teacher would be a Saviour through whom I become a new creature.

From here on we move dogmatically, and not existentially, elaborating a "project for thought" which none the less has the merit of showing the "condition of Error" to be "polemic" against the Truth; and so the learner, having lost the condition of his pure relationship to God, is constantly in the course of forfeiting the relationship, though sustained, to be sure, by the antecedent and irremovable relationship which the creature must always bear to his Creator. Kierkegaard also recognizes that this is a condition of "exile," and that to be exiled by one's own self is to be bound.[31] Beyond this, however, the analysis is formal, and the condition brought by the Teacher, who is also Himself the condition, is appropriated by faith understood as a "leap." Yet at this point such a leap is clearly a self-coercive act, and not a spontaneous response to grace within or love without, and as such the act is necessarily as polemic against the Truth as any other self-assertion under the condition of the self's exile from the true. Kierkegaard is at this stage one of the violent ones who would take the Kingdom by storm.

Clement of Alexandria, in whose work will be found the original of this argument, had perhaps a sounder intuition here; for, accepting the Platonic opposition between idea and ignorance, he transposed the terms into a new key. He moved from the Platonic *idea* to the Christian *Word,* from the Platonic $\nu\hat{\omega}$ to the Christian $\theta\epsilon\hat{\omega}$, from the Platonic ignorance to the Christian *knowledge of ignorance*—which is itself a preparatory learning. Know thyself, for Clement, meant learning many existential things: that we are mortal, that we are human beings, that we must seek to know for what we were born, and what our relation to God is, etc.[32]

Just as he transposed the Platonic intellectualism into existentialist contexts, so in a daring comparison Clement converts the Socratic method into Christian reticence:

Alcibiades: Do you not think that I shall know about what is right otherwise?
Socrates: Yes, if you have found out.
Al.: But you don't think I have found out?
Soc.: Certainly, if you have sought.
Al.: Then you don't think I have sought?
Soc.: Yes, if you think you don't know.

So (continues Clement) with the lamps of the wise virgins lighted at night in the great darkness of ignorance, which the Scripture signified by "night." Wise souls, pure as virgins, understanding themselves to be situated amidst the ignorance of the world, kindle the light, and rouse the mind, and illumine the darkness, and dispel ignorance, and seek truth, and await the appearance of the Teacher.[33]

It is the waiting that is difficult, which Kierkegaard had not at first learned; for the knowledge of our ignorance is the learning that this ignorance is what the Scriptures call "night." We "all go into the night":

I said to my soul, be still, and let the dark come upon you
Which shall be the darkness of God. . . .

I said to my soul, be still, and wait without hope
For hope would be hope for the wrong thing; wait without love

For love would be love of the wrong thing; there is yet faith
But the faith and the love and the hope are all in the waiting. . . .[34]

This is the position of our culture today. "I do not deny God," says
Heidegger. "I state his absence. My philosophy is a waiting for God. Here
is the problem of our world. Not in gloom."[35] But if not in gloom, then we
wait expectantly, and we trim the lamps of our ultimate concern, learning
that we are mortal, that we are human, learning for what we were born,
everywhere making ready the place where in truth the Bridegroom may
dwell.

III

Perhaps it would be better to say that we are "waiting for Godot,"[36]
and that this is a truer representation of the problem of our world. We
move about a little, we talk, we contrive abstractions about our situation,
we sit, the earth turns; but meanwhile we do nothing. We wait. We wait
for "Godot"—for something, anything that promises to come and free us
from our condition, whether this something be "God" or the "Second
Coming" or the "new Order" or the social revolution or the nine-day diet.
Man waits for help from the outside. And his waiting arises out of his
refusal to accept his condition—his finiteness, his mortality, his responsibility for employing his proper powers to become free through himself.
Meanwhile he continues to talk, and he projects his finite existence into the
infinite and there petitions his unrealized potentialities, in the form of the
"supernatural," or "cause and effect," or the "moral law," or Mephistoph-
eles, to come to his aid and release him into freedom. And the world
turns, and man talks, his guilt increasing in geometric ratios, as the infinite
projections of his responsibilities and powers return upon him as categorical moral demands, browbeating him into impotence and fear or driving him into fantasies and forms whereby he may serve as priest and judge
to his own delinquencies.

On behalf of Clement it may be said that he understood quite well that
the language of religion was a language of symbols and parables, and that
by reason of these he aimed to capture man beneath his rationalized projections.

John the apostle says: "No man hath seen God at any time. The only-
begotten God, who is in the bosom of the Father, He hath declared Him"—
calling invisibility and ineffableness the bosom of God. Hence some have called
it the Depth, as containing and embosoming all things, inaccessible and boundless.[37]

And when the Scripture says, "Moses entered into the thick darkness where God was," this shows to those capable of understanding, that God is invisible and beyond expression by words. And "the darkness"—which is, in truth, the unbelief and ignorance of the multitude—obstructs the gleam of truth.[38]

When Clement speaks of the "Saviour Himself" it is in the language of metaphor: for he is "our spiritual garden . . . into whom we are planted, being transferred and transplanted, from our old life, into the good land. And transplanting *contributes to fruitfulness*."[39] In like manner Jesus is also the Light, and the shepherd, and the door; Clement returns once more from the Teacher to the axioms to which the Teacher points: "the righteous man will seek the discovery that flows from love, to which if he hastes he prospers. For it is said, 'To him that knocketh, it shall be opened; ask, and it shall be given to you.' "[40]

On behalf of Kierkegaard it may be said that, while he was not a poet, as he proclaimed himself to be, he was aesthetic enough to recognize the place of the parable—such as Faust, Don Juan, the Wandering Jew, Hamlet, Abraham sacrificing Isaac, Job—and that, while he was an inveterate logician, he was not a dull one, which led him paradoxically not into his own cleverness but into the Paradox—unless, indeed, the Paradox is precisely the projection of his own cleverness. For "the paradox is not a concession but a category, an ontological definition which expresses the relation between an existing cognitive spirit and eternal truth."[41] Twelve years earlier he proclaimed his necessity for finding "the *idea* for which I can live and die."[42] So Christ was for him the incarnation of a category, the Paradox in whom his subjective concern for the relation between an existing cognitive spirit, himself, and eternal truth, the Wholly Other, was visibly reconciled. And this was fortunate. For the "infinite qualitative difference" which his logic asserted betwixt himself and his projected "God" would have recoiled on him as the Great Destroyer, which he partly intuited: for "God [he held] cannot be the object for man because God is the subject, and for that very reason the reverse is absolutely true: when a man denies God he does not harm God but destroys himself."[43] He partly intuited the metaphysical posturing of his cleverness when he sensed that taking cognizance of God and His infinite qualitative difference was sinful—for had not Sören Kierkegaard, who passionately longed with all his inwardness for the sense of the *presence* of God, effectively banished Him—thus "denying" Him and his own father's dominance at the same time—by the very incommensurateness of the categories of time and eternity? "God is near enough," he would argue in "What It Means to Seek God," "but no man can see God without purity, and sin is impurity, and therefore no one can take cognizance of

God without becoming a sinner."[44] However, "purity" in this context is not a moral category, but a category of transparency, by reference to which "cognizance" of any kind breaks up the transparency of the pure category, making it "impure." But—and here is the psychological as well as the logical equivocation—impurity is sin, a moral category. The Paradox could only justify this infinite offense by bringing transparency, as God, into cognition, as the world, and so lifting the cognitive part to deity.

Once again, fortunately, Kierkegaard was saved by his aesthetic sense, which converted the Paradox into the Pattern and the Paradigm. This is later, of course (as in his *Training in Christianity,* 1850); but it confirmed for him his earlier recognition that "in the same degree . . . thou dost direct the attention exclusively to the definite things a man must believe, in that same degree dost thou get away from faith."[45] Or, still better, as he put it in 1845, some men find it so hard to find God that they "prove that God exists, and find evidence necessary"; but the author of such a proof "has *placed himself outside,* he does not deal with God, but considers something about God."[46]

IV

Clearly, this being *outside* the true relationship with God comes close to the heart of the problem as to where the true is to be found. It also describes trenchantly the condition of modern man, of whom Rilke complains that

> . . . we, spectators always, everywhere,
> looking at, never out of, everything![47]

We stand even outside our own experiences. Utilitarian society has produced the utilitarian man, who can sanction nothing which does not receive the approval of the causal account of things rendered by the operational reason. Significance is attached to externals, and man has placed his understanding *outside* the immediacy of his own being, which Kierkegaard's "deeper self" asserts and which calls for understanding from within. For we are "the hollow men"—devoid of inwardness:

> The eyes are not here
> There are no eyes here
> In this valley of dying stars
> In this hollow valley
> This broken jaw of our lost kingdoms . . .

And we remain "sightless, unless The eyes reappear."

Language too has been sapped of its image-evoking power.

> Alas!
> Our dried voices, when
> We whisper together
> Are quiet and meaningless
> As wind in dry grass . . .[48]

Words have become *things,* like other external objects, to be manipulated causally within the predicative order of "truth" and "reality" as reduced rationalistically to a logic of identity which has lost its metaphysical reference. So modern man must identify thought with the abstract organization of data, neglecting the symbolic and metaphorical origins of language arising out of the experienced moment of the subjective node of time and thought and being. Perhaps behind all this lies the intellectualistic subordination of reality to the *notion* of being as the ontological myth of the principle of identity superimposed upon the world of "becoming." Such subordination leaves us standing *outside* of "being," the projected myth of the principle of identity. If so, a *theo*logy, working within the structure of the projection, would be equally mythical and rationalistic, hovering conceptually

> Between the idea
> And the reality . . .[49]

A distinguished Roman Catholic theologian writes:

A complete abandonment of all symbolism, or attempt at its abandonment, could only result in a sort of bizarre rationalism, as was the case with the odd character of medieval legend, Till Eulenspiegel, half clown and half sage. Till's aim was to mock all human pretense by taking every allegorical or figurative expression in an absolutely literal sense, and to treat every symbol in the same spirit. In this way he held up the "mirror" (Spiegel) to human pretense, but in so doing drove himself into an arid and sterile spiritual desert.[50]

Good, and it is surely true that a bizarre rationalism, such as we know it today, would result from the abandonment of all symbolism. But Tyl—Tyl Eulenspiegel!—he was a mirror all the same. And did he not, perhaps, reveal the *outside*-ness of the projected symbols which covered the abstract nakedness of scholastic rationalism? Clowns, it has been said, are the gods of ous circuses—the "type of the incomplete and lonely hero who is able to give back to the dull unknowing public a compressed picture of itself . . . [one whose] performance . . . is sufficiently improvised, sufficiently drawn up from a deep subconscious understanding of the world, to make it resemble the creation of a poem . . ."[51] Is it not the ubiquity of *both* the clowns and the crucifixions of Georges Rouault that makes his painting "the most humanly and morally pathetic art of our time" and elevates it (as Jacques Maritain has witnessed) "to hieratic grandeur and eloquence?"[52] Could not Tyl, the half-clown, have been going about the streets of Madrid looking for a man of flesh and bone, carrying the lantern of his lonely inwardness ironically in his hand?

A distinguished Protestant theologian has written:

According to Holy Scripture God's revelation is a ground which has no sort of higher or deeper ground above or behind it, but is simply a ground in itself, and therefore as regards man an authority from which no appeal to a higher authority is possible. Its reality and likewise its truth do not rest upon a superior reality and truth, are under no need of an initial actualization or legitimation as a reality from any such point, and so are also not measured by reality and truth such as might be found at such another point, are not to be compared with such, nor judged and regarded as reality and truth in the light of such. On the contrary, God's revelation has its reality and truth wholly and in every respect—i.e. ontically and noetically—within itself, etc., etc. . . .[53]

Would not a little first-class spoofing from some Tyl Eulenspiegel be highly edifying here?

"You here?" said the young girl. "Is there no fire there, then?"
"There? No," answered Ulenspiegl.
"But that bell that peals out so sadly?"
"It doesn't know what it's doing," replied Ulenspiegl.
"And that doleful trumpet? And all the people running?"
"The number of fools is infinite," (said he).[54]

Or perhaps if some ironist with a talent for logic and cleverness—perhaps Kierkegaard himself—might come, carrying his modest lantern of logical analysis in his hand, and lifting his light to the pages (as though it were not already as plain as the daylight), exclaim: How really wonderful! Twelve complete lines without a single predication of the pure category of being! And four absolute terms for the Absolute, told like the beads of a rosary from "God" to "revelation" to "reality" to "truth" and back to "God" again, turning "ontically" and "noetically" into itself!—a most remarkable tautology in which the assertion that there is nothing "higher" than the "highest" is consistently maintained throughout save for that tiniest and almost unnoticeable break where the term "authority" is smuggled in almost as though it were but one more equivalent term for "God" (instead of being a sly confession of guilt for having placed oneself *outside* the human in order to take cognizance of God *without* becoming a sinner by cognizing Him in the pure transcendency of the hypostatized notion of "the highest"): for "revelation" may equally well show that what is authoritative about God is precisely that He is not authoritarian and wants my acceptance of my true nature and not my obedience to "His" depersonalizing command.

And knowing that "humour is also the joy which has overcome the world,"[55] and musing on the fact that *Dogmatiks* are almost uniformly humorless, he might sketch briefly another Scenario[56]:

Whether a Tautology is a Beginning
Prologue in Heaven
Dramatis Personae: Kierkegaard, a Dane; The Protestant
Theologian; Chorus of Noetic Ideas, robed in transparency
and seated in a circle.

Kierkegaard sits by the fire, reading in a subdued voice from the GUILTY?/ NOT GUILTY? of his *Stages on Life's Way,* listening to the sound of the unbridled flow of the sentences of Frater Taciturnus. The Protestant Theologian, seated in the magic circle of noetic transparencies reading from Karl Barth's *Kirchliche Dogmatik,* Vol. I, Pt. I, Section 8, ch. 2, "The Root of the Doctrine of the Trinity," p. 350, leaves the charmed circle and goes across to the Dane in order to protest the formula that "faith is subjective certitude of the objectively uncertain."

Kierkegaard: Shall we begin by being in complete disagreement, or in agreement upon something which we will call an assumption?

Prot. Theo: —— —— —— ——

Kierkegaard: With what assumptions do you begin?

Prot. Theo.: From none at all: revelation has its reality within itself.

Kierkegaard: That is quite possible; perhaps you do not begin at all?

Prot. Theo.: I not begin! I who have projected a *Kirchliche Dogmatik* in five volumes, with each volume subdivided into two parts of some five to six hundred pages each?

Kierkegaard: Ye Gods! what a hecatomb you are sacrificing.

Prot. Theo.: But I begin from nothing other than God's revelation which has its ground within itself.

Kierkegaard: Is that not from anything?

Prot. Theo.: No, it is just the opposite. In this way everything is understood from *before* the beginning. With revelation as my surrogate, so to speak, to guarantee the authority of what I say, my task is exclusively to direct attention to the definite things a man must believe; though I must admit (and here I quote from myself, Section 8, ch. 2, p. 356) that "there is no reasonable way in which we could or can contradict either Arius or Pelagius, Tridentine Catholicism or Servetus, Schleiermacher or Tillich directly out of the Bible, as though their false doctrines were already contradicted there to such and such an extent *totidem syllabis et literis.* . . . On the contrary we may and must argue on the basis of Scripture which must be discovered afresh from time to time, if we do not wish to argue as arbitrarily and as untheologically as our adversaries apparently do."

Kierkegaard: How shall I ever get over that difficulty—of your actually beginning without a beginning (though perhaps not in actuality). For I was about to say (and here I quote from myself, *Christian Discourses,* "The Lilies and the Birds," p. 322) that "thou shalt *first* seek God's kingdom. But then in a certain sense it is nothing I shall do. Yes, certainly, in a certain sense it is nothing; thou shalt in the deepest sense make thyself nothing, become nothing before God, learn to keep silent; in this silence is the beginning, which is, *first* to seek God's kingdom. In this wise, a godly wise, one gets to the beginning by going, in a sense, backwards. The beginning is not that with which one begins, but at which one arrives, and one arrives at the beginning backwards. The beginning is this art of *becoming* silent. . . ."

V

Now, of course, the crucial difference here is not merely between the *credo ut intelligam* of Anselm and the existentialist's "I seek in order to find that I am already found." It is rather to convey the sense of the way in which the two traditional theologians (LaFarge and Barth) cited above stand on the *outside* and consequently do not deal with God or reality. This is due to the fact that they are "rationalists"—in a particular sense of that term. They are rationalists in the sense in which Epictetus was a rationalist and Heraclitus was not; in the sense in which Aquinas was a rationalist and Augustine was not; in the way in which Descartes was a rationalist and Pascal was not; in the way in which Kant was a rationalist and Goethe was not; in the way in which Locke was a rationalist and the depth psychologist is not; in the way in which Barth is a rationalist and Heidegger, Marcel and Tillich are not. Barth's use of language is rationalist, his logic is rationalist, his psychology is rationalist. He does not distinguish, as Kierkegaard does, between a "first self" and a "deeper self," or between the conscious ego and the unconscious, as the depth psychologist does. Therefore he cannot recognize that the disrelationship with God is in the first instance made "dialectically" manifest as alienation, or disrelationship with ourselves. He does not recognize with Kierkegaard, in that passage so decisive for Kierkegaard's understanding of the Self, and thereby for his entire "theology," that the Self becomes a Self by relating itself to its own self, and by willing to be itself the self is grounded transparently upon the Power which posited it.[57] Because of this Barth has no category of "Presence" such as we find in Marcel, nor can he recognize that the presence of the self to itself (*présence à moi-même*) cannot be taken for granted and is the condition *sine qua non* of the Presence. This disrelationship of the self within itself must therefore be projected outward upon "reality" and a qualitative difference is set up between the non-rational me and the transcendent purity, in one form or another, of the pure idea. For this reason Tillich can protest against "the supranaturalistic consummation of the dialectical movement in Barth's dogmatics"[58] and fail to "arouse [his] interest."[59]

There is today a more crucial reason why the problem of Barthian "rationalism" must be regarded as more than a theologian's quarrel: it is that it is one of the primary factors preventing a recovery of faith within the Church as well as within the remnants of "Christendom." From the psychological point of view what is needed is a means of re-establishing man's connection with life. "To live," writes Marcel, "in the full sense of the word is not to exist or subsist, to limit oneself to existing or subsisting, but it is to make oneself over, to give oneself."[60] Heretofore the culture itself provided archetypal symbols in terms of which the person could project the conscious and unconscious elements of his psyche toward a symbolic goal, which would help at once to harmonize his experience, give meaning and direction to his life, and sustain him in his negative encounters—with dread, anxiety, death, guilt and nothingness—by relating his inner "drives" to the conventions and mores of the culture. Today we can see how the traditional symbols have been dropping away, and are becoming less "true," as the contexts within which they functioned and were serviceable cease to be life-affirming. The medieval matrix of images, with its two-storied hierarchical structure compounded with Biblical, Hellenic and Gnostic myth elements appears to fall almost entirely "outside" the reality of the contemporary man. The Christ symbol also has been receding from the center of the Western consciousness. About the time that Nietzsche was discovering the "death of God" in Germany, Carlyle remarked to Browning, while looking at an image of the Crucifixion in the countryside near Paris: "Ah, poor fellow! *Your* part is played out!" The point is important since, from a psychological point of view, the Christ symbol functions as a "symbol of the Self" (Jung); and, for the Western psyche, some aspect of the Christ symbol has served as the center around which the symbolism of "individuation" has been experienced. Now, with the great objective symbols falling or fallen away, contemporary man has been thrown back upon the Self itself as the primary archetype of the Real. If so, the self must be seen as gathering up all other symbols of a subordinate kind evoked from within our relevant history and as opening into a significance rooted in the cosmos and universal in scope.

The path of this development is most apparent in the plight of the artist. As one moves from Dante to Bunyan to the *Waste Land* one witnesses the progressive loss of informing myths and symbols until emptiness itself becomes a symbol of our condition. As the heroes and saviours and gods recede as available archetypes through whose deeds the problems of the inner life may be portrayed and formulated, the artist is thrown more and more upon "himself": his work becomes confessional—that is, he exploits his own ambiguities and ambivalences, moving like the mythological hero courageously and dreadfully into the feared inner realm of the "unconsciousness," employing his art to gain a deeper self-knowledge and a possible hold thereby upon "reality." What he discovers is manifold:

> so many selves (so many fiends and gods
> each greedier than every) is a man
> (so easily one in another hides;
> yet man can, being all, escape from none)

> so huge a tumult is the simplest wish;
> so pitiless a massacre the hope
> most innocent (so deep's the mind of flesh
> and so awake what waking calls asleep)

> so never is most lonely man alone
> (his briefest breathing lives some planet's year,
> his longest life's a heartbeat of some sun;
> his least unmotion roams the youngest star)

> —how should a fool that calls him "I" presume
> to comprehend not numerable whom?[61]

Strange how the primary wonder is here renewed: not precisely as Kant was moved by "the starry heavens above," though the planets and sun and stars are metaphorically juxtaposed to evoke the infinite microcosm within; and when the poet gazes into so unfathomable a deep of mind, it is not unlike Kierkegaard's "first" wonder: "When the sea lies deep and still, inexplicable, when the wondering mind gazes dizzily down into its depths. until the unknown seems rising up to meet it . . ."[62] Especially is the similarity apparent if we note the evocation of the threat of death in the adroit paraphrase of Tennyson's "Crossing the Bar":

> and so awake that waking calls asleep
> (but such a tide as moving seems asleep)

There are many signs, in both literature and painting, that the artist is moving into the "second wonder" of the "deeper self," effecting a realistic recovery of the Christ symbol released from the two-storied framework of earlier times and moving far, far deeper than the sentimentalized "Poor fellow!" whom Carlyle and his time so confidently patronized. It is all in Rouault's poem, as it is also in his Christ figures:

> Peace seems scarcely to rule
> Over the anguished world
> Of shadows and appearances
> Jesus on the cross will tell you better than I.[63]

This Christ figure is not elevated either magically or supranatural-istically into some "otherworldly" "being": he is permitted to remain where he is, turning us into an awareness of our compounded culpability and irresponsibility. He solicits all the images of our pain; and he "receives" them, "accepting them" in such a way as to console us into the courage to accept them ourselves. Otto Rank is persuaded that the way of psychology is the way to a new person with a "new soul" emerging by "rebirth," and that "the road beyond psychology leads to a point where art and religion meet, join, and transform each other."[64] Where this is taking place most fruitfully it is taking the form of a search for a faith beyond dogma—for the simple reason that in any of the dogmatic patterns the depth dimension is ignored and the "Church" becomes judgmental and oppressive. Inevitably the believer projects the pure forms of perfection or of power or of justice, and the ratio of the discrepancy between what he finitely is and what he infinitely ought to be is the perpetual intimidating measure of his guilt. He can do nothing. Whatever he does must compound the offense. He can only strive to learn what is "edifying in the thought that over against 'God' we are always in the wrong." He must reduce himself to zero, and commit himself thereafter to "saving" others by bringing them into a like relation, meanwhile surrendering his "soul" to whatever institution or leader (*Führer*) or dogma may be currently serving as surrogate for the Absolute. "We make an idol of truth even!" said Pascal.

Now (1) if it is to be otherwise, the problem of the *Meno* must be solved not intellectualistically, but in terms of our depth experience, precisely after the manner of Augustine. He knew the *Meno* well. "But where shall I find Thee? If I find Thee without memory, then I am unmindful of Thee. And how shall I find Thee, if I do not remember Thee?" "For the woman who lost her drachma, and searched for it with a lamp, unless she had remembered it, would never have found it." "How, then, do I seek Thee, O Lord? For when I seek Thee, my God, I seek a happy life. I will seek Thee, that my soul may live. . . . (But) How do I seek it? Is it by remembrance, as

though I had forgotten it? . . . Truly we have it, but how I know not."
Then, finally, the depth disclosure bursts through: "For behold, Thou wert
within, and I without (outside!), and there did I seek Thee: I, unlovely,
rushed heedlessly among the things of beauty Thou madest. Thou wert with
me, but I was not with Thee."[65]

There is, however, (2) a danger here: the danger, namely, that one
might become entranced and permit his ambition to be directed "down-
wards," like Thomas Mann's probing through the collective unconscious
into the bottomless "well of time"; and one might become a fugitive or
vagabond there, for "no matter to what hazardous lengths we let out our
line" the more the unfathomable foundations of humanity "withdraw
again, and further, into the depths."[66] One might unwittingly commit the
indiscretion of holding oneself up as a medium of self-knowledge to God
and not rest in the riddle. Also there is the danger of merging the Self
(atman) with the Self of the All (Atman), or of elevating the Self as a
Symbol into an idea of the universal whereby the "rationalism" in which
the ego is unaware of its depth dimensional otherhood reinstates itself after
all and things are just as they were.

If it is to be other than this, the symbols of the new self-understanding
must be related to the historical experience, both of the individual and of
culture, and to mythopoetic ventures of both into self-understanding,
noting particularly what is typical and what is directional in this—symbols
of journey and return, of alienation and exile, of covenant and promises, of
defiance and acceptance, of descents and ascents, of deaths and resurrec-
tions, of flights and encounters, of quests and hordes, of Leviathans and
Lucifers, and so on. Then these must be assimilated to the primary myths
and "master images" of that people, and imaginatively related to its drama
of faith and infidelity, whereby the first representative man moves by
episode and elaboration toward the second Representative Man in whom
the collision of all the opposites is summed and sustained, and whose "way"
becomes thereby the Parable and Paradigm for the new birth into new life
and being.

Such a theology, however, (3) must be prepared to surrender those
orientations of orthodoxy which have been guilty of the unconscious
rationalization of beliefs which stand in the way of the free and open adventures of faith, and which, on behalf of security and protection against
the inroads of Grace, refuse to acknowledge the dimension of depth. The
Church will resist this. It will not wish to consider that the Lantern may
have passed from its grasp without its being observed that the light that
was in men was a curious darkness formed, so to speak, from the absence

of a light which was there by definition but not in fact. But "grace is insidious," as Péguy says:

When it doesn't come from the right it comes from the left. When it doesn't come straight it comes bent, and when it doesn't come bent, it comes broken. When it doesn't come from above it comes from below. . . .[67]

And there are signs that a "Church" is coming into being, outside the official Church (whose conceptual and symbolic forms have already placed it *outside* its own myth of "being"), where the quest for meaning has become authentic and where men move, in fear and trembling, into the source of Joy. By way of the sometimes strange and new alignments of our understanding effected in that "rendezvous between accomplices who, in spite of themselves, cannot resist meeting,"[68] we are catching glimpses here and there of Rilke's truth—that "to love is to give light with inexhaustible oil."[69]

Once again, however, (4) the historic Church may find it as perplexing to find its way of structuring its views which are slowly slipping away from it as Kierkegaard's man who comes to the "second" wonder: he may be discovering that he already has what he inwardly sought, but his misfortune is that he stands and loses it. Particularly will this be true of the doctrine of the person and the work of Christ. For the definitions demanded by a substantialist intellectualism caught between the conceptual opposites of being/non-being and eternity/time are superfluous now; yet they stand between God and man like the moon eclipsing the earth from the sun. What is missing is the depth dimension; but a theology of depth points not at the Teacher but at that to which the Teacher is pointing. In this way is He the instructing Parable and the informing Paradigm of the deeper secrets of the human condition.

. . . a man once said (concerning parables): Why such reluctance? If you only followed the parables you yourselves would become parables and with that rid of all your daily cares.
Another said: I bet that is also a parable.
The first said: You have won.
The second said: But unfortunately only in parable.
The first said: No, in reality: in parable you have lost.[70]

So with the recession of the classical framework for doctrine: it becomes clearer day by day that the elaborate system was a parable of the imposture in human pretension trying to house God within our ideological projections. Everything was in order: both "time" and "eternity" were in place; and "Christ the Mediator" appeared uniting the two (by definition) in the Mystery of the Eternal Presence. It was discovered one day that the

Scriptures bore witness to something else—to a way and a truth and a life and a Lantern. The Lantern was not in the definition, and though the Presence was undoubtedly there in the Mystery it remained absent from the world.

So undoubtedly we have lost a great deal: for in losing the substantialist matrix of images we have lost the deification of our projections. But we have lost it only in parable; for when the projections fall the misplaced power of our striving returns to the self where it is, and what we have lost in parable we may win in reality.

Finally, then, there is Nietzsche's problem, which deletes its author so easily, rising quietly into the autonomy of its own paradox, and presiding there, like a Presence, over all our "dialectical" twistings and turnings. Before one seeks for men, one must have found the Lantern. *"Wird es die Laterne des Zynikers sein müssen?"*[71] Will it have to be the Lantern of the Cynics?

The answer, of course, is "No." But it is useful, all the same, to have an ironist occasionally, with his lantern of mockery, to remind us of our finitude. Even Augustine observes how men can more easily count than be wise, for they "hold gold more dear than the light of a lamp." Yet "even a beggar kindles a lamp for himself, but few have gold," and wisdom, whether in merchant or beggar, still "seeks the eye by which it can be seen." And when wisdom's true lovers come to it and seek it, "it shows itself to them joyfully along the way and runs forward to them with all foreknowledge."[72] "Alas, those who abandon you and . . . who love, instead of you, your beckonings *and forget what you beckon for* . . . who turn themselves from your light, and cling to the shadow of it!"[73]

This wisdom obtains at all times, of course. It only waits to be specified by the seeker. In Diogenes, the Cynic, it is specified as irony, that dry light of the rationalistic mind, which shines in the emptied, flattened daylight at the demise of every view of life that stands *outside* but not within the inner concerns of people. Christ comes in every darkness carrying his Lantern, illumined by the light of "Grace," and beckons the "lost" ones into the place where the object of the search can in truth exist, into a knowledge of the love of God, into themselves where that which is sought is given, and where all things become new.

8

Christian Root-Terms*: Kerygma, Mysterium, Kairos, Oikonomia

BY ERICH PRZYWARA, S.J.

The thought of Paul Tillich, in its innermost intention, is directed to the examination of Christian root-terms. This focus emerges early, in his interpretation of Schelling, who himself had sought for a "philosophy of revelation," not for the purpose of taking up revelation into a final philosophical concept (as did Hegel) but rather to understand revelation in terms of its own immanent concepts. As Schelling was dependent upon Boehme and Franz von Baader, who developed such an immanent philosophy of revelation, so Tillich in his turn interpreted this tradition in his first works,[1] attempting to draw from it the final consequences for the development of a possible "Christian grammar." Such a grammar, for Tillich, culminates in the *kairos,* around which his whole thought moves.[2]

Christian root-terms can be understood materially or formally. Taken *materially,* root-terms refer to the content of Christian revelation and point to the fulfillment of its particular revelation. This centrality of a *particular* revelation appears in the history of thought from Irenaeus to Augustine in terms of the *admirabile commercium* or the *commutatio:* the "spiritual barter" between God and man fulfilled in Christ as the "Mediator" who functions as a dynamic "medium."

The special material root-term of the Christianity of the Middle Ages, particularly in Thomas Aquinas, was the *ordo universi* in a *perfectio universi:* that is, "sacral ordering of all," understood as the ground of revelation in the prologue of John the Evangelist and in the Epistles to the Ephesians and Colossians. (Christ "before the foundation of the world" to "the new heavens and the new earth" as *archē, anakephalaiēsis,* and *synhestēken* of the "whole creation," of the "whole cosmos," of "everything

* Translated by Calvin Schrag.

in heaven and earth.") This material root-term, having the same intention of meaning as the original Christian "spiritual barter" is now expressed in terms of a "Christian ordering of all" in Christ as *Logos* and the Holy Spirit as *Paraclete*.[3]

Out of this interpretation in the Middle Ages arose the special root-term of the Reformation: "justification by faith alone." In it there is a return to the situation of the Epistle to the Romans and the Epistle to the Galatians. As Paul counters the "sacramental justice" of Judaism with a "divine justification" by the justice of God, so the Reformation counters the static institutional justice of the Middle Ages with a dynamic "justification," in which the pure receptive potentiality of man becomes the divine expression of justice in the dialectical claim of justice and grace. The Reformation doctrine of "justification" as the article by which the Church stands or falls (*articulus stantis et cadentia ecclesiae*) excludes all juristic thinking in its appeal to the primordial *mysterium* of *Deus irae et gratiae* which (according to Romans 11) is the "abyss of the deep and the high (*bathos*)," expressed in Luther's "volcanic" experience, made a cardinal principle in the cosmic theosophy of Jacob Boehme, and today again emphasized in Paul Tillich's philosophy of religion.[4]

But this material root-term of "justification through faith alone" has met in our day a counter root-term in the rediscovery of the cult emphasis in the Epistle to the Hebrews: the *High Priesthood of Christ in the Holy Temple,* whom "God ordains and not man"; a High Priest not only in heaven but "announced from the *Agora,*" in the markets of the world. Christian salvation is thus seen not as a simple ontic "barter," nor merely as an aspect of a divine dialectic, but rather has its determinate center in the "Here He is"— as in the conclusion of the prophecy in which Ezekiel names the "new temple." It is this new root-term which occasioned the rise of the so-called "liturgical movement" in Catholicism following the First World War. In a similar manner, a liturgical-sacramental Protestanism grew following the Second World War.[5] Eastern Orthodox Christianity has seen in these Catholic and Protestant movements a renewal of spirit, since from the very beginning, the Epistle to the Hebrews with its teaching on the High Priesthood of Christ has been the determining charter of Eastern Orthodoxy.

One must clearly distinguish the material Christian root-terms from the *formal* Christian root-terms. The latter do not refer to the content of the Christian revelation in so far as this has its determinate center in the fact of revelation itself, but rather refer to the form in which the totality of revelation appears concretely: in the annunciation, or *kerygma;* in the sacramental *mysterium;* in the historical *kairos;* or in the trans-historical *oikonomia,* the "order of salvation."

The formal root-term, for ancient prophetism as for the new evangelism, is the *kerygma. Kerygma,* derived from *kēryssein* and *kēryx* and rooted in *geryo,* means basically "to sound" (as also animals "make sounds"). "Sound" is here understood as the "sounding" of a state, military or sacred authority which through a "crier" calls together the people, the militia, or the believers for a public gathering, for training, or for a sacrifice. In so far as the authority "sounds out" through a "crier," the crier becomes the representative of the authority, the "messenger" or "he who is sent." As representing messenger he is a "herald" in the original meaning of the term. *Kerygma* means, therefore, official messenger announcing the official message, and is thus internally bound up with a "kingdom": a kingdom in a free public gathering, a kingdom over which the warriors engage in battle, or a kingdom before God in the act of sacrifice. *Kerygma* also appears in the story of the Apostles and in Paul as the central form of the Messianic message (cf. Is. 16:1); as the message of the Messiah as announced by John the Baptist (Matt. 3:1); as the message of the Messiah in his own words (Matt. 4:17); as the message of the Messiah through his Apostles as "messenger in the whole world" (Matt. 10:7; Mark 16:15); as "narrator of the message of Christ the Crucified" (I Cor. 1:21, 23). So also *kerygma* is inextricably bound up with the *basileia* as the "Kingdom of God" or the "Kingdom of Heaven": that is, as "messenger of the Kingdom." In this sense *kerygma* is simply *evangelion* in the historical meaning of the word— not in the sense of a fortuitous "happy message" but as a message from the Roman Caesar to the whole of the Roman Empire, whose message is in itself "holy" (following from the divine character of Caesar), quite independently of whether it comprises a message of punishment or clemency. Therefore, *evangelion* in its historical form means "message of the kingdom," just as *kerygma* means "official message," thereby presupposing a kingdom. In this similarity of *kerygma* and *evangelion* there is finally the *Pater immensae Majestatis,* as expressed in the *Te Deum:* the Divine Majesty which proclaims itself through its messengers, the *kerygma* and the *evangelion.*

Kerygma and *evangelion* are therefore necessarily rooted in the "Word of God" as expressed by the Gospel of John, leading back to the *Logos* as the "Word of God." As this Word of God is the one *Logos,* the one "Word" of the *kerygma* and *evangelion,* so the root of all Christian *kerygma* and *evangelion* is the one "I am with you" in the *Logos.* This central form of the *kerygma* provides the formal criterion in the theology of Origen, since for him all revelation-words of the old and new covenants, in his method of *analogia fidei,* become a *kerygma* of the "Logos of God," so that all faith and all life in faith is a "participation in the Logos"; thus, leading to a *Logos* Christianity.

During the late Middle Ages this centrality of the *kerygma* of the *Logos* became the foundation of the medieval Dominican teaching on the *ordo praedicatorum,* which was a reaction against the centrality of liturgy among the Benedictines. In extreme Calvinism or Zwinglianism, the absolute form of this central *kerygma* arises in preacher-centered worship, wherein all sacraments and liturgy are only pictorial remembrances and commemorations, and the sermon itself becomes the determining principle. Karl Barth's theology provides the interior metaphysics for this centrality of the *kerygma;* for him the *kerygma* is ultimately rooted in the mystery of the Trinity itself.

The second formal Christian root-term, *mysterium,* is so basic to Pauline thought that today both the Catholic *"Mysterien* theology" and the Protestant liturgical-sacramental movement take the word *mysterium* as a designation of a new Pauline emphasis in contradistinction to a "Pauline *kerygmatic."* In its etymological meaning, *mysterium* means "concealed truth" (*terein*). It has at one and the same time a tellurian and a psychic-spiritual meaning. This separation into a tellurian and a psychic-spiritual dimension opens the view into the inner duality of the historical *Mysterien.* The telluric side is expressed particularly in the *mysterium* of the *hieros gamos,* holy marriage, which stands in the center of the Babylonian Mysteries. The psychic-spiritual side is expressed in the specific ancient Greek Mysteries which affirm a metaphysical-religious "resurrection in death."[6] This telluric-spiritual dualism posits a "terrifying abyss" as the essence of the *mysterium.* In the words of the learned philologist, Walter Otto, *mysterium* is the "repetition of a divine event" in the cult whereby "man is ethereally lifted to the divine and works together with the divine."[7]

With the concepts of a spiritual marriage and a resurrection in death we are already in the center of the Christian *mysterium.* Mystery in the Christian sense signifies, in the Gospel of Matthew, "the mystery of the Kingdom of God" (13:11) and in Paul, in whom the "Gentiles are fellow heirs, members of the same body, and partakers of the promise" (Eph. 3:6), as well as the "cosmic *mysterium"* of the "all in all in Christ." This Christian mystery finds its constant renewal in the self-fulfillment of the Church as the body and the consummation of the one Christ (I Cor. 12:12 ff.; Eph. 5:25 ff.), and therefore, as the new living celebration of marriage in its members (as *epi-chor-hegume-non* and *synbibazomenon*), and as a marriage feast in which there is the objective *memoria et praesentia* in the bread and the cup of the "body and blood of the Lord."

This is the Magna Charta of the Christian *mysterium* and forms the basis of the *Mystagogical Catechism* of Cyril of Jerusalem, as well as of Augustine's sermons (*Tractatus in Johannem* and *Enarrationes in Psalmos*), wherein Christianity is acknowledged as the new, living cult which under the sign of the one bread and the one cup celebrates the one true mystery— wherein the crucified and resurrected One in his resurrection is now married to the many members in one body (I Cor. 12:12).

Both *kerygmatic* Christianity and Christianity as *mysterium*, taken alone, are susceptible to an overemphasis of a trans-historical Christianity. In the version of Origen, *kerygmatic* Christianity tends to become an intelligible structure understood as a "System in the Logos," and a Christian-Platonic *topos noëtos*. The danger of a pure trans-historical *mysterium* Christianity can be seen in Eastern Orthodoxy in which the Platonic *topos noëtos*, the ideal world of the icon, and the ideal world of a trans-historical liturgy converge. But Christianity essentially implies the incarnation of the divine in the human, in which the eternal God fully becomes historical man and continues to live in the historical Church, in humanity, and in the world as the Christ who is the same yesterday and today and forever (Heb. 13:9). It is at this juncture that *kairos*, the third formal Christian root-term, makes its appearance. This is the root-term which has particular significance for Paul Tillich's philosophy of religion.

Christianity inextricably means eternity in time: Absolute, Divine Eternity in relative human time, and thus within the duration of yesterday, today and tomorrow. The full implication of this notion can only be grasped by exploring three words used by the New Testament Greek to express the mystery of historical time: *chronos, kairos, aiön*. *Chronos* denotes simply the duration of time in a temporal succession. *Aiön* has reference to the content of a temporal or a world age, in the sense of an "early age," "middle age," and "modern age." As *chronos* focuses primarily upon the *successive* character of time—"chronology" is thus made possible by virtue of which one becomes conscious of the transitoriness of time—so *aiön* crystallizes the "relative eternity" of this transitoriness into an "absolute eternity," as expressed in the liturgical form: *per omnia saecula saeculorum*. In contrast to the emphasis on transitoriness in *chronos* and the emphasis on eternity in *aiön*, *kairos* emphasizes the situational Appositeness, "right time," in the manner of the Latin word *opportunitas*—the "opportune moment." The right time as opportune is rooted in a "pre-established Plan" but becomes concretely opportune in specific historical circumstances. It is opportune by virtue of an ideal "determination from above" and by virtue of a "real situation below." *Kairos* is "time in the right measure," which is at one and the same time a trans-temporal measure and an inner-temporal "measure of real circumstances."

It is in this sense that the Lord, in his parting words to his Apostles when they asked concerning the "time" of the coming Kingdom, distinguished the *chroni* as *kairoi*, "which the Father has fixed by his own authority" (Acts 1:7). That is to say, the Father as "originator without origin" (*principium sine principio*) enters the temporal succession *chronoi* by an interruption at the opportune moment's *kairoi*. As this entering into time is essentially Messianic, the word *kairos* is particularly applicable to the Christ: for the Lord himself, in the Gospel of John, speaks of "my *kairos*" (7:6). However, in so far as the Messianic *kairos* in its essential content is set over against Satan as the "ruler of this world" (John 14:30; II Cor. 4:4) and the "anti-Christ," the word *kairos* indicates also the time for this opposition, as is expressed in Luke: "And when the devil had ended every temptation, he departed until an opportune time" (4:13). Thus, the *kairos Christi* is essentially the "*kairos* of salvation" as this salvation occurs in the conflict between God and Satan, between Christ and the anti-Christ.

It is this duality in the *kairos* which Paul Tillich, in the tradition of Jacob Boehme, Franz von Baader, and Schelling, as well as of the Russians, Tschaadajev, Frank, Chestov, and Berdyaev, has expressed in his concept of the Divine as "Ground and Abyss." In his criticism of Rudolf Otto, Tillich argues that the Holy must be understood as an intrusion through the realm of meaning which is its abyss and its ground.[8] In his *Religionsphilosophie* he argues that theism and atheism are rooted in this divine "Ground and Abyss": "in every theism . . . an abyss of atheism is present."[9] In the same writing he speaks of a "differentiation of the Holy into the Divine and the Demonic," wherein the demonic is "the Holy which contradicts the Divine." *It is here that we see the tradition of Origen becoming transparent in the thought of Tillich,* wherein "the Kingdom of Satan as the Ruler of this Age" is understood as the last antithesis to God, which itself is taken up in the final "divine synthesis" of the "complete restoration" in which "God is all in all" (I Cor. 15:28).

But the fourth formal Christian root-term gives the answer to such dubious undertakings in Tillich's thought. Beyond all the contraries of the "Kingdom of God" and the "Kingdom of Satan" in the history of salvation stands the *oikonomia tu pleromatos ton kairon;* rooted in "the mystery of his will according to his purposes" (Eph. 1:8), in which are "united all things, things in heaven and things on earth" (Eph. 1:10). All *kairoi* in their inner history of salvation within the duality of the "Kingdom of God and His Christ" and the "Kingdom of Satan and his anti-Christ" are grounded, live, and move in an *oikonomia tu pleromatos ton kairon,* wherein resides the inscrutable and unsearchable abyss of God's Being; God's "abyss in depth and height" (Rom. 11:33) which alone the *Pneuma,* the Spirit of God, can comprehend (I Cor. 2:11). Although the Epistle to the Romans comes close to affirming a final dialectic between God and Satan, it moves exclusively in the "depths of the riches and wisdom and knowledge of God," from whom and through whom and to whom are all things (Rom. 11:33–36).

The history of salvation is thus finally and exclusively grounded in the appearance within history of the "inscrutable justice and unsearchable ways" of the one *bathos,* the one *oikodespotes,* the one *oikonomia,* as the sovereign ordering of the incomprehensible and unsearchable "height and depth of the divine abyss." For this reason, *Catholicism has this Christian root-term* oikonomia, *as its most fundamental term.* If the divine *oikodespotes* and *oikonomia,* ruling and ordering, belong together, and if the Divine became human entering the world and history, then He is present in this world as human ruler and as One who orders through law. Catholicism sees the dialectical character and double significance of the *kairoi* as rooted in the final Christian root-term, *oikonomia,* and represented in the ordering of the Church through ecclesiastical lords. Hence, Majesty and Glory are the final "sound" and "breath" of this divine-human *oikonomia.*[11]

9

Myth, Symbol and Analogy

BY GUSTAVE WEIGEL, S.J.

One of the characteristic traits of the Gospel of St. John is the device often used by the author whereby an obviously figurative statement of Christ is interpreted by his hearers with gross literalism.[1] This is, of course, a stylistic artifice but it points up clearly the nature of the Christian *kerygma*. It is clear from the four Gospels, and most of all from the Gospel of John, that the verbal formulas are not always to be understood in their *prima facie* vulgar sense.

Little satisfaction is achieved by attempting to construct historiographically the events of the life of Christ, as the bewildered quest of "the historical Jesus" showed. Today the majority of theologians are of the mind that not too much can be accomplished by the rigid application of the rules of the modern historian's sober craft to the New Testament documents. Nor is this a new persuasion, for the Alexandrine expositors in the tradition of Clement and Origen looked on principle for a meaning of the words far below the surface. We call their approach pneumatic, spiritual, mystical, allegorical, typical, symbolic. This kind of interpretation was dear to the Christians for many centuries. The medieval distich—

> *Littera gesta docet, quid credas allegoria,*
> *Moralis quid agas, quo tendas anagogia—*

gives it high importance, for the *credenda* of Scripture were assigned to the allegorical sense. What is more, for many medieval doctors, such as St. Thomas, the anagogic and moral senses were in their way symbolic.[2]

However, the tendency to seek first the symbolic sense of the scriptural dicta always had an opposition. The Antiochians in the spirit of Theodore of Mopsuestia were uncomfortable with symbolic hermeneutics. They preferred to stick to the letter. It was not so much that they advocated a puerile literalism, but rather they wished to transpose the *kerygma* and *didache* into simply intelligible propositions in the light of common logic and the philosophic assumptions of their times.

These two rival hermeneutical orientations simultaneously march down the centuries of the Christian era. The Fathers and the earlier Scholastics had a keen eye for the symbolic content of revelation while the Age of the Reform was strongly inclined to remain with the more obvious burden of the words. This inclination with time helped to produce the historicism of the nineteenth century with its chimeric search for the "historical Jesus." Today, a reaction against rationalistic historicism has brought us back again to the possibilities of allegory and symbol.

Thomas Aquinas wished to mediate between the two tendencies and his views prevailed in the Catholic Church. He gladly admitted the validity of allegorical interpretation but gave the primacy to the text as it stood; it was the "historical" or "literal" sense (the literary sense, as we would say today) which must first engage the attention of the interpreter. In its light there could be a transition to the allegorical dimensions of the message. The "historical" sense was basic and only under its guidance could an appeal be made to the "spiritual" meaning.

The multiplicity of scriptural senses does not make the Scriptures equivocal or in any way multiple in meaning. As was said above, there are many senses in the Scripture without implying that the same word has many meanings. The multiplicity of senses derives from the fact that the objective things signified by the words can in turn have a symbolic function with reference to other things. Consequently there is no confusion in Scripture, for all the senses are founded on one alone, namely, the literal sense. Moreover, when arguing from Scripture, evidence must be drawn exclusively from the literal meaning. Allegorical interpretation is no argument, as St. Augustine saw.[3] This involves no loss of scriptural content, because there is nothing necessary for faith to be grasped from the symbolism which is not clearly expressed elsewhere by the literal sense.[4]

St. Thomas had solved the problem of hermeneutics, at least to his satisfaction. He was both Antiochian and Alexandrine; he could go along with both without any negation of the valid insights achieved by either camp. Thomas' philological method would hardly come up to the standards set today, but the textual critic and philological investigator on the Thomistic principle must be considered as formally, even though subsidiarily, engaged in the theological enterprise.

Perhaps the weightiest objection to fundamentalist literalism, or even to the moderate historicist position of Aquinas, was clearly put by Reinhold

Niebuhr. "I do not know how it is possible to believe in anything pertaining to God and eternity 'literally.' "[5]

The support for this objection is found in the finitude of human conception and the inevitable bondage of human language to the finite. God is the Infinite, the Trans-human, the "wholly Other." Hence human language and human thought cannot express Him as He is. At most they can only point to the ultimate reality, Tillich's ground of being, in terms of existentialist concern.

In the place cited, Niebuhr makes it clear that he cannot subscribe totally to Rudolf Bultmann's call for "demythologization." This does not mean that Niebuhr and Bultmann are in disagreement as to the nature of the Biblical message. For both of them it is a stimulus to existentialist reflection, and in the reflection "revelation" is achieved. The difference between the men, and Tillich would go along with Niebuhr, is that Bultmann thinks there is too much myth in the Scriptures, while Niebuhr, admitting the presence of myth, would consider that much of the so-called myth is really valid symbol. We have here two concepts in play: myth and symbol.

So much has been written about these two terms that one is afraid to say any more about them.[6] Yet something more must be said, for there is much confusion on this score. For Bultmann the Scriptures must be demythologized, not because myth can ever be eliminated from the formulation of the Biblical message but because the mythology employed by the Bible stands in the way of modern man's achievement of the Biblical truth. By Biblical mythology Bultmann means the ancients' accepted image of the universe in terms of their physics, cosmology, psychology and sociology. That image is so thoroughly in conflict with the image functioning in our day that the former inevitably alienates our age, which does not believe in miracles, angels, demonic possession, anthropomorphic divinity, autocracy, slavery and other constituents of the classical world vision. The Biblical message must therefore be couched in harmony with the image accepted by current man in order to be effective in our day. Just how this is to be done is not so clear. Although Bultmann wishes to reform the expression of the *kerygma*, he does not want to rewrite the Scriptures nor does he want to edit out large or small sections of the books.

There is one fundamental assumption in the demythologizing plea which has not been criticized sufficiently. Is it true that myth is a barrier to the correct understanding of substance? The Greeks had various terms for "word." Three of them are relevant to our purpose: *rhema, mythos* and *logos. Rhema* was neutral; it referred to the material vocal (or written) sign, much as does the Latin *vox* or *sermo. Mythos* implied the image-evoking value of the word. *Logos* referred to the intellectual content of the term, rendered in Latin as *ratio*. Every word is simultaneously *rhema, mythos* and *logos*. Any word can be considered from all of these three viewpoints. Thoroughgoing demythologization, in consequence, can only be achieved in completely wordless communication. That is something humanly difficult, if at all possible. The myth dimension of human communication is no obstacle to correct understanding. Ronald Knox somewhere points out that the scriptural phrase "the bowels of his mercy" is not English, for we would rather speak of a man's kind heart. The observation is true enough, but the initial distraction of the image does not rob it of its power to communicate accurate meaning. With time and familarity we may even ignore a term's image so that we can say that the sun rises and the sun sets, though the astronomical assumptions of today's prevailing myth reject any notion of the sun's movement around the earth.

The mythological component of language is no defect of language; only a sign of man's dependence on image for thought. Effective works of literary communication fuse the functions of imagery and thought evocation, with the consequence that it would kill the precise message of the writer if we were to change his imagery. The reader will not grasp such images exactly as the writer formed them in his own fantasy, but the *ratio* is still carried genuinely by the kindred image produced.[7] To demythologize the Scriptures means to substitute a different message from the one contained there.

One cannot help but suspect that the champions of demythologization unconsciously want to change it. They seem to manifest a loss of nerve because of which they cannot retain the Biblical burden as they find it. Of course they recognize so many good things in it. Hence they hope that a radical reconstruction will give us something better to take its place. This is an understandable endeavor, but why call its result Christianity?

Barth, Tillich and Niebuhr seem to see the flaws in the project of demythologization. But, with Bultmann, they feel that there is a *scandalum pusillorum* involved in Biblical rhetoric. They do not, however, bridle at the presence of myth in the Scriptures, because they readily appreciate that only children, young or old, identify *logos* with *mythos*. They recognize that an adult easily and effectively distinguishes between the two. The difficulty vexing the existentialist theologians concerns not the *mythos* but the *logos* of the Bible. This difficulty is eminently and properly theological because it stems from the theological principle that the *logos* of Scripture cannot be taken literally since no human *logos* is equipped for the task of revealing the transcendent God.

What, then, is the solution of existentialist theology? Neither demy-thologization nor fundamentalist or historicist literalism, but in their stead symbolism. Perhaps the most stimulating definition of theological symbol-ism was given by Tillich when he said:

> One of the things I always forbid my students to say is "only a symbol." This bad phrase is rooted in the confusion of sign and symbol. Signs point to some-thing in which they do not participate at all. Symbols participate in the power of what they symbolize.[8]

If we may examine this statement somewhat, it seems true to say that a symbol is a sign but not simply a sign. It is more than a sign because it shares in the reality which it signifies. The green light at the street crossing is a simple sign of an open street because its being is totally alien to the being of the street. Open street and green light are only mythically con-joined. In the phenomenon of fire, however, smoke is a constituent element of the integral phenomenon, and thus smoke is a symbol of fire. It is not all of it; it is not even its essence, but it shares existentially in the essential being of fire.

In this sense the Scriptures must be understood as symbolic statements. Hence when they speak of God as Lord, as Creator, as Father, as King, we are in the realm of symbolism. It is not stated that God is literally any one of these things, but rather that lordship, contingent reality, paternity and dominion have their roots in God, the ground of being, and in their way point to Him in telling fashion. When Jesus as the Christ is called God, we are not told that Jesus of Nazareth was God, but rather that in the encounter with the phenomenon of Jesus God was revealed to man definitively under the guidance of man's ultimate concern.

Similarly Niebuhr can take the third chapter of Genesis and see in it not merely a myth of primal innocence and its loss but rather the symbolic affirmation of man's estrangement from God through the fact of sin. The myth in its literal dimensions is not the object of concern. What concerns us is the symbolic affirmation that man, any man, from his origin estranges himself from transcendental righteousness through the selfishness operative in all his works. Niebuhr in this position considers himself as reading the symbol differently from Tillich. As Niebuhr sees it, Tillich has man es-tranged from God by the mere fact of creation, while the Bible shows man estranged not by creation but by sin. However, the difference seems not to be too great, for Niebuhr's man will inevitably sin as soon as he is created.

Seeing symbol where Bultmann sees only myth gives the symbolists a great advantage. They have no need of demythologizing. On the contrary, they see the definitive value of the Bible precisely in its effective symbolism. In Scripture we are faced not with "pre-scientific myths" but "permanently valid symbols."[9] In consequence they can wholeheartedly agree with the current cry that theology should take its categories from the Scriptures, where the history of revelation is most genuinely given.

However, the symbolist pays a price for his advantages. The historical concreteness of the Biblical accounts, patent to any reader, is swallowed up into a trans-historical awareness of existence. Christ is risen indeed, but this does not state that Jesus of Nazareth physically rose from the dead. We are only told symbolically that the man of perfect faith rises above death, which then loses its existentially constrictive menace. The man of faith lives "eternally," in dimensions beyond time.

In such a hermeneutic it is postulated that the Bible as a record of revelation does not teach history, for history is not a matter of ultimate concern. Tillich has been reported as being quite explicit on this point.[10] As a record of revelation, the Scriptures make no historiographic statements and to look for such betrays a misunderstanding of their nature. If a historian uses the Bible as something less than a record of revelation he is using a document of dubious trustworthiness, because any historiographic value in the books is completely irrelevant to the real significance of the reports. The Bible is a record of revelation and not the historiographic presentation of secular events. The symbolists make much of the meaning of history, but as theologians they ignore on principle any historiographic validity of the Bible.

The eminent Orientalist William F. Albright grows somewhat uneasy with this hermeneutical method. He has called Tillich a "modern gnostic."[11] "Tillich has grafted C. G. Jung on Schelling's pantheism . . . and produced a theological system which resembles traditional Christianity only in superficial aspects."[12]

Tillich and the symbolists deny such an accusation vehemently. They see themselves as very genuine Christians, following a middle way already previsioned dimly in the Reformers. Unlike fundamentalists, who consider every proposition of the Bible or of dogmatic intent as a statement of secular event or secular fact, they reject literalism. The symbolist insists that he does not take the affirmations literally but he equally insists that he takes them seriously. In his position he avoids the unseriousness of absurd literalism and the equally unserious treason of those who will not take the scriptural affirmations as statements of truth. The truth, of course, is existential, the answers to man's ultimate concern. Biblical propositions indeed speak of history, but not historiographically.

This is brilliant. But it nonetheless gives the impression that history is no longer a concrete flux but rather a non-fluid comprehensive abstraction, dialectically opposed to the non-historical. In this opposition history becomes so dehistorized that it can stand in homogeneous polar relationship with meta-history. *Contraria sunt eiusdem speciei.* Can thoroughgoing trans-historical symbolism do justice to the historical preoccupations of the Christian message? It is understandable that so able a historian as William F. Albright should become irked when history, which he knows through lifelong work, suddenly means something which for him is not history at all.

It is all very well for Niebuhr to say that his symbolic approach to the record of revelation must not be identified with Bultmann's ideas on demythologization. Proximately they are not the same, obviously. Ultimately, however, there is a high degree of coincidence. Bultmann is still concerned with the mythical level of revelational language, but the symbolists on principle ignore it from the outset. They concentrate on the trans-historical meaning of mythical expression and thus render it a symbol. Bultmann makes a plea for demythologization. He is too late; the symbolists have effectively anticipated his need.

Bultmann's call appears to show that there are unresolved problems in symbolist hermeneutics. Undoubtedly, the main obstacle confronting the symbolists is the refusal of the human community to share their assumption that religious truth can be equated with the answers to man's ultimate concern, which latter is irrevocably a subjective experience. Professor Ben F. Kimpel of Drew University put it very well:

No religious individual believes that his experience constitutes the source of his security. The source of the security is the reality in which he believes, and to which he orients his life in complete trust. Hence he wants to know the nature of this reality. . . .

A belief about the nature of the divine reality is, therefore, not the criterion by which a religious individual proposes to select from among the competing claims to knowledge those beliefs which are true. An earnest religious individual wants to know the divine reality, and yet, his earnestness is not a sufficient condition for selecting true beliefs from other beliefs which may be held with equal earnestness. Earnestness is a condition for learning but it is not a criterion by which the character of belief can be ascertained.

According to religious faith, the criterion for the truth-character of interpretations of the divine reality is a knowledge of the divine reality.[13]

The symbolists use the word "serious" very often. On last reduction does their seriousness coalesce with Kimpel's earnestness?

In the light of the dissatisfactions aroused by both symbolic and de-mythologized hermeneutics, a rapid glance at the generic solution of Aquinas might be helpful. Passing over the positive core in demythologiza-tion, let us face the strong point in the symbolist position. The symbolists cannot see how any human word can be applied literally to God. Therefore they must look for a non-literal meaning in the affirmation.

Perhaps we are being misled by the word "literal." Is it simply true that we cannot use any word "literally" of God? It is universally recognized that we refer to God with words. The symbolists do it no less than others, and Tillich has said that God "is not the 'ineffable' simply and uncondi-tionally; but on the basis of his ineffability much can and must be said about him."[14]

As Tillich has seen, symbolism is similar to Thomistic analogy. Now, Thomas cannot be logically compelled to choose one or the other of the members in the disjunction: literal or symbolic. On his principles of pred-ication the disjunction is a false one, for he can logically add a *tertium* with ease. He did so when he insisted that the Biblical content was simul-taneously literal and symbolic, though the literal enjoyed a normative primacy in theological dialogue.

The ambiguous word in our current hermeneutical discussions is "literal." Aristotle distinguished literal predications by establishing the dichotomy between univocal and equivocal.[15] With something less than pro-found insight, he placed analogy, an inferential process known to Plato and the mathematicians before him, under equivocation. Mathematics and philosophy continuously reworked the concept up to the time of Thomas. Aquinas then produced his own theory without, however, explaining its totality explicitly. Yet the general lines of his doctrine can easily be de-tected in his writings.[16]

According to Thomistic thought, a word in its literal sense can be pred-icated univocally, simply equivocally, or analogously. In all three in-stances we are dealing with the word literally. The symbolic power in the term need not be touched at all. When I say "rook," the word may mean a crow or a chess piece. This ambiguity occurs by reason of the literal power of the word. A simple equivocation faces us, and in fact we do not en-counter the same word in two cases. It is not *una vox*, except as *rhema*. Actually two different words are offered us, though the sign structure is equal—*aequa vox*.

But when I speak of the leg of a man and the leg of a table there is neither univocity nor simple equivocation. In both cases the word is used literally. It is absurd to say that the leg of the table is a symbol of a human

leg, for it is neither the symbol nor the sign of it. Of course it is true that
the leg of a table is analogous to the leg of a man. The proposition, this is
the leg of the table, immediately affirms something literal of the table, and
on ultimate reduction also affirms that there is a proportion between a
human leg and a table leg. This proportion is literally true. The partial
function of a human leg with respect to a man is equivalent (not equal!)
to the partial function of a table leg with respect to the table. We rightly
use the term "leg" in both instances literally, but with analogy. And let it
be remembered that analogy must not be reduced to metaphor, though any
truth content of a metaphor is derived from the prior principle of analogy.

Analogy or proportionality is not the conquest of a mystical perception
nor the object of an experience so baffling as that suggested in some of the
descriptions of the symbolists when they try to explain the existential perception of the ground of being. Any child recognizes the similarity which
really exists between two relations. What is more, analogy can be employed in reasoning, for the mathematics of proportion is a purely logical
achievement.

The recognition of the role of analogy seems to explode the difficulty
against the literal predication of human terms to God. Could it be that
that eloquent symbolist, Karl Barth, glimpsed this when he declared, probably in irritation, that *analogia entis* was the invention of Antichrist? Whoever invented it certainly drove a powerful wedge between the horns of the
supposed dilemma: univocal literalism or unliteral symbolism. The concept
of analogy tells us that there is the a priori possibility of analogous literalism.
Nor need we assign the discovery of analogy to Antichrist. The demon is the
simia Dei (ape of God). He can only misleadingly imitate God. Now, which
is the real thing and which the fraudulent copy: analogy or gnosticizing
symbolism? We must discern the spirits, and in the relatively long history of
Christianity the analogous understanding of the scriptural statements concerning God has a record of piety whereas cavalier impatience with the letter
has always been suspect.

Nor need the symbolist fear that the "utter otherness" of God is denied
by an analogous understanding of the formulas which speak to us of God.
In a proportion we do not say that the half of an orange is in any way
equal to the half of a melon. We only say that in ratio of whole and half
they are equivalent. When the Scriptures call God our King, they are not
saying that God is our Nero. It is only affirmed that Nero's proper power
in his limited field of direction is relatively equivalent on his side of the
equation to the absolute dominion of God over us on the other side. There
is no univocity; no equality. We all know that we cannot conceive God's

dominion absolutely. We only conceive it relatively to what we know of human dominion, for proportionality is a reality of the order of relation. Nor does this give us only formal knowledge. When I am told that the boy before me looks like his father, I know something about the father I have never seen.

Analogy does not immediately answer the problem which Bultmann tries to solve by demythologization, though indirectly it can offer us a different solution. The historiographical aspects of the Scriptures can be safeguarded, nor need they be cast into the discard. Analogy pervades all language.[17] It is vexing to a foursquare rationalist that this is so, for he wants only univocal terms so that all valid inference can be restricted to an Aristotelian syllogism.

But reality itself stubbornly resists the rationalist's prejudice. The realism so characteristic of the English language accepts analogy without a qualm, so that the same word can be a substantive, verb and adjective— all with different levels of meaning. The genuine root-meaning is not precisely the same in all instances but an analogical perception makes diverse uses easily intelligible without confusion. Now, "history" is a chameleon word in English. It can mean the flux dimension of empirical reality. It can mean historiography. It can mean a philosophy of history. And it can mean a theological interpretation of history.

The formulas of Christian revelation, scriptural or non-scriptural, are in large part theological interpretations of history. For this function the methodological precision and detailed accuracy in the presentation of historical data are not called for. Historical data can be referred to in many ways. Folklore does it. So does epopoeia. Theological interpretation rightly telescopes the data or even poetizes them, but the genuine data are referred to, even if the reference is not to ultimate sources nor given with rigid definition.

It is true enough that the methodologically exact historian uses the scriptural monuments at his own risk, but it is equally true, as experience has proved, that historiography can successfully and profitably use the Scriptures in its work. The rhetorical exaggerations and fanciful reconstructions inevitable in a small people's chauvinism are not imprecisions. They are merely evidence that in the selected literary genre precision in the offering of data was not contemplated.

In the light of this rapid sketch we can glimpse values and defects in symbolism and demythologization. With the symbolists we can consider as unserious and rather puerile the assumption that the Biblical writers were writing history with the purpose a modern historian pursues in his work.

This is fundamentalism, which always runs the risk of becoming ridiculous. On the other hand, to refuse to see any kind of historiography in the Scriptures seems willful and unfaithful to the books before our eyes. Scriptural historiography is analogous to ours. It must be understood not by the canons of Bernheim but by the modes and styles of the past, and according to the theological purposes of the authors. To ignore, overlook or discard the analogously historiographical dimensions of the Bible is to change a record of flux into static Platonic didacticism. Seriousness, earnestness, plain unvarnished candor prevent such a procedure.

Part V

Religion and the Realms of Reason: Philosophy and Science

10

Faith and Reason in the Thought of Erasmus and Luther*

BY HEINRICH BORNKAMM

The historical impact of the Reformation is shown by the fact that this movement did not remain confined to its original concern, namely, the reorganization of the Church; from the depth, like a submarine earthquake, it exerted a profound effect upon the entire epoch with its spiritual, political and social problems and institutions, agitating it into turbulent waves. In this process it was inevitable that the Reformation should come in contact or in conflict with other revolutionary movements which were in existence before and alongside it—humanism, peasant revolts, the idea of the national state, the social remolding of the cities, etc. It could be said especially of the conflict with humanism that two "reformations" came together. The struggle between Luther and Erasmus was hardly of less ardent concern to the educated persons of the time than Luther's fight against the Roman Church. For here it was not a question of coming to terms with those who chose to cling to tradition, but with those who themselves were innovators and pioneers. The epoch-making dialogue between Luther and Erasmus is a prelude to the problems which have plagued modern man since the time of the Reformation.

In the year 1518 Erasmus published for the second time his most important religious work, the *Enchiridion militis christiani*. Erasmus was not disappointed in his hope that the booklet would be more favorably received than at the time of its first publication (1503). But Erasmus found himself unable to exercise any further control over that new wave which seized his booklet and tempestuously carried it away. With his ideas of religious reformation he had drifted into the sphere of influence of another, stronger mind. This remained the tragic situation of his life.

* Translated by Anne Liard Jennings.

Whatever Erasmus was able to offer to his time stemmed from *devotio moderna,* the late medieval spiritual movement in which the fervor of the great mystics had subsided into a delicate inwardness, striving to express itself in deeds. This attitude, combined with the moralistic tendency of the late classical philosophy, produced for Erasmus a balance between the Bible and antiquity, a "Christian philosophy," which had reigned in its classical form in the early Church, extending from the time of the Apologists to Jerome and Augustine. Erasmus considered it his lifework to revive that epoch. His severe and simple admonishments were oriented toward that goal: "With true courage you should resolve to lead a perfect life, and never waver from that resolution. The human spirit has never forcefully imposed upon itself a command which it failed to obey. . . . That which appears unattainable at the beginning is rendered less difficult with time, easy with exercise, and finally even pleasant with habit."[1] "See to it that you become spirit."[2] He firmly believed that man is capable of carrying out such an exhortation—the exhortation of Christ, the "father of philosophy." And he was profoundly convinced that this was the message of true philosophy and of the Bible. The latter contains in all its widely varying books the same ever-recurring truths which are directly accessible to the moral intellect of all people and all times. With the help of allegorical interpretation it is only necessary to know how to extract these truths from historical reports and the whole time-bound disguise, much in the same manner as with all other literature.

Luther, after an excruciating struggle, had long ago recognized the incompatibility of that which Erasmus bound together in simple comparisons. In his eyes the unproblematic "Christian philosophy" necessarily appeared as a step backward from the far more grandiose scholastic synthesis of reason and revelation—a synthesis which he had tried and discarded as untenable. And, while Erasmus urged man to enhance his powers, calling upon all pedagogic means, appeals and enticements at his disposal, Luther had learned to tear man away from any kind of introspective reflection, and to direct his trust exclusively toward the forgiving and rejuvenating power of God's love. His interpretation of the Bible was in keeping with his realistic concept of man. For him the factual occurrence, the "flesh and blood" of the Biblical story, was of prime importance. He rejected the devious moral-spiritual interpretation of Erasmus as an arbitrary addition, as the mere exercise of human thought. The intellectual realms of the two great spiritual rulers of their time were bound to conflict sooner or later. With astounding penetration Luther very early foresaw those issues which later led to conflict. As early as October, 1516, he informed the famous man with all due respect, through Spalatin, that he could not hope to understand the Old Testament law if he endorsed the (allegorical) interpretation of Jerome instead of that of Augustine.[3] And in March, 1517, he wrote: "I take less and less delight in Erasmus . . . The human element is more important to him than the divine . . . One sees things differently when one attributes such wide significance to human capabilities, than when one knows of nothing else but divine grace."[4]

The conflict developed in three phases. The first phase was formed by a struggle of which neither party was aware and which neither desired—the struggle for the favor and support of the young generation, whose most able representatives sided with the Reformation. Erasmus went into seclusion and was not always successful in his efforts to prevent being taken for a partisan of one or the other feuding group. Under pressure from his friends and Catholic nobles, such as George of Saxonia and Henry VIII of England, he tried to clarify matters in his precarious position by attacking Luther at that point where Catholic and humanistic lines of thought met: namely, in the problem of free will. In his work *De libero arbitrio* (1524) the dogmatic solution of the problem was of no concern to him. He candidly admitted being a skeptic, "whenever it is permissible under the infallible authority of the Holy Scripture and the decisions of the Church, to which I shall always willingly subordinate my opinions, regardless of whether I comprehend its orders or not."[5] It was the method of allegory— the possibility of shifting at will from concrete statements to figurative ones—which produced this mixture of skepticism and loyalty to authority in him. It was not the question as such that interested him, but rather the moral consequences of the denial of free will. His most effective weapon was the natural desire of man for intellectual harmony, for a reasonable picture of God and man, whereby justice would be done to both sides: a small but indispensable measure of freedom, and a great deal of grace. With his reply *De servo arbitrio* (1525) it is as difficult today as it was for Luther in his own day to overcome that ally of Erasmus, the desire for rationality. Unlike his opponent, he was unable to keep open the doors of skepticism and authoritarianism as well. Furthermore, he was not only concerned with the moral consequences, but the question itself was of vital importance to him: the question of human freedom, seen from the perspective of the reality of God. Only *this* kind of freedom was his concern, not the philosophical question of determinism, the possibility of making a free choice in matters of everyday life. In contrast to Erasmus, Luther had incomparably less faith in man and incomparably more faith in God. By producing a sober attitude in man with regard to his own capabilities

Luther wished to render man accessible to the power of God, so that his spiritual rebirth might occur. Erasmus quite correctly perceived the difference to lie in the fact that Luther attributed very little significance to education and very much significance to the Holy Ghost.[6] Luther's present concept of man also contained a new psychology—not as root, but as fruit. Erasmus' man was the rational being of late antique popular philosophy, characterized by a high degree of consciousness, self-control, and self-determination. Luther's man had a different countenance: entangled in ability and impotence, will and inertia, incomprehensible to himself, fleeing from God and striving toward him—a totality of indistinguishable, incalculable forces, never to be grasped rationally.

For Luther man is unfree before God with regard to good—a servant of sin. At the same time he is also "unfree," that is, not autonomous—governed by grace. He is a tool of the Holy Ghost, who keeps and protects him from his former self—and unfree on that very account.

While this freedom in servitude, this self-realization of the ego in surrender, had been a meaningless paradox, so much the more incomprehensible for him was the concept of God which Luther worked out with an astounding consistency found in no other work but his powerful reply to Erasmus. This concept was lacking in all rational harmony, since the problem of God, according to Luther, could not be mastered by analytic intellect; on the contrary, this problem extends beyond the limits of human thinking, and therefore must lead to incommunicable conclusions, statements which defy systematization on the theological as well as the philosophical basis. The Bible does not tell of God in such a way that it might be construed as a "Christian philosophy," but in a way that ever anew creates a grasp of God's reality in human consciousness. It always remains the same reality, although it can be viewed from various aspects: majesty and omnipotence of God, as compared to our status as created beings—responsibility, guilt, and helpless subjection of man—deliverance through Christ and the divine word alone. The inner unity of all aspects lies in their consistent presentation of God as the true God, and of man as the true man. Luther establishes these aspects as paths leading into a dark jungle; they start out at various distant points, but they all emerge in one hidden clearing. Whoever walks to the end of any of these paths meets the real God face to face. For the intellect, which sees the problem from the outside, these aspects remain full of contradictions. But contemplative faith, which has walked the paths, comprehends that in final analysis these contradictions are only apparent and are the result of the limits of our thinking with respect to God. Luther hoped that the light of eternity would resolve these conflicts.

After this alignment of forces, obviously no further agreement between Luther and Erasmus was possible. To be sure, Erasmus came forth with another reply, uttered in a tone of unwarranted irritation, but he failed to contribute any new ideas. Luther let him say the last word. Nevertheless, a third, although brief, exchange of views occurred. In a pamphlet of 1533 Erasmus voiced his ideas about a reunification of the Church.[7] Again his program displayed the same combination of skepticism and authoritarianism: dogmatic questions should be let alone as much as possible, but no interference with the tradition and unity of the Church should take place; for only in the Church could man find security and stability. Luther responded amiably, but in no uncertain terms: the Evangelical, that is the Protestant, side would always be favorably disposed toward a concordance of love, but a concordance of faith should not be established at the expense of conscience and truth.[8]

Although in the course of time Erasmus withdrew from active participation in the making of Reformation history, and neither of the opposing sides agreed with him, he nevertheless remained a towering figure in the intellectual world. With his Christian rationalism he was prophetical. In the pedagogically oriented religion which he initiated a wealth of disparate themes lingers on: skepticism and an ensuing indifferent tolerance, an awareness of tradition and a need for security, a reduction of Christianity to an easily grasped morality, faith in education as a factor of basic importance to man, disregard for ecclesiastical institutions and high esteem for the Church as a political and moral authority, a tendency to resolve Biblical statements into allegory and metaphor, and in spite of all this, almost aesthetic respect for traditional forms and dogmas.

In comparison to the highly modern air of this complex of contradictory motifs, Luther's plain and unpretentious spiritual heritage takes on an almost meager look, despite its undeniably superior religious power and historical impact; here we encounter a religious conviction which continually issued the same firm and finite statements about God and man, which placed conscience and truth above everything else and left the consequences to Providence. Nevertheless, we must ask ourselves whether Luther's faith did not also contain constructive forces of spiritual edification and education which counterbalanced the Erasmus-inspired doctrine, indeed were superior to it.

Although it is impossible for us to discuss here in detail the theological justification of Luther's position with regard to Erasmus, we should, nevertheless, like to recall three important conclusions arising from these considerations; furthermore, we should like to add three points which characterize the contrast between the two opposing sides above and beyond the extensive literary controversy.

1. While Erasmus reduced the philosophical and religious material of antiquity and of the Old and New Testament to a unified, timeless rational philosophy, Luther stressed the difference between philosophy and theology. By doing so Luther rendered a service to each discipline, since he set limits to both and did not demand from either intellect or faith more than it could offer. Within the area where these two must overlap, to be sure, especially in determining the nature and purpose of man, he favored faith over reason, since he did not conceive of man as existing in isolation, but always took God's reality as his standard and basis.

2. The allegorical interpretation of Erasmus abolished the historical individuality of the Biblical books and neglected the historical process of religious revelation in reducing it to the common level dictated by his philosophy. On the other hand, Luther's passionate interest in the accounts and facts of the Bible led by a direct path to historical Bible research, even though Luther's methods were alien to the premises and extent of modern Bible interpretation.

3. As far as psychological veracity is concerned, Luther's concept of man was far superior to that of Erasmus. The former saw man as he is, the latter as he wished him to be. Luther's psychology was more modern than that of Erasmus.

4. Both men made magnificent contributions to the educational progress of their time: Erasmus with his commendable training of an elite, which however remained aloof and isolated and soon exhausted itself in trivial artistic endeavors. Luther's merits are not less significant; he never ceased to thank Erasmus for the new linguistic knowledge, and he subjected this new knowledge to a vital challenge in interpretation, sermon, and literature. Moreover, he sought to make these fruits of linguistic scholarship available to the whole people, a thought which had scarcely occurred to Erasmus. One cannot balance these two contributions against each other; but we must esteem each individually in terms of its significance in the cultural history of mankind.

5. Erasmus, the scholar, stood apart from the problems of nature which came to the fore at that time; Luther, on the other hand, with his affinity for everything real and concrete, was astoundingly well attuned to natural phenomena. We cannot call Luther unjust when he once ironically remarked that Erasmus regards the creatures as a cow observes a new gate.

And he added with delight: "We are now facing the sunrise of a new life, since we are beginning to regain that knowledge of creatures which we lost through Adam's fall."[9]

6. Not Luther but Erasmus is the author of the idea of the Christian state, which generally forms the foundation for the absolutism of the sixteenth to eighteenth centuries. Erasmus had directly ascribed to the ruler the responsibility for the cultivation of religion, the foundation of public welfare.[10] A realist even here, Luther, on the contrary, always expressly designated State and rulers as secular, and only requested the nobles to assume temporary emergency duties for the sake of reorganizing the social structures of which they were members. The religious overtones, and finally the religious self-glorification, of the modern political State can be traced back to the Christian humanism of Erasmus, not to Luther.

May these examples help to clarify the question of whether the simplicity of the faith-oriented conscience in Luther was not more abundant in spiritual force than that manifoldness of intellect which Erasmus offered—being unable to offer that one thing which he himself also sought.

The Predicament of the Christian Historian

BY GEORGES FLOROVSKY

Veritas non erubescit nisi abscondi.
—Leo XIII

I

"Christianity is a religion of historians."[1] It is a strong phrase, but the statement is correct. Christianity is basically a vigorous appeal to history, a witness of faith to certain particular events in the past, to certain particular data of history. These events are acknowledged by faith as truly eventful. These historic moments, or instants, are recognized as utterly momentous. In brief, they are identified by faith as "mighty deeds" of God, *Magnalia Dei.* The "scandal of particularity," to use the phrase of Gerhard Kittel,[2] belongs to the very essence of the Christian message. The Christian Creed itself is intrinsically historic. It comprises the whole of existence in a single historical scheme as one "History of Salvation," from Creation to Consummation, to the Last Judgment and the End of history. Emphasis is put on the ultimate cruciality of certain historic events, namely, of the Incarnation, of the Coming of the Messiah, and of his Cross and Resurrection. Accordingly, it may be justly contended that "the Christian religion is a daily invitation to the study of history."[3]

Now, it is at this point that the major difficulties arise. An average believer, of any denomination or tradition, is scarcely aware of his intrinsic duty to study history. The historical pattern of the Christian message is obvious. But people are interested rather in the "eternal truth" of this message, than in what they are inclined to regard as "accidents" of history, even when they are discussing the facts of the Biblical history or of the history of the Church. Does not the message itself point out beyond history, to the "life of the Age to come"? There is a persistent tendency to interpret the *facts* of history as images or *symbols,* as typical cases or examples, and to transform the *"history*

of salvation" into a kind of edifying *parable*. We can trace this tendency
back to the early centuries of Christian history. In our own days we find ourselves in the midst of an intense controversy precisely about this very matter.

On the one hand, the essential *historicity of Christian religion* has been
rediscovered and re-emphasized, precisely during the past few decades, and
a fresh impact of this reawakened historical insight is strongly felt now in all
fields of contemporary theological research—in Biblical exegesis, in the study
of Church history and liturgics, in certain modern attempts at the "reconstruction of belief," and even in the modern ecumenical dialogue. On the
other hand, the recent plea for a radical *demythologizing* of the Christian
message is an ominous sign of a continuing anti-historical attitude in certain
quarters. For to demythologize Christianity means in practice precisely to
de-historicize it, despite the real difference between myth and history. In
fact, the modern plea is but a new form of that theological liberalism, which,
at least from the Age of the Enlightenment, persistently attempted to dis-
entangle Christianity from its historical context and involvement, to detect its
perennial "essence" (*"das Wesen des Christentums"*), and to discard the
historical shells. Paradoxically, the Rationalists of the Enlightenment and the
devout Pietists of various description, and also the dreamy mystics, were
actually working toward the same purpose. The impact of German Idealism,
in spite of its historical appearance, was ultimately to the same effect. The
emphasis was shifted from the "outward" facts of history to the "inward"
experience of the believers. Christianity, in this interpretation, became a
"religion of experience," mystical, ethical, or even intellectual. History was
felt to be simply irrelevant. The historicity of Christianity was reduced to
the acknowledgment of a permanent "historical significance" of certain ideas
and principles, which originated under particular conditions of time and
space, but were in no sense intrinsically linked with them. The person of
Christ Jesus lost its cruciality in this interpretation, even if his message has
been, to a certain extent, kept and maintained.

Now, it is obvious that this anti-historical attitude was itself but a particular form of an acute historicism, that is, of a particular interpretation of
history, in which the historical has been ruled out as something accidental
and indifferent. Most of the liberal arguments were, as they still are, historical and critical, although behind them one could easily detect definite
ideological prejudices, or preconceptions. The study of history was vigorously
cultivated by the Liberal school, if only in order to discredit history, as a
realm of relativity, or as a story of sin and failure, and, finally, to ban history
from the theological field. This "abuse of history" by the liberals made even
the "lawful" use of history in theology suspect in the conservative circles. Was

it safe to make the eternal truth of Christianity dependent in any way upon
the data of history, which is, by its very nature, inextricably contingent and
human? For that reason Cardinal Manning denounced every appeal to history, or to "antiquity," as both "a treason and a heresy." He was quite
formal at this point: for him the Church had no history. She was ever abiding in a continuous present.[4]

After all—it has been persistently asked—can one really "know" history,
that is, the past? How can one discern, with any decent measure of security,
what actually did happen in the past? Our pictures of the past are so varied,
and change from one generation to another, and even differ from one historian to the next. Are they anything but subjective opinions, impressions, or
interpretations? The very possibility of any historical knowledge seemed to
be compromised by the skeptical exploits of the learned. It seemed that even
the Bible could no longer be retained as a book of history, although it could
be kept as a glorious *paradeigma* of the eternal Glory and Mercy of God.
Moreover, even if one admits that Christians are, by vocation, historians, it
can be contended that they are bound to be bad historians, or unreliable
historians, since they are intrinsically "committed" in advance. It is commonly agreed that the main virtue of a historian is his impartiality, his
freedom from all preconceptions, his radical *Voraussetzungslosigkeit*. Now,
obviously, Christians, if they are believing and practicing Christians, cannot
conscientiously dispense with their formidable "bias," even if they succeed in
preserving their intellectual honesty and integrity. Christians, by the very
fact of their faith and allegiance, are committed to a very particular interpretation of certain events of history, and also to a definite interpretation of the
historic process itself, taken as a whole. In this sense, they are inevitably
prejudiced. They cannot be radically critical. They would not agree, for
instance, to handle their sacred books as "pure literature," and would not
read the Bible simply as the "epic" of the Jews. They would not surrender
their belief in the crucial uniqueness of Christ. They would not consent to
rule out the "supernatural" element from history. Under these conditions, is
any impartial and critical study of history possible at all? Can Christians
continue as Christians in the exercise of their profession? How can they
vindicate their endeavor? Can they simply divorce their professional work,
as historians, from their religious convictions, and write history as anyone
else may do it, as if they were in no way informed by the faith?

The easiest answer to this charge is to declare that all historians have a
bias. An unbiased history is simply impossible, and actually does not exist.[5]
In fact, "evolutionary" historians are obviously no less committed than
those who believe in the Biblical revelation, only they are committed to

another bias. Ernest Renan and Julius Wellhausen were no less committed than Ricciotti or Père Lagrange, and Harnack and Baur no less than Bardy or Lebreton, and Reitzenstein and Frazer much more than Dom Odo Casel and Dom Gregory Dix. They were only committed to different things. One knows only too well that historical evidence can be twisted and distorted in compliance with all sorts of "critical" preconceptions, even more than it has been done sometimes in obedience to "tradition."

This kind of argument, however, is very ambiguous and inconclusive. It would lead, ultimately, to a radical skepticism and would discredit the study of history of any kind. It actually amounts to a total surrender of all claims and hopes for any reliable historical knowledge. It seems, however, that, in the whole discussion, one operates usually with a very questionable conception of the historical study, with a conception derived from another area of inquiry, namely, from the natural sciences. It is assumed in advance that there is a universal "scientific method" which can be applied in any field of inquiry, regardless of the specific character of the subject of study. But this is a gratuitous assumption, a bias, which does not stand critical test and which, in fact, has been vigorously contested, in recent decades, both by historians and by philosophers. In any case, one has, first of all, to define what is the nature and specific character of "the historical" and in what way and manner this specific subject can be reached and apprehended. One has to define the aim and purpose of historical study and then to design methods by which this aim, or these aims, can be properly achieved. Only in this perspective can the very question of "impartiality" and "bias" be intelligently asked and answered.

II

The study of history is an ambiguous endeavor. Its very objective is ambiguous. History is the study of the past. Strictly speaking, we have at once to narrow the scope of the inquiry. History is indeed the study of the *human* past. An equation of human history and natural history would be an unwarranted presupposition or option. Much harm has been done to the study of history by such naturalistic presuppositions, which amount, in the last resort, to the denial of any specific character of human existence. Anyhow, "the past" as such cannot be "observed" directly. It has actually passed away and therefore is never given directly in any "possible experience" (to use the phrase of John Stuart Mill). The knowledge of the past is necessarily indirect and inferential. It is always *an interpretation*. The past can only be "reconstructed." Is it a possible task? And how is it possible? Actually, no historian begins with the past. His starting point is always in the present, to which he belongs himself. He looks back. His starting point is his "sources," the primary sources. Out of them, and on their authority, he proceeds to the "recovery" of the past. His procedure depends upon the nature and character of his information, of his sources.

What are these sources? What makes a certain thing a source for the historian? In a certain sense, almost everything, *omnis res scibilis,* can serve as a historical source, provided the historian knows how to use it, how *to read the evidence.* But, on the other hand, no thing at all is a historical source by itself, even a chronicle, or a narrative, or even an autobiography. Historical sources exist, in their capacity as sources, only in the context of a historical inquiry. Things are mute by themselves, even the texts and speeches: they speak only when they are understood; they render answers only when they are examined, as witnesses are examined, when proper questions are asked. And the first rule of the historical craft is precisely to cross-examine the witnesses, to ask proper questions, and to force the relics and the documents to answer them. In his admirable little book, *Apologie pour l'Histoire, ou Metier d'Historien,* Marc Bloch illustrates this rule with convincing examples.

Before Boucher de Perthes, as in our own days, there were plenty of flint artifacts in the alluvium of Somme. However, there was no one to ask questions, and there was therefore no prehistory. As an old medievalist, I know nothing which is better reading than a cartulary. That is because I know just about what to ask it. A collection of Roman inscriptions, on the other hand, would tell me little. I know more or less how to read them, but not how to cross-examine them. In other words, every historic research presupposes that the inquiry has a direction at the very first step. In the beginning there must be the guiding spirit. Mere passive observation, even supposing such a thing were possible, has never contributed anything productive to any science.[6]

This remark of a conscientious and critical scholar is revealing. What he actually suggests is that all historical inquiry is, by definition, as a true inquiry, "prejudiced" from the very start—prejudiced because directed. Otherwise there would have been no inquiry, and the things would have remained silent. Only in the context of a guided inquiry do the sources speak, or rather only in this context do "things" become "sources," only when they are, as it were, exorcised by the inquisitive mind of the historian. Even in the experimental science, facts never speak by themselves, but only in the process, and in the context, of a directed research, and no scientific experiment can ever be staged, unless an "experiment in mind" has been previously performed by the explorer.[7] Observation itself is impossible without some interpretation, that is, understanding.

The study of history has been sorely handicapped by an uncritical and "naturalistic" conception of historical sources. They have been often mistaken for independent entities, existing before and outside of the process of the historical study. A false task was consequently imposed on the historian: he was supposed to find history *in* the sources, while handling them precisely as "things." Nothing could come out of any such endeavor but a pseudo history, a history made "with scissors and paste,"[8] a "history without the historical problem," as Benedetto Croce aptly has styled it.[9] Certain historians have deliberately sought to reduce themselves to the role of reporters, but even reporters must be interpretative and selective, if they want to be intelligible. In fact, historical sources cannot be handled simply as "relics," "traces," or "imprints" of the past. Their function in the historical research is quite different. They are *testimonies* rather than traces. And no testimony can be assessed except in the process of interpretation. No collection of factual statements, no compilation of news and dates, is history, even if all facts have been critically established and all dates verified. The best catalogue of an art museum is not a history of art. A catalogue of manuscripts is not a history of literature, not even a history of handwriting. No chronicle is history. In the sharp phrase of Benedetto Croce, a chronicle is but a "corpse of history," *il cadavere*. A chronicle is but "a thing" (*una cosa*), a complex of sounds and other signs. But history is "an act of the spirit," *un atto spirituale*.[10] "Things" become "sources" only in the process of cognition, in relation to the inquiring intellect of the student. Outside of this process historical sources simply do not exist.

The question a historian asks is the question about *meaning* and *significance*. And things are then treated as *signs and witnesses* of the past reality, not simply as relics or imprints. Indeed, only signs can be interpreted, and not "pure facts," since the question about meaning points beyond pure giveness. There are things insignificant and meaningless, and they cannot be understood or interpreted at all, precisely because they are meaningless, just as in a conversation we may fail to understand certain casual remarks, which were not intended to convey any message. Indeed, historical cognition is a kind of conversation, a dialogue with those in the past whose life, thoughts, feelings, and decisions the historian endeavors to rediscover, *through the documents* by which they are witnessed to or signified. Accordingly, one can infer from certain facts, words or things, *as from a sign to the meaning,* only if and when these objective things can be lawfully treated as signs, that is, as bearers of meaning, only when and if we can reasonably assume that these things have a dimension of depth, a dimension of meaning. We do not assign meaning to them: we should detect meaning. Now, there is meaning in certain things, in our documents and sources, only in so far as behind them we are entitled to assume the existence of other intelligent beings.

History is accordingly *a study of the human past,* not of any past as such. Only man has history, in the strict sense of this word. R. G. Collingwood elaborates this point with great clarity. Close similarity between the work of an archaeologist and that of a paleontologist is obvious: both are diggers. Yet, their aims are quite different. "The archaeologist's use of his stratified relics depends upon his conceiving them as artifacts serving human purposes and thus expressing a particular way in which men have thought about their own life." In the study of nature, on the other hand, there is no such distinction between the "outside" and the "inside" of the data. "To the scientist, nature is always and merely a 'phenomenon,' not in the sense of being defective in reality, but in the sense of being a spectacle presented to his intellectual observation; whereas the events of history are never mere phenomena, never mere spectacles for contemplation, but things which the historian looks, not at, but through, to discern the thought within them."[11] Historical documents can be interpreted as signs because they are charged with meaning, as expressions or reflections, deliberate or spontaneous, of human life and endeavor.

Now, this meaning is available for others only in so far as a sufficient identification can be achieved between the interpreter and those whose thoughts, actions, or habits he is interpreting. If this contact, for any reason, has not been established, or cannot be established at all, no understanding is possible and no meaning can be elicited, even if the documents or relics are charged with meaning, as it is, for instance, in the case of an undecipherable script. Again, "testimonies" can be misunderstood and misinterpreted, just as we often misunderstand each other in an actual conversation or fail to find a "common language"—then no communication is possible; just as we may misinterpret a foreign text, not only because we simply make mistakes in translation, but also when we fail to enter congenially into the inner world of those persons whose testimonies we are deciphering. An *Einfühlung* into the witnesses is an obvious prerequisite of understanding. We are actually deciphering each other's words even in an ordinary conversation, and sometimes we fail sorely to achieve any satisfactory result. The problem of semantics, that is, of intelligent communication—a communication between intelligent beings—is inherent in the whole process of historical interpretation. In the phrase of Ranke, "history only begins when monuments become intelligible."[12] One should add that only "intelligible documents" are, in a full sense, *historical* documents, historical *sources*—as H. I. Marrou puts it, *"dans la mesure où l'historien peut et sait y comprendre quelque chose.*"[13] Consequently, the person of the interpreter belongs to the actual process of interpretation no less than the data to be interpreted, just as both partners in a conversation are essential for a successful dialogue. No understanding is possible without some measure of "congeniality," of intellectual or spiritual sympathy, without a real meeting of minds. Collingwood is right in pointing out that

historical inquiry reveals to the historian the power of his own mind. . . . Whenever he finds certain historical matters unintelligible, he has discovered a limitation of his own mind, he has discovered that there are certain ways in which he is not, or no longer, or not yet, able to think. Certain historians, sometimes whole generations of historians, find in certain periods of history nothing intelligible, and call them dark ages; but such phrases tell us nothing about those ages themselves, though they tell us a great deal about the persons who use them, namely that they are unable to re-think the thoughts which were fundamental to their life.[14]

It is the first rule of the true *exegesis:* we have to grasp *the mind of the writer,* we must discover exactly what he intended to say. The phrase, or the whole narrative, or the whole document, can be misunderstood when we fail to do so, or when we *read* our own thought *into* the text. No sentence, and no text, should be dismissed as "meaningless" simply because we fail to detect meaning. We misread the text when we take literally that which has been said metaphorically, and also when we interpret that which was meant to be an actual story just as a parable.

You cannot find out what a man means by simply studying his spoken or written statements, even though he has spoken or written with perfect command of language and perfectly truthful intention. In order to find out his meaning you must also know what the question was (a question in his own mind, and presumed by him to be in yours) to which the thing he has said or written was meant as an answer.[15]

It is true of our actual conversations, in the intercourse of the current life. It is true of our study of the historical sources. Historical documents are *documents of life.*

Every historian begins with certain data. Then, by an effort of his searching and inquisitive mind, he apprehends them as "witnesses," or, as it were, "communications" from the past, that is, as meaningful signs. By the power of his intellectual intuition, he grasps the meaning of these signs, and thus recovers, in an act of "inductive imagination," that comprehensive setting in which all his data converge and are integrated into a coherent, that is, intelligible, whole. There is an inevitable element of guess, or rather of "divination," in this process of understanding, as there is, unavoidably, a certain element of guess in every attempt to understand another person. A lack of congenial guess, or imaginative sympathy, may make any conversation impossible, since no real *contact of minds* has been established, as if the participants spoke different languages, so that utterances of one person did not become messages for the other. In a sense, any act of understanding is a "mental experiment," and divination is always an indispensable element therein. Divination is a kind of mental vision, an indivisible act of insight, an act of imagination, inspired and controlled by the whole of one's acquired experience. One may suggest it is an act of "fantasy," but it is fantasy of a very special kind. It is a *cognitive fantasy* and, as Benedetto Croce eloquently explains, without it historical knowledge is simply impossible: *senza questa ricostruzione o integrazione fantastica non e dato ne scrivere storia, ne leggerla e intenderla*. It is, as he says, a "fantasy in the thought" (*la fantasia nel pensiero e per pensiero*), a "concreteness of the thought" which implies judgment and is therefore logically disciplined and controlled, and thereby clearly distinguished from any poetical license.[16] *"Understanding is Interpretation,* whether of a spoken word, or of the meaningful events themselves," as it was stated by F. A. Trendelenburg: *Alles Verständniss ist Interpretation, sei es des gesprochenen Wortes oder der sinnvollen Erscheinungen selbst.*[17] The art of hermeneutics is the core of the historical craft. And, as it has been aptly put by a Russian scholar, "one must observe as one reads, and not read as one observes."[18] "To read," whether texts or events themselves, means precisely "to understand," to grasp the inherent meaning, and the understanding intellect cannot be ruled out of the process of understanding, as the reader cannot be eliminated out of the process of reading.

Historians must be critical of themselves, probably even more critical of themselves than of their sources as such, since the sources are what they are, that is, "sources," precisely in proportion to the questions which the historian addresses to them. As H. I. Marrou says, "a document is understood precisely in the measure in which it finds a historian capable of appreciating most deeply its nature and its scope," *dans la mesure où il se rencontrera un historien capable d'apprecier avec plus de profondeur sa nature et sa portée.*[19] Now, the kind of questions a particular historian is actually asking depends ultimately upon his stature, upon his total personality, upon his dispositions and concerns, upon the amplitude of his vision, even upon his likes and dislikes. One should not forget that all acts of understanding are, strictly speaking, personal, and only in this capacity of *personal acts* can they have any existential relevance and value. One has to check, severely and strictly, one's prejudices and presuppositions, but one should never try to empty one's mind of *all* presuppositions. Such an attempt would be a suicide of mind and can only issue in total mental sterility. A barren mind is indeed inevitably sterile. Indifference, or neutrality and indecision, are not virtues, but vices, in a historian as well as in a literary critic, as much as one should claim "objectivity." Historical understanding is ultimately an intelligent response to the challenge of the sources, a deciphering of signs. A certain measure of relativity is inherent in all acts of human understanding, as it is inevitable in personal relations. Relativity is simply a concomitant of relations.

The ultimate purpose of a historical inquiry is not in the establishment of certain objective facts, such as dates, places, numbers, names, and the like, as much as all this is an indispensable preliminary, but in *the encounter with living beings.* No doubt, objective facts must be first carefully established, verified and confirmed, but this is not the final aim of the historian. History is precisely, to quote H. I. Marrou once more, "an encounter with the other" —*l'histoire est rencontre d'autrui.*[20] A narrow mind and an empty mind are real obstacles to this encounter, as they obviously are in all human relations. History, as a subject of study, is *history of human beings,* in their mutual relationship, in their conflicts and contacts, in their social intercourse, and in their solitude and estrangement, in their high aspirations and in their depravity. Only men live in history—live, and move, and strive, and create, and destroy. Men alone are *historic beings,* in a full sense of the word. In the historical understanding we establish contact with men, with their thoughts and endeavors, with their inner world and with their outward action. In this sense, Collingwood was undoubtedly right in insisting that "there are no mere 'events' in history."

What is miscalled an "event" is really an action, and expresses some thought (intention, purpose) of its agent; the historian's business is therefore to identify this thought.[21]

In this sense, Collingwood insisted, "history proper is the history of thought." It would be unfair to dismiss this contention as a sheer intellectualism, as an unwelcome ghost of obsolete Hegelianism. Collingwood's emphasis is not so much on the thought as such, but on *the intelligent and purposeful character of human life and action.* In history, there are not only happenings and occurrences, but actions and endeavors, achievements and frustrations. This only gives meaning to human existence.

In the last resort, history is history of man, in the ambiguity and multiplicity of his existence. This constitutes the specific character of historical cognition and of historical knowledge. Accordingly, methods must be proportionate to the aim. This has been often ignored in the age of militant and doctrinaire positivism, and is still often forgotten in our time. Objective knowledge, *more geometrico,* is impossible in history. This is not a loss, however, since historical knowledge is not a knowledge of *objects,* but precisely a knowledge of *subjects*—of "co-persons," of "co-partners" in the quest of life. In this sense, historical knowledge is, and must be, *an existential knowledge.* This constitutes a radical cleavage between the *"study of Spirit"* and the *"study of Nature,"* between *die Geisteswissenschaften* and *die Naturwissenschaft.*[22]

III

It has been often contended, especially by the historians of the old school, that historians are led, in the last resort, in their study, by the desire "to know the past as an eyewitness may know it," that is, to become, in some way, just a "witness" of the past events.[23] In fact, this is precisely what the historian cannot do, and never does, and never should attempt to do, if he really wants to be a historian. Moreover, it is by no means certain that an eyewitness of an event does really "know" it, that is, does understand its meaning and significance. An ambition to perform an impossible and contradictory task only obscures the understanding of that which a historian actually does do, if only he does a "historical" work.

The famous phrase of Leopold von Ranke, suggesting that historians "wish to know the actual past"—*wie es eigentlich gewesen*—has been much abused.[24] First of all, it is not fair to make of a casual remark by the great master of history a statement of principle. In any case, in his own work, Ranke never followed this alleged prescription of his, and was always much more than a chronicler. He always was aiming at an interpretation.[25] Obviously, historians want to know what actually has happened, but they want *to know it in a perspective.* And, of course, it is the only thing they can actually achieve. We can never remember even our own immediate past, exactly as we have lived it, because, if we are really *remembering,* and not just dreaming, we do remember the past occurrences in a perspective, against a changed background of our enriched experience. Collingwood described history as "re-enactment of past experience,"[26] and there is some truth in this description, in so far as this "re-enactment" is an integral moment of "understanding identification," which is indispensable in any conversation. But one should not mistake one's own thoughts for the thoughts of others. Collingwood himself says that the objects of historical thought are "events which *have finished* happening, and conditions *no longer in existence,"* that is, those events which are "no longer perceptible."[27] Historians look at the past in a perspective, as it were, at a distance. They do not intend *to reproduce* the past event. Historians want to know the past precisely *as the past,* and consequently *in the context of later happenings.* *"Un temps retrouvé,"* that is, recaptured in an act of intellectual imagination, is precisely *"un temps perdu,"* that is, something that really *did pass away,* something that has been really lost, and only for that reason, and in this capacity of a "lost moment," can it be searched for and rediscovered.

Historical vision is always *a retrospective vision.* What was a future for the people of the past, is now for historians a past. In this sense, historians know more about the past than people of the past themselves were ever able to know. Historians are aware of the impact of the past, of certain past events, on the present. As historians, we cannot visualize the glorious *Pentekontaetia* of Pericles, except in the perspective of the subsequent doom and collapse of Athenian democracy. Or, in any case, such an attempt, even if it were possible (which it is not), would in no sense be a historical endeavor. A perspective and a context are constitutive factors of all true historical understanding and presentation. We cannot understand Socrates properly and historically if we ignore the impact of his challenge and thought, as it has been actually manifested in the later development of Greek philosophy. Indeed, we would know much less about the "true," that is, historical, Socrates if we endeavored to see him, as it were, *in vacuo,* and not against the total historical background, which for us includes also that which for Socrates himself was still an unrealized and unpredictable future.

After all, history is neither spectacle nor panorama, but a *process.* The perspective of time, of concrete time, filled with events, gives us the *sense of direction* which was probably lacking in the events themselves, as they actually happened. Of course, one can make an effort to forget, or to ignore, what one does actually know, that is, the perspective. Whether one can really succeed in doing so is rather doubtful. But even if this were possible, would this be really a historical endeavor? As has been recently said, "to attempt to make oneself a contemporary of the events and people whose history one is writing, means, ultimately, to put oneself in the position which excludes history." *No history without a retrospect,* that is, without perspective.[28]

No doubt, retrospection has its dangers. It may expose us to "optical illusions." In retrospect, we may discover in the past, as it were, "too much," not only if we happen to read anything into the past events, but also because from a certain point of view certain aspects of the past may be seen in a distorted or exaggerated shape. We may be tempted to exaggerate unduly and out of proportion the role and impact of certain historic personalities or institutions, because their images have been disproportionately magnified in our apprehension by the particular perspective in which we are looking at them. And very often the perspective is simply imposed upon us: we cannot change our position. We may be tempted to establish wrong ancestries of trends and ideas, mistaking similarities for actual causal links, as has been done more than once in the history of Early Christianity, and indeed in many other fields. In brief, we may look at the past in a *wrong* perspective, without knowing it and without any means of correcting our vision. In any case, our perspective is always limited. We can never have a total perspective. Yet, on the other hand, we can never see the past in no perspective at all. The ultimate aim of the historian is indeed to comprehend the whole context, at least in a particular "intelligible, that is self-explanatory field" of research (the phrase is Toynbee's). Obviously, this aim is never achieved, and for that reason all historical interpretations are intrinsically provisional.

The historian is never content with a fragmentary vision. He tends to discover, or to presuppose, more order in the flux of events than probably there ever was. He tends to exaggerate the cohesion of various aspects of the past. As H. I. Marrou describes the historian's procedure, he endeavors, *for the sake of intelligibility,* to substitute "an orderly vision," *une vision or-donnée,* for that "dust of small facts" of which the actual happening seems to consist.[29] No historian can resist doing so, and no historian can avoid doing so. It is at this point, however, that utter caution must be exercised. Historians are always in danger of overrationalizing the flux of history. So often instead of living men, unstable and never fully "made up," historians describe fixed characters, as it were, some typical individuals in characteristic poses. It is, more or less, what the painters of portraits sometimes do, and by that device they may achieve impressiveness and convey a vision. This was the method of ancient historians, from Thucydides to Polybius and Tacitus. This is what Collingwood described as the "substantialism" of ancient historiography, and it was what made that historiography, in his opinion, "unhistorical."[30] But the same method has been persistently used by many modern historians. It suffices to mention Mommsen (in his *Roman History*), George Grote, Taine, Ferrero. To the same category belong the numerous stories of Christ in modern historiography from Keim and Ernest Renan to Albert Schweitzer. In a sense, it is a legitimate device. A historian tends to overcome, in a synthetic image, the empirical complexity and often confusion of individual bits, and occurrences, to organize them into a coherent whole, and to relate the multiplicity of occurrences to the unity of a character. This is seldom done in a logical way, by a rational reconstruction. Historians act rather as *inductive artists,* go by intuition. Historians have their own visions. But these are *transforming visions.* It is by this method that all major generalizations of our historiography have been created: the Hellenic mind; the medieval man; the bourgeois; and the like. It would be unfair to contest the relevance of these *categorical* generalizations, which must be clearly distinguished from the *generic* generalizations. And yet, it would be precarious to claim that these generalized "types" do really exist, that is, exist in time and space. They are, as it were, *valid visions,* like artistic portraits, and, as such, they are indispensable tools of understanding. But "typical men" are different from real men of flesh and blood. Of similar character are also our sociological generalizations: the city-state of Ancient Greece; the feudal society; capitalism; democracy; and so on. The main danger of all these generalizations is that they overstress the inner "necessity" of a particular course of behavior. A man, as a "type" or a "character," seems to be predestined to behave in his "typical" manner. There seems to be a typical pattern of development for each kind of human society. It is but natural that in our time the mirage of "historical inevitability" had to be exposed and disavowed, as a distorting factor of our historical interpretation.[31] There is indeed an inherent determinism in all these *typical* and *categorical* images. But they are no more than a useful shorthand for the "dust of facts." The actual history is fluid and flexible and ultimately unpredictable.

The tendency toward determinism is somehow implied in the method of retrospection itself. In retrospect we seem to perceive the *logic* of the events, which unfold themselves in a regular order, according to a recognizable pattern, with an alleged inner necessity, so that we get the impression that it really could not have happened otherwise. The ultimate *contingency* of the process is concealed in the rational schemes, and sometimes it is deliberately eliminated. Thus, *events are losing their eventuality,* and appear to be rather inevitable *stages of development or decay,* of rise and fall, according to a fixed ideal pattern. In fact, there is less consistency in actual history than appears in our interpretative schemes. *History is not an evolution,* and the actual course of events does not follow evolutionary schemes and patterns. Historical events are more than happenings; they are actions, or complexes of actions. History is a field of action, and behind the events stand agents, even when these agents forfeit their freedom and follow a pattern or routine, or are overtaken by blind passions. Man remains a free agent even in bonds. If we may use another biological term, we may describe history rather as *epigenesis* than as "evolution," since evolution always implies a certain kind of "pre-formation," and "development" is no more than a disclosure of "structure."[32] There is always some danger that we may mistake our conceptual visions for empirical realities and speak of them as if they were themselves factors and agents, whereas, in fact, they are but rational abbreviations for a multiplicity of real personal agents. Thus we venture to describe the evolution of "feudalism" or of "capitalistic society," forgetting that these terms only summarize a complex of diverse phenomena, visualized as a whole for the sake of intelligibility. "Societies," "categories," and "types" are *not organisms,* which only can "evolve" or "develop," but are *complexes* of co-ordinated individuals, and this co-ordination is always dynamic, flexible, and unstable.

All historical interpretations are provisional and hypothetical. No definitive interpretation can ever be achieved, even in a limited and particular field of research. Our data are never complete, and new discoveries often compel historians to revise radically their schemes and to surrender sometimes their most cherished convictions, which may have seemed firmly established. It is easy to quote numerous examples of such revision from various areas of historical study, including church history. Moreover, historians must, from time to time, readjust themselves to the changes in the surrounding world. Their vision is always determined by a certain point of view, and thereby limited. But the perspective itself unfolds in the course of actual history. No contemporary historian can commit himself to the identification of the Mediterranean world with the *Oicoumene,* which was quite legitimate in the ancient time. These limitations do not discredit the endeavor of historians. It may even be suggested that a "definitive" interpretation of events would eliminate the "historicity" of history, its contingency and eventuality, and substitute instead a rational "map of history," which may be lucid and readable, but will be existentially unreal. Again, our interpretations are also facts of history, and in them the depicted events continue their historical existence and participate in the shaping of historical life. One may argue whether the "Socrates of Plato" is a "real" Socrates, but there is little doubt that this Socrates of Plato had its own historical existence, as a powerful factor in the shaping of our modern conception of "philosopher." It seems that our interpretations disclose, in some enigmatic way, the hidden potentialities of the actual past. It is in this way that traditions are formed and grow, and the greatest of all human traditions is "culture," in which all partial and particular contributions of successive ages are melted together, synthetically transformed in this process of melting, and are finally integrated into a whole. This process of formation of human culture is not yet completed, and probably will never be completed within the limits of history. This is an additional reason why all historical interpretations should be provisional and approximative: a new light may be shed on the past by that future which has not yet arrived.

IV

It has been recently suggested that "if history has meaning, this meaning is not historical, but theological; what is called *Philosophy of history* is nothing else than a *Theology of history,* more or less disguised."[33] In fact, the term "meaning" is used in different senses when we speak of the meaning of particular events or of the sets of actions and events, and when we speak of the Meaning of History, taken as an all-inclusive whole, that is, in its entirety and universality. In the latter case, indeed, we are speaking actually of the ultimate meaning of human existence, of its ultimate destiny. And this, obviously, is not a historical question. In this case we are speaking not of that which has happened—and this is the only field in which historians are competent—but rather of that which is to happen, and is to happen precisely because it "must" happen. Now, it can be rightly contended that neither "the ultimate" nor "the future" belongs to the realm of historical study, which is, by definition, limited to the understanding of the human past. Historical predictions, of necessity, are conjectural and precarious. They are, in fact, unwarranted "extrapolations." Histories of men and societies are history, but the History of Man, a truly universal and providential History, is no longer just history.

In fact, all modern "philosophies of history" have been crypto-theological, or probably pseudo-theological: Hegel, Comte, Marx, even Nietzsche. In any case, all of them were based on beliefs. The same is true of the modern substitute for the Philosophy of history, which is commonly known as Sociology, and which is, in fact, a *Morphology of history,* dealing with the permanent and recurrent patterns or structures of human life. Now, is Man, in the totality of his manifold and personal existence, a possible subject of a purely historical study and understanding? To claim that he is, by itself is a kind of theology, even if it turns out to be no more than an *"apotheosis of man."* On the other hand—and *here lies the major predicament of all historical study*—no historian can, even in his limited and particular field, within his own competence, avoid raising ultimate problems of human nature and destiny, unless he reduces himself to the role of a registrar of empirical happenings and forfeits his proper task of "understanding." In order to understand, just historically, for instance, "the Greek mind," the historian must, of necessity, have his own vision, if not necessarily original, of the whole range of those problems with which the "noble spirits" of Antiquity were wrestling, in conflict with each other and in succession. A historian of philosophy must be, to a certain extent, a philosopher himself. Otherwise he will miss the problems around which the quest of philosophers has been centered. A historian of art must be, at least, an *amateur*—otherwise he will miss the artistic values and problems. In brief, the problem of *Man* transpires in all problems of *men,* and accordingly cannot be skipped over in any historical interpretation. Moreover, in a certain sense, historical endeavor, as such, aims in the last resort at something which, of necessity, transcends its boundaries.

The process of historical interpretation is the process in which the Human Mind is built and matures. It is a process of integration, in which particular insights and decisions of various ages are accumulated, confronted, dialectically reconciled, vindicated or discriminated, or even discarded and condemned. If history, as the process of human life through ages, has any meaning, any "sense," then obviously the study of history, if it is more than a matter of curiosity, must also have a meaning, a certain "sense." And if historical understanding is the historian's "response" to the "challenge" of that human life which he is exploring, it is of utter importance that historians should be prepared, and inwardly equipped, to meet this challenge of human existence in its fullness and in its ultimate depth.

Thus, contrary to the current prejudice, in order to be competent within his proper field of interpretation, a historian must be responsive to the whole amplitude of human concerns. If he has no concerns of his own, concerns of the others will seem nonsensical to him, and he will hardly be able to "understand" them and hardly competent to appraise them. A historian indifferent to the urgency of the philosophical quest may find, with full conviction, that the whole history of philosophy has been just a story of intellectual vagaries or "vain speculations." In the same way, an areligious historian of religion may find, again with naïve conviction and with an air of superiority, that the whole history of religions has been but a history of "frauds" and "superstitions," of various aberrations of the human mind. Such "histories of religion" have been manufactured more than once. For similar reasons, certain sections and periods of history have been denounced, and consequently dismissed and ignored, as "barbarian," "dead" or "sterile," as "dark ages," and the like. The point is that even a pretended neutrality, an alleged freedom from bias, is itself a bias, an option, a decision. In fact, again contrary to the current prejudice, commitment is a token of freedom, a prerequisite of responsiveness. Concern and interest imply commitment. Now, obviously, one cannot be committed in general, *in abstracto.* Commitment is necessarily discriminative and concrete. And consequently, not all commitments would operate in the same manner and not to the same effect. In any case, the openness of mind is not its emptiness, but rather its comprehensiveness, its broad responsiveness, or, one is tempted to say, its "catholicity." Now, there is here more than just a gradation, as it were, in volume or capacity. "The whole" (*to kath'olou*) is not just a sum total of various "particularisms" (*ta kata merous*), even if these particularisms are dialectically arrayed (as they were, for instance, in the Hegelian map of intellect) or discriminated as "stages of the progress" (as was done, for instance, by Auguste Comte). Particularisms must be done away, and catholicity of mind can be achieved only by a new, integrating reorientation, which would necessarily imply a certain radical discrimination. For in the last resort one cannot evade the ultimate discrimination between "yes" and "no"—and the compromise of "more or less" is just "no" in polite disguise.

In any case, historical interpretation involves judgment. The narrative itself will be twisted and distorted if the historian persists in evading judgment. There is little difference, in this case, between discussing the Greco-Persian War and World War II. No true historian would escape taking sides: for "freedom" or against it. And his judgment will tell in his narrative. No historian can be indifferent to the cleavage between "Good" and "Evil," much as the tension between them may be obscured by various speculative sophistications. No historian can be indifferent, or neutral, to the challenge and claim of Truth. These tensions are, in any case, historical facts and existential situations. Even a denial is a kind of assertion, and often a resolute one, charged with obstinate resistance. Agnosticism itself is intrinsically dogmatic. Moral indifference can but distort our understanding of human actions, which are always controlled by certain ethical options. An intellectual indifferentism would have the same effect. Precisely because human actions are existential decisions, their historical interpretation cannot avoid decisions.

Accordingly, a historian, precisely as historian, that is, as interpreter of human life as it has been actually lived in time and space, cannot evade the major and crucial challenge of this actual history: *"Who do men say that I am?"* (Mark 8:28). For a historian, precisely in his capacity of an interpreter of human existence, it is a crucial question. A refusal to face a challenge is already a commitment. A refusal to answer a certain question is also an answer. Abstention from judgment is also judgment. An attempt to write history, evading the challenge of Christ, is in no sense a "neutral" endeavor. Not only in writing a "Universal History" (*die Weltgeschichte*), that is, in interpreting the total destiny of mankind, but also in interpreting any particular sections or "slices" of this history, is the historian confronted with this ultimate challenge—because the whole of human existence is confronted with this challenge and claim. A historian's response prejudges the course of his interpretation, his choice of measures and values, his understanding of human nature itself. His response determines his "universe of discourse," that setting and perspective in which he endeavors to comprehend human life, and exhibits the amplitude of his responsiveness. No historian should ever pretend that he has achieved a "definitive interpretation" of that great mystery which is human life, in all its variety and diversity, in all its misery and grandeur, in its ambiguity and contradictions, in its basic "freedom." No Christian historian should lay such claims either. But he is entitled to claim that his approach to that mystery is a comprehensive and "catholic" approach, that his vision of that mystery is proportionate to its actual dimension. Indeed, he has to vindicate his claim in the practice of his craft and vocation.

V

The rise of Christianity marks a turning point in the interpretation of history. Robert Flint, in his renowned book, *History of the Philosophy of History,* says:

The rise of ecclesiastical history was more to historiography than was the discovery of America to geography. It added immensely to the contents of history, and radically changed men's conceptions of its nature. It at once caused political history to be seen to be only a part of history, and carried even into the popular mind the conviction—of which hardly a trace is to be found in the classical historians—that all history must move towards some general human end, some divine goal.[33]

Contemporary writers are even more emphatic at this point. For, indeed, the rise of Christianity meant a radical reversal of man's attitude toward the fact of history. It meant actually the discovery of the *"historic dimension,"* of the *historic time.* Strictly speaking, it was a recovery and extension of the Biblical vision. Of course, no elaborate "philosophy of history" can be found in the books of the Old Testament. Yet, there is in the Bible a comprehensive *vision of history,* a perspective of an *unfolding time,* running from a "beginning" to an "end," and guided by the will of God, leading His people to His own goal and purpose. In this perspective of dynamic history early Christians have assessed and interpreted their new experience, the Revelation of God in Christ Jesus.

Classical historians held a very different view of human history. The Greeks and the Romans were indeed a history-writing people. But their vision of history was basically unhistorical. They were, of course, desperately interested in the facts of history, in the facts of the past. It might be expected that they would accordingly be well qualified for the historian's task. In fact, by their basic conviction they were rather disqualified for that task. The

Greek mind was "in the grip of the past." It was, as it were, charmed by the past. But it was quite indifferent and uncertain with regard to the future. Now, the past itself acquires its historic character and significance only in the perspective of the future. "Time's arrow" was totally missing in the classical vision of human destiny. Great historians of Greece and Rome were not, in any sense, philosophers. At their best, they were fine observers, but rather moralists or artists, orators and politicians, preachers or rhetoricians, than thinkers. Ancient philosophers, again, were not interested in history, as such, as a contingent and accidental flux of events. They endeavored, on the contrary, to eliminate history, to rule it out, as a disturbing phenomenon. Philosophers of ancient Greece were looking for the permanent and change-less, for the timeless and immortal. Ancient historiography was emphatically pessimistic. History was a story of unavoidable doom and decay. Men were confronted with a dilemma. On the one hand, they could simply "resign" and reconcile themselves to the inevitability of "destiny," and even find joy and satisfaction in the contemplation of harmony and splendor of the cosmic whole, however indifferent and inimical it might be to the aims and concerns of individuals and societies. This was the *catharsis* of tragedy, as tragedy was understood in the classical world. Or, on the other hand, men could attempt an escape, a "flight" out of history, out of this dimension of flux and change —the hopeless *wheel of genesis and decay*—into the dimension of the changeless.

The ancient pattern of historical interpretation was "cosmic," or "natural-istic." On the one hand, there was a biological pattern of growth and decay, the common fate of everything living. On the other hand, there was an astronomical pattern of periodical recurrence, of circular motion of heavens and stars, a pattern of "revolutions" and cycles. Indeed, both patterns belonged together, since the cycles of the earth were predetermined and controlled by the circles of the heavens. Ultimately, the course of history was but an aspect of the inclusive cosmic course, controlled by certain inviolable laws. These laws were implied in the structure of the universe. Hence the whole vision was essentially fatalistic. The ultimate principle was *tyche* or *heimarmene,* the cosmic "destiny" or *fatum.* Man's destiny was implied and comprehended in that astronomical "necessity." The Cosmos itself was con-ceived as an "eternal" and "immortal," but periodical and recurrent, being. There was an infinite and continuous reiteration of the same permanent pattern, a periodical renewal of situations and sequences. Consequently, there was no room for any pro-gress, but only for "re-volutions," re-circula-tion, *cyclophoria* and *anacyclosis.* Nothing "new" could be added to the closed perfection of this periodical system. Accordingly, there was no reason, and no motive, to look forward, into the future, as the future could but disclose that which was already preformed in the past, or rather in the very nature of things (*physis*). The permanent pattern could be better discerned in the past, which has been "completed" or "perfected" (*perfectum*), than in the uncertainty of the present and future. It was in the past that historians and politicians were looking for "patterns" and "examples."

It was especially in the later philosophical systems of the Hellenistic age that these features of "permanence" and "recurrence" were rigidly emphasized—by the Stoics, the Neopythagoreans, the Platonics, the Epicureans alike. *Eadem sunt omnia semper nec magis est neque erit mox quam fuit ante.*[34] But the same conviction was already dominant in the classical age. Professor Werner Jaeger admirably summarizes the main convictions of Aristotle:

> The coming-to-be and passing-away of earthly things is just as much a stationary revolution as the motion of the stars. *In spite of its uninterrupted change nature has no history* according to Aristotle, *for organic becoming is held fast by the constancy of its forms in a rhythm that remains eternally the same.* Similarly the human world of state and society and mind appears to him not as caught in the incalculable mobility of irrecapturable historical destiny, whether we consider personal life or that of nations and cultures, but as founded fast in the unalterable permanence of forms that while they change within certain limits remain identical in essence and purpose. This feeling about life is symbolized by the Great Year, at the close of which all the stars have returned to their original position and begin their course anew. In the same way cultures of the earth wax and wane, according to Aristotle, as determined by great natural catastrophes, which in turn are casually connected with the regular changes of the heavens. That which Aristotle at this instant newly discovers has been discerned a thousand times before, will be lost again, and one day discerned afresh.[35]

In this setting of thought there was no room for any conception of "history," whether of the world or of man and human societies. There was a *rhythm* in the cosmic process, and consequently in the destiny of man, but *no direction.* History was not going or moving anywhere. It was only rotating. It had no end, as it had no goal. It had only structure. The whole of ancient philosophy was, in fact, a system of "general morphology" of being. And it was also essentially political or social. Man was conceived as an essentially "social being," *zoon politicon,* and his personal uniqueness was hardly acknowledged at all. Only "typical" situations were regarded as relevant. Nor was the uniqueness of any event acknowledged. Only "patterns" were relevant. There was a great variety of views and shades of opinion within this general and common pattern of the Greek and Hellenistic thought; there were inner tensions and conflicts therein, which must be carefully discerned and acknowledged. But the basic vision was the same in all these variations on the same theme: an "eternal Cosmos," the "endless returns," the ominous "wheel of genesis and decay."[36]

Against this kind of background, and in this perspective, Christianity meant an intellectual revolution, a radical reversal of standards, a new vision and orientation. Christianity is an *eschatological religion* and, for that very reason, is *essentially historical*. Recent theological controversy has sorely obscured the meaning of these terms, and some explanation is required to prevent confusion and misunderstanding.

The starting point of the Christian faith is the acknowledgment of certain actual events, in which God has acted, sovereignly and decisively, for man's salvation, precisely "in these last days." *In this sense these facts*—Christ's coming into the world, his Incarnation, his Cross and Resurrection, and the Descent of the Holy Spirit—*are eschatological events:* unique and "ultimate," that is, decisive, "critical" and crucial, wrought once forever, *ephhapax*. In a certain sense, they are also *final events,* the accomplishment and fulfillment of the Messianic prophecy and promise. In this sense, they assume their significance in the perspective of a past history which they "conclude" and "fulfill." *They are eschatological because they are historical,* that is, because they are situated in a sequence of the antecedent events, and thereby validate retrospectively the whole series. *In this sense, Christ is "the end of history,"* that is, of a particular "section" of history, though not of history as such. History, as such, is far from being terminated or abrogated by Christ's coming, but is actually going on, and *another eschatological event* is anticipated and expected to terminate history, *the Second Coming*. This entire pattern of interpretation is definitely *linear,* running from the beginning to the end, from Creation to Consummation, *but the line is broken, or rather "bent,"* at a particular "crucial" or "turning" point. *This point is the center of history,* of the "history of salvation," *die Heilsgeschichte*. Yet, paradoxically, "beginning," "center," and "end" coincide, not as "events," but in the person of the Redeemer. Christ is both *alpha* and *omega,* "the First" and "the Last," as well as the center. *In another sense, Christ is precisely the Beginning*. The *new aion* has been inaugurated in his coming. "The Old" has been completed, but "the New" just began.

Time was in no sense "devaluated" by Christ's coming. On the contrary, time was validated by his coming, by him and through him. It was "consecrated" and given meaning, the new meaning. In the light of Christ's coming history now appears as a "pro-gress," inwardly ordered toward "the end," to which it unfailingly precipitates. The hopeless "cycles" have been exploded, as St. Augustine used to say. It was revealed that there was no rotation in history, but, on the contrary, an unfolding of a singular and universal purpose. In this perspective of a unique and universal history, all particular events are situated in an irreversible order. "Singularity" of the events is acknowledged and secured.

Now, it can be contended that the Biblical vision of history was not, in fact, a "history of man," but rather "the history of God," the story of God's rule in history. Indeed, the main emphasis of the Bible is precisely on God's lordship, both in the world at large and in history in particular. But *precisely because history was apprehended as "God's history," the "history of man" was made possible.* Man's history was then apprehended as *a meaningful story* and no longer as a reiteration of the cosmic pattern, nor as a chaotic flux of happenings. The history of men was understood in the perspective of their salvation, that is, of the accomplishment of their destiny and justification of their existence. Man's action has been thereby justified and stimulated, since he was given a task, and a purpose. God has acted, and His ultimate action in Christ Jesus was a consummation of His continuous actions in the past, "at sundry times and in diverse manners." Yet, His manifold actions were *not simply particular cases* or instances of a certain general law, *but* were *singular events*. One can never suppress personal names in the Bible. The Bible can never be, as it were, "algebraized." Names can never be replaced by symbols. There was a dealing of the Personal God with human persons. And this dealing culminated in the Person of Jesus Christ, who came "in the fullness of time," to "complete" the Old and to "inaugurate" the New. Accordingly, there are two basic themes in the Christian understanding of history.

First, there is *a retrospective theme:* the story of the Messianic preparation. Secondly, there is *a prospective theme,* opening the vistas of the "end of history." *The Christian approach to history,* so radically different from that of the ancient world, *is by no means just a subjective reorientation of man in time.* An existential revaluation of time itself is implied. Not only was the human attitude changed when a new and unique term of reference was inserted into the flux of events, but the character of historical time itself has been changed. What was of decisive importance was that God's revelation in Jesus Christ was of an *ultimate* character, disclosing *a new dimension of human existence.* The decisive contribution of the Christian faith to the understanding of history was not in the detection of the radical "historicity" of man's existence, that is, of his finite relativity, but precisely in *the discovery of perspective in history,* in which man's historical existence acquires relevance and meaning. Therefore, the modern existentialist emphasis on "man's historicity" is, in fact, neither historical nor distinctively Christian. It is, in many instances, rather *a relapse into Hellenism*. "Man's historicity" means, in certain existentialist interpretations, nothing more than man's essential temporality, his inextricable involvement in the comprehensive context of passing occurrences, which brings him, finally, to extinction, to death. This diagnosis reminds one, however, more of the tragic insight of the Ancients than of the jubilant News of the Gospel. The original Christian *kerygma* not only intended to expose the misery and "nothingness" of sinful man, and to announce the Divine judgment, but above all it proclaimed the value and dignity of man—God's creature and adoptive child —and offered empirical man, miserable and spiritually destitute, God's "enemy," and yet beloved of God, the way of salvation. It was not only a condemnation of the Old, but an inauguration of the New, of "the acceptable year of the Lord."

Now, it is precisely at this point that a radical disagreement among Christian interpreters arises. Is there anything else to happen "in history" which may have any ultimate existential relevance for man, after Christ's coming? Or has everything that could be accomplished *in history* already been achieved? History, as a natural process, is, of course, still continuing—a *human history*. But does the *Divine history* continue as well? Has history any constructive value now, after Christ? or any "meaning" at all? It is sometimes contended that, since the ultimate Meaning has been already manifested and the *Eschaton* has already entered history, history has been, as it were, "closed" and "completed," as a meaningful process, and eschatology has been "realized." This implies a specific interpretation of the "turning-point" of history which was the coming of Christ. It is sometimes assumed that there was, indeed, a *sacred history* in the past, just up to the coming of Christ Jesus, in which it was "consummated," but that after him there is in history only an empty flux of happenings, in which the nothingness and vanity of man is constantly being exposed and manifested, but nothing truly "eventful" can ever take place, since *there is nothing else to be accomplished within history*. This assumption has been variously phrased and elaborated in contemporary theological thought. It may take a shape of the "realized Eschatology," and then meaning is shifted from the realm of history to the realm of sacramental experience, in which the *Eschaton* is present and re-enacted.[37] It may take the shape of a "consequent Eschatology," and then history appears to be just a great *Interim* between the great events in the past and in the future, between the "first" and "second" comings of the Lord, devoid of any constructive value, just a period of hope and expectation. Or else history may be "interiorized," and the realm of meaning would be confined to the experience of individual believers, making "decisions."[38] In all these cases, history as an actual course of events in time and space is denied any "sacred" character, any positive significance. Its course is apprehended as a continuous unfolding of human vanity and impotence.

It has been, in fact, recently suggested that "a Christian history" is simply nonsense. It has been contended that "the message of the New Testament was not an appeal to historical action, but to repentance," and that this message "dismantled, as it were, the hopeless history of the world."[39] This radical eschatologism, which simply "dismantles" all human history, is open to serious theological doubt. Indeed, it is a theological, and not a historical, assumption. It is rooted in a one-sided theological vision in which God alone is seen active, and man is just an object of Divine action, in wrath or mercy, and never an agent himself. But it is this "inhuman" conception of man, and not "the message of the New Testament," which makes nonsense of human history. The message of the New Testament, on the contrary, makes sense of history. In Christ, and by him, Time was itself, for the first time, radically and existentially validated. History has become *sacred* in its full dimension since "the Word was made flesh," and the Comforter descended into the world for its cleansing and sanctification. Christ is ever abiding in his Body, which is the Church, and in her the *Heilsgeschichte* is effectively continued. The *Heilsgeschichte* is still going on. It is obviously true that in practice it is utterly difficult to discern the pattern of this ongoing "history of salvation" in the perplexity of historical events, and historians, including Christian historians, must be cautious and modest in their endeavor to decipher the hidden meaning of the particular events. Nevertheless, the historian must be aware of that new "situation" which has been created in history by the Coming of Christ: there is "now" nothing "neutral" in the human sphere itself, since the Cross and Resurrection, since the Pentecost. Accordingly, the whole of history, even "the hopeless history of the world," appears now *in the perspective of an ultimate, eschatological conflict*. It was in this perspective that St. Augustine undertook his survey of historical events in his story of the "Two Cities." It may be difficult to relate the *Heilsgeschichte* to the general history of the world. On the other hand, the Church is *in the world*. Its actual history may be often distorted by worldly accretions. Yet "salvation" has also a historical dimension. The Church is the leaven of history. As Cyril C. Richardson has aptly observed recently, the history of the Church bears a *prophetic* character, no less than the sacred history of the Bible. "It is a part of revelation—the story of the Holy Ghost."[40]

One may suggest that in the modern "hyper-eschatologism," with its

implicit radical devaluation of history, we are facing in fact a revival of the
Hellenic anti-historicism, with its failure to ascertain any constructive value
in temporal action. Of course, eschatologists of various descriptions protest
their allegiance to the Bible and abhor and abjure all Hellenism. They
would indignantly repudiate any charge of philosophism. However, the close
dependence of Rudolf Bultmann upon Martin Heidegger is obvious. In fact,
they advocate the same position as the Greek philosophy, so far as the
understanding of history is concerned. Obviously there is a profound difference between a subjection to the *fatum,* whether it is conceived as a blind
heimarmene or as a "fiery Logos," and the proclamation of an impending
and imminent judgment of the eternal God. Yet in both cases *human action*
is radically depreciated, if for different reasons, and is denied any constructive task. This makes the understanding of history an impossible and even a
nonsensical endeavor, except in the form of a general exposure of man's
vanity and pride, of his utter impotence even in his ambition and pride.
Under the guise of prophecy, history of this kind is in danger of degenerating
into homiletic exercise. It is true that, in a certain sense, the modern radical
eschatologism may be regarded as a logical consequence of the reduced conception of the Church, which was so characteristic of certain trends of the
Reformation. The Church was still recognized as the area of an "invisible"
action and operation of God, but she was denied precisely her historical
significance. The modern recovery of the integral doctrine of the Church,
which cuts across the existing denominational borders, may lead to the recovery of a deeper historical insight and may restate history in its true
existential dimension.[41]

Strangely enough, for those who reduce the Church to the role of *an
eschatological token* and refuse to regard her as a kind of *proleptic eschatology,* history inevitably becomes again essentially a "political history," as it
was in classical times. It is again conceived as a story of states and nations,
and as such it is denounced and condemned. Paradoxically, it ceases to be,
in this interpretation, the history of man. It is assumed that man has nothing
to do, that is, to create or to achieve. He simply expects judgment, or, in any
case, stands under it. But in fact, man is becoming—or, indeed, is failing to
become—himself precisely in his historical struggle and endeavor. Eschatologism, on the contrary, condemns man to a dreamy mysticism, that very
trap and danger which eschatologists pretend and attempt to evade. He is
doomed to detect and contemplate, unredeemably, the abyss of his nothingness, is exposed to dreams and nightmares of his own vanity and spiritual
sickness. And a new mythology emerges out of these unhealthy dreams.
Whatever kind of "man's historicity" may be claimed as a discovery of such

an impoverished Christianity, the actual historicity of man is thereby, implicitly or often quite explicitly, denied and prohibited. Then history, in such an interpretation, actually becomes "hopeless," without a task, without a theme, without any meaning. Now, the true history of man is not a political history, with its utopian claims and illusions, but *a history of the spirit*, the story of man's growth to the full stature of perfection, under the Lordship of the historical God-man, even of our Lord, Christ Jesus. It is a tragic story, indeed. And yet the seed matures, not only for judgment, but also for eternity.

The Christian historian does not proceed actually "on Christian principles," as is sometimes suggested. Christianity is not a set of principles. The Christian historian pursues his professional task of interpreting human life in the light of his Christian vision of that life, sorely distorted by sin, yet redeemed by Divine mercy, and healed by Divine grace, and called to the inheritance of an everlasting Kingdom. The Christian historian will, first of all, vindicate "the dignity of man," even of fallen man. He will, then, protest against any radical scission of man into "empirical" and "intelligible" fractions (whether in a Kantian fashion or in any other) of which the former is doomed and only the latter is promised salvation. It is precisely the "empirical man" who needs salvation, and salvation does not consist merely in a kind of disentanglement of the "intelligible character" out of the empirical mess and bondage. Next, the Christian historian will attempt to reveal the actual course of events in the light of his Christian knowledge of man, but will be slow and cautious in detecting the "providential" structure of actual history, in any detail. Even in the history of the Church "the hand of Providence" is emphatically hidden, though it would be blasphemous to deny that this Hand does exist or that God is truly the Lord of History. Actually, the purpose of a historical understanding is not so much to detect the Divine action in history as to understand the human action, that is, human activities, in the bewildering variety and confusion in which they appear to a human observer. Above all, *the Christian historian will regard history at once as a mystery and as a tragedy—a mystery of salvation and a tragedy of sin.* He will insist on the comprehensiveness of our conception of man, as a prerequisite of our understanding of his existence, of his exploits, of his destiny, which is actually wrought in his history.[42]

The task of a Christian historian is by no means an easy task. But it is surely a noble task.

~~~~~~~~~~~~~~~~~~~~~~~~~~~~~~~~~~~~~ *12*

A Philosopher's Assessment
of Christianity

BY CHARLES HARTSHORNE

Religion is devotion and, through devotion, character-creation and re-creation. Irreligion or secularism is lack of devotion: there is a plurality of desires and aims not unified or criticized in the light of any supreme aspiration.[1] The secularist has no "pearl of great price" for which lesser things may be given up. An inferior religion is one whose supreme object of devotion is unworthy of this status.

Christianity, following Judaism, accepts unreserved devotion to the God of all things as the inclusive principle of action. As the Gospel of Mark has it, "Thou shalt love the Lord thy God with all thy heart, and with all thy soul, and with all thy mind, and with all thy strength."[2] There can be few more emphatic utterances in the world's literature. Four times over in one short sentence, the phrase "with all thy" is reiterated. *Nothing* of ourselves is to be withheld; we are to have *no* devotion, appreciation, concern, or interest that is not directed to the divine. When, then, we are told that the second "great commandment" is to love our neighbor as ourselves, this must not be taken to mean that some part of us not expressed in the love toward God is to manifest itself in self-love or neighborly love. All our being is to be expressed in the relation to deity, hence any love of neighbor must already be embraced in this relation, and the second commandment constitutes not an addition to the first, but only an explication of part of its meaning. Every legitimate love, interest, or valuation of any kind is to be embraced in that valuation whose object is not a mere totality of good things, but is one being and one good. The conclusion that I draw is that the Christian must think of the divine as the all-inclusive reality. For to recognize anything as real outside God is to express at least some slight interest in it, an interest by hypothesis not directed to God. An all-inclusive interest cannot have a less than all-inclusive object!

167

It will probably seem to some that I am confusing Christianity with pantheism. My position, however, is that, if the term "pantheism" means only that the divine reality includes all things, then Christianity necessarily is a form of pantheism; and if, nevertheless, we wish to maintain a verbal contrast between "theism," in a Christian sense, and "pantheism," we must define the latter term more carefully than is usually done. Certainly, some doctrines historically called "pantheistic" are incompatible with Christianity. If, for example, our own inclusion in the divine is so construed that our freedom must be taken as an illusion, then, far from embracing all our valuations, the relation to God cannot properly embrace any. For valuation implies the possibility of free decisions among really open possibilities, and the notion of a plurality of valuing agents, such as oneself and one's neighbors, implies that free decisions are effected not exclusively by one agent, God, but by many agents. However, this corollary of freedom need not prevent the many agents from being included within the one supreme agent. Let us remember that in many Christian documents it is said that God is love. Surely to love another person is not to make the other's decisions for him; just the contrary, it is to respect his freedom and to accept his decisions as objects of appreciative awareness. To love is to savor the free self-development of the persons loved, who are thus able to mold our own being by furnishing us with values we should otherwise miss. Accordingly, love—and, I believe, in its highest as well as its lowest aspects—involves passivity as well as activity. If, then, God is constituted by love in its perfection, this means not that He makes our choices for us, but rather that, by a willing passivity, He accepts and experiences these decisions as ours. He need not approve of their having been made in order to take them as real, and to add them to the content of His own perceptual experience, thus allowing Himself to be molded by them.

One reason why this idea of God is not easily accepted is the influence of the formula "God has created us." If He has created even our decisions, then in what sense are they *our* decisions? "Creating" here must mean "made possible"; it cannot mean made inevitable or *uniquely* possible. Other acts than those we perform must also have been made possible for us by God, and it must be we, not God, who effect the decision as to *which* of these divinely furnished possibilities to actualize. And if God is aware of our decision, He cannot, in this relation, be "wholly active"—in spite of the use of this expression in some theological systems.

Various attempts have been made by theologians to defend the notion that God knows all things in a wholly active manner. To me such accounts are meaningless or self-contradictory. I realize that they are offered as having what is called analogical (or symbolic) rather than literal meaning. And, admittedly, the divine experience is different in kind, and not solely in degree, from ours; but should this not lead to the conclusion that the divine passivity is itself different in kind from ours—rather than that there is no passivity in it? We human creatures are very limited in our passivity, in our willingness and ability to permit others to mold the content of our experiences. The most sensitive, sympathetic, responsive person you can find is largely unresponsive to all but a very few persons—at a given moment, at any rate—and his responsiveness even to these persons has narrow limits. Is there anything godlike in the way in which some people continue their own line of activity—for example, criminals bent on tricking us—with a minimum of deviation due to our feelings? Having discussed these matters in other writings, I must be content here to reassert my conviction that a notion of divine passivity, in principle elevated above all ordinary forms of passivity, is as intelligible as a notion of divine activity, similarly elevated above ordinary forms—nay, that the two notions are aspects of one and the same idea. Passivity *is* activity so far as it is receptive to, or engaged in taking account of, the activity of others; and the higher the activity the more comprehensive the receptivity. Thus man is receptive to influences that leave the atom or the stone unaffected, "impassible"—to use the theological expression.

Let us now face the question of the rationality or philosophic defensibility of the idea of an all-inclusive divine life, permissive of and passive to our decisions. "Rational" here means supported by some cogent reason, or evidence, and opposed by no equally cogent reason. Let us consider first what opposing reasons there could be.

The time-honored philosophic argument *against* any belief in God is what is called "the problem of evil." If God cannot prevent evil, He is weak; if He can, but will not, prevent it, He is wicked—or at least not good. Notice that the argument assumes that it makes sense to talk about "preventing" evil. Particular evils can indeed be prevented. Thus one can prevent suffering by bringing about lapse of consciousness. But here the absence of evil in the unconscious state is matched by an equal absence of good. Again, one may be able to prevent an individual from harming himself or others by confining him in a padded chamber. But he will probably do little good to himself or others in these circumstances.

May it not be true that the conditions which make good possible are the very ones which make evil also possible? What, indeed, are the conditions of good? They seem to be chiefly two: spontaneity or free self-development and social relations with other beings likewise free. But are not these also the factors which make the greatest evils possible? If the social interplay is harmonious, there is contentment or joy; if it is discordant or mutually frustrating, there is distress or suffering. Further, if the socially related beings are making their own decisions, and in so far as they are, it depends upon them collectively whether harmony or discord results. No one individual can decide unilaterally that there shall be harmony; for an individual cannot give up all personal preference and conform purely passively to the preferences of others. To be an individual is to have and act upon some distinctive preference or other. But even collectively, individuals cannot, absolutely speaking, elect harmony; for none of them fully understands the others, and still less can they entirely anticipate how the others will act, if it is true—and I believe it is—that no deliberate act can in all its features be the wholly inevitable result of antecedent causes. Suppose, then, we take God into account. Can He be thought unilaterally to bring about absolute harmony among created individuals? My suggestion is that no such idea is tenable; not because God is weak, but because the idea is self-contradictory. Free beings, beings with genuine dynamic individuality, must, so far as they are such, harmonize themselves together as best they can: they cannot *be* harmonized by a higher power, except to the extent that this power limits their freedom, and therewith their extent of individuality. All freedom is indeed within limits; but within these limits, what an individual does is his decision alone.

Consider in this light the absurdity inherent in the complaint which runs as follows: Why did God do this to me?—where (let us suppose) "this" is an injurious act done by some human being. The human injurer did the deed, yet we hear of God "doing" it. Did both, then, perform the same act? No doubt one can be ingenious in attempting to make sense out of such double agency. By analogy one may say that Hitler could order his underlings to slaughter many unoffending persons, and thus, in a sense, he did the fearful deeds, yet also the underlings did them. I maintain, however, that, in so far as Hitler's underlings had literally no choice as to their acts, it was not they who acted but solely Hitler. If, nevertheless, the acts were theirs, this is because certain details in the effecting of the orders must always be left undecided by the political superior, and must be determined, not without freedom, by the underlings. These details may be trivial and of little or no importance to the victims; but they serve to make the particular concrete acts those of the underlings. Furthermore, one cannot know that there was *no* psychological possibility of disobeying the orders. One can only estimate probabilities and improbabilities here; impossibility is beyond our ken.

Shall we, then, suppose that the divine ruler, infinitely more cunningly and completely than any dictator, determines our human acts down to the last detail, so that a murder, say, is really and literally an "act of God"? I believe this to be blasphemous and unphilosophical. Unlike Hitler, divine love cannot *wish* to suppress freedom, it cannot be supposed to exert incomparably superior power to the tyrant's end of managing the lives of others. Love always wishes the other to be partly self-determining; God cannot wish to cut off the conditions of freedom that make evil possible, for then He would cut off also those that make good possible, and this would not be "preventing evil" in the sense in which one could want evil to be prevented. One can very well wish that a certain murder, for example, had not occurred or that the murderer's mother had not so brought him up that criminal conduct was a probable outcome; but to wish that God had guided the process so exactly as to make the mother's very decisions for her, or the murderer's, is, it seems, to wish that they had been people and yet not people. If there are agents other than God, there are decisions, however important or trivial they may be, which God has not made.

I am aware that examples from hypnotism have been used to show that a choice can be entirely determined (causally predictable) and yet seem a genuine choice to the hypnotized subject. But to say that actions may be predictable "in all detail" in such cases is to speak very loosely indeed. Obviously the full concrete properties of actions can never be covered precisely by verbal instructions, and the consciousness of choice can be viewed, in conformity with our doctrine, as due to the details which were *not* prescribed, such as the exact instant of each movement, the accompanying "rationalizations" as to why the act was done, and many other aspects. In addition, there can hardly be proof that the act is the *inevitable* result of the hypnosis, rather than merely the very probable one. I conclude that little is shown here beyond what we should suppose in any case, that freedom has narrow limits. It does not follow that it can or could be prevented from causing conflict and suffering.

But, one may ask, what about evils in nature apart from man? The fact that animals devour one another is often held to render animal life a wretched and morally hideous spectacle. Most naturalists will, I believe, agree with me that this is mostly anthropomorphic nonsense. A creature lives scores, hundreds, millions of seconds, and then, perhaps for a second or two, more or less, it undergoes a painful process of being killed. To be preyed upon, which we as spectators sometimes suppose a large fraction of animal existence is really, for almost any one individual, a vanishingly small fraction of its life. And surely it matters not at all to an animal that what kills it is another animal (rarely of the same species!) rather than a falling tree. But, you ask, is not death itself an evil? Certainly—*if* living forever would be a good thing. But would it? The longer an animal has lived, if it has any memory (and if not, how much does continuance of the same individual animal signify?), the more the basic traits of its life must have lost the charm of novelty. (Watch any very young animal to see what is meant by this charm.) Persistence of individuality has little importance without memory, and it has little importance with memory unless there are contrast and novelty. But unlimited assimilation of novelty seems to contradict sameness of individuality, for (except in God Himself) must not all individuality be limited in potentialities? Thus the finitude of life span of the creatures is not an evil, unless it be an evil that they are not God.

But surely premature death is an evil, and so are the numerous pains and distresses to which animals are subject! My suggestion here is that spontaneity, some humble degree and kind of self-determination, is essential to enjoyment even in the lower animals; and this is enough to exclude any absolute control over the details of their actions. Yet only such control—for example, over the cells in our bodies—could guarantee the prevention of all discord or suffering, or premature death. Early death is not, save in man, much of an evil, for it is not foreseen as such nor is it long remembered by the survivors. There seems to be little point in the complaint of some sensitive souls that animals cannot even know that they "accomplish" any good by their sufferings. Animals are not *compelled* to live, they feel like living (or they should be unable to do so), and while they live they are always "compensated" for their efforts. When this is no longer true, they die, as animals in captivity often do.

It may be remarked in passing that, while there is a good deal about nature in the Gospels, there is no puzzling over animal suffering. Nor does one find much of this among naturalists, for nearly all of whom (in my experience, as more or less one of them) nature seems predominantly a spectacle of happiness so far as one can interpret it psychologically at all. What naturalists do often feel is a keen sense of the havoc which man, the one shockingly destructive creature on this planet, can do both to his own kind and to creatures generally. The other species tend, for long ages, to coexist with one another, the individuals mostly dying either in extreme immaturity, before they have much individuality to lose, or at the first onset of old age, before they have suffered from the poor health and dullness of senility. If anyone can conceive of a better scheme for promoting spontaneous happiness or zestful living I should like to hear of it! But man, and only man, is capable of wiping out numbers of entire species, or even much of the life on the planet. Here is indeed a "problem of evil." A believer can only suppose that the risks of human freedom—in scope extending far beyond that of the other animals—are not too high a price for the opportunities inherent in that same freedom.

The solution of the problem of evil, then, is not that evils are designed to make various forms of good possible, but that various levels and kinds of freedom are designed to make various levels and kinds of good possible and probable, although the probability of some negative values is inseparable from freedom. *Opportunities justify risks,* but nothing justifies evils, nor needs to, since evils are not intended or designed at all, unless by more or less perverse human beings, or devils. Evils simply happen, as lines of free action intersect. In all this I presuppose a philosophy of freedom, such as is found in Bergson, James, Peirce, Dewey, and some other illustrious philosophers. Of course, there are also distinguished thinkers who do not accept this view.

What can it mean thus to seek to justify religious doctrines by appealing to views which are defended by seemingly reasonable thinkers, but attacked by other thinkers? I do not know what more we can say than that a decision reached after an honest weighing of the arguments which have been advanced is as close to a rational justification as we can come in these matters.

But, so far, our justification in the present essay has been chiefly negative. We have sought to refute the atheistic argument based on the reality of evil. Is there any more positive justification for belief in the reality of the divine? How, indeed, does one know of any reality? One does not so much "prove" that one's wife or neighbor exists as one perceives their existence. Is there perhaps a perception of divinity? It must be admitted that, if such perception occurs, it has not the same sort of obviousness and intersubjective communicability as characterizes ordinary perceptions. Hence the mere *claim* to perceive or experience God is hardly a rational justification, in the normal sense. There remains what used to be termed "proofs for the existence of God." Since proofs must in the end have premises which are not themselves proved, one cannot escape the necessity, at some point, of appealing to perception, to direct awareness. Still, I believe that the proofs are relevant. Their function is to elicit the content of a realization of God which, as a distinguished British philosopher, H. H. Price, has recently maintained, is in the depths of every man's experience.

The proofs are *reductio ad absurdum* arguments directed against alleged alternatives or substitutes for theism. If successful, they leave the theistic idea as sole residual legatee, after it has turned out that apparent alternatives are not genuine, since experience furnishes no coherent meaning for them. In the process, one becomes more conscious of the basic traits of experience which do furnish meaning for the theistic view. For example, to the theistic conception of God as the divine power which orders the world there are the following apparent alternatives: (1) there is no co-ordination or mutual harmony between the parts of the world; (2) there is co-ordination but no common subordination of all the parts to one superior power; (3) there is co-ordination and there is also a common subordination to a superior power, but this power is *not* divine, that is, worthy of inclusive devotion because supremely good.

I do not find any of these alternatives to possess coherent meaning. The parts of the world must fit together, at least in the sense that they do not prevent one another's existence; if this mutual fitting is not due to subordination of all to one supreme or ruling power, then it consists in universal adjustment of each to all; but this is absurd, because there can be no adjustment to an environment unless its members are mutually adjusted, for otherwise they do not form a definite or coherent environment; and so the solution is presupposed, not exhibited by this account; and finally, nothing except superior goodness can render universal subordination intelligible. There can, to be sure, be more or less wicked temporary rulers, but their power is largely indirect and derivative, and presupposes the power of the good, for instance, as embodied in traditions and in the virtues of subordinates, as well as the power of the ruler's minds over their bodies and the influence of the subjects' bodies over their minds. No intelligible account seems, to me at least, to be available in any of these cases that does not involve the principle that power inheres in that which has value to offer. Supreme power, able to co-ordinate all things by subordinating all to itself, must offer supreme value.

The subordination of all to one power does not mean complete determination of all by one will. In accordance with our foregoing discussion, it means rather that all things are self-determining (and mutually determining) *within limits,* and it is the setting of these limits which constitutes the divine ordering of the world. Causal regularity, without which nothing could exist, is not a rigid affair, but an approximate and statistical pattern, allowing for all sorts and levels of free play. The present state of science fits this notion far better than did the science of the eighteenth or the nineteenth century.

Anything like a full evaluation of the theistic proofs is a task I must reserve for another place. At present we face other problems. How far is Christianity constituted simply by the love of God taken as inclusive of love of neighbor? Do not other religions—Judaism and still others—accept the two Great Commandments to which Jesus referred? Must one not have some specific belief concerning Jesus himself, or concerning the Trinitarian nature of God, to classify oneself as a professing Christian? I mention these queries, not to answer them but merely in order not to seem to overlook their significance. I have no Christology to offer, nor do I wish to criticize any. But there is one aspect of the view that God was incarnate in Jesus which I do wish to mention. Jesus was a man who suffered, mentally and physically, in intense degree, and not alone upon the cross. Thus his acceptance of suffering symbolizes the supreme value of humility. The first of men dies the death of a slave. But should we not go further? Jesus was termed the Christ, the self-manifestation of God. Yet, according to many theological and philosophical doctrines, being divine means precisely, and above all, being wholly immune to suffering, in any and every sense. In that case, the Stoic or Buddhistic sage would be more nearly divine than was Jesus.

On the contrary, as we have already seen, reasons can be given for positing supreme passivity, as well as supreme activity, in God. We have also maintained that all things, of any importance whatever, must be recognized as literally embraced in the divine reality. But surely suffering has some importance. Hence there must be suffering in God. If it be not so, then to wish to remove suffering must be to feel an interest that is not an interest in God. We should, I think, take literally the saying, "Inasmuch as ye have done it to the least of these, ye have done it unto me" where "me" refers to God Himself, and not to any man as man, not even Jesus. Not, indeed, that deity is to be conceived as thirsty, say, in the sense of having a human body, deficient in moisture, as His very body, but that the feelings of suffering involved are somehow within the divine experience, as analogously the sympathetic spectator of a thirsty man imaginatively shares in his sufferings. In the divine case, however, there is not mere imagination, but sheer, intuitive participation.

Is the doctrine of a suffering deity, thus sketched, distinctively Christian? One does not easily find it outside Christianity, not even in Judaism, although in Jewish mystical writings it does seem to occur. Did Jesus hold the view? At least he nowhere asserts or, so far as I can see, even suggests that God is immune to feeling, suffering, or passivity. And the parable of the prodigal son, or even the expression "Father," rather seems to imply the contrary.

Passing over the Trinity[3] as outside my present concern (it is usually held to be beyond the reach of philosophic speculation or natural reason), I now propose to consider a different feature of historic Christianity. This is the view, so well embodied in Dante, of personal immortality as the basis on which divine justice can apportion rewards and punishments for human actions. I confess I see in this conception substantial elements of irrationality, not in the sense of doctrines above reason but of doctrines below and contrary to it. For example, if there is an irreducible factor of chance in social existence as such—as we have maintained there is—then in any heaven there must be chance, or else no sociability; and where there is chance there will be "injustice," if this only means that weal and woe are in no exact proportion to the past deeds of the agent himself. (And if there is no sociability, then will it be heaven?) The theory of justice in the sense in question seems incompatible with the nature of existence. Not that God is *un*just, rewarding actions inappropriately, but that He is not engaged in rewarding or punishing in this bookkeeping sense at all. Acts bring consequences in the course of social interaction, to which every agent, and not simply God alone, contributes decisions. The world is not a police court, nor anything much like it. Such a court is a highly specialized aspect of life, a social expedient, designed to set limits to human anarchy and destructiveness, including the destructiveness of private vengeance, but the cosmos, one may surmise, is run on rather different principles. Its aim seems to be zestful creaturely activity, the creation of intense and predominantly harmonious experiences, in order that these may be appreciatively appropriated by the divine love, of which our own love is a faint image.

A formidable objection may here be interposed: Will not the legitimate demand for justice among men be weakened if we reject the notion of divine justice? There is a grave possibility of confusion here. A parent who helps one child to develop his powers and neglects the needs and potentialities of another is unjust. A judge who rules in favor of an accused person because of some legally irrelevant bond of interest between himself and that person is unjust. These are cases where some decision concerning the fate of another individual has to be made. But suppose one child suffers because another child is jealous, envious, perhaps because of the innate good looks or quickwittedness of another child. The parent will use such influence as he or she has to mitigate this evil; nevertheless, if the envious child has freedom of choice at all—it may be an almost grown-up child—then the exact weal or woe of the children as dependent emotionally upon one another will not be entirely determined by the parent. Any parent, even the heavenly one, must permit individuals wittingly or unwittingly to reward or punish each other in free (and therefore somewhat random) social interchange. Naturally a human judge, assigned the role of pronouncing punishments for crimes, ought not to have favorites. Were he to do so he would not be loving his neighbor as himself, for men in society need fairly administered rules of distribution and enforcement of contract, because their love for one another is so limited and so unpredictable or anarchic. But God's love is all-sufficient, and it *is* His justice.

The question confronting God's love is this: Within what limits can the creatures be allowed to be their own and each other's destinies? It is these limits of freedom which provide for the cosmos the predictability which legal forms aim to achieve for human society. But the cosmic stabilities, or laws of nature, are maintained in more subtle ways than by special rewards or punishments for past acts, and there seems no reason to suppose that endless prolongation of individual existences is necessary or desirable simply in order to make the laws effective.

But there is an aspect of the matter not clearly covered by the foregoing, or by most discussions of the subject of immortality. How can our lives be integral to the divine good without achieving thereby a sort of immortality that is in a very genuine sense personal? If I am real in God now, surely nothing of the divine reality which I thus help to constitute can be destroyed. God does not lose elements from His experience, does not forget what He has once enjoyed, but with ideal perfection of vividness retains it forevermore. This is Whitehead's great doctrine of the immortality of the past, as having its ultimate apotheosis in the nature of God. All that we actually succeed in being or experiencing is a divine treasure that can nevermore be lost. Furthermore, there is a divine evaluation of such treasure, a consciousness of what it contributes or fails to contribute (in comparison with what may have been possible for us).

In this sense, then, there is indeed a "divine judgment" upon our lives, a judgment from which nothing can be hid and before which no pretense is of avail. Those who are willing to contribute poorly will "have had their reward"; they will not have enjoyed the sense of contributing adequately which they might have enjoyed. Why ask for a motive for loving God, and for making service to Him the ultimate end? Either the motive for loving God is His lovableness, or it is something else. If it is His lovableness, then that is sufficient, and all that is required is to make men as aware of the divine good as possible. If the motive must be something else, then God is deficiently lovable, which is blasphemous.

It may be objected that it is the very lovableness of God which makes us desire to survive death, so that we may achieve a higher consciousness of Him than the conditions of this life make possible. But how cogent can this argument be? If the conditions of life after death are radically different, as they must be if God is to be apprehended in essentially better fashion, then how much will it mean to speak of the same human individual in the two cases? And why is it so important that there be such continuation of ourselves as such? It may indeed be highly desirable that there be clearer and fuller creaturely consciousness of deity than we human beings now enjoy.

But must *we* be those more God-conscious creatures rather than the inhabitants, say, of some other planet, or than our remote descendants upon earth? After all, God is the inclusive end, and He can possess the values of creaturely response to Himself on any possible level, wherever such responses occur, and whether or not it is ourselves who achieve them. And as to our own motivation, we have, it seems, the same reason to try to achieve on earth such consciousness of God as is open to us, whether or no it may lead to still fuller consciousness of our own hereafter.

I am not pronouncing upon the question: Is there individual survival after death? I certainly do not know how to refute the testimony of Sherwood Eddy and others concerning their apparent communications with deceased persons. I am saying only that I see no religious or philosophical necessity for the idea, which has often promoted selfishness rather than neighborly love.

It may seem that not much is left of historic Christianity in my account, so far. But I can, at least, add one more factor. If anything is Christian, it seems that prayer must be. Now, God, as I have been conceiving Him, is a responsive being, taking our lives into His own, and making them into whatever immortal treasure they are capable of constituting. He is conscious of us, and of our thoughts and feelings. To be sure, we do not need to put these thoughts or feelings into words for God to know about them. But we do need to put them into words if they are to take on distinct and conscious character, rather than remaining inchoate and subconscious. For human consciousness is essentially linguistic. If, then, our relation to God, our response to Him, which religion holds is to be the inclusive response, is not to remain lacking in conscious clarity it must take on verbal form. But such form must consist either in talking, if only to ourselves, *about* God or else of talking *to* Him, it must be either in the third or in the second person. Yet, since third-person statements are natural only in the absence of the party concerned, and since God is never absent but always in effect a witness and auditor, it is the second person that is appropriate. Hence prayer is rationally justified.

What about petitionary prayer? To ask God for something seems to be impertinent, a process of suggesting what He should do. On the other hand, *if we have wishes* at all, they can be verbalized, consciously formed and recognized, in connection with the divine presence (which once more is the all-inclusive object of valuation) only as requests, or at least as expressions of wishes—"We would like to have such-and-such, and hence, *if* it is in conformity with Thy providential concerns, would like to have Thy influence favor its occurrence." I seem, then, to see these as the rational alternatives, religiously speaking: either we transcend all wishes or we admit something like petitionary prayer in some form. The first seems not entirely possible, if desirable. The second seems, then, to remain. I confess the dilemma troubles me.

So far we have spoken of direct rational justification for Christian doctrines. There remains the question: Is it not, perhaps, reasonable for human reason to admit its own limitations, and to concede that faith may transcend reason? In some sense, I suppose this may be correct. But to define the sense is not easy. Yet certain things I can dimly see. Let us not forget that an animal without reason has a sort of equivalent of faith. It has in its way that which the religious man has in his, but which the irreligious man tends to lack, namely, integrity, unity of aim through conformity to the divine unity of all things. For what is animal "instinct" but this? The animal takes impulsively the role which God, by His creative guidance of nature, assigns to it. The small details of animal action are not thereby fully determined, in my opinion; nevertheless, the animal is always doing what it can to express its dominant inner drive. But man lacks impulses definite enough to determine his role; he must formulate *conscious* objectives, and in doing so he is capable of departing widely from his proper place in the scheme of things, making himself, as it were, less than a man.

Faith, I suggest, is the acquirement, on the more conscious level, of that integral adjustment to the whole of things which inherited impulse furnishes to all creatures below the conscious level. This agrees with our contention that God is experienced, not just proved indirectly, for if proof were required, animals could not respond to divine guidance at all. (I regret that I cannot take space to try to explain this strange way of speaking, as I fear some will find it.) It follows that one man may surpass another, not so much in the clarity of his thought concerning God as in the vividness and steadiness of his perceptual experience of the divine. "Blessed are the pure in heart, for they shall see God" is not necessarily contrary to reason, and may even receive some support from it.

Yet, even though this be granted, many questions remain unsettled. Clearly, an ecclesiastical organization claiming revelation may or may not represent the pure in heart, and if it claims infallible revelation, some of us would be inclined to see in this very claim itself the expression of pride rather than of purity. Human reception of divine messages is not, it seems, itself divine, and only as received is the message available. Here I am taking the Protestant position. Its difficulty is that it is not easy to draw a line between Christian and non-Christian faith, if no agency exists which has the right to define the content of Christian doctrine. But possibly this is not wholly a disadvantage. Perhaps drawing the line is as much the expression of pride and hate—or of cowardice—as of devotion and charity.

In conclusion: I discern some degree of rational justification for a religion of complete, all-inclusive devotion to One in whose Life all good and all actuality are embraced, to whom prayer may properly be addressed, and whose loving acceptance even of our sufferings is supremely symbolized in the human life depicted in the Gospels.

Christian Faith and the Growing Power of Secularism*

BY KARL HEIM

Secularism is usually traced to two causes. The first cause is modern man's conception of the world as a closed causal system—a conception resulting primarily from Newtonian physics. In the light of the discovery that the world process conforms inexorably to law, belief in God comes to be thought of only as a relic from the philosophical museum of our ancestors. The world process has become calculable, and thus there is no longer a need for a personal ruler of the world. Fritz Mauthner can begin his four-volume work on the history of atheism in the West with the statement: "God has died. The time has come to write His history."[1]

The second cause of secularism is said to be the technological age in which we live—the technological and industrial control of the surface of the earth. The iron machines, with which man believed he could rule the earth, have mercilessly ground to pieces all metaphysical systems.

Now, these two causes are surely responsible for the fact that modern this-worldliness has spread over the earth like an epidemic, just as certain residential conditions in the harbor district of Hamburg were responsible for the fact that cholera spread rapidly after it had first appeared there. But the presence of this strange disease of secularism is by no means explained by these external conditions. If we want to fight a disease we must draw a sharp distinction between two questions. The first question asks: What is the original cause of the disease? The second question asks: What helps the disease to spread?

That the original cause of secularism lies neither in modern physics nor in the technological age, is shown by two facts:

* Translated by George Norby.

1. Secularism has existed since long before modern physics and the machine age. Democritus, Epicurus, and Lucretius (d.55 B.C.) were secularists. The didactic poem of Lucretius, *De rerum natura,* which Goethe esteemed so greatly, is a document of a rather highly developed this-worldliness. Lucretius writes: "While human life lay miserably crushed beneath the yoke of Religion—who showed her head along the region skies and glowered on mortals with her hideous face—a Greek it was, a mortal man, who first dared to oppose her, a man whom neither the temples of the gods, nor lightning-flash, nor threatening thunder of the ominous heavens, have subdued." And, "For all I care, one may call the sea Neptune and the grain Ceres, if only one frees himself in reality from miserable Religion." Similar statements were made by the mocker, Lucian.

2. More important in analyzing the origins of secularism, however, is a second, equally well-known fact. The real discoverers of the physical conception of the world and of causal calculability, like Kepler, Galileo, Descartes, and Newton, were by no means led to secularism by the mathematical laws which they regarded as the basic formulas of the world process. Their belief in the Creator was not shaken for a moment by the causal mechanism which they discovered. And their belief was not a remnant of the religious tradition—a remnant which they retained in conformity with custom. On the contrary, they were led to a deeper awe before God by the numbers, by the mathematically expressible natural laws, in which the mystery of the world revealed itself to them.[2] The simple mathematical relations which, according to Kepler's law, chart the movements of cosmic bodies, were regarded by the great astronomer as the most irrefutable proof that the world is not ruled by accident, but that a thinking Spirit stands behind it. Descartes, a convinced Christian belonging to the religious circle of Port-Royal, converted to the Catholic faith Queen Christina of Sweden, the daughter of Gustavus Adolphus, while giving her philosophical-mathematical instruction. Similarly, the law of gravitation was conceived by Newton as a proof of the reality of a thinking Creator.

This kind of interpretation was also characteristic of the great inventors who brought about the technical age. In his analysis of the technical age, Hans Lilje cites as an example from recent times the inventor of the steam locomotive, Schmidt, whose invention was received in all parts of the world. Schmidt did not come upon the idea of the steam locomotive in a rational way; it came upon him as a vision which, according to his firm conviction, was sent to him by God. Only after this vision did Schmidt subject what he had seen to calculation, and thus express it in a mathematically correct form. Oswald Spengler could therefore assert that all secularism, that is, the divorce of the mathematical-mechanical view of the world from faith in God, is nothing else than a phenomenon of old age—a phenomenon which appears in the late autumn of every great culture and announces its end. At the high point of a cultural development both aspects of the world, the religious and the causal, are with equal force present to the human spirit. The spirit still has the power to speak and to understand these two languages in which reality reveals itself. The causal necessity of nature and the Christian idea of the Lordship of the divine will, as this is expressed in the doctrine of predestination, are only two different forms of expression for the same destined necessity. Only in a culture which has become old does the spirit lack the power to grasp the unity of the religious aspect of the world and the causal aspect of the world. In this situation the two aspects are separated from each other. Nature is deprived of its spiritual principle, and thus secularism arises, which can find in nature nothing more than a lifeless body (*corpus mortuum*).

In the present essay we shall not share the optimistic view which understands secularism as merely a passing phenomenon of a dying culture. We shall have to take secularism more seriously. This much is clear, however: if modern physics and the technical rationalization of human life have contributed to the spread of secularism, they are not its real causes. The cause of secularism lies in a deeper dimension.

What is the original cause, the ultimate ground, of secularism? It is true that secularism appeared in the last stage of the polytheistic religions (from Democritus to Lucian). In its mature form, however, *secularism has grown only in the soil of the Christian culture of the West*. In the highly developed non-Christian cultures, as for example in the Indian or Chinese culture, the forms of life and thought have been so profoundly nurtured by the religious faith out of which they grew that the entire cultural edifice would have perished had the transcendent presupposition been removed. Just as the members of the body begin to decay if the heart stops beating, so these cultural edifices would not have been able to endure if the heartblood of religion had ceased to sustain them. This was true of the Vedic culture; and of the Confucianism of ancient China and the Zen culture in Japan—with their gardens, their architectural style, and their painting. This was also true of the ancient Egyptian culture. With the aid of an unsurpassed technology, swarms of Egyptian workers erected monumental structures which have their meaning only in transcendent reality. None of these cultures could produce secularism, could produce a world culture dissolved from its transcendent ground. If their religious substance was lost, they perished. Only in the Christian West, in a culture which was ruled during the Middle Ages by the Church and which thus grew under the influence of the Bible, has man, without destroying his whole culture, divorced himself and his world from the creative ground and sought to live his life unto himself. Indeed, having torn itself away from faith in God, this culture has seemed, especially since the Renaissance and the development of the empirical sciences, to have blossomed forth; and, nourished by technical inventions, it has evolved into an imposing world view and way of life that is turned in upon itself; it has evolved into a system which has had a revolutionary power and has overthrown all cultures with which it has come into contact. Much of the secularism in India, China, and Africa is only an offshoot of the originally Christian culture of the West—an offshoot which is now having a sterilizing and destructive effect on these cultures.

We must keep this fact in mind if we wish to understand the origin and nature of secularism. Secularism in its present form originated in that part of the world which was influenced by the biblical view of the relationship between God, man, and the world. How was this possible? In all non-biblical religions (I do not include Mohammedanism in this category, since its origin lies in the Old Testament faith in God) there is always a point of identity between God and the creaturely world. In the first stage of the non-biblical religions, the powers of nature which nourish and threaten us are worshiped as gods. In a later stage this worship of the powers of nature is transformed into the mystical belief that being, in which we and all beings participate by virtue of the fact that we are, is itself eternal and absolute. We need only go behind the realm of individualization, in which being differentiates itself, and we shall be in the eternal realm and be united with the Absolute.

In contrast to this fundamental view of the non-biblical religions, which assumes the unity of divine and creaturely being, the Bible sees the relationship between God and the creature in another light. In the hymn which forms the conclusion of the First Letter to Timothy (I Tim. 6:16), God is invoked as the King of kings and the Lord of lords, who alone has immortality. Thus God alone has eternity; in contrast to God, all the rest of creation—we human beings as well as every plant and every stone—have only time. The whole creation (*ktisis*) is subject to corruption (*phthora*). Existentially understood, this means: we creatures always possess only the being of this moment; we have only the Now. The past is not possessed by us any more. Even memory is something present. And we do not yet possess the future. We no longer have the past within our power—not even our former conscious experiences; for every falling brick or automobile accident can bring an end to our memories of yesterday. The future we do not yet have within our power; it is a mere possibility. All that we have is thus the point of transition to which the future continually comes and, "scarcely greeted," slips away from our hands to become the past.

We therefore live entirely from hand to mouth. Together with all creation, we are totally dependent on the Power which gives us being from moment to moment, which grants us being for a moment only to take it back again immediately. This Power is the Creator, who alone has true being, that is, immortality, and who therefore is the only Giver of true being. Thus there arises the relationship between God and the creature which is described, for example, in Psalm 104: "When thou hidest thy face, they are dismayed; when thou takest away their breath, they die and return to dust. When thou sendest forth thy breath, they are created; and thou renewest the face of the earth!" Our creaturely existence is sustained from moment to moment by the breath of God (*ruach*). In the moment that the breath of God ceases to sustain us we sink into the nothingness out of which we were created.

Thus a relationship between God and the creature is given which is completely different from the identity of divine and creaturely being which is assumed in all non-biblical religions. The biblical God is omnipresent; He is everywhere, in every stone, in every fly, as the One who gives them being in every moment: "In Him we live, and move, and have our being." But this omnipresence of God has nothing to do with identity between Him and His creatures. The eternal being of God remains outside the being of every creature. The being of God is never dependent on the creature. God's being and creaturely being always remain apart. As soon as the creature approaches God and attempts to lose itself in Him and become one with Him, it encounters the electrically charged wire which, as soon as it is touched, thrusts the creature back to its finitude. According to Kierkegaard, temptation is the way in which God always repels the pious worshiper who would like to become one with Him. Thus God always remains invisible to the creaturely eye. To see God means to die. The sight of the gods is the original sin of man. It is a confusion of the two modes of being, human and divine, which are mutually exclusive. This idea is not understood in the non-biblical religions. For them everything transitory is a symbol for the primordial unity of the opposites. It is Buddhism which has lovingly endured and cultivated the sight of the gods.

If we maintain the biblical view of the relationship between God and the creature, we find ourselves, together with the entire created world, in a thoroughly painful and humiliating situation. At every moment we receive our being anew from a Power which transcends us, and which is therefore incomprehensible to us and unattainable by us—which we cannot make into an object either of our knowledge or of our will. According to the Bible, this peculiar and humiliating situation is not our ultimate and true destiny. Our present situation is an interim between a pristine state—an original community with God from which we and all creation have fallen and which we can therefore no longer conceive—and a final state awaited by all creation, in which the servitude of the past, and thus of time, is overcome—a condition which we are not yet able to conceive. We are so completely immersed in our present situation of estrangement from God that we are unable to see our situation and become conscious of it. In order to see ourselves we should have to be outside of ourselves and acquire distance from ourselves. If we are totally immersed in our present situation, we cannot know that we are fallen, and thus that we live in an interim between an original state and a final state. Such knowledge comes to us only when God reveals Himself to us. But this can occur only if God comes to us from outside our present situation: only if God comes to us in such a way that we are repelled by His coming, for His coming makes us painfully conscious of our present situation, of our dependence on a Power with which we can never become identical. Our painful situation is made manifest when God, from outside our situation, draws near to us through His Word and revelation. Because man must be repelled by this approach of God, who is outside his situation—must be repelled by the divine act which makes him conscious of his fallenness—the Word of God is always given with the Cross in which mankind denies the approach of God.

We have now discerned the presuppositions from which secularism arises with a kind of necessity. Although God is, on the one hand, the omnipresent reality from which every being continually receives its being, He is, on the other hand, entirely outside creaturely being. Over against God, creatures possess a certain autonomy: this is implied in the biblical concept of "world." The world has a being which stands over against the being of God, its Creator. Between God and the world there is no point of identity. There is rather an absolute disjunction between the two. We can love *either* God *or* the world. He who loves God does not love the world. "Do you not know that friendship with the world (*philia toe kosmoe*) is enmity with God?" (Jam. 4:4). Whoever wants to be a friend of the world has become an enemy of God. Thus, biblical religion, unlike non-biblical religions, gives a specific weight to the world and everything which is and occurs within it. The cares of this world choke the Word (Matt. 13:22). "What will it profit a man, if he gains the whole world?" (Matt. 16:26). "The children of this world are wiser than the children of light" (Luke 16:8). "Demas has fallen in love with this world" (II Tim. 4:10).

In such language, God is contrasted not merely with the sin of evil men, nor merely with the history of mankind. The specific weight which the Bible calls "world" is constituted by the entire cosmos, with its vegetative, animal, and astral processes. The world is, figuratively speaking, placed on one side of the scale of balance; on the other side of the scale lies God with the infinite weight of His presence. A decision between the two is demanded. If one side of the scale rises, the other side must sink. This disjunctive relationship between God and the world, the exclusion of every point of identity between the two, is, according to the Bible, what makes it possible for every human being to decide for the world and against God. *Philia toe kosmoe* is the biblical expression for secularism. Secularism is the possibility man has of abstracting himself from God and the question of eternity; of regarding them as an "ideological superstructure" (Marx); and of attempting to be a child of this world ("to love the world and what is in the world" [I John 2:15]) and thus to cling to a finiteness resting in itself.

Hence man must choose one of two possibilities: the autonomy of the world or the absoluteness of God. And this choice is, according to the New Testament, not merely a choice between two modes of human existence. Man is only the representative of a cosmic will. On the one side is God's claim to be the beginning and the end of the cosmos; on the other side is the love of the cosmos for itself ("The world loves its own"). Our human self-love is thus only the human expression of the love with which the entire fallen creation loves itself.

But we must now make another statement. The world cannot actualize the first of these two possibilities—it cannot make a decision for God—through its own power. "The world lies in darkness." The world cannot free itself from darkness by itself. The decision for God, the return to the Source, is only possible if God makes it possible by loving the world and giving His Son to the world. So long as God does not draw the world to Himself, the world has only the second possibility. If the world actualizes the second possibility, however, if it moves in the dimension which is opposed to God, and if we human beings participate in this movement and thus are *echthroi* (enemies), as Paul says in Romans 5, then a fact always remains which makes the human situation painful and questionable, and which oppresses even the "child of the world." This fact is that we creatures are completely temporal. We possess only the Now. We do not yet have the future, and the past has slipped out of our hands. Our temporal character—our bondage to the present—is revealed to us in the awareness of our limitation.

Thus, the world and we human beings can stand over against God and can want to find rest in ourselves, only if we attempt to overcome the creaturely limitation which reminds us of our dependence and to destroy the bondage to the present which lies in this limitation. How can the world and we human beings do this? We can do this only if the world suggests to itself and to us that it possesses something apart from God which is eternal in itself and which is therefore able to endure beyond the moment without being continually sustained by the Creator. Now, when this happens the world becomes a reality resting in itself, and the Creator who breathes into us the breath of life is regarded as a superfluous "ideological superstructure." With the attempt of the world to give to itself its own eternity and thus to free itself from God, a radical secularism appears. At this point secularism assumes a demonic form and becomes an overt enterprise against God: for the world wants to claim for itself the eternity which belongs to God alone; it wants to dethrone God and be divine itself.

Secularism attempts to take possession of a being which is self-sustaining and self-subsistent. Now, the cosmic reality always has two poles: the ego and the outer world, consciousness and objective reality. These two poles prescribe the two directions which secularism must follow in order to attain its goal. On the one hand, secularism seeks to find in consciousness, in the spiritual hemisphere of the world, an element which by its own power endures beyond the moment. This element is the ego which grasps the future and the past in a synthesis and thus is lifted above the flux of time. This belief in an eternal ego, in a soul which has its eternity in itself, is the first form of secularism—its Platonic form.

At the beginning of our era the Platonic form of secularism was challenged by the Apostolic message of the resurrection. Unlike the adherents to the Platonic form of secularism, the Apostles maintained that the soul can endure after physical death only through the resurrection, that is, only through a creative act of God. The Platonic belief in the natural immortality of the soul represents man's first great attempt to secure an eternity which is not dependent on God. It is found once again, in its most demonic form, in Fichte, who sought to reconcile it with the message of the New Testament. Since the fourth decade of the nineteenth century, the Platonic belief in immortality has largely disappeared from the consciousness of educated men. But the impulse that led to the Platonic belief in immortality is still present. This impulse is manifest in the logic and psychology of our academic philosophers, where the human ego always appears as a fixed mid-point which remains identical with itself while its images fluctuate, and therefore makes thinking possible. Every case of amnesia in connection with brain injury seems to show, however, that I by myself do not have the power to remain identical with myself even for two seconds—much less for the time that I need in order to make a judgment or a calculation. I am able to unite yesterday's memories with today's consciousness only because the Creator holds me from second to second above the abyss of nothingness, into which I am continually falling. If the Creator should cease to do this, my consciousness would immediately disappear like sand which runs through the fingers.

But the belief in immortality, and thus the belief in the autonomous ego which does not need God, is only one of the forms of demonic secularism—and a form which now belongs largely to the past. A second form of secularism, which came to the fore with the development of natural science and rules our technical age, attempts to find an eternal element in objective reality. The divorce of technology and the scientific investigation of nature from the biblical faith in the Creator was not caused by the discovery of new facts and natural laws. Genuine facts, and natural laws established by observation, can never place the reality of the Creator in question; they can only correct false notions of the way in which this Creator governs the world. The Bible knows that the Creator is incomprehensible. We can never express His will in formulas. Every notion of the way in which He governs the universe must be continually corrected by new facts. Even if all the marvels of the universe could be explained by natural laws, the reality of the Creator would not be placed in question for one moment. It would only be shown that God in governing the universe follows definite laws which He has established for all time.

For the Old Testament, therefore, natural law is not an argument against the reality of God, but it is an expression of the immutable faithfulness of the Creator, who has made life possible for us human beings by establishing a constant order of nature. Thus the Old Testament reads, after the story of the flood: "While the earth remains, seedtime and harvest, cold and heat, summer and winter, day and night, shall not cease" (Gen. 8:22). According to the word of the prophet, God does not will to be unfaithful to His people any more than do the sun and moon will to change their course. Facts and observed laws are therefore unable, by themselves, to shake man's faith in God. Man can lose his faith in God only if he goes beyond his experience and fits his observations into a dogmatic metaphysical system, with which he attempts to explain the process of nature in terms of elements which have in themselves the power to endure beyond the moment, and thus to be eternal in themselves.

Experience shows us nothing enduring, but only a continual flux of phenomena. Everything in the universe is in the process of passing out of being. One seeks to overcome this impression, which must lead to despair if one is without God, by constructing a metaphysical system. One posits beneath the flux of phenomena a substrate which endures through its own power. In his work, *The Spirit as Adversary of the Soul*,[3] Ludwig Klages has shown that as soon as the concept of duration and of something enduring appears, the human spirit reads into nature that which satisfies its own spiritual needs. Thus arises the dogma of the preservation of substance, which regards the changing form of substance as the process of nature. According to Kant's *Critique of Pure Reason,* this belief arose out of man's need to possess an enduring substrate in the flux of time.

The simplest form of the belief in substance is the older atomism. Even in ancient times—in Democritus and Epicurus—the doctrine of atoms was a declaration of war against faith in God; it was an attempt to remove man's fear of the divine. "Nothing exists but atoms and the void; everything else is illusion." The world process appears as a continual mingling of small bodies which are indestructible, and thus eternal through their own power. In this system of thought matter has received the property which, according to the Bible, belongs to God alone. Materialism deifies the world.

In the nineteenth century the very concept of matter became problematical. Since J. R. Meyer and Wilhelm Ostwald, matter has been regarded as only a form of energy. As soon as this first support of man's this-worldliness was lost, man sought for another support. The belief in an enduring substrate of the world process, in which the world claims a demonic independence from God, has assumed another form: the cosmic law of the preservation of energy. As a working hypothesis, the principle of the preservation of energy has, of course, a fully scientific status. As soon as one makes this working hypothesis into an assertion concerning the universe, however, one has gone beyond empirical observation and has formulated a metaphysical statement. That this working hypothesis has been made into a cosmic law, and thus into a metaphysical statement, is shown by the Russian physicist Chwolson in his critique of Haeckel's *Riddle of the Universe:* the energy quantum, which can be neither increased nor decreased, has been interpreted, on non-empirical grounds, as self-sustaining and self-subsistent, as something resting in itself.

This consequence of the cosmic law of the preservation of energy shows clearly the law's demonic character. To the first axiom of thermodynamics has been added a second axiom, the so-called law of entropy. From this second axiom an eschatology has been developed which is directed against biblical eschatology. Because energy is continually being dissipated, the energy quantum of the universe leads to a frozen state in which all life and movement cease. This is the eschatology of the secular view of the world.

The secularism of modern technology is not the product of technological inventions as such. In themselves these inventions could lead to a deeper sense of awe before the Creator. Man does not create the powers which are operative in his technological inventions. He only releases these powers, by learning from nature its secrets. The engineer or technologist is thus only an agent of God. He places himself at the disposal of the divine work of creation. He spreads the sail in order to let the tiny vessel of human existence be driven by the wind of the divine creative power. If modern technology produces secularism, there is only one reason for this: behind technology and its work has appeared the demonic belief that matter or the energy quantum is eternal in itself and sustains itself through its own power. Like the belief in immortality, this belief in an eternal substrate behind the transitory being of the world is a demonic movement against the Creator.

Of course, the metaphysics of matter or energy is given conscious expression only in rare instances, as in Haeckel's *Riddle of the Universe* or in Ostwald's philosophy of nature. The conscious metaphysics of matter or energy supports the more or less unconscious mode of life which is popular secularism. Secularism is most powerful as *popular* secularism, that is, as the mode of life of unphilosophical, unchurched masses who repudiate all philosophical speculation as ideology; in other words, secularism is most powerful as practical materialism. According to Kierkegaard, the fact that flesh and the sensuality of man are directed against God means that they become spiritual in a certain sense, namely, as the demonic denial of the spirit. Communism is perhaps the religious passion of the Russian soul; if this is so, however, it is so in the negative form of frenzy against the spirit. The most consistent form of secularism is manifest when man clearly sees that he possesses only the moment and does everything within his power to exploit this moment. Thus arises the insane cult of the moment as it is found in the pleasure-seeking of a tired city dweller, who only wants to get drunk and forget himself.

If this is the deepest meaning of secularism, how are we to fight against it? We have seen that secularism is the form in which the fallen world demonically seeks to replace God, from whom it receives its being in each moment of its existence. As long as we live in a state between the Primal Fall and the End, this movement of rebellion against God will never cease. Indeed, according to Scripture, it will become still greater and in the last days will reach its climax in an anti-Christian world power.

Perhaps we are now at the beginning of this last development. But if we understand this, it does not mean that we should fatalistically resign ourselves to our situation and look back with longing to the past. Just the opposite is the case. We are now standing before the frontal attack of the anti-Christian power. This situation requires us to summon all our powers. What can we do? We cannot overcome spiritual processes, such as those which are leading to the anti-Christian power, by seeking to return to an earlier stage of development in which these spiritual processes were not yet present. The spiritual disease of our time can be overcome only if it breaks out—if it festers as the anti-Christian power. The only way to conquer secularism is to let it destroy itself by its own consequences. And we can accelerate this process if we, through our witness, bring to the consciousness of the present world the meaning of the entire process.

The secular movement which has arisen in the age of natural science and technology is youthful and vital only among peoples who, previously in possession of a mythological view of nature and a primitive way of life, are suddenly provided with a causal-mechanical view of the world and, at the same time, with all the achievements of modern technology. These peoples believe that a new age has dawned, in which man will plumb the secrets of nature and so become lord of the earth and lord of his destiny. But this springtime of secularism, which is represented in Germany by such books as Büchner's *Power and Matter* and Haeckel's *Riddle of the Universe* and is now appearing in other parts of the world, is only the first stage of secularism. This first stage is still manifest here and there among groups of workers. But among the leaders of the technological movement, whose thoughts are assimilated thirty years later by the workers, the first stage has given way to a deep disillusionment.

In the first place, all the principles of the old physics of matter and energy have in our time been placed in question. The absolute and self-sustaining quanta and standards, with which physics had previously worked, have, one after the other, been relativized. This relativizing process was brought to a kind of conclusion by Einstein. Not only have the constant body and the constant energy quantum been dissolved. Even absolute space and absolute time, which Newton presupposed as self-evident, have become relative constructs. There is nothing that can be called self-sustaining and self-subsistent any more. All standards are valid only from a given point of observation. Contemporary physics cannot find anything eternal in nature; there is no substrate resting in itself which could be placed over against God.

Far from being a hindrance to faith, this relativism prepares for a reawakening of the biblical understanding of our human situation: for relativism, which has made its way into all areas of life and thought, is nothing else than man's confession that he is completely temporal; that he sees nothing which could endure in itself and through its power; that the absolute constructs to which he subjects the world process are only necessary fictions which he presupposes in order to exist. But this transformation of the physical view of the world has affected only a small group of educated men.

Much more important are the practical attitudes toward life which have been made possible by the technological age in its second stage of development. The technology of machines, which seemed like a miracle to primitive man and gave him the impression that man had found the meaning of his existence and had subjected the entire world, has in its second stage of development just the opposite effect. With a compelling urgency the technology of machines brings to the consciousness of man in this second stage the perplexing question of the meaning of his life. According to the renowned inventor Diesel, "The hope that technology will save us or will miraculously effect our moral improvement is a kind of modern idolatry." Shortly before his death, Diesel asserted: "Whether all this has a purpose, whether it will make men happier, I am unable to say."[4] Hence at the end of his scientific career the great inventor stood before the unanswered question of the meaning of his life. Just when we have, in accordance with the biblical injunction, made the earth subject to us, and possess everything which the world can offer, we confront, with an ever more compelling urgency, the question: "What is the meaning of all this? Is not everything vanity and a chasing after wind?" This question has been asked not only by men who have been excluded from all the good things of this earth, but traditionally also by a man like Solomon who had everything at his disposal—houses, vineyards, pleasure gardens, ponds, menservants and maidservants, dancers, and every kind of diversion. Possessing all the treasures which this world can offer, Solomon realized that this world has no meaning in itself.

To this another statement must be added: the technology of the industrial age has deprived of meaning the daily work of large numbers of human beings. This technology has, as Oswald Spengler says, unleashed the satanism of the machine. Man has become a slave to an impersonal power, by which he had expected to be blessed. The machine age has made clear to us that, once the world has forgotten God, it unleashes demonic, destructive powers. The demonic character of modern industrial life is manifest in its production of ruthless strong men, who coldly step on the lives and health of thousands. Technology has unleashed the demonic urge of man to go beyond all human measure and to play with human life. Only in the age of modern industry have we learned to understand completely why Jesus characterized Mammon as a satanic power.

In Europe and America the secularism of the technological age is now to a great extent in its second stage of development, while in other parts of the world it is in its first stage. We can fight secularism only by helping it develop into its second stage. In the first stage of secularism man believes that he can become lord of all things through technological invention; in this stage man has no need for God. In the second stage of secularism man, having produced a multitude of technological inventions, finds that he has not become lord of all things, but has become enslaved and empty; in this stage he can ask the question concerning the reality of God, the ultimate meaning of his existence, in a more radical way than he could if he lived in a more peaceful situation.

Today we live in a situation similar to that which existed in the first centuries of our era, when the sun had set on the gods of the ancient Greek world and they had begun to die. At that time the messengers of Jesus were called atheists (*atheoi*). They deprived the world of its gods, in order to prepare a place for the living God. In the present situation Christians should follow the precedent of the early Church: they should join those who deprive the world of its gods and who oppose all man's attempts to claim for himself and for his world the eternity and absoluteness which belong to God alone. In other words, *contemporary Christians should support those who relativize world and man.*

When the relativizing process has come to an end, and man realizes that nothing in himself nor in his world is eternal, he asks with a new urgency the question of eternity—the question concerning that which is *truly* eternal. When this has occurred in our time, Christians will have a positive task which is far greater than their negative one. Like the Christians of the early Church, they are called upon to establish the Cross of the Christ in a world which has become disillusioned with its own gods; they are called upon to witness with new tongues to God's act of reconciliation, through which a demonically torn humanity receives salvation and the technological control of the world becomes meaningful as a participation in the creative work of God. But this witness must be expressed in such a way that it can be understood in the contemporary world.

Wherever the message of the Christ confronts human beings who live in a primitive stage of cultural development, it works through its own religious power; in order to be received, the message does not need to be supported by a social ethics or a comprehensive world view. The situation is different if the Christian message encounters a highly sophisticated secularism acquainted with the entire range of natural science and technology. Christians can combat such a secularism only if they work out a position which is as comprehensive as it is informed. Thus today the Christian community faces a new task. It needs to formulate a social ethics which places all questions concerning human social life in the light of the Bible. And it also needs to work out an interpretation of life and the world from the standpoint of the Cross—a biblical philosophy of faith in opposition to the philosophy of unfaith.

If one looks over the history of the Church, one can compare its present situation only with that of the Church in Augustine's time, when the expectation of the imminent return of the Christ had grown faint and the Church faced for the first time the task of interpreting the basic thoughts of the Bible in terms of the life and thought of Western culture. If we are to fulfill this task, we need not only the witness of the divine Spirit, which is in all times the most essential need, but also a rigorous thinking which occurs in faith. It cannot be doubted that the biblical writers' knowledge of historiography and natural science was more limited than that of educated men in our own time. We calculate in terms of Sirius millions of years, while the biblical writers moved within the framework of only a few thousand years of world history. When God uttered His Word of revelation, He did so in terms of the limited world view of the men who first received it. We have the task of expressing the content of the Word of God in terms of the world view of the present time without losing or changing this content—just as a musician may have the task of transposing an eighteenth-century composition into a contemporary orchestral idiom without losing any of its original musical quality.

And so secularism in our time places before the community of the Christ a new, difficult task. All the demonic enemies of Christianity are now forming a solid front. A tremendous battle is being prepared between the demonic powers and the message of the Cross. A great hour has come. Perhaps it is the last hour. May this great hour find men who know the signs of the time —who are prepared to fight the enemy and to suffer, die, and thus conquer with the Christ.

Knowledge and Faith:
From the Pre-Socratics to Heidegger*

BY KARL LOEWITH

The present essay originates in a quandary: Has not all philosophy since the beginning of Christianity had to labor under a cross? Unable to be Christian —for then it would no longer be philosophy—it cannot be non-Christian or pre-Christian, as though it had never heard about Christian revelation at all. This is clearly the case for the course of modern philosophy. The ambiguity begins, indeed, with Descartes's attempt to prove the existence of God without faith, through reason alone, from the facts of self-consciousness. His philosophical proof of God, which he chose to dedicate to the unbelievers on the theological faculty of Paris, may be thought of as a support for Christian faith, but it can just as well be thought of as a criticism of it. From Descartes' proof of God modern thought moves to Hegel's philosophy of religion, and from Hegel's "speculative Good Friday" to Nietzsche's Anti-Christ and from there to Heidegger's treatise on Nietzsche's statement about God's death, all in a characteristic ambiguity.[1]

The more we ponder this development the more our quandary compounds itself. In the entire history of modern philosophy it can never be clearly ascertained whether philosophy's appropriation of the Christian tradition is an attack or a defense. What began with Descartes and Spinoza[2] as a rational criticism of revelation and led, in Kant's religious work, to the remarkable inversion that true faith, that is, morally reasonable "faith," required no certain faith at all, found expression in the nineteenth century in Dilthey's program of a historical critique of reason, and culminated more recently in Heidegger's proclamation of "essential" thinking for which both scientific reason and faith are the "degeneration of thought."

Is there a way out of the labyrinth? What road lies open beyond the

* Translated by Harold O. J. Brown.

modern perplexity which has reached the end of the rational desire to know and yet cannot come to terms with faith? Perhaps it will be best to begin with some preliminary reflections concerning that crossroads where the philosophical desire for knowledge met Christian faith for the first time. By so doing we may discover some clues for reconciling the antinomies which have plagued this problem throughout the history of the Christian West. We reserve for our closing pages our assessment of the relations of faith and knowledge in the nineteenth and twentieth centuries.

I. THE HELLENIC SYNTHESIS

To inquire into the relation between knowledge and faith may seem to presuppose that philosophical knowledge has necessary and intrinsic relation to faith. This presupposition, however, finds no warrant in the history of Greek thought, from which our later philosophy is derived. It holds only for philosophy in the Christian Era. Both the separation of knowledge and faith and the attempt to harmonize them are peculiar to Christianity. For this reason we must start by seeking to determine how the Greeks understood the relation of faith to knowledge.

Classical philosophy does not confine itself to the either-or of knowledge and faith in the Christian sense, but addresses itself to the difference between *episteme* and *doxa*. *Doxa* may be translated as opinion as well as belief. The latter is at stake when we speak of "orthodoxy." Measured against *episteme* as true knowledge, *doxa* is but belief in the sense of a simple acceptance of some truth, not faith in the New Testament sense of *pistis*. What *doxa* holds to be true is in reality but a semblance, a seeming truth. One thinks or believes that one knows what is true, but does not really know the truth.

This difference between *doxa* and *episteme* is fundamental for all philosophical reflection. There is for antiquity no transition from faith in the invisible to knowledge of the empirical and demonstrable. There is instead the possibility of ascending from opinion to true knowledge. All his life Socrates did nothing else but question the unexamined opinions of his contemporaries in order to bring them gradually to real knowledge, or at least to the admission of their lack of knowledge. Faith in the Christian sense, which is no mere taking-to-be-true and not-yet-knowing, allows no similar transition to evident knowledge, because Christian faith is not conceived as an initial step to demonstrable knowledge.

The New Testament concept of faith does not exist in Greek thought. For Plato *pistis* means a subordinate form of *doxa*. To move within *pistis* means for him to move within sensory understanding. Not until Proclus (A.D. 410?– 485) did *pistis* come to rank above *gnosis;* but here, too, faith was still understood as a higher sort of insight. For Plato it is absurd to assume that faith must precede insight and open the way to a higher truth.

It is not surprising, therefore, that our modern distinction between orthodox believers, heretics, and unbelievers had no counterpart in antiquity. Heresies can only exist where there are orthodoxies, and atheists only where there are believers. In antiquity, atheism was not a religious departure from faith, but a political deviation with respect to the religious bases of the *polis*.[3] Atheism is *asebeia* (impiety), and this is an offense which is punished by the *polis*. Socrates was accused of *asebeia* because he did not honor the gods of the *polis*, but other, new divinities. Because such innovations in religious matters generally proceeded from philosophers and poets, the poetic and philosophical interpretation of the divine came in conflict with the officially recognized political religion, not with the Church and its theologians (neither of which existed). Protagoras, Anaxagoras, Aristotle, Theophrastus were all accused of *asebeia*, and preferred to emigrate or to disappear for a time. Today it is not easy to imagine Sartre on trial before a public court on account of his dedicated atheism, or Jaspers because of his unorthodox philosophical faith, or Heidegger because of his talk about the holy. The worst that might happen is that their writings would be listed on the papal Index!

II. FROM PAUL TO PASCAL

A decisive innovation came into the pagan world in the form of the radically different, unpolitical Christian faith. In the first centuries the Christians were actually seen and described by the pagans as atheists, or as innovators politically dangerous to the State in that they did not believe in or worship the old gods of the *polis* and the *kosmos*.[4] Conversely, the pagans did not appear to the Christian apologists as atheistic, but as superstitious, believing in all too many gods and demons. They were therefore paradoxically called "polytheistic atheists." Real atheism became possible only with the victory of Christianity over religious paganism, through the dismantling of the pagan cults and the discrediting of their many gods, which had sanctified the world and all human activity. Indeed, it was not until the exclusive Christian faith in the one otherworldly Creator God finally became unbelievable in later centuries that the world, the *kosmos* and the *polis*, became godless and secular to an extent it had never been for the Greeks and Romans, not even for Epicurus.

The Christian view of the relation of Faith to knowledge receives its decisive expression in the theology of St. Paul. Paul distinguishes philosophical knowledge, as the wisdom of this world, from the true wisdom of faith, by comparison with which the wisdom of this world is folly before God. Faith itself is characterized in the New Testament as certainty, not certainty on the basis of theoretical evidence but certainty on the basis of an unconditional trust in things which cannot be seen and understood. Paul's alternative between worldly, evident insight and faithful trust in the invisible and uncertain survives not only in theology and its concept of faith but in philosophy and its concept of knowledge as well. Until the eighteenth century, philosophy described itself as "worldly wisdom," in contrast to an entirely different wisdom which is not of this world.

But pre-Christian, classical thought does not move within this alternative of worldly knowledge and otherworldly faith. Greek philosophy wants to know what is, even what God or the divine is. And where there is knowledge there are supposed to be proofs, even proofs of the existence of God. These proofs do not presuppose any faith, but demonstrate the divine in its relation to the visible world, or as directly known in the cosmos. Thus ancient theology is par excellence theological ontology and cosmology, but not a theology of faith. The Greeks did not ask so much about the *existence* but rather about the *essence* of the divine, about the nature of the gods.[5] The existence of the gods was generally taken for granted. The nature of the gods seemed to manifest itself in the ancient natural world and consequently could be proved by natural theology.

All Christian proofs of God, from Paul to Anselm, ask primarily about God's *existence*. Because the Christian God is an otherworldly, invisible Creator of all that is, His existence must be proved, since it cannot be shown from that which already is. The Biblical God cannot be seen simply in His creation. In order to see the whole visible world, heaven and earth, as creation, one would have first to know about its Creator, and one knows of Him only through faith in His Word in Scripture. The really *Christian* proofs of God have no intention of somehow establishing faith in God; rather, they take faith for granted, in order to make it intelligible to natural reason.[6] To the extent that they try to prove more, they are justly subjected to philosophical criticism. Both the proofs of God by the believing theologians and their critique by philosophers presupposed that philosophical knowledge and Christian faith are two different things.

So far is Greek theology from being in conflict with philosophy that theology was thought to be philosophy's most characteristic product, the highest knowledge of the highest being, particularly in its contrast to the popular religion of the *polis*. The question is not: Can one know God or must one first believe in Him? but rather: Does philosophic wisdom provide a more satisfactory understanding of the divine than popular religion? Greek philosophy, which had to come to terms with popular stories of the gods and with myths, therefore has an entirely different attitude toward knowledge than Christian philosophy, which has to come to terms with the dogmatic claim of a revealed faith. Yet, because knowledge in the Christian Era finds itself in this awkward relation to faith, it cannot avoid looking about to see if there is not a reasonable way, in spite of everything, in which fallible knowledge can approach self-confident faith.

Augustine

Such a way was broached by Augustine with exemplary clarity in his work, *Concerning the Usefulness of Faith*. Augustine follows the Epistle to the Hebrews in his definition of faith: unconditional trust in things which one cannot see or know as one can visible things.[7] His first question bears upon the priority of faith to knowing insight. He wishes to show that, far from being contrary to reason, preliminary subjection to faith is demonstrably reasonable: it is rational for one to believe *before* one knows. If the decision to believe were against reason, *fides* would be but *credulitas*. Augustine illustrates the difference between genuine faith and mere credulity by the difference between being *studiosus* and being *curious*. Both the merely curious and the earnestly industrious person want to know something, just as the credulous and the faithful person both believe something. The difference, however, is that the curious person wants to know much that does not concern him, whereas the faithful person seeks to know only that which is useful and profitable to him, because it serves the salvation of his soul. But admitting that the *credulity* and *faith* of these people are not the same thing, it is still possible that both sorts of belief are false paths, if we are concerned with nothing less than knowing with unconditional certainty what is helpful to the eternal salvation of the soul, because it is the truth of the Christian religion. How sad it would be for the welfare of the soul if *credulitas* and *fides* differ only as do occasional intoxication and habitual alcoholism? If this were the case, Augustine says, then it would not only be impossible to have faith in the religious sense but one could not even have a friend or trust one's parents nor simply engage in business with others. All of human life, most notably community life, is based on mutual trust, loyalty, and faith in things which cannot be seen and known.

As an example of the usefulness and reasonableness of belief *before* all perception, knowledge, and insight, Augustine gives the following instance: one cannot love and trust one's parents unless one believes that they are one's parents. But whether they really are one's parents can never be known with certainty, in the case of the father not at all and of the mother not with complete certainty. One accepts the mother's word, or that of relatives, servants, and doctors, but if someone should draw the conclusion, since this is not certain, I am likewise not obliged to love and obey my presumed parents, one would act not only foolishly but highly immorally. In contrast, he who fulfills his filial duties faithfully, even if it should later be discovered that his presumed parents are not really his parents at all, would have acted in a morally right manner. If, then, trust, faith in something unseeable and unknowable, is found rationally justifiable in merely human relationships in which unconditional, unrestrained trust might seem out of place, how much more will it be necessary first of all to trust God, in order to come into any relationship with Him at all?

In the same way, Augustine says, the natural relationship of trust between individuals is necessary to and basic for access to Christian faith and its proclamation in the Church. A man learns of the Christian message only through hearing it preached by others who already believe. If one is to believe, one must first of all be willing to listen to others who already believe; one must be willing to learn and let oneself be instructed in the Christian religion by a teacher. In this initial relationship of teacher and pupil, we must reasonably presuppose that the pupil will trust his teacher and, conversely, that the teacher will trust the pupil. The teacher believes that the pupil will really allow himself to be instructed in the Christian faith and is not merely curious or out to dupe the teacher. Whoever first critically tests the trustworthiness of the one he is supposed to trust, putting him on trial, only shows thereby that he has no confidence and also mistrusts his own trust. Trust will never follow from mistrust.

Here a great difficulty arises, which Augustine examines in detail. How shall the unbelieving fool, who indeed seeks after truth but has not yet found it in faith, ever find the religiously informed or wise man, who already is well acquainted with Christianity? The fool would have to be a sage himself in order to be able to recognize the wise man as such. While seeking for the right teacher, how can one keep from falling prey to a teacher of falsehood, especially when so many philosophical schools and religious sects claim the same authority and maintain that they possess the truth? How can one be certain that *fides* in an *auctoritas* is no mere *credulitas* in a false authority? This, says Augustine, is an exceptionally difficult question, which gets one into the greatest perplexity. Even visible signs of Christian truth, such as conversions or miracles, are of little avail. How is one supposed to recognize such manifestations of God as signs, without knowing beforehand what they are signs of? A waymarker cannot be recognized as a waymarker if one does not already know what a way is.

The difficulty, says Augustine, is so great that only God Himself can solve it, when He brings foolish man into the way to faith and thus to believing insight into the truth of the Christian religion. We are unable to ask inquiringly about the true religion if God does not exist and come to our help even in our seeking. The divine authority, to which I am to give faith, must give me that very faith. Even when faith is no mere decision and no mere leap but is inspired by God Himself, it is still a daring wager, the wager of letting oneself go. Faith does not presume knowledge of the outcome of the undertaking.

If we analyze what is existentially a wager, we have a *circle,* in which what is to be proved is already assumed, namely, God, His revelation and faith in it. Augustine's last word on the relation between faith and knowledge is a sort of cyclical movement which turns back upon itself.[8] He sees no contradiction between emphasizing against the Manichaeans that faith must precede insight and stressing against an irrational leap into faith that it is *reasonable* for faith to precede reason.

So much for Augustine's philosophical clarification of the usefulness and reasonableness of faith. No long explanation is necessary to make it plain that man's natural presupposition of faith (in relation to parents, teacher, friends, physicians, judges) is no mere preliminary step from which one can ascend immediately to faith in God's revelation in Christ. Just as the natural authorities (in the relations of parents and children, teachers and pupils, physicians and patients, experts and laymen) do not of themselves lead to the recognition of the God of the Bible as a supreme authority, so natural faith does not lead to Christian, qualified faith.[9] The unnatural aspect of Christian faith and of Christian hope lies in the fact that both are commanded: we *ought* to believe and *ought* to hope, even if our natural tendency is not to believe in a unique revelation of God in a particular man.

Natural and Christian faith have in common only this negative quality, that both are faith in things which cannot be seen. No one could tell by looking at him whether Jesus is the Christ and the Son of God, nor could one tell by looking at Hitler whether he would be the destined leader and a political savior or a vicious seducer. In each case it had to be believed or disbelieved, and in each case those who believe in themselves find believers as well as unbelievers. Whether or not one has been mistaken in one's trust cannot be fully determined from the consequences of the acts of the person in question. If we assume that faith in Christ had not had the historical result which we call Christendom (supposing the possibility that Christianity had remained a historically insignificant sect), the visible failure would prove just as little as a visible success for or against faith in Jesus as

Christ. Historical success indeed speaks for itself, because nothing succeeds like success, but it proves something if one already believes in the course of history as such and is thus historically faithful.

If, however, in spite of the negative common ground of all natural and revealed faith, there is found no continuous transition from natural faith in natural authorities to Christian faith in Christian authorities, how, then, is Christian authority and faith in it to be documented and proved to man's natural reason? Again Augustine gives us the clue. Originally he sought truth in philosophy and in different religious sects, without finding it. At the peak of a crisis of his life he made the decision to let himself be instructed in the Christian religion, that is, he subjected himself freely to an authority believed in before the fact, in order to become whole again. When, in spite of passionate seeking, he did not find the object of his search, then the question of the method of his search (*modus quaerendi*) necessarily arose. Had he been looking for truth in the correct manner and direction? To ask that question was but to ask another question: Whence do we find the right direction of questioning, how shall we enter upon it, if not through some divine *authority*, in the double sense of governor and originator? Thus it is necessary for the sought-for true authority itself to confirm the faith and induce agreement with it. Authority becomes authority only when one accepts it, agrees with it, and believes it. It is not sufficient that it is itself trustworthy, true authority. But how does the confirmation take place? Obviously only if the authority, to which one is to grant faith, itself gives us faith in it.

Once again we have a *circle* which defies the application of an external measuring rod. Indeed, Augustine bases the necessity and the reasonableness of faith in authority on the fact that *human* reason is corrupted by the Fall. Since that time authority is necessary for reason's re-establishment. Sin and forgiveness are themselves knowable as such only if one has already placed oneself on the ground of Christian faith. The presupposed and contingent faith in a determining authority cannot be replaced by any sort of retroactive critical consideration. For precisely this reason it would be very serious if we were to err with respect to that which we recognize as determining authority. When it is a question of the conversion of our direction of questioning and way of life, of a rueful conversion of man to the true God as the *saluberrima auctoritas*, then a deception with regard to believed authority would be very unfortunate. Yet Augustine adds here: "It would be still less fortunate if no authority were to set us in motion." In the last analysis he relies upon the fact that God stands at the head of all things, even of our seeking after Him.

Without this circular establishment of faith, nothing could be decided; without God's own confirmation, faith cannot be believed.

Clearly, Christian *fides* and ancient *religio* are far apart, at least with respect to the aforementioned difference between pre-Christian atheism and the atheism of later times. It now remains to show that doubt has become more total and intensive as a result of Christianity. Philosophical skepticism and its sharpening into Christian doubt have exacerbated the problem of defining the *certitude* of faith.

In the history of philosophy, this problem of truth as certainty is usually traced to Descartes, because he based scientific truth on the certainty of knowledge. He sought to eliminate all uncertain knowledge by means of methodological doubt, in order to attain indubitable truth. Eventually Descartes's determination of objective truth by means of the subjective certainty of knowledge was brought to its dialectical conclusion in Hegel's *Phenomenology*. In absolute knowledge, truth per se and my certainty coincide.

The story told by histories of philosophy is sadly in need of modification. The quest for certainty is much older than the new science of Descartes. It is presupposed in the Christian view of truth as saving truth about the *unum necessarium,* truth about the one thing which is necessary, and of the certainty necessary for it.

This urgency of a saving truth is what makes philosophical skepticism unbearable yet so central for Tertullian and Augustine, for Luther and Pascal. For this reason they all grappled with philosophical skepticism: Tertullian and Augustine, with classical skepticism; Luther, with the *professio sceptica* of Erasmus; and Pascal with the doubt of Montaigne, which rested upon the classical arguments. The struggle of the certainty of faith with philosophical skepticism has indeed been a constant theme of European intellectual history. (One of its most poignant contemporary manifestations is the correspondence of Paul Claudel with André Gide.)

The certainty of faith is crucial for Luther. Blessedness and damnation rest upon certainty. He writes against Erasmus, "What is more like accursedness and damnation than uncertainty, and what is more blessed than certainty?" Erasmus' essay *On Free Will,* Luther says is an uncertain book, and for that reason dangerous. "The Holy Spirit is no skeptic. He has written no uncertain madness in our heart, but a powerful, great certitude, more certain and steadfast than that we are now living creatures, or that two and three are five." Among those necessary things of which one must be fully certain, Luther reckons the doctrine of the captive will. Whoever does not know what the will can or cannot do cannot know what God's Will and His Grace can do. Particularly in the question of the freedom of the will one must decide in the most certain manner possible, with a straightforward yes or no. Whoever is uncertain in such things is no Christian. Luther calls this certainty of faith the *assertio fidei*. "Asserere" means to insist firmly on a teaching, to confess it in faith before God and men.

Such assertion may in fact be necessary for a confession of the *unum necessarium*, but what has such a confession, or—existentially put—such an *engagement* to do with knowledge? Whoever questions this existential certainty of the faith-decision because he sees, like Erasmus, uncertainty and darkness everywhere, even in the Bible, and for this reason is unwilling to make an apodictic decision, is, according to Luther, possessed by the devil, who seeks to use philosophy and other doctrines of man to turn men away from the Bible.

The paradigm of decisive certainty of faith is the Christian who lets himself be killed as a witness to the truth of his faith. How can someone who is not fully certain of Christian teaching, Luther asks, offer himself for it? But, one must rejoin, does such potentiality of sacrifice for a faith prove anything about the truth of what is believed? The men around Cromwell, Napoleon, Lenin and Hitler were no less certain of their faith; they sacrificed themselves and, above all, sacrificed others for it, killing and being killed. On the other hand, it is undoubtedly not just chance that there have been few philosophical martyrs. Even Socrates did not die as a pre-Christian martyr, but as a citizen of Athens and a skeptical philosopher, who remained an ironist to the end. Philosophers, if they are really seekers after truth and do not have merely firm convictions, are rarely so sure of their cause that they could let themselves be killed and could involve others in sacrifice for the sake of truth. Generally, in the face of conflict they withdraw from the public state or distinguish between an esoteric and an exoteric sense of their writings. One can ask oneself whether a merely reflective person can possibly have such unshakable convictions as a Christian or even non-Christian religious witness to truth. Plato and Aristotle always left room for things to be more or less true or certain, and they did not disdain, even in philosophy, to speak of probability, because with their knowledge they were aware that not all knowledge is true and certain in precisely the same way.

Among all Christian thinkers, Pascal gives scientific skepticism the most liberty, and he constructs his proof of God's existence in the form of a mathematical probability, in order, as far as possible, to meet the objections of the skeptics. Even the certainty of faith gives man no security. Behind and beyond Pascal's recognition of uncertainty in matters, both of knowledge and of faith, he has an unconditional demand for a last certainty, one which would make all that is knowable and demonstrable relative, because it seeks the certainty of the salvation of the soul.

III. KANT'S CRITIQUE

Kant's analysis adds a new turn to the discussion of knowledge and faith. In the *Critique of Pure Reason*[10] Kant distinguishes opinion, belief and knowledge as different ways of holding a thing to be true. An opinion is a way of holding something true which is inadequate both subjectively, as mere opinion, and objectively, with respect to the truth of the opinion. Belief is a way which is indeed subjectively adequate, as one can be certain in one's belief, but is objectively lacking in validation. Only scientific knowledge is sufficient both in its own certainty and in the objective truth of what is known. It would be unreasonable merely to "opine" or to "believe" truths which are scientifically demonstrable: I do not *think* that $2 + 3 = 5$, and I do not *believe* it; I *know* it.

In contrast to these three levels of theoretical acceptance of truth, Kant describes several practical ways of accepting things as truth, namely, doctrinal, moral, and pragmatic. A *doctrinal* faith, for example, is the faith in a wise Creator of the world, whose existence can indeed never be proved on the basis of the natural world, but who is more than a mere opinion, because He has a foundation in the demonstrable regularity of nature. A *moral* faith is the faith in a future life and in a God who judges our acts. This moral faith cannot be proved either, but is to be assumed as the basis of our moral reason. It is true that we cannot "know" anything about this God, but we can have moral certainty; at the least it is not certain that there is *no* God and *no* future life. *Pragmatic* faith is illustrated when a physician, though lacking assured knowledge of the cause of the sickness, prescribes a cure. A touchstone for the certainty of this faithful acceptance of something as true might be a wager. The higher the stakes the more the uncertainty of our faith will tend to reveal itself.

For all the force of his argument, Kant is not invulnerable to criticism. In objection to Kant one must ask whether Christian faith can be classified as "doctrinal," "moral" and "pragmatic," and thus be included in the general concept of acceptance as truth. One must even ask whether Christian faith may be compared with knowledge and opinion at all. Whoever really "believes," in the Christian sense, does not only hold something to be true; he is certain of his faith and of what he believes. Faith, as it speaks to us from Job and Paul, from Augustine, Luther and Pascal, is a hard-won, unconditional confidence. Christian faith is something more than and different from mere doctrinal, moral or pragmatic assurance of the truth of a statement. For this reason alone, Christian faith is no mere acceptance of a fact as true. Basically it does not concern itself with anything factual at all; it is personal faith in a person.

This distinction is quite clear in Augustine:[11] even the demons believed Jesus, but they did not *believe in* Him. Whoever believes in God believes Him, but not everyone who believes Him believes in Him. Thus indeed the Christian believes the words of the Apostle Paul, but he does not believe in him. To believe in someone means to turn unconditionally to him, to have full trust in him, to expect everything from him. In the Christian view this unconditionally hopeful faith is itself a gift of God, conjointly willed by man, because the directed fulfillment of God's will is the very nature of faith as the Christian understands it.

Kant's distinctions between theoretical and practical reason as well as opinion, knowledge and faith are not much in fashion today. Hegel criticizes Kant's concept of reason as one of mere understanding. And the concept of "understanding" which has come to the fore since Dilthey has still further obscured the difference between opinion, knowledge and faith. Much can be *understood*, it is claimed, but little can be known with certainty. The reasonable distinctions between opinion, knowledge and faith have vanished. It is part of the signature of our time that those who cannot stand up against the skepticism of knowledge are receptive to all the variations of religiosity and refurbish philosophy as a substitute for religion.

IV. FROM HEGEL TO HEIDEGGER

Hegel has had a fateful influence on the history of the dialogue between philosophy and religion. In an essay explicitly devoted to "Faith and Knowledge," he attacks the disjunction between the two as dialectically false. He maintains that "our progressive education" has risen so far above the old contradiction between philosophy and religion that this contradiction has come into the orbit of philosophy itself by way of the distinction between mere *understanding* thought and speculative, *reasoning* thought. At the same time, Hegel points out, reason has asserted itself so strongly in religion that criticism of miracle-faith has lost ground. The traditional religious doctrine of the transformation of bread and wine into the Body and Blood of Jesus Christ, he declares in his early philosophical and theological works,[12] is an inconceivable miracle only if one thinks of bread and wine externally, as two lifeless objects. If one conceives of them in their inward sense, in terms of one's spiritual and intellectual relationship to them and of their meaningfulness, these lifeless and meaningless objects become transformed into supersensual symbols, just as believable as they are conceivable.

Hegel later develops this line of thought as the explicit theme of a special chapter called "Struggle of the Enlightenment with Superstition" in his *Phenomenology of the Mind*. The antagonism of faith and enlightenment is illusory, he claims, because each has been penetrated by the other without knowing it. Both "enlightened" knowledge and religious faith, which seemed a dismal superstition to the Enlightenment, are superseded according to Hegel in what he calls the absolute knowledge of the Absolute. Here he sees the reason of philosophy and the faith of Christian religion balance as formally different perceptions of the same absolute content. In a similar manner, the Catholic theologian F. von Baader[13] blames the unnecessary falling-out of knowledge and faith for much of the disintegration in religious and political society and tries to show that the conflict between knowledge and faith is at bottom only a conflict between two faiths.

Neither Baader's reintroduction of reason into Christian faith nor Hegel's inclusion of faith within philosophy has ended the opposition between knowledge and faith. Indeed Hegel's mediation between philosophy and religion gave fresh impetus to the old contradiction. Bruno Bauer and Ludwig Feuerbach[14] claimed to discover a hidden atheism in Hegel's philosophy of religion. Marx and Kierkegaard drew equally radical but opposite conclusions: Marx's atheistic "materialism," which sees revelation only in the dialectic of secular history, has as a prerequisite a decisive *unbelief* in a supernatural redemptive event. Kierkegaard opposed both Hegel's philosophical theology and historical Christianity, held fast to God's unique revelation in Christ and gave up everything else in historic Christianity. His reduction of the traditional content of faith to the single point of decision for revealed faith makes it clear again to many that Christian faith does not rest on rational inquiry, that is, skeptical knowledge, but is rather a *scandal* for all worldly knowledge.[15]

The Twentieth Century

Kierkegaard's paradoxical faith underlies but does not really determine the inner structure of the theological and philosophical development of the nineteen-twenties. Kierkegaard's attack on existing "Christendom" aroused Protestant theology to a new flight into ecclesiastical dogmatics. His attack on the philosophical "system" has led to an existential philosophy, which conjures up "ciphers of transcendence" or thinks on "being" in the place of faith in God. In the writings of Jaspers the difference between philosophy and the Christian religion diffuses into a "philosophical faith" which interprets the relation of the soul to God as a movement of existence toward transcendence. Heidegger[16] has sought to avoid the "malicious destiny of being," which lets thoughtful questioning degenerate, on the one hand, into the knowledge offered by the sciences and, on the other hand, into faith. He affirms that essential thought is itself a reverent "remembrance" and that questioning is the "piety" of thought.

In general, contemporary German philosophy neither wants to know what is true in the light of deserved skepticism nor does it hold to traditional Christian faith. It flees into formless religiosity, loves to cite poets, and replaces the lack of religious substance by overtaxing philosophy. Few can or will distinguish among what is mere opinion (*doxa*), true knowledge (*episteme*), or genuine faith (*pistis*). Hegel's criticism of his romantic contemporaries[17] is still applicable today: the spirit of the times has become so pitiable that man today demands not insight into what eternally is but edification through "dumping all the disciplines of thought together" for the satisfaction he gets out of thinking that he has thereby subordinated subjectivity to the essence of being. Hegel warns that something may appear deep without having any foundation, seeming mysterious and hidden only because there is nothing behind it which can be explained! Philosophy must be on her guard, he admonishes, against the desire to be edifying and the temptation to nibble at the "bait" of the holy. How much Hegel himself, in spite of his having delineated the problem, contributed to its obfuscation by abandoning Kant's sober thinking becomes clear in the writings of his opponents.

A CONCLUDING REFLECTION

On the basis of Heidegger's analysis of the circular nature of all understanding,[18] we have today been all too easily satisfied that this vicious circle is not a fault, and that it is not crucial to escape from it; we are only supposed to enter into it in the proper way. The popular justification of the circle is contradicted, however, by the fact that the circle of presupposed faith is only closed and inaccessible through other presuppositions as long as one holds oneself within the faith once won. If it is correct that no one is born as a believing Christian, and that no man is Christian by nature, but becomes one through conversion and rebirth, then the closed circle of the presupposition of faith is open, before the winning and after the loss of faith —in the decisive step from the questioning, seeking and investigating man to the believing Christian, or from there back into doubt. Only here, at this point, can the man who *wants to know* and the man who *wills to believe* meet, rather than stand opposed as if at an invisible border.

If Jaspers complains that there is no real communication with theologians and that every conversation with them breaks off at particular points without any understanding having been reached, then the reply must be that one can hardly expect a believer, who believes that he has found the truth in his Christian faith, to be open to the uncertainties of philosophy in unlimited communication. The only possible philosophical point of attack, nevertheless, ought to be the simple fact that *even faith has a history,* that it arises from seeking and doubting. The questioning and investigating spirit of philosophy, which wills to know, occurs in time and in fact *before* the certainty of faith, because even the person who has become a faithful and confessing believer was once a seeker of truth, a philosophizer. On the other hand, the philosophizer himself can indeed attain faith and be converted, and this even with the help of skepticism and philosophy, as Pascal and Augustine show, but never *because of* philosophy.

Today, existentialism is underbidding and overtaxing philosophy precisely because it claims to overcome the limits of rational thought by decisions of faith albeit non-Christian ones. The existentialist wants to decide what cannot be known. It is characteristic of his decisiveness that it removes itself, in one leap, toward a faith and away from the uncertainty of knowledge.

Strictly speaking, there can be no "Christian philosophy." One can conceive of a "Christened" philosophy, that is, after a philosopher has become Christian, but the relationship between philosophy and Christianity is then a relation of Christian faith to Christian knowledge, not a relation between philosophy as such and Christianity. The most that Christian faith can demand of philosophy is that it not exclude the possibility of a divine truth which is self-revealing. If there is such a divine self-revelation of truth and if man is capable of grasping it as such, it is superior in principle to every human seeking for truth. Even Socrates came this far and attained this insight.

In Plato's *Phaedo,* Socrates is discussing with his friends and pupils his imminent departure from this life. Many questions come up, the answers to which remain uncertain. One of his pupils says to him: "I feel myself (and I daresay that you have the same feeling) how hard or rather impossible is the attainment of any certainty about questions such as these in the present life. And yet I should deem him a coward who did not prove what is said about them to the uttermost, or whose heart failed him before he had examined them on every side. For he should persevere until he has achieved one of two things: either he should discover or be taught the truth about them; or, if this be impossible, I would have him take the best and most irrefragable of human theories, and let this be the raft upon which he sails through life—not without risk, as I admit, if he cannot find some word of God which will more surely and safely carry him."[20]

15

God and Causality*

BY GABRIEL MARCEL

We cannot avoid reflecting whether or not the notion of causality is applicable to God, especially if we consider the development which that notion has undergone in the course of the history of thought since the Middle Ages. Without a doubt we are nowadays generally inclined to hold a mechanistic conception of causality which really has nothing in common with the conception St. Thomas might have held; yet the intention of the present essay is to concentrate our attention on that "causality of being" about which the best modern interpreters of Thomism speak. It will quickly become apparent that we cannot understand the latter notion unless for the word "causality" we substitute the notions of communication and generosity.

Indeed, in my opinion, we men of modern times have hardly any right to preserve a concept as burdened with ambiguities as is that of causality. We may retain it only if there is clear agreement that our use of it is not unequivocal.

Let us commence with an analysis of generosity, emphasizing always the existential rather than the notional context. The generous man is the one who gives and who to a certain extent gives for the sake of giving, not with calculation, that is to say, not to gain a favorable reputation in the eyes of the beneficiary, not to bind him in any way.

We need to dig a little deeper to discover the true nature of the generous man's gift. For this gift, taken in itself, can appear ambiguous to us; we may not know exactly what it is and what its purpose is. But where generosity shines forth it puts an end to this ambiguity. It embraces an affirmation of the freedom of the beneficiary to such a degree that the receiver can only regard himself as free. The generous act runs sometimes quite deliberately the risk of being unrecognized or wrongly interpreted. It cannot escape this risk without losing its true character.

Here an account of meanness appropriately enters in. Generosity cannot

---

* Translated by Robert W. Flint.

fully reveal itself except to a generous soul; the mean or vicious soul will always find a way to belittle the generous act or to find its very motives mean. It could indeed happen that generosity, like a sudden light, might dissipate these clouds, these belittling interpretations. But at the same moment it would raise the beneficiary in some fashion to the level of the benefactor. In any case, nothing in this area is inevitable; nowhere more than here do we see the limits of a psychological determinism founded on a supposedly complete enumeration of people's true motives and incentives.

Let us ask how generosity may look from the perspective of the idea of causality we commonly hold. This question is admittedly difficult to answer. One might answer it by saying, for example, that even a supposedly perfect generosity is motivated by the stake which the generous person has in the person he intends to overwhelm with his kindnesses. Cannot this motivation be interpreted as a mode of causality? It is clear enough that one tends here to confuse cause and reason. But let us go a little deeper. It is obvious that the more definite the character of a kindness, the more circumscribed it is, and the more it seems to be a way to remedy a deficiency itself definite. I recall, for example, someone who discovered, during the occupation of France, that my wife and I were poorly warmed, and spontaneously brought us a little of his provision of wood. But the problem of causality in generosity changes somewhat if the act is no longer a matter of giving a definite thing to someone definite. Moreover, even in the instance I have just described, what touched us deeply was our recognition of the genuinely charitable thought itself. In a certain way it gave itself to us. And this observation can be generalized.

The more one meditates on generosity the more it appears as a gift of oneself. The generous person is one who gives himself in what he gives. But here we must guard ourselves from the snare of the causalist interpretation. The latter interpretation inevitably reduces things to the material level. Generosity, however, especially when considered in the absolute, is an instance of *spirit speaking to spirit*. Once again I ask: What advantage is there in wanting to extend to this domain a notion of causality which otherwise seems to me retrograde, even to the level of physical explanation?

The main point, however, which concerns us in this inquiry lies elsewhere. It is especially from reflecting on the problem of evil—and on how this problem should not be posed—that I have been led to think it necessary to abandon conceiving God as a cause. I have come to think that cause is an essentially profane category. Theological meditation needs to concentrate above all on the idea of a holy God, that is to say, on transcendence. (There is no little danger here that in our attempt to protect God's transcendence we will attenuate His contact with the world in which we must laboriously find our way.)

I will cite an example here, at once definite and banal, in order to ascertain, gropingly, how—and within what limits or with what corrective—it may or may not be possible to introduce a purified notion of divine causality. A young man, seemingly quite healthy and vigorous and with the best prospects for the future, was suddenly seized with what was first believed to be merely a stiff neck. But other symptoms appeared, and it turned out that it was a cancer, already well advanced and spreading at a rate that made its cure impossible.

In my present philosophical perspective it is clearly not my task to state this agonizing problem in medical terms. Only the pathologist has the authority to pronounce on the physiological development of this disease. Moreover, we know that in current pathology knowledge of the etiology of the disease is in its beginnings. One might ask, however, if even here in considering the origins of disease the common notion of causality is applicable. It may well be that reality is much more complex and that one is in the presence of a synergy with innumerable factors, certain of them being even today almost indiscernible. I shall not press the point. In the problem we are concerned with now we must first put ourselves into what one might, somewhat crudely, call the conscience of the patient who sees himself called upon to face a situation which, if one considers it objectively, appears to be desperate.

Under these conditions the question which interests me, and not only me but existential philosophy as well, is above all that of knowing whether this young man, whom we shall here assume to be a believer, can, in some sense or other, attribute what we have a right to call his trial to a causal action of God. I have already had occasion to say several times, notably in the review *Présence,* that nothing seems more offensive to me for spirit and for faith itself than the pedagogical idea of a trial set up by some divine schoolmaster to discover as if by the help of a quiz whether I the patient—we must indeed dramatize by personalizing—am able or not to put this suffering, this anguish, to good use. Here, what I have already said concerning the importance of emphasizing the transcendence or the holiness of God seems to me to carry all its weight. By referring the youth to God's causality I do something very grave: I refer Him to a process which is nothing if not human and bound to empirical and even sociological conditions.

But can I, on the other hand, go to the opposite extreme and simply say that what happens to me is not only contingent but, absolutely speaking, insignificant and even indifferent to a transcendent God who would not bother with such trifles? That would be, I think, to fall into an error as hostile as can be to what is most substantial and, let us say, most sacred in the Christian affirmation. If an individual is of infinite worth because he was created in the image of God, a trial which exposes him to the temptation of absolute despair and denial cannot in any way be regarded as insignificant to God; it could be so only from a Stoic or pantheistic perspective. What seems necessary to me is somehow to suppress my preoccupation with causes; these should only preoccupy scholars or technicians to the extent that they may legitimately hope to discover the causes of a particular evil, to get a grip on it and fight the battle in my behalf or in behalf of others with some chance of success. To abandon divine causality seems to me of the greatest importance; this amounts to saying that the causal order remains empirical and dependent on the modalities of possible action, but that there is everything to lose in judging causality as transferable to the level of transcendence.

Is there a way, here, of making use of what Père Le Blond has said on the subject of generosity? Perhaps, but within what limits? Certainly not to work out, on whatever level, a complete explanation of what happens to me. But rather that the divine generosity, in which I must immediately believe, may be imagined perhaps as grace, able not only to help me accept my fate (this would still be only a transposed stoicism) but to transmute it. But, one may say, have I not the right, I the patient, to pray that God may cure me? Certainly, but should this prayer not be joined with the Lord's Prayer that "thy will be done on earth as it is in heaven"? I desire to unite myself to this Will, to be sure, but certainly not to reason about it retrospectively and to persuade myself that God's Will is the source of my trouble.

We are here, after all, at the very heart of the problem: for it is a matter in the last analysis of knowing whether that Will may be considered etiologically, that is to say, as a cause toward which one reascends like the historian who tries to determine retrospectively the causes of a given event—even a cancer. It seems to me that we cannot proceed in this way without a wholly illegitimate objectification which will result in treating God as one cause among others. I am well aware that one may be tempted here to appeal to the traditional distinction between the first cause and the secondary causes; but I do not believe that it could in any way solve our problem.

I am, moreover, very far from deceiving myself about the difficulties and dangers of a position in certain respects entirely negative, as that toward which I have aimed in the foregoing remarks. It is too obvious that we are climbing here toward an extremely narrow ridge, and that we are in particular continually exposed to the Manichaean temptation. What is indeed more simple and more seductive in appearance than to imagine a radically evil will at the root of my trouble, to which the Will of God will oppose itself? Shall we merely suppress the difficulty resulting from the convenient but suspect notion of a laissez-faire divine toleration of what is perhaps an evil or demoniac will which remains nevertheless under the control of God? I do not know whether this recourse is entirely avoidable, and I even fear that it may not be; but it troubles me because here also I discern suspect analogies to human conditions, too human, in which a sort of celestial management is involved. In the last analysis, recourse to this basically anthropological notion of a *permission* has only a limiting value; it expresses very clumsily our legitimate refusal to imagine a divine causality in imagining which we would risk compromising the holiness of God.

I fear, then, that I must personally hold myself to a sort of *docta igno-rantia* (learned ignorance) which consists finally in saying this: the explanation of causes that I have when I hold myself to a consideration of empirical conditions is existentially inadequate. That is to say, the explanation is profoundly inadequate with respect to a certain need for a higher intelligibility, and this need, it seems to me, I cannot deny without betraying some essential part of my being. On the other hand, I will not succumb to the temptation of doubling this explanation, which cannot be more than empirical, by a theological pseudo-explanation. It appears that I must resist that temptation and bring all my efforts to bear on the way in which I can, with God's grace, transfigure suffering and make it significant, make it even illuminating both for myself and for others.

How can I avoid mentioning here a striking book which appeared some time ago and which is called: *The Story of a Struggle* (*Récit d'un combat*)? The author, Madame Sorana Gurian, recounts there with a strange precision the struggle she had carried on for two years against a cancer which has now become generalized.

I penetrated the strange and burning region of sorrow. I learned to trace in my body those landscapes of tangled nerves, of twisted and bloody muscles, of the dark veins which are for the soul the tortuous paths up nightly calvaries. . . . For a brief moment I understood that this was so, that nothing was meaningless (this under the influence of morphine and its fluid peace). The sense of the injustice done to me transformed itself into intense satisfaction: I would pay *my* debt, and nothing could reproach me for having fled my just punishment. . . . The effect of the morphine passed off, I started again to suffer agonies. The wind of the insurrection whistled. Everything became delusive.

A very old missionary has just visited her, and she suddenly says that perhaps it was the Angel who took this slightly mocking shape. She confesses, she takes communion. But the sense of ineffable peace she had experienced does not last. She lacks the conviction that this suffering could be useful to others and confer on them a mysterious dispensation. "I was quite willing to suffer if that might be in a sense . . . in order to ransom others." But is not that still another temptation? Nevertheless, she could write: ". . . with the cancer, someone else lived in me. And this was no longer the idea of death: it was a sort of light which I did not understand."

But this suffering light, what is it? It will certainly be extinguished as soon as some theologian rashly attempts to explain to the sick person that her illness was willed and caused by God, for the sake of some greater good. This arithmetic is no better than the utilitarian arithmetic of a Bentham. It excludes in the last analysis what ought first to be taken into account, and that is communion, compassion. Let us clearly understand, I repeat, that every causal reference should be excluded here, except for the medical person who attempts either to heal or to prevent. But to the condemned person, to the tortured one, is it enough to say: "we have hope that in a few years from now science will have progressed; it is hard on you, but you arrived too early"? No, this in no way constitutes an answer. That which, on the other hand, can be helpful—I will say *mysteriously* helpful—is to make the patient recognize that she can, if she will, enter into a communion of sufferers which in a certain respect is an aspect of the Church, an aspect meant to exist only under conditions which infinitely transcend those of an earthly trial: the Church Triumphant, consubstantial with the very Will of God.

I must, nevertheless, add that in so far as I have written these lines at my worktable in relative comfort, so far do they seem to me suspect. We are here in an existential order where the highest truths cannot be decently set forth by anyone, in any context. But this is not to say that the only truths in this life, therefore, are those to which science has access: on the contrary, there exist truths on a much higher level. They are in communion with the inexpressible secret of all destiny.

~~~~~~ Part VI

Religion and the Vocation of the Church

16

Rudolf Sohm's Theology of Law and the Spirit

BY JAMES LUTHER ADAMS

According to Luther's conception of the Two Kingdoms, the Christian believer belongs to two realms, "one of which is the kingdom of God under Christ and the other is the kingdom of the world under civil authority." These two realms exist under quite different kinds of authority, the one under the love and spirit of Christ, the other under legal restraints; the one under the guidance of the Holy Spirit in conjunction with Word and sacrament, the other under the rule of law. In Luther's view, then, "temporal government has laws which do not reach farther than over person and property and what is external on earth; for God will not permit any one to rule over the soul of man but Himself. Where temporal power presumes to give laws to the soul, it touches God's rule and misleads and destroys the souls."

This view, adumbrated in Luther's treatise *On Secular Authority,* has long been a subject of controversy, for example as it relates to claims regarding the spiritual and political significance of the Lutheran Reformation and regarding the influence of that Reformation. A generation ago the controversy found sharp focus in the opposition raised by Karl Holl to Ernst Troeltsch's adverse evaluation of Luther's conception of the two realms, an evaluation that attributed to Luther abject subservience to the power of any State able to establish itself. This particular controversy necessarily involved a discussion of the relations between law and gospel. Since that time the debate in certain quarters has assumed a more restricted scope having to do with the respective roles of law and Spirit within the Church. This discussion, which was vigorously promoted before the First World War, appears now to be gathering momentum again. The roster of the contemporary participants in this discussion includes a substantial number of Protestant scholars. Much of the controversy has centered in the questions: What is the role of the Holy Spirit, of charismatic authority, in the Church? Is there any place for a sacrosanct legal authority in the Church? Does not any rule of law, any legal order, in a Protestant church deprive it of its distinctive evangelical character and freedom, and does it not drive a Protestant church into an essentially Roman Catholic bondage to canon law? Does not law in the Church lead to idolatry? Is not charismatic authority in essence incompatible with divinely sanctioned legal authority, whether the latter officially establishes "pure doctrine" or a particular, fixed ecclesiastical order?

A key figure for understanding this controversy is the eminent German jurist and church historian Rudolf Sohm (1841–1917), who viewed charismatic authority (in conjunction with Scripture and the sacraments) to be completely incompatible with any "divine church law." The German literature dealing with Sohm's thesis is abundant, and it continues to grow. Almost every month a new treatment of Sohm appears.[1] The presentation of his outlook set forth in this essay can provide only a partial background for the understanding of the issues of the current discussion.

At first blush the non-Lutheran Protestant may understandably show little positive interest in the questions that have been raised by Sohm, particularly in so far as they are concerned with the validity of canon law. Is not "divine church law" a matter for live discussion only in Protestant-Catholic polemics? Why need one bother to defend the authority of the Holy Spirit as over against that of canon law? Actually, however, Sohm's characterization and defense of charismatic authority bears affinity to conceptions of the Holy Spirit which are familiar in free-church tradition and (still more) in the "left wing" of the Reformation, to which many Protestant denominations and sects trace their lineage. To be sure, Sohm never explicitly recognizes this affinity.

In the face of the history of ecclesiastical legalism and tyranny and of recurrent forms of rigidity in Christian belief and practice, Sohm raised a vigorous protest against any constitutional legalization of the Church, whether this legalization be Roman Catholic or Protestant. Besides appealing to Luther's doctrine of the Two Kingdoms (whereby he found an avenue to a New Testament norm for authority in the Church), he asserted that in Luther's doctrine of the invisible Church the Protestant should recognize a norm that was implicit, if not articulate, in the primitive Church's understanding of itself. In spelling out his conception of the New Testament and Lutheran norm, Sohm developed what we might call a theology of church history in terms of loyalty to or deviation from the norm. This normative theory of periodization offers a striking analogy to Anabaptist theories charting the periods of the creation, fall, and redemption of the Church. Sohm sets forth a basic norm for the Church; he then traces the stages by which the Church "fell" away from the gospel; and, finally, he discerns the recovery of the norm in Luther (and its subsequent perversion in the Protestant churches). Sohm's view of the norm and of defection from it differs in important ways from that of the Anabaptists. We need not consider here the difference between his norm and theirs. It is of special interest, however, to observe that, whereas the Anabaptists discerned the "fall" in the alliance of Church and State (with the consequent coercion in matters of faith), Sohm placed the "fall" much earlier, in the advent of church law. In this connection, one should note also the contrast between Sohm's and Harnack's identification of the "fall" of the Church; Harnack saw it in the "acute Hellenization" of Christianity, and Sohm identified it with the legalization of Christianity, in the advent of a legally constituted church under the episcopate.

Despite the intrinsic interest to the Nonconformist of this theology of church history, Sohm's writings on the constitutional history of the Church are not well known in the United States. Since American Protestants are generally little concerned with canon law or its history, it is not surprising that Sohm's *magnum opus* on the history of canon law (*Kirchenrecht*, I, 1892; II, 1923, published posthumously) has not appeared in English translation. But in 1904, Walter Lowrie's *The Organization of the Church* gave an extensive interpretation of the first volume of this work. Other aspects of Sohm's scholarship are more familiar in the English-speaking world. His classic study of ancient jurisprudence, *The Institutes of Roman Law* (1884), appeared in English in 1892, and his widely known *Outlines of Church History* (1888) in 1895, and both works have received numerous reprintings. For a time Sohm's theology of church history was given favorable attention in the United States through the efforts of the short-lived Sohm Foundation, which was inaugurated two decades ago under the leadership of Sohm's American Lutheran disciple, Professor John O. Evjen.

In Germany Sohm's work has received much attention, largely because of his massive learning and because of the radical challenge he has offered to regnant views. Almost fifty years ago Harnack said of Sohm's anti-legal and pneumatic doctrine of the Church that "with the exception of the Catholic view, it is the most coherent and complete which has ever been put forward."[2] Harnack's judgment is the more significant because he rejected Sohm's view that the primitive Church was solely under charismatic authority and possessed no legal constitution. Recently Heinrich Bornkamm has asserted that "even though the over-sharpened consequences which Sohm drew from his ingenious basic idea have elicited later justified criticism, his work nevertheless remains up to now the immovable starting-point for every discussion of Luther's doctrine of the church."[3] Yet, relatively few German scholars have been willing to accept Sohm's normative conception of the Church. On the other hand, Emil Brunner a decade ago asserted that Sohm "has raised questions which have not yet been answered. . . . In truth, we have not yet done with Sohm, no, not for a long time to come."[4] In his book, *The Misunderstanding of the Church,* Brunner shows a marked sympathy for certain aspects of Sohm's outlook; indeed, in general, he accepts and also sharpens Sohm's normative periodization of church history. Following upon the publication of Brunner's book, Karl Barth, in a section of his *Kirchliche Dogmatik,* has dealt sharply with Brunner as "Sohm's successor" —thus initiating a quite new phase in the theological debate with Brunner. Meanwhile, Rudolf Bultmann has devoted a substantial section of his *Theology of the New Testament* to a somewhat favorable interpretation of Sohm. It appears that Brunner's prediction that "we have not yet done with Sohm" is to be vindicated.

In accord with Luther's Two-Kingdom theory, Sohm was particularly concerned to dissipate every confusion between the kingdom of Christ and the kingdom of the world. In his view, the most disastrous confusion can appear when the Christian Church admits into its structure the authority that belongs to the political realm, the alien principle of legal direction and restraint. The primitive Christian *Ecclesia* under the charismatic authority issuing from Christ and the gospel had excluded this alien principle. But again and again the Christian Church has adopted it. Instead of remaining the Body of Christ under the guidance of the Holy Spirit, the Church has tended to become a worldly, secular authority and organization, a second state, as it were, exercising legal control, including coercion, over its members. In effect, this is to secularize the Church from within. Sohm epitomizes his view in the axiom, "Ecclesiastical law stands in contradiction to the nature of the *Ecclesia.*" From Sohm's point of view, this axiom at the same time grasps the substance of Luther's theory of the two realms, and it presupposes the New Testament norm of pneumatic or spiritual authority which is the charter of the freedom that belongs to the Church of Christ. The enemy of this freedom is law, "divine church law." Christ has delivered us from law.

Coming from a jurist, this radically negative evaluation of law in the Church sounds strange. A striking paradox lies at the center of Sohm's whole enterprise as a historian and interpreter of canon law. As a jurist he devoted much of his career to teaching the theory and history of law. In addition to his classic treatment of Roman private law, *The Institutes,* he published a number of learned studies of Germanic law; he was concerned also with the history of the law of associations. In an autobiographical statement which he prepared at the request of a law journal, Sohm speaks of choosing his profession of jurist because of his conviction that (secular) law is a great benefactor of mankind, a primary means of social control and human fulfillment. But when he turned his attention to the search for the characteristic authority of the Christian *Ecclesia* he found that legal concepts were completely inappropriate. The Christian *Ecclesia* was informed by a power of a different order. This power he called charismatic, the power of the Holy Spirit. We shall presently observe that he connected this conception of authority with the view that Christian faith requires primary orientation to an invisible rather than to a visible church. Canon law belongs to a faith that attaches itself to a visible church. Before considering these matters, however, we should examine the concept of law in contrast to which he posits the charismatic authority of the *Ecclesia*. Without an awareness of Sohm's definition of law, one misses the peculiar character of the contrast he envisages for the two realms. An understanding of his concept of law is the more necessary in view of the fact that even his disciples sometimes assert wrongly that for Sohm law is "only the command sanctioned by physical coercion." It is much more than this.

What, then, is law according to Sohm? Law, he says, determines, defines, and distributes the relations of power in terms of justice.[5] Its immediate task through the State is to promote human freedom and justice by bringing congruence out of the struggle of different wills against each other (*bellum omnium contra omnes*). It achieves this through the formal definitions of rights and obligations. In thus attempting to bring order and right into man's power relations, the immediate purpose of law is to regulate *external* freedom. It does away with external hindrances (such as are characteristic of the kingdom of this world). But law has a broader task, namely, the congruence of the human will with the divine will. It aims at external freedom for the sake of inner freedom. In this connection one must observe certain contrasts between legal regulations and moral law. The moral imperative is obligatory in terms of its content, which demands inner assent to natural, intrinsic authority; it gives rise to an ethical community that has conventional law but not legal rules; and it is oriented to the present, that is, to the situation of the individual case. On the other hand, the legal statute or the formally established right is rooted in a national community, and it is obligatory without reference either to the present consent of the individual or to special cases. In the realm of law, moreover, one confronts the power of previously articulated forms (statutes, laws, custom); the past appears as the impartial judge of the present. "The nature of legal authority lies not in its being carried out by force, but in this, that it is formal in nature—that is, that it rests on the basis of definite events of the *past*, without possibility of criticism, without consideration of whether or not it appears to be really justifiable in the present." In addition, law must be enforced; "it tends towards coercive realization." The State as the instrument of the national community and as the executor of law is accordingly the power over power relations, the power that enforces law. At the same time, constitutional and statutory law give realization to a moral law or to an ideal of justice residing in a community, through mediating agencies and forces that find their ultimate source in a belief in divine justice. In the general community life, law is therefore at bottom a moral and religious necessity. In sum, then, law is concerned with achieving external freedom in the context of power relations, it defines abstract rights and obligations within the framework of a national community, its validity is bound up formally with precedents out of the past, it is ultimately oriented to moral law and divine law, and it can legitimately effect enforcement by means of coercion.

Now, church law shares these features of law, Sohm finds, but in a special way. In its earliest stage Christian ecclesiastical law identifies the Church with the bishop, giving him legal rights in perpetuity. Later on (in the Middle Ages), canon law, adopting categories from Roman law, defines the Church as a corporation possessing the power of the keys to bind and loosen and to mediate the divine life. This corporation is an external, superindividual, compulsory institution whose leaders hold office by virtue of formal rights and obligations. These authorities dispense salvation through the sacraments and through penitential disciplines. The canon law purports to guarantee legitimacy and continuity for offices and doctrines. Thus the guarantee binds the Church to the past, and the regulations obtain without possibility of criticism. In the Middle Ages this legally constituted church becomes a sovereign world power, and that in a twofold fashion: in the secular imperial constitution and in the church constitution. As a consequence the canon law is a second law alongside the imperial constitution, and both constitutions are under the aegis of a church that claims ecclesiastical monopoly. This corporation in the last resort enforces its multitude of legal regulations by resort to coercion and with the claim to absolute divine authority. The inevitable outcome of "the divine church law" is the doctrine of papal infallibility; and, paradoxically, the papal authority *ex cathedra* can in the name of tradition subvert both Scripture and church tradition. Merely human law assumes the status of divine law. The *Ecclesia* which was ruled by the Spirit and was thus a spiritual entity has become a secularized corporation under canon law and papal autocracy. (In the Enlightenment, Sohm observes, the idea of the corporation persists in Protestantism, albeit under the aegis of freedom. Here again the *Ecclesia* of the Spirit has disappeared in so far as the Church is viewed as a voluntary association created by human consensus or contract.) The whole process of legalization, according to Sohm, is a process of secularization. The Church becomes simply a worldly organization, making a divine claim for its corporation law. In the name of Christ, who delivered the Christian from subservience to law, the Church again subjects men to "divine church law." It loses the authority appropriate and peculiar to the *Ecclesia*. It adopts merely worldly authority, and it proceeds then to give this worldly authority an absolute, divine sanction.

Luther, with his doctrine of the Two Kingdoms and with his doctrine of the invisible Church, set out to liberate the Church from its legalized Babylonish captivity. Returning to the spiritual concept of the earlier *Ecclesia,* he rejected the idolatry and the ecclesiastical monopoly of the "fallen" Church, he cast into the flames the *Corpus Iuris Canonici,* and he assigned temporal power with its law to the State (under God and not under the Church). The Reformation protest was not a legal protest. It was a religious protest toward the end of making the Church the province of the freedom of the Word and of making it again a spiritual entity such as it was at its beginning.

In contrast to the Church ruled by "divine church law," Sohm asserts, the primitive Christian *Ecclesia* was under the direction of the Holy Spirit effective in the Body of Christ. His description of the *Ecclesia* is probably the most familiar aspect of his whole theology of church history. It represents the essential norm against which the process of legalistic secularization has exercised its insidious power. The primitive norm is rooted in the Pauline faith that Christ has delivered the Christian from the law and has brought him into the glorious liberty of "the people of God," the Body of Christ. It is rooted also in Jesus' affirmation, "My kingdom is not of this world." The *Ecclesia* came into being not by law or might but rather out of faith in Christ; it is the outcome of the working of *agape.* As the Body of Christ the *Ecclesia* is one and universal. Every assembly, whether large or small, is a manifestation of the one *Ecclesia,* of the whole of Christendom. This view is supported by the words of Jesus, "Where two or three are gathered together in my name, there am I in the midst of them" (Matt. 18:20). Where the Lord is, the head of the Body, there is Christendom with all the promises made to her. As the Body of Christ the *Ecclesia* is constituted by many members who are called by the Holy Spirit to various tasks. It is organized in terms of the distribution of gifts of grace (*charismata*) which both call and qualify the individual Christians for different activities. It is an organization given by God, not a corporation emerging out of merely human consensus. The decisive bearers of *charismata* are endowed with the gift of teaching the Word—apostles, prophets, teachers; other bearers of *charismata* exhibit other gifts. The activities of the *Ecclesia,* indeed all the fruits of the Spirit, are charismatic in origin. Those leaders endowed with the gift of teaching have the power of the keys: to preach the Word and to apply it spontaneously from case to case. In the course of time the teaching offices become closely related to responsibilities incident to the conduct of the eucharist. In no case do these bearers of spiritual gifts have a right to their offices. They may be replaced as the Spirit moves, though the apostles enjoy a special status. The leaders depend upon the permission of the assembly, upon charismatic free recognition and obedience. The confirmation of leaders is not a "corporate" action of the assembly as if the assembly were sovereign or democratic. It depends upon the witness coming from God. The obedience to the Spirit is given as a response of love, not out of obligation to law. The efficacy of the Spirit is always connected with Word and sacrament. Under the power of the Spirit the *Ecclesia* is obedient to a living, not to a dead, Word. It is thus not bound to the past.

The question arises as to why this pneumatocracy waned in favor of a legal organization. The causes were many, in Sohm's view. Charismatic leaders became less and less available. Heresy, instead of being combated by the living, authentic Word, was fended off through increasing bureaucratization. The conduct of the eucharist, the administration of the Word, baptism, ordination, church property, and church discipline, gave rise to an officialdom. In this process the doctrine of apostolic succession emerged, the division between clergy and laity appeared. Authority passed from the charismatic leader, a *person,* to a monarchic bureaucracy of permanent *offices* less and less dependent upon the confirmation of the members. The offices took over the control of the elements of the eucharist. This constituted the reification or thingification of piety. The decline and the legalization can be traced in this shift from the charisma of *persons* under the Word to the charisma of *offices* in control of *things.* Charisma becomes an object at the disposal of the hierarchy. Sohm does not explicitly describe the decline in this way, but this is the burden of his account of the transformation of charismatic into legal authority.[6]

A description of institutional changes, however, is insufficient to explain the corruption of the primitive charismatic *Ecclesia.* Something spiritual lies back of this corruption which despiritualizes, depersonalizes, and legalizes the *Ecclesia*. This spiritual corruption Sohm calls "small faith."

Mistrust appears, that is, lack of trust in the power of the divine Spirit. Fear raises its head, fear of sin, fear that the power of sin may be greater than that of love. Small faith demands props, crutches, external securities for the conserving of right order in the *Ecclesia*. Small faith longs for legal regulation, formal limits, guarantees for the maintenance of Christendom. Out of this small faith of the Christian epigones, Catholicism came into being. . . . As soon as small faith won the upper hand, as soon as fear of sin became greater than trust in God, legal right followed as a historical necessity. Out of the power of sin, which won room even in Christendom, came the need for church law, and with it came Catholicism.[7]

Sohm is not content to leave the explanation here. He states his position with unsurpassable sharpness. Catholicism—any Christianity dependent on divine church law with respect to doctrine or polity—is precisely an expression of original sin. It is man's pious, "divinely sanctioned" means of escaping from spiritual freedom into the visible security of the Grand Inquisitor, who adds to the "rewards" for piety the gorgeous lushness of worldly success. Why did the *Ecclesia* "fall" into "small faith," into the false faith of Catholicism? Sohm's answer is memorable:

The reason is not far to seek: Because the natural man is a born enemy of Christianity. . . . The natural man desires to remain under law. He strives against the freedom of the gospel. . . . He longs for a legally appointed church, for a kingdom of Christ which may be seen with the eyes of the natural man, for a temple of God, built with earthly gold and precious stones, that shall take the heart captive through outward sanctities, traditional ceremonies, gorgeous vestments, and a ritual that tunes the soul to the right pitch of devotion. . . . Before all, he longs for an impressive, authoritative constitution, one that shall overpower the senses, and rule the world. He desires, as the key-stone of the whole, a fixed body of doctrine that shall give certain intelligence concerning all divine mysteries, presented to him in literal form, giving an answer to every possible question. . . . He desires a rock which his eyes can see—the visible church, the visible Word of God. Everything must be made visible, so that he may grasp it. From these impulses of the natural man, born at once of his longing for the gospel and his despair of attaining it, Catholicism has arisen. Herein lies the secret of the enormous power it has had over the masses who are "babes"; it satisfies these cravings. *The natural man is a born Catholic.*[8]

"The natural man is a born Catholic." He wants an absolutized, visible church to which he may attach himself and from which he may receive guarantees. In short, he is an idolater. The Christian needs something to protect him from the temptations of "small faith" and to maintain his trust in Christ and the Holy Spirit and in a living Word. Actually, the primitive *Ecclesia* by its "fall" has revealed a limitation that may have been inherent in that *Ecclesia*. It left the way open for Christians to put their faith in a tangible absolute.

Here Sohm's conception of the significance of the Lutheran Reformation becomes decisive. According to Sohm, Luther offered a corrective to the primitive *Ecclesia* and also to legalized Christianity by his doctrine of the invisible Church. Faith in a visible church is the "small faith" of the natural man, the natural-born Catholic. Faith in the invisible Church alone protects one from the natural man's idolatry. This conception of Sohm's has elicited such vigorous debate that we should cite here at considerable length the passage in which he sets forth his most radical application of the doctrine of the invisible Church.

The Church in the religious sense—the Church as the people of God on earth —is a matter of faith and "what one believes, that one cannot see"; it cannot be seen with the eye of the natural man. The existence of the people of God (the *Ecclesia*) indicates the existence of a new life, of a superworldly life in the midst of the world, of a life through Christ with and from God. That there is such a life cannot be demonstrated by the reason or comprehended by it. The Church of Christ, therefore, does not exist for the unbeliever. It exists only for him who is himself a partaker of this life. . . . He recognizes it by means of its signs of life (the *notae ecclesiae*), especially by the preaching of the divine Word, to forms of which the Sacraments also belong. The believer perceives and comprehends the communion of saints which supports and nourishes him. He experiences the power which flows out of the people of God, out of the living Word, into his soul and assures him that such a word is the Word of God directed to him. The signs of life of the Church of Christ (*externae notae ecclesiae*) are manifest in the external visible Christianity, the fruits of which are peace, joy, righteousness, and works of Christian love. But it is a fellowship of these things that outwardly appear not by virtue of an external common possession but only as the fellowship of the invisible spiritual life out of which word and work arise. Therefore no one is able to see this fellowship to which word and work belong unless it be a believer. . . .

The Church in the religious sense, the people of God on earth, is, even as far as it possesses the Word and Sacraments not an external corporate fellowship. It can therefore not have an objective, institutional existence founded in any way on the possession of holy things physically perceptible. The Church in the sense of the Lutheran Reformation is not a holy institution, but a holy people (Luther: a holy Christian people which believes indeed in Christ); further, it is not a people to which a certain (although not outwardly recognizable) group of persons belong, but a people whose members are determined by the presence of a spiritual stream of life continually active in it. The people of God, the Church of Christ, exists where the new life through Christ with and of God manifests itself, life of super-earthly strength—today powerful in you, tomorrow in another. The people of God is not in any way an institutionally or personally organized, corporate society. The people of God is invisible. . . .

The Church of Christ is invisible. Therefore there is no visible fellowship which as such might be the Church of Christ. Even in as far as it possesses and administers Word and Sacraments the visible "bodily" Christianity is not the Church of Christ. It possesses Word and Sacrament only outwardly, apparently. Just to the extent that it is the true Word of God that is operative in the visible Christianity, it is an action not of the visible but of the concealed, invisible Christianity. . . . Visible Christianity does not have the Spirit of God, is not the people of God, does not have the Word of God. . . . It is only the Christian World, not the Christian Church. Even in as far as it produces a fellowship of Word and Sacrament, it is only world, and not Church at all. There is no visible Church.

Thus Word and confession of visible Christianity are always only word and confession of the Christian world, never word and confession of the Christian Church (the Church of Christ). The word of the Christian world, as is self-evident, is not religiously binding; it is the fallible word of man, not the infallible word of God. An externally visible confession (word) of the invisible Church of Christ cannot be formulated at all. There is no infallible church.

The Church of Christ is not a confessional church. Had it a visible confession it would not be invisible. Its nature is not that of formulated doctrine but of participation in a spiritual, divine, holy life, which can be associated with the most varied kinds and types of spiritual confession. Therefore, according to the unquestionable Protestant doctrine of faith, the Christian Church (the true Church, the Church in the religious sense) is spread over all confessions. It is super-confessional. . . . The word of the gospel, of the good news of the Kingdom of God in the hearts of men can never be comprehended in the word of men. The Christian faith must always strive for an expression by which it can make intelligible the content of its assurance. There is no Christianity that is not dogmatic. There must always be dogmatics, but never dogmas which with their fixed forms finally assume sway over the nature of Christendom. . . . There is no *one* dogma, nor *one* doctrine, which is the sole means of grace. Protestantism in general does not know a faith in a doctrine of the church, nor a faith in the Scriptures. That would be mere assumption. Faith in the Protestant sense is trust that triumphs over the world and death. We can believe only in a living personality; in Christ and through Christ in God. No doctrine of any kind saves. Faith alone saves. . . . No kind of visible fellowship based on doctrine, but only the invisible fellowship of the Church of Christ can be the fellowship in which alone there is salvation. There is no visible church which is the sole possessor of the power to save.[9]

Sohm's interpretation of the Two Kingdoms has led him to make the earthly kingdom visible and the spiritual one invisible. Although he asserts at times that the invisible Church is always becoming (ambiguously) visible, one may question with many scholars whether his concept of the Church is in accord with Luther's. In any event, Sohm is well aware of the fact that it is not the concept that obtained in the primitive *Ecclesia* itself (though he holds that the idea was implicit in the view that the *Ecclesia* is a stranger on the earth).

Luther's concept of the Church is different from the concept of apostolic Christendom. But in our knowledge of the nature of Christendom we also are not bound by apostolic Christianity. Luther brought forth his church-concept out of the depths of his own life with God, out of the gospel which had not attained to the knowledge of the invisibility of the people of God. Therefore it became Catholic. The discovery of Luther, that the Church is invisible, carried within it the dissolution of Catholicism.[10]

"Out of the depths of his own life with God, out of the gospel" which had been newly experienced by him. These words point to one of the most important things at stake for Sohm in the appeal to the invisible Church (and to charismatic authority): inwardness is the indispensable condition of the working of the Word and the Spirit. In Sohm's view, faith in the invisible Church is a sign not only of the Christian's dependence upon a grace from beyond this world but also of the interiorization of piety.

This emphasis on the inwardness of true piety is succinctly expressed in Luther's assertion that every man must do his own believing. It is made very explicit in the paragraph of his treatise *On Secular Authority* which we cited at the beginning of the present essay: "Temporal government has laws which do not reach farther than over person and property and what is external on the earth; for God will not permit any one to rule over the soul of man but Himself."

In his pursuance of this theme Sohm brings his constructive position to a focus. The motive that runs through his whole protest against "divine church law" is his pathos for inwardness. Ecclesiastical law is the identification of the divine with external, finite machinery. Again and again Sohm asserts in one way or another that "one apprehends the Word of God not in some *form* or other but in its inner power. Christianity has only to follow that Word which by the power of an inner, free assent it *recognizes* as the Word of God." "God is *beyond* all legal ordering. He is not the source or object of any kind of law; he is only the source and goal of the inner life of the individual. The relation to God is no legal relationship, it is never a substantial part of any sort of *external* common life. Indeed, it is a relation of *person to person*—that is the secret of religion. It is this which is expressed in the faith in the love of God and in the righteousness of God springing from love." Sohm goes so far in his emphasis on inwardness as to say that the polity of the Church, a merely secular concern, is a matter of indifference. Thus he appears to view everything ecclesiastical as externality, as institution, as tradition, as "world." The inwardness of the working of the Spirit delivers from all bondage to the finite order and to the past—even from bondage to "apostolic Christianity." It is the absolute opposite of law.

What shall we think of Sohm as a theologian of law and of the Spirit? Any adequate evaluation of the great jurist today, over sixty years after the publication of his first massive volume of *Kirchenrecht,* should take into account a host of writings dealing with Sohm's views pro and con. We can here raise only a few of the important issues. These issues have to do with historical questions, and they have to do with theological questions regarding his treatment of law and the Spirit and of the relations between them.

Despite the extraordinarily vigorous and extensive literature that has appeared on Sohm, the crucial historical questions he has posed (particularly with respect to the primitive *Ecclesia*) remain, as Bultmann has said, unsolved. Harnack's double-organization theory continues to stand over against the Sohman view of the early Church, for there are signs of "constitutional" as well as of charismatic authority almost from the beginning. Bultmann suggests that the difference between Harnack and Sohm issues from the fact that the former is concerned with historical and sociological motifs while the latter is interested in the *Ecclesia*'s self-understanding.

Sohm's work illustrates the opportunities and the perils that attach to historical analysis, particularly when that analysis is conditioned by a theological presupposition which is to be vindicated at all cost. Sohm's Lutheran piety and his Two Kingdom theory have sharpened his scent for data that otherwise might not be taken sufficiently into account. Certainly, Sohm's work represents a turning point, indeed a point of no return, in the development of New Testament scholarship during the past century. Before his time, as Olaf Linton has shown, the consensus of scholarly judgment favored the attempt to understand the Church, in antiquity or today, in terms of corporation or association theory. Since his time that consensus no longer exists. Sohm as a jurist in command of the immense lore regarding associations and as a theologian accepting the dualistic view incident to the Two Kingdom theory spent most of his effort to show, on the one hand, that the primitive Church (and any Christian church) cannot be understood as a corporation based on law, consensus, contract, or voluntary association and, on the other, that the Church must be interpreted in its own terms. His singling out of charismatic authority as a unique and decisive feature of the primitive *Ecclesia* can never properly be gainsaid. By directing attention to the role of charismatic authority Sohm has done much to stimulate in ecclesiological theory the reinstatement of the doctrine of the Holy Spirit. Thus he has shown that a Church that today makes no room for charisma does not stand in continuity with the early *Ecclesia*. Moreover, Sohm's description of the *Ecclesia* as being in principle one and universal, rather than being a congeries of autonomous congregations, is now generally accepted. And with respect to his axiom that "legal regulation contradicts the nature of the Church," we must agree with Bultmann that this view is irrefutable if such regulation is interpreted as constitutive and not merely regulative. In this connection we should observe also that Sohm's periodization of the history of the Church in terms of alternative attitudes toward church law offers a highly instructive perspective.

These insights of Sohm are the valid increment that has issued from his application of the Two-Kingdom theory. Yet, Sohm's search for a norm consistent with this theory probably caused him to give a distorted account of the structure of authority in the primitive *Ecclesia*. His characterization of the *Ecclesia* is unquestionably lopsided. In presenting the evidence for the role of charisma he centered attention on the Pauline churches, and he thereby ignored the predominantly monarchic system of the Jerusalem community and of the congregations of the pastoral Epistles. He failed also to consider the Oriental background of the primitive community's conception of authority. This failure is understandable in the light of the state of research in Sohm's time. The current investigation of the Qumram community promises to reveal much regarding Oriental and Jewish conceptions of "constitutional" authority. Here and also in the primitive *Ecclesia* one finds signs of a complex, organic constitution where "inclinations toward monarchy, oligarchy and democracy were present together, without being mutually exclusive or even in conflict."[11] Apart from these considerations, however, we must observe that Sohm gave no attention to early Christian theological thinking about law. He allowed his own juristic conceptions to dominate his analysis. He even ignored the kerygmatic or charismatic interpretation of law implicit in the judicial procedures of the *Ecclesia* itself, procedures that were sanctioned by St. Paul's admonition that Christians should eschew the civil courts (I Cor. 6:1–11). These procedures, which perhaps initially had more to do with the cure of souls than with legal regulation, subsequently developed into the *episkopalis audientia*.[12] In this connection we should add that Sohm overlooked the role of tradition in general, even of tradition initiated by charismatic authority. Thus he neglected to observe that the principle of hierarchy obtaining within the original *Ecclesia* possibly served as a formal model for the later, "legalized" Catholic hierarchy.

When we evaluate Sohm's work as a theologian of law and Spirit we must adopt an equally ambiguous judgment. It is understandable and justifiable if in face of an absolute "divine church law" he assumed that the alternative for the Christian Church is *aut papa—aut nihil*. But not so much can be said for his view of church law that is merely regulative. Here he adopted a *laissez-faire* attitude, so long as charisma could find a place. Sohm's attitude, as well as his lack of concern for New Testament conceptions of law, was conditioned by a nineteenth-century conservative, positivist, formal conception of law—scarcely a Christian interpretation of law. As a consequence, he overstressed the static, abstract character of law and the bondage of law to the past. Indeed, he seems to have been willing to leave regulative law, including church polity, undisturbed if it made no absolute claims. But we must ask, If the Word can be alive, why not also law? Here Karl Barth's view is particularly pertinent and cogent. With considerable persuasiveness (and probably following Bohatec's interpretation of Calvin) Barth rejects Brunner's support of Sohm's antilegalism, by demanding law in the Church, *living* law, if the Church is to be faithful to its mission in the changing historical situation. Actually, Sohm's interpretation of the Two-Kingdom theory led him to an acute dualism. Thus he was able to see no direct connection between law and Spirit, even between law and love. And he was able to see nothing of inwardness in law. Law is external, Spirit is sheer inwardness, love is appropriate only in immediate person-to-person relations. Not that law offers nothing to inwardness: it promotes external freedom for the sake of internal freedom. But law and love, justice and love, in Sohm's view, must be kept in separate spheres.

Accordingly, in an address delivered in 1895 at the Twenty-eighth Congress of the Inner Mission, Sohm warned emphatically against any mixing up of the Christian work of love with the social question in any consideration of the theme "Christian-Social." "The social question," he said, "is *only* a question of justice, no question of love." If the Christian is to concern himself with justice, he should leave the Church out of it and proceed to fulfill his worldly vocation or to work as a citizen in a worldly voluntary association. Indeed, Sohm in these ways devoted himself to the extension of suffrage and to the elevation of the working classes against the complacent dominance enjoyed by the bourgeoisie; he had a theory of periodization regarding the history of the social classes—from the medieval aristocracy to the modern bourgeoisie to the contemporary emergence of the worker in his search for dignity and rights. But, in Sohm's view, one should not expect the Christian faith or the Christian Church to suggest a direction in the search for justice: "the social classes do not demand or crave for love, they crave for their right."

Considering Sohm's lament over the invasion of law into the Church, one would expect him to desiderate the separation of church and state. But so far from being sympathetic with the left wing of the Reformation and with the Nonconformist tradition, he is very critical of any movement that "weakens the power and meaning of church organization." He takes a dim view even of Pietism's formation of *ecclesiolae in ecclesia*. The Church as a legal entity within the community requires "as an equal" the support of the State. "The separation of church and state would mean the disappearance of the Church from the law!" On the other hand, the Church "in the religious sense," as we have seen, stands so high over the earthly reality that it no longer touches the earth. So does Sohm interpret the Two-Kingdom theory. It should be added, however, that in his view the Church in both the religious and the legal sense must not be subjected to coercion; this view he derives from the Two-Kingdom theory of the separation of powers. In this connection he has nothing but praise for Liberalism for its resistance to coercion in religion.

If we turn now to consider Sohm's conception of Spirit we find again the dualism we have noted in other aspects of his outlook. Charisma works only spontaneously, from case to case. He sees no connection between charisma and Logos. Thus he gives no attention to ways in which the charisma relates itself to the analysis of the empirical reality in face of which it will offer love. Nor is there any suggestion that any sort of casuistry is required. In the dimension of Spirit he seems to prefer a purely dispositional ethic, and he gives no indication as to how response to the Spirit involves responsibility for the consequence of action or inaction. Moreover, he fails to consider how Spirit effects consensus among Christians. Some sort of automatic predetermined harmony is relied upon for the Church "in the religious sense." This harmony presumably ensues if faith does not allow itself to be yoked to contingent actualities.

It is at this point, however, that Sohm's conception of the invisible Church achieves genuine positive significance. The Christian's faith in and loyalty to the invisible Church, as we have seen, protects the Christian from idolatry and also from *bondage* to the past. The Christian *Ecclesia* is not to be identified with the worldly ecclesiastical institution, for that is only the Christian "world," not the Christian Church. "Visible Christianity," he says, "does not possess the Spirit of God, it is not the people of God, it does not possess the Word of God." Therefore, it is to be properly understood only in its relation to the critical and creative energies of the invisible Church. Here Sohm approaches the articulation of what Paul Tillich calls "the Protestant principle." He would readily accept Tillich's statement that "although the Church represents the Kingdom of God in history, it is not the Kingdom of God. It can be perverted into a representation of the demonic Kingdom." But in face of Sohm's dualism of visible-invisible, Tillich, insisting that "there is not a visible and an invisible church as two 'churches,' " would deplore Sohm's docetic derogation of the empirical Church over against the spiritual Church. In this respect Tillich comes nearer than Sohm to Luther's conception of the visible-invisible Church. Sohm's dualism, supported by his pathos for inwardness (a kind of *hybris*) led him astray.

For his part, Sohm so much derogates the "worldly," visible Church that he says its organization is a matter of indifference. In his view, no polity can guarantee the working of the Spirit which gives birth to love among the brethren; no polity may be accepted as a norm. To absolutize a norm for the organization of the Church would constitute the reversion from Spirit to law. The sense of the dualism between the visible and the invisible Church, however, prevents Sohm from indicating whether (apart from an absolutistic church) there is any polity that is more or less receptive to the promptings of the Spirit than another. Nor does he show how the invisible Church operates in order to make an impact upon the organization of the visible Church. There is "no line of connection" from the spiritual Church to polity. To find such a line, according to Sohm, is "un-Lutheran."

Sohm's view is that within any polity, except one in which "divine church law" prevails, room can be made for charismatic authority. But if this room is to be found, he insists, we must be able to respond to the Power that is able to exorcise our demonic attachment to the false faiths of ecclesiasticism and of "culture." "One thing is certain," he says. "It is not our culture that will save us, but the gospel alone." In this faith Rudolf Sohm undertook his entire lifework. The question remains, however, as to whether he was able to achieve an adequate understanding of the relationship between (what Tillich has called) the vertical and the horizontal dimensions of Christian faith. The present volume is dedicated to a man whose understanding of these realities is more adequate because it presupposes a more critical and creative relationship between the Two Kingdoms.

17

Preaching: Genuine and Secularized*

BY RUDOLF BULTMANN

What do we mean by *preaching?* Obviously, preaching is not the simple communication of facts. The reporting of a discovery made by scientific or historical research is not preaching. Likewise, preaching must be distinguished from teaching or instruction: the presentation of mathematical or philosophical subjects, for example, is not preaching. Why not? Because preaching means a declaration which speaks directly to the hearer and challenges him to a specific reaction. *Indirectly,* of course, the communication of facts can be preaching. If, for example, I hear a historian speak on the historical concept and European politics of nazism I immediately perceive in it an appeal, a challenge to serious political reflection. Philosophical instruction as well can indirectly take on the character of preaching. When it clarifies the essence of human existence and the meaning of conscience and decision it can lead the reader or auditor to reflect about himself, and bring him to the burning question of the genuineness of his existence; thus it functions as an appeal. I do not hesitate to call this sort of communication or reflection true preaching. But when I am asked about the *difference between genuine and secularized preaching,* the obvious presupposition is that genuine preaching is religious, or specifically Christian, preaching. It is only of such preaching that we can say that it becomes secularized. The appeal of a communication or teaching can indeed be secular, but not secular*ized.*

In what, then, does the character of religious, and particularly of Christian, preaching consist? It goes without saying that it is direct address, a calling. Thus in the New Testament it is often called *kerygma,* the heralding, or *evangelion,* the message. The call which rings out and is heard in it is the *call of God.*

For many people today, *art* is such preaching, be it poetry or the plastic arts. But is anything expressed in art but man himself, in his rich and

* Translated by Harold O. J. Brown.

abysmal possibilities? Does it not bring to the hearer or viewer an awareness of his own possibilities, now joyful, now horrifying? It is admittedly possible for art to become indirect preaching, when it lays bare human existence in its depths, bringing to light the problematical nature of man and his limitations. But is it therefore God speaking, or only man, probing to the ground of his being, speaking to himself?

How, then, does God speak to man?

The Old Testament knows God's call ringing in nature: "The heavens declare the glory of God; and the firmament sheweth his handy work" (Ps. 19:1). This preaching forces man to marvel, to fear and stand in reverence, so that he becomes aware of his smallness in the face of the might of God displayed in nature. But this preaching is not an appeal which draws one to reflection. It is secularization when God's call in nature is understood as the order and purposiveness of natural events, from which one would draw the conclusion of the wisdom of God. Seen thus, nature really proclaims nothing to us, for the wisdom thus perceived is but the wisdom of man, not of the Creator.

According to the Bible, however, God's heralds are above all *men,* in the Old Testament the prophets, in the New Testament Jesus of Nazareth and the Apostles. What they preach is not their own thoughts and judgments, but the call of God, which they must proclaim, whether they will or not. "The lion hath roared, who will not fear? the Lord God hath spoken, who can but prophesy?" (Amos 3:8). The words of such messengers are words with *authority,* with an authority such as human speech otherwise does not have. The herald does not speak on his own authority and claims no status for himself; as Paul says, "For we preach not ourselves, but Christ Jesus the Lord" (II Cor. 4:5). This preaching cannot be discussed; it is the simple challenge to faith.

True Christian preaching is therefore a proclamation which claims to be the call of God through the mouth of man and, as the word of authority, demands belief. It is its characteristic paradox that in it we meet *God's* call in *human* words. This paradox is most clearly expressed in the Gospel of St. John. Here, outlined in all clarity, is the stroke in which Jesus, a man, claims to speak the Word of God as the Revealer. The words which he speaks are God's words; he is not speaking from himself alone. The prologue of the Gospel expresses the paradox in the sentence, "The Word became flesh." And this paradox is also valid for the Church's preaching. "He that hearth you heareth me; and he that despiseth you despiseth me" (Luke 10:16), Jesus says in St. Luke's Gospel. In this sense, St. Paul says that God, in that through Christ He has reconciled the world to Himself, concomitantly instituted the "service," the "word" of reconciliation, and thus Paul can say, "Now then we are ambassadors for Christ, as though God did beseech you by us" (II Cor. 5:20). The preaching of the Church has its meaning as the Word of God, for the preacher does not present his own opinion, and does not admonish and console of himself, but rather transmits the Word of God as the authoritative Word.

With all this we have simply characterized preaching according to its *form,* but this formal description is of decisive importance as it gives the standard by which genuine preaching is to be judged. In particular, it says: (1) That Christian preaching is not the *propagation of a philosophy,* that it does not pronounce general truths, concerning the reasons for which one can speculate, which one can discuss. It is authoritative direct address, transmitted through men and demanding faith. Everything depends upon the Church's awareness of this in its preaching, that it may really strike the hearer as direct address in his concrete situation, so that he knows himself questioned, challenged, comforted, so that he cannot draw back. (2) This means that *preaching must not be confused with teaching.* This is not to say that a sermon cannot instruct and stimulate the thinking of the hearers; indeed it should and, with all the boring sermons one is constrained to hear, it is to be hoped that some will be more interesting. But all that is instructive and interesting in the sermon is justified only when the sermon points up the questions which are inherent in this or that area of life, and what answers they receive in the light of the Word of God.

Preaching is secularized also when it is *ethical instruction,* because this can be found outside of the faith and can be had from pagans like Socrates. If we look at the content of the moral imperatives, there is no specifically Christian ethics; and if one would characterize, say, the commandment of love as a specifically Christian commandment one should remember that St. Paul said that all the commandments of the Law were comprehended in the commandment of love (Rom. 13:9). These commandments, however, can be known to every man before he has heard the Christian message. Every man has a conscience, and can know what is good and what is evil. True Christian preaching does not have special demands to make with respect to ethics, but it should make two things clear:

The first is the question which each man must ask himself, how his actual conduct corresponds to those well-known demands. And if he then admits—as is to be expected—that he is not perfect, but rather that he errs often and ever again, it has to guide him, so that he will not comfort himself with simply looking at his shortcomings as a "not-quite-yet" and getting along with his efforts to surpass this (as surely as such efforts are demanded), but will rather ask himself for the deepest reason for this continual "not-quite-yet." Thus he may become aware that he lacks the strength to master the evil that is in him, to become free of himself, the "old man," and can only say with the publican, "God be merciful to me a sinner" (Luke 18:13). True preaching must show man that he is in need of forgiveness, and its paradox is revealed when it, as human speech, speaks God's forgiveness.

Preaching is secularized when the liberation which it imparts to man in God's forgiveness is made into the business of the psychotherapist, who intends with his methods the liberation of man from what he has become through his past. God's forgiveness is then no longer necessary. The analyst has replaced the confessor. And yet it is clear from the fact that so many men take refuge in the analyst that they are dependent upon authority and long for it; it is, above all, clear from the fact that the patient so often becomes "tied" to his analyst.

The second thing that true preaching has to say in the matter of ethics deals with the *commandment of love*. It has to show that a man can fulfill this commandment only when he has been freed from himself for pure devotion to others. Freedom is not a natural attribute of man, but is an occasional event, and it occurs only when man is freed from himself by the word of forgiveness and so becomes open for the demanding question which he encounters in his neighbor.

Just as Christian preaching can hardly be equated with ethical instruction or therapeutic treatment, *neither is it doctrinal instruction*. Doctrinal instruction is not direct address; it is not an authoritative Word demanding faith. This seems to be the case only when one attaches to the instruction the demand that what is said must be believed. It is true that the content of preaching may also be formulated in dogmatic language. For example, the fact that preaching says to man that he needs God's forgiveness can be brought to expression in the doctrine of original sin. But the believing acceptance of such preaching is expressed only in the confession "God be merciful to me a sinner" and not in agreeing with any doctrine of original sin.

In truth, strange as it may sound, preaching is secularized when the sermon or instruction presents doctrinal statements which are to be believed. Doctrinal statements have the character of general truths, which one can hold to be true. But holding something to be true is not believing it. Luther knew this when, in explaining his second article of faith, he subordinated all dogmatic statements to one sentence, "I believe that Jesus

Christ . . . is my Lord," or when, in his lecture on Romans, he said, "Believing in Christ means being directed towards him with all your heart, and orienting everything according to him." Believing in Christ does not mean holding high ideas about his person to be true, but believing in the Word, in which he speaks to us, through which he wants to become our Lord.

In talking about Christ we have imperceptibly passed from the formal characteristics of Christian preaching to its *content*. Of what does this consist? In the Christmas story the angel's message resounds: "Behold, I bring you good tidings of great joy, which shall be to all people. For unto you is born this day . . . a Saviour" (Luke 2:10 f.). Correspondingly, the Epistle to Titus reads, "For the grace of God that bringeth salvation hath appeared to all men" (Tit. 2:11). The content of the message is thus an event, a historical fact: the appearance of Jesus of Nazareth, his birth, but at the same time his work, his death and his resurrection. Paul can also say that the content of his preaching is Christ's Cross, or he can say, "That if thou shalt confess with thy mouth the Lord Jesus, and shalt believe in thine heart that God hath raised him from the dead, thou shalt be saved (Rom. 10:9).

Does this mean that true Christian preaching would be the *communication of a historical fact?* Yes and no! It is the communication of a historical fact which is at the same time more than a historical fact, so that its communication is something more than mere communication.

When the angelic message calls Jesus' birth that of the Saviour, and when the Epistle to Titus calls his appearance that of the grace of God to all men for salvation, we are using the language which we characterize as that of eschatology. Eschatology deals with the "last things," with the end of this world and the dawn of a new world. The angel's message and the words of Titus answer man's question and longing: "When will the salvation of the world come? When will the great day dawn, when the Light will shine forth to dispel all the darkness of earthly life?" This, then, is the content of preaching: the appearance of Jesus is the end of the old world and the dawn of the new. Thus St. Paul understood it when he said, "But when the fulness of the time was come, God sent forth his Son" (Gal. 4:4). Therefore he can address his readers, "Behold, now is the accepted time; behold, now is the day of salvation" (II Cor. 6:2). And therefore St. John's Gospel has Jesus say, "He that heareth my word, and believeth on him that sent me, hath everlasting life, and shall not come into condemnation; but is passed from death unto life" (John 5:24).

Jesus' appearance is thus seen not as within history but as the *end of history.* But the paradox of preaching is this, that the event which puts an end to history has occurred within history. The communication of this event is consequently something different from the usual communication of historical events, and is correctly understood only when it is understood as the call to see in this appearance the end of the world. But in what sense?

Earliest Christianity did not become aware of this paradox; according to its opinion, the end of the world was imminent. But what can we say today, as the world continues to exist and history continues to run on?

Now, according to the New Testament at least, Christian preaching says that Jesus' appearance was not an event in the world but means the end of the world. Accordingly, preaching is secularized wherever Jesus is understood as an appearance in history, as a phenomenon of intellectual history, as a hero and model of piety, as the bearer of a new, pure ethics, wherever there is talk of the beneficial influences which emanate from him, no matter how high the words.

But how can genuine preaching today preach this paradox? In no wise by giving a story of Jesus' life and deeds, for this would be dissolving itself into a historical report. Genuine preaching preaches him as the end of the world, when it *preaches him as Lord.* "Jesus Christ is Lord," is the oldest Christian confession. What does it mean? It means this: *to let that same paradox rule one's own life* and, living in this world, to be raised above it, to have already loosed oneself from it. It means not basing one's life on what is temporary, on the world that can be understood in its laws, utilized and ruled. It means to see in the purposes of worldly activity no ultimate purposes, in the meaning of worldly work no ultimate meaning. It means, as long as we are in the world, to withdraw from the world into that attitude which Paul characterizes as the attitude of *as though they did not:* "And they that weep, as though they wept not; and they that rejoice, as though they rejoiced not . . ." (I Cor. 7:30). It therefore also means to let want and suffering bring a man not to despair but rather into that dimension which lets him repeat after Paul, "For when I am weak, then am I strong" (II Cor. 12:10), because he hears the Lord say to him, "My grace is sufficient for thee: for my strength is made perfect in weakness" (II Cor. 12:9). Finally, it means to learn to understand the lordship of the Lord as the gift of freedom, in which man becomes free of himself and is a new man.

To accept Jesus as Lord in this sense means to *believe.* To believe means at once to trust and to obey. But it does not mean to accept some particular doctrines about Christ. True enough, the early Church has expressed all that Christ means in doctrinal formulas, and these teachings have perpetuated themselves in ecclesiastical tradition. As the symbolic expression of what

Christ is for us, may they continue to be pronounced. When it happens, however, that they are laid down for men as laws of faith they are abused, and in the place of true confession there is the acceptance of doctrines.

True preaching is that which preaches Jesus Christ as Lord, whatever its words and ideas. Thus it is crucial that he be present as Lord in the preached word itself, and that where this word resounds the end of the world be present to the auditor, in that it places before him the decision, whether he will belong to the old or to the new world, whether he will remain the old man or become a new man.

Where does this word resound? The Christian Church would let it resound in every divine service. Nevertheless, it would be false to think that only the official minister can be the proper preacher. At one point in his commentary on the Epistle to the Romans, in criticizing false dogmatic faith, Luther says that the heretics indeed confess and boast that they believe in Christ

according to that which the Gospels tell of Him, that He was born, suffered, and died. But they do not believe in that which characteristically belongs to Him. And what is it? The Church, that is, every word from the mouth of a preacher of the Church or of a good and holy man, is a word of Christ, Who said, "Who hears you, hears Me." It is necessary to believe in Christ, whereever and through whomever He may speak. Therefore, one must be earnestly concerned, that we be not stubborn in our own fashion, that we not resist Christ and be unbelieving, of Whom we do not know when, where, how and through whom He speaks to us. And it almost always happens here and there, in some manner and through someone, where and as we do not suspect it.

Yes, one may finally ask whether preaching can always be only in the spoken word, whether it cannot also occur *through silent action*. Certainly a deed, too, can have the nature of an address. But we are concerned with a deed which can be effective as Christian preaching, that is, not with any effects of the Christian religion in Western civilization but with the proof of Christian love of man for man. The act of love opens to him who receives it the way to become free from himself, as he is drawn into the kingdom of the rule of love and is guided to accept with it the human, spoken word of preaching as the Word of God.

Religion, Power, and Christian Faith

BY PAUL L. LEHMANN

I. POWER AND RELIGION

The religious character of power may be understood from a comparison between the primitive and the contemporary world as regards the phenomenon of power. It is, of course, difficult to say when the primitive world left itself behind. But, for purposes of this comparison, the primitive world is the stage of man's relation to nature and society at which man's thoughts are associational rather than analytical, mythological rather than metaphysical; and at which social stability and the controls over nature are haphazard and rudimentary. The contemporary world stands at the other pole of social and historical development. Man's relations with nature have been brought under the refined and predictable control of technical science and there are philosophical and political traditions by which social relations can be interpreted and guided.

However, despite the immense contrast in culture and civilization between the primitive and the contemporary world, there are remarkable similarities in relation to power. Both worlds may be said to be dominated by power. In both power is at once obvious and elusive, and the hopes and fears, the lives and destinies of men are shaped by nothing so much as by power. In the primitive, as well as in the contemporary world, power is most concretely and vividly experienced as the impact of nature upon man. Indeed, the problematic character of power arises primarily with reference to the indeterminate and capricious processes and possibilities of the natural as distinct from the human order. Power is a problem because its operation is more menacing than benevolent, and thus threatens human existence with meaninglessness and extinction. Both in the primitive and in the contemporary world, the dominating and the problematic character of power either tempts men to futility in the face of power or gives impetus and urgency to the quest for the understanding and the control of power.

But neither the primitive nor the contemporary world has a clear view of the nature of power or of the possibilities of its control.

These basic similarities between power in the primitive and the contemporary world are accompanied by notable differences. One difference is that in the primitive world power was regarded as initiated by personal intention, whereas the contemporary understanding of the operation of power is technical. This difference, in turn, leads to a different estimate of the nature of power and of the possibilities of its control. The primitive world looked behind the operation of power and responded to a world of volitional mystery as the key to the meaning and control of power. The operation of power was the work of "powers" upon whose behavior and favor men depended for existence and significance. The operation of power was so complex as to deprive the primitive world of an adequately unitary interpretation of the powers which controlled it. At best, the primitive world achieved a limited pluralism, the sublimest expression of which is the pantheon. Although the pantheon emerges from the kind of reflective analysis and social stability which make for culture and civilization, it symbolizes nevertheless the maturest wisdom of the primitive world about power. This wisdom declares that power is a religious phenomenon. Power is a religious phenomenon because it defines the transcendental foundation of the world. Transcendence is the dimension of reality and meaning from which the world and human existence are derived, and with reference to which they can be understood. Since power, more than any other single aspect of the scheme of things, is all-pervasive and unsettling, it also articulates the dependent character of all existence. The correlation of transcendence and dependence in the apprehension and experience of power gives to power its religious character. It inspires the search for the meaning of power in terms of deity and occasions experiments in ritualistic control. The cults of the gods are the recognition and response of the primitive world to the religious phenomenon of power.

The contemporary understanding of power is technical. Technics are a precisely refined compound of reason and instrumentality at which man has arrived in the course of his attempt to comprehend and to control the impact and the processes of nature. Nature is the necessity which is the mother of invention; and the most brilliant invention of all is the scientific method by which the caprices of nature are brought under the predictable stabilities of law. At first, the accent fell upon phenomenological investigation and interpretation. But when the premises and the promises of this search achieved instrumental organization and expression in the machine, the focus of attention shifted to the problem of control. Technics are science with the accent upon control; and technics express the maturest wisdom of the contemporary world about power. This wisdom declares that power is not a religious but a natural phenomenon. It is not necessary to look *behind* the operation of power for a dimension of meaning in terms of which to direct the control of power. It is necessary instead to look *into* the operation of power in order to discover there the processes at work. The reward of this inquiry is the knowledge that is the key to the skills and the organization by which power can be controlled. Power is not transcendent but immanent; it defines the possibilities of meaning and achievement inherent in the infinite dynamic of the world. Power is no less all-pervasive and unsettling. But far from articulating the dependent character of all existence, the disturbing omnipresence of power is a stimulus to fearless and enlightened ingenuity. This correlation of immanence and ingenuity in the apprehension and experience of power gives to power its scientific and technical character. The mastery of power is a matter not of ritual but of training. It is not the pantheon but the laboratory and the factory which express and symbolize the response of the contemporary world to power.

Certainly these contrasts accrued to the advantage of the contemporary world and seemed to overshadow any kinship between it and its primeval past. And then, in May, 1945, nuclear fission—the sublimest fruit of the laboratory and the factory—went awry. At Hiroshima, power stood exposed in terrifying nakedness. Once again, as often in those distant and forgotten centuries, men were overwhelmed by the menacing combination of intensity and intention in the operation of power. Although not for long, even the gods were called into play. The untutored were confident that scientific pride had at last overstepped its boundaries, and that upon its lofty head fire had quite properly been cast down from heaven. Those among the tutored who were, so to say, "in the know," not only shrank from recommending the awful uses to which their knowledge had been and could be put, but took up the belated task of repairing the moral framework without which power would deprive men both of existence and of meaning.

At the college where I was teaching at that time, an attempt was made to loosen the paralysis of suspense and uncertainty with which students had returned for the opening of the term after Hiroshima. A panel of the faculty was asked to discuss with the students the question of "Culture and Religion in an Atomic World." I was asked to join with a colleague from the Department of Physics, and one from the Department of History, and to state the case for religion. A crowded and protracted session left one paramount impression. It was that the contemporary world had turned a corner after which there was no turning back. The operation of power and the knowledge upon which it was based had shattered rather than fulfilled the dreams which that power had inspired. It was then that I became vividly aware of how thin is the line that separates sophistication from superstition. This generation of college students, along with the world which had replaced superstition by sophistication, had been brought back by a naked exposure of power to the reactions and questions of its distant forebears. It was as though the bomb that fell on Hiroshima had torn the scales from its eyes and a long-forgotten dimension of reality had been suddenly apprehended as too clearly inescapable and too dimly understood. Fear and anxiety lent critical urgency to the questions of the meaning and the purpose of existence. One felt an unspoken and impatient longing for some sign of deliverance to be supplied by religion. This could be the one alternative to futility.

It was, of course, not possible to take up again the transcendental pluralism of ancient polytheism. On the other hand, the immanental pluralism of a culture whose recipe for living included assorted varieties of humanism, positivism, mysticism, and political and economic anarchy, suddenly seemed obsolete. Yet from the parallel which we have tried to sketch a constructive possibility does emerge. There is a fundamental connection between power and religion which is basic to the proper understanding of each and to the prospect of the meaningful operation of power in the world.

The connection between power and religion arises from the relation of each to reality. Reality is experienced as at once dynamic and binding. The dynamism of reality is the relentless intensity of change in the relations of nature and society and in the efforts of man to find himself at home in both. The binding character of reality is the relentless persistence of intention, of pattern and direction, of order and meaning, in, with, and under the intensity of change.

Now, it is with this being bound by intention, by pattern and direction, by order and meaning, with this factor of limitation in human existence that religion is intrinsically concerned. As Professor Tillich has put it, religion is "ultimate concern," "unconditional seriousness," about the meaning of life. "This unconditional seriousness is the expression of the divine in the experience of utter separation from it."[1] Religion, as the stem of the word suggests, is man's recognition of the fact that he is bound, and his response to this fact. Primitive religion did, of course, accent the capriciousness and arbitrariness of the limits within which man's existence was set. The result was that under the impact of the intensity of change, the world of meaning and control became a splintered field of multiple and willful intention. But the basic orientation of primitive religion was sound. It is the boundedness of reality, its essential connectivity, which raises the question of the purposefulness of change and suggests a possibility of meaning and control from the other side of the boundary.

Power, on the other hand, is concerned with the dynamics of change. The complex of relations in nature and society in which man finds himself is characterized by variation under pressure. Man takes his time about exploring the world in which he lives. But the march of events is always ahead of him, and reminding him that it is later than he thinks. Under the drive and the tempo of this mobility, it becomes imperative to know how things happen as they do and how they can be effectively controlled. What the primitive world did not grasp was that the dynamics of change is a question of energy, not of divinities. Consequently, it did not see that the organization of energy is a matter of technics, not ritual. The insight into power as technically organized energy is the sound achievement of the contemporary world.

The technical organization of energy, however, does not exhaust the dynamism of reality. If it did, there would be no problem of power. More accurately, if the technical organization of energy exhausted the dynamism of reality, the problem of power would be a matter of mathematics rather than of the meaning of human existence. If the problem of power were a matter of mathematics, the destruction of Hiroshima would not have shaken the foundations of our culture, so confidently laid by the laboratory and the factory. The point is that the effective control of energy is more than a matter of technical organization. It involves the question of the purposes for which and the authority by which the control of energy is exercised and achieved. There is a will-to-power, as well as a knowledge of power; and the effective organization of power includes both. This is why the problem of power is basically and ultimately a problem of the meaning of human existence.

The problem of meaning is the link between power and religion. The resistance of our culture to this fact, as well as the tenacity of our technical illusions, is nicely indicated by the current addiction to semantics. Semantics regards the problem of meaning as essentially a problem of communication. If people would but learn to think and talk in such a way that the words which they used were precisely and dependably labeled with the intended meaning, human relations might be expected to take on the dynamic integration characteristic of process and reality. The techniques are at hand. What is called for is the discovery and arrangement of the "powers" of language with an analogous precision and procedure to that already applied to the "powers" of numbers.

It is not strange that semantics should have moved beyond its proper boundaries and for many intellectuals in our day have taken on the proportions of a cult. This pseudo religion indeed emphasizes the connection between power and religion. But the problem of meaning arises at a much deeper level than that of communication.[2] The problem of meaning arises, for an individual as well as for a culture, whenever the organized energies and the insistent purposes of existence fail to correspond. The control of energy sooner or later requires validation and direction in terms of the insistent purposes of life; the insistent purposes of existence sooner or later require implementation through the organized energies of existence. Power that cannot be bounded by purpose threatens existence with meaninglessness and annihilation; purposes that fail of integration with the organized energies of existence lose persuasiveness and point. Religion that ignores power degenerates into pious illusion and ceremonial triviality; power that ignores religion devours itself. On the boundary of the problem of meaning, the capricious and immanentist views of life break down. The key to the problem of meaning is the problem of power because in the phenomenon of power the dynamic and intentional experience of reality comes to concrete and decisive focus. Power is a problem because the energies by which things happen in the world do not carry their own authority, and the authority by which the energies of the world are organized and controlled is not self-vindicating. It is the office of religion to resolve the problem of meaning by integrating the organization and the exercise of power with the fulfilling purposes of life.

II. RELIGION AS POWER AND POWER AS RELIGION

The religio-technical phenomenon of power may now be defined. *POWER is the energy and authority by which whatever happens in the world occurs.* As energy is the principle of relatedness and change in what occurs, authority is the principle of legitimacy, of validation, in what occurs. Before suggesting how religion resolves the problem of power, it is necessary to admit and to dispose of the ways in which religion has aggravated the problem of power. Religion has corrupted power in two main ways. On the one hand, religion has coveted power for the sake of preserving and furthering the ideas and institutions of religion. On the other hand, religion has made possible the worst forms of the pursuit of power for the sake of power. In the first case, religion departs from its true office in relation to power and claims to be power itself. In the second case, power usurps the true office of religion in relation to power and claims to be supreme.

Religion often has and still does masquerade as power. This is possible because religion is a genuine source of motivation and meaning in the attempt of man to organize his life in the world. This source of motivation and meaning in religion is revelation. But ever and again religion works itself out in ideas and practices which are identified with revelation itself. Religion achieves in this way a power over men, a hold upon the energies and authorities of life, quite at variance with its authentic function in the world.

Voltaire was not the first to suggest that religion was a hoax because it was the invention of priests in order to perpetuate their own power. This point had been made as early as the sixth century before Christ from within Hinduism by those who were outraged in reason and in conscience by the pretensions and the behavior of the religious. As an account of the origin of religion, this view is a polemical error, true to a tendency in all polemics to "throw out the baby with the bath." Nevertheless, the objection does underline a fatal tendency in all religion to stifle the critical vitality of the relation of men and the world to deity by sanctifying what is not sacred. This is as true of religion at the reflective level of doctrine as at the unreflective level of rite.

It is, of course, difficult to hold the line between religion as the source of motivation and meaning in life and the deification of the energies and the authorities by which whatever happens in the world is organized and controlled. The personification of the processes of nature which plays a major role in early religion so closely intermingles the objective and the subjective factors in religion that the gods seem to be mere projections of man's responses to an uncertain and perilous world. A more careful examination discloses, however, that what really is involved here is the intimate relation between the dynamic and the divine aspects of power. The awesome power of the energies of nature, including the physiology and psychology of man himself, is at once overwhelming and essential to the continuity and the meaning of existence. Blood, for instance, is one of the most notable cases in point. Blood is the sacred secret of superhuman strength because through the blood the power of the gods passes imperceptibly into the man who drinks it. There are other beverages which, *mutatis mutandis,* have the same office. The ninth book of the Rig-Vedas celebrates the god Soma. Soma appears originally to have been a drink immemorially associated with the gods. It is not only the drink by which the gods are moved to grant the requests of their worshipers but also the drink whereby the gods gain strength and courage themselves. Soma, writes George Foot Moore, "is itself a divine power. . . . The belief in its efficacy with the gods passes easily into the notion of power over the other gods."[3] Soma is a drink. Soma is a god. The interchangeability is due to the mystery and the efficacy of power. This power is at once the energy and the authority by which the man who has it is elevated above his fellows and above the processes of nature. Thus religion is sacred energy and the race is on for its possession and control. The deification which obliterates the line between the divine and the natural and human aspects of this energy also blurs the difference between the gifted and the unscrupulous in the possession and distribution of this energy. Hence the immense peril of all mediation in religion. It is difficult to keep mediation from becoming a monopoly. And let it be said quite bluntly that the monopolists of mediation are the priests. The power of the priesthood is the power of sacred energy. And even when the exercise of this power is circumscribed by the independent and purposive character of revelation, the monopoly is hard to break.

The best proof of this is supplied by the history of Christianity. Contrary to its analysis of power, Christianity has its own distortions of power by religion. The two most influential instances are Roman Catholicism and theocratic Calvinism. Roman Catholicism is a particularly virulent form of sacerdotalism. By a curious paradox, Calvinism has inspired both democratic and theocratic forms of power, which in the latter instance have made for a particularly virulent kind of political and economic royalism.

The aggressive power politics of Romanism has been an open secret for centuries. It seeks to bring all forms of public life under allegiance to and censorship of the Roman Church. What is not generally understood, however, is that this religious distortion of power has a foundation and logic of its own. It is the foundation and logic of sacerdotalism. The foundation of sacerdotalism is the conception and the transmission of power as sacred energy. And the logic of sacerdotalism is that the sacredness of this energy, and consequently its effectiveness, can be guaranteed only by a sacramentally ordered institution, functioning by means of a priestly succession, and culminating in an infallible sovereign over thought and behavior. The doctrines of grace, of papal infallibility, and of temporal power are inseparable in principle, however variously and cautiously they may be applied. It was the monopoly of this sacred energy which made kings and peoples in other days tremble under the bans of excommunication and the interdict. It is the monopoly of this sacred energy which still gives to those who are distraught in mind or in emotion, whether sophisticated or superstitious, the safety and the serenity they require. It is the monopoly of this sacred energy which deprives religion of its critical relation to power. Religion is no longer the source of motivation and meaning in the attempt of man to organize his life in the world. Instead, religion is the deification of a particular pattern and structure of the exercise of power. The pattern and structure of power are deified because they are effectively removed beyond the possibility of ultimate criticism and must ultimately be reverentially acknowledged and adored.

Theocratic Calvinism is an attempt to solve the problem of power on some other foundation than that of sacerdotalism, namely the divinely ordained power of the magistracy. This distortion of the relation of religion to power was a possibility for Calvinism because of the pivotal position in Calvin's thought of the doctrine of election. Calvin's view was that everything that happens in the world is the working out of the divine will, operating to achieve the purposes of God. This meant that the energies of nature and the sovereignties of history were ordered by divine providence and that the responsibilities and the fulfillment of individual life were ordered by divine predestination. Although the behavior of Calvinists often suggested as much, it is an error to regard the working out of the doctrine of election in providence and in predestination as deterministic. Calvin never held that everything was set up in advance so that men were deprived of freedom of choice and it made no difference what they did. His position was exactly the contrary. The free choices of men were real, and their responsibility for the world made sense precisely because nothing that happened in the world could elude the divine will and because one did not have to prove that any given course of action would really work in order to find it worth doing at all. Here was a way of taking the world seriously without either deifying it or taking it for granted. Here was a clear alternative to the Lutheran abandonment of the struggle to deal with power in the world, according to which existing power was accepted as a punitive defense against anarchy and the authentic possibilities of motivation and meaning were transferred to the world to come. Here was also a clear alternative to the program of the nonconformist sects which sought to narrow the range of the responsibility of Christians for the world to perfectionist Christian communities which could let the rest of the world go by.

But the theocratic experiment in Geneva and the theocratic temper of the Puritan mind proves that it is easier for men to accept the benefits of providence than it is for them to live by the destiny that God has set out for them in the world. Calvin's substitute for the hierarchy and for the rule of kings and princes was the magistracy. Magistrates were to be elected by the people and to rule by divine mandate. Under this rule, the energies of nature would be responsibly related to the needs of men and there would be order and peace in the world. However, owing to the combined pressures of human recalcitrance, Romanist apostasy, and sectarian anarchy, the magistracy came more and more under the domination of the clergy and sought to enforce the pattern of the Decalogue upon the pattern of the community. The "due process of law" and the "duly constituted authority"—these bulwarks of democracies to come—were first tried out theocratically. And the experiment proved to be abortive, partly because the law and the magistrate were effectively removed from critical re-examination in terms of the divine sanction claimed for them and partly because enforced conformity deprives power of a meaningful relation to order. The political error of sixteenth-century Geneva was afterwards to be repeated in economic terms according to which the favorable possession of the goods of life was a proof of the divine favor. Whenever a given form of power is regarded as divinely sanctioned, and thus, in principle, beyond the possibility of effective change, religion has lost its true office in relation to power and masquerades as power itself.

The second way in which religion has aggravated the problem of power is that religion has made possible the worst forms of the pursuit of power for the sake of power. Religion can do this because religion is concerned with the ultimate boundedness of existence. Whenever this passion for ultimate boundedness is dissociated from its transcendental ground and aim, it spends itself by lifting partial and passing organizations of energy and sovereignty to the level of ultimate significance. The corruption here is not that divine sanctions are applied to existing forms of power so as to place them effectively beyond the criticism of divine and human judgment. The corruption is, conversely, that existing forms of power are placed effectively beyond criticism by their own dynamics. Power is, so to say, self-justifying. What makes it persuasive is not the awesomeness of faith but the contagion of ideology. What keeps it going is not the tranquillity of order but the relentless tempo of its own momentum.

The totalitarianisms of our days are, of course, only too obvious cases in point. The religious character of totalitarianism is that it nourishes and feeds upon the passion of men for ultimate boundedness. But the distortion of religion which is produced thereby is that the religious dimension of existence is completely imprisoned by the self-justifying and impeccable efficiency of technical organization and control. And not only religion is thus imprisoned but other concerns of men as well: their cultural and national aspirations, their need for security and for community, for creative happiness and hope. All these things are subordinated to, indeed, consumed by, the pursuit of power for the sake of power. It is not so important that one of these totalitarianisms is outspokenly atheistic and materialistic and the other two have been less so. The important fact is that modern totalitarianism is an organization of the energies and sovereignties of existence which is possible because of the technical character of power and the almost infinite momentum and minuteness which technics has given to the will-to-power. And religion makes this possible in the sense that, when it is imprisoned by totalitarianism, religion intensifies the self-justifying dynamic of totalitarianism.

The totalitarianisms of our day are, however, only the most obvious instances of power masquerading as religion, for the democracies have fallen into the same organizational and ideological patterns. Democracy is not, in principle, committed to the pursuit of power for the sake of power. But under the menacing pressure of totalitarian dynamics and the inescapable modification of previous political and economic structures required by the technical character of power, the democracies have become unsteady. They have adopted an ideology of their own instead of exploring ways of adapting the technical character of power to the true office of religion in providing motivation and meaning for the exercise of power in the world. According to the ideology of democracy, political and religious freedom depend upon economic freedom and economic freedom means the organization of goods and services with maximum rewards for private initiative and a minimum of political and religious restraint. The impact of technics upon this conception of economic freedom has led in practice to political regulation and even to economic restraints, some self-imposed and some monopolistic. But the bearing of these changes upon the foundation and the structures of democracy has been increasingly defined in ideological terms and less and less in terms of a constructive democratic faith. A constructive democratic faith requires a re-examination of the relations between democracy and religion in the light of the religio-technical character of power. The attempt to preserve democracy by lauding its economic achievements is materialism. The effort to perpetuate democracy by making difference of mind a sign of disloyalty and by reducing loyalty to the legal devices of an oath is to make "the road ahead" the byway of self-justification. In both respects, the totalitarian enemy has become a Trojan horse. Religion in such a case, however Christian it may sound and however free it may be, has become the prisoner of the pursuit of power for the sake of power. And power becomes religion whenever this imprisonment occurs.

III. POWER AND CHRISTIAN FAITH

The religio-technical character of power implies that there is a constructive as well as a corruptive relation between power and religion. The constructive relation between religion and power is supplied by the role of religion in giving motivation and meaning to the energy and the authority by which whatever happens in the world occurs. It is this enabling and enlightening function of religion which integrates the organized energies with the insistent purposes of existence, the relentless momentum of change with the equally relentless persistence of pattern and direction, of order and meaning, in, with, and under change. Religion has always been a source of power in the sense that it has made it possible for man to endure all sorts of otherwise intolerable conditions. But, in addition, *authentic religion has always enabled man to see that the power by which he can endure the world requires him to change the world.* The power to act is identical with the power of meaningful purpose. When the energies and the sovereignties of existence are organized and exercised with reference to the enabling power of meaningful purpose, the problem of power is resolved. The problem of power is resolved because the exercise of power corresponds with its nature. The possession and the use of power are divested of both deification and self-justification. Technics and politics make sense because they serve the meaning and the purposeful dynamics of reality.

The identification of the power to act with the power of meaningful purpose is the unique achievement of Christian faith. The Christian analysis of power is based upon the monotheistic assertion that the dynamic and the delimiting aspects of power belong to God alone and that every existing organization and exercise of power—including the power of religion—is subordinate to the divine purpose and subject to the criticism of the divine will. The Hebrew prophets are the architects of this view and break new ground in the analysis of power in the world. Prophetic religion is irreconcilably opposed to polytheism and to pantheism of every sort. The prophets are likewise sternly set against the tight monopoly of mediated power. What they declare is that power is not sacred energy but righteous will.[4] Upon this will the world depends for its existence and fulfillment. And when the energies and the sovereignties of life are organized and expressed in accordance with this righteous will, they give to life both security and meaning.

In this prophetic tradition Jesus stands, and upon it he builds. He is, indeed, its fulfillment because he takes up, in and over the world, the actual exercise of power according to the will and purpose of God Himself. In the New Testament, as well as in the thought of the Church, Jesus is viewed not only as the unique revelation of God and the saviour of men and the world. He is also acknowledged as the lord of life. It is this integration of deity, deliverance, and lordship in the person and work of Jesus Christ that gives to Christian faith its constructive relation to the problem of power.

The constructive relation of Christian faith to the problem of power may be stated by saying that *Christianity makes it possible for men to live by the grace of the triune God*. A classical and a contemporary contribution of Christianity to the organization of the energies and sovereignties of existence must suffice to make this plain.

The late Professor Charles Cochrane[5] has reminded us that the Graeco-Roman commonwealth was based upon a great and untenable experiment. The experiment was the "creative politics" of the *Pax Augusta*. The aim was to provide a stable order of life in nature and society based upon the character and destiny of the ruler. The virtue of the ruler was defined in terms of the classical conception of justice, itself derived from the permanent excellences of the soul. And the expectation was that the *"virtus et fortuna"* of the ruler would guarantee security and give motive and meaning to existence. Here was a *"logos* of power," a way of understanding and ordering the energies and sovereignties of life, which could give ultimate and abiding significance and effect to technics and politics. But the Pax Augusta failed. And Professor Cochrane's thesis is that it failed because it was based upon a defective *logos* of power. Chiefly because the successors of Augustus proved to be neither wise enough nor good enough to cope with the complexities of nature and the pressures of the will-to-power,[6] the gulf between the integrity of the ruler and the fortunes of the state widened and men were left without a clear sense of meaning and direction in the world. Confidence in reason and in virtue not only declined; it was paralyzed by the nemesis and the nonsense of blind chance.

Meanwhile, Christians had been reading the Bible and reflecting upon the significance of Jesus for the world. They began with the conviction that all dynamics and authority centered in and derived from him. Under the impact of the life, death, and resurrection of Jesus, it seemed to them both urgent and possible to make the choice between futility and meaning at the *beginning* rather than at the *end* of the search for an order of tranquillity and peace. Jesus could have been another supreme disillusionment, as Augustus had become. Whether or not he was depended upon the issue of power. Christians took the line that Jesus was "the power of God and the wisdom of God" (I Cor. 1:24). And this courageous act of faith and will brought fresh illumination to the mind. It now appeared that God was the *presupposition* of all thought and experience, not an inference from them.

The energies and sovereignties of life were neither capricious nor under the control of fate but were the expression of the divine will and purpose. Jesus became the continuing clue to the order and purpose of the world, distinguished but not separated from the God who had set up the structure of nature and of human nature. To *see* the world like this was the enabling and enlightening work of the Spirit.

Here was a way of thinking and behaving entirely different from what Christians had found in classicism or classicism had found in itself. Men, who were by nature bent upon a secure and true community of life, were lifted to a new level of insight and understanding on which they discovered that God had purposed them for companionship with Him and had so arranged all things that they were delivered from every paralysis of circumstance. No longer were men's hopes tied to a final order of society in which fate triumphed over meaning and responsibility. Here was a new and constructive *"logos* of power" in terms of which technics and politics could be pursued. The trinitarian understanding of power regards change not as the nemesis but as the instrument of sovereignty; and sovereignty as authentic, not when it keeps order but when it orders all things under the critical judgment of the divine will and purpose.

The trinitarian reconstruction of the disintegrating order of the Pax Augusta may be paralleled by the contemporary bearing of Calvinisim upon democracy. Democracy is at the moment in serious straits because its classical foundation has been undermined by the impact and complexity of circumstance not unlike that which underminded the ideals of the Augustan age. Technics have changed the social and economic bases of democratic political traditions and institutions. Consequently, we are going through a crisis of motivation and meaning which takes the form of an intense division over loyalty and responsibility, with the resultant disintegration of both. The problem is whether the technical organization of energy and the political organization of sovereignty can be correlated so as to check the will-to-power by the power to will the authentic purposes of life. On this point Calvinism, divested of its theocratic errors, has something constructive to offer.

The resources of Calvinism for the reconstruction of political democracy in a technical age lie in the way in which Calvinism has rethought the loyalty and the responsibility essential to a democratic community. The key is the conception of grace.

It will be recalled that the theocratic errors of Calvinism were the result of a too-consistent application of the doctrine of divine election to the exercise of power and the possession of goods. But this consequence need not have been drawn. Indeed, the doctrine of election served Calvin in exactly the same way that the doctrine of the Trinity had served Christianity in the Graeco-Roman world. Here was the foundation for a meaningful and responsible ordering of the energies and sovereignties of existence. And Calvin worked, if anything, more directly at the problem of the exercise of power than the trinitarian theologians had done. If a man wanted to know how he could come by the power of meaningful purpose and how he could carry it through, the answer was: by grace. Grace is the reconciling and enabling power whereby man can deal with the complexities and the unpredictabilities of nature and his fellows as God has dealt with him. Grace is *common* in the sense that the energies of life are the gifts of God and not the achievements of men. These energies are, therefore, opportunities for checking the will-to-power by the power of purpose. Grace is *special* in the sense that to each man has come the promise of reconciliation and renewal from the Sovereign and Creator of all things and an orbit in which this promise is to be obediently received and applied. The Christian community is the orbit in which grace is received; the Christian's vocation is the orbit in which it is applied.

The political structures which conform to the power of grace are necessarily constitutional. Calvin himself was a child of his time and suspicious of the sovereign will of the people. But this was an unfortunate hesitation before the implications of his own position. The people are sovereign because God has drawn all men into the ambit of His grace. This is a *derived* sovereignty which can never be transposed into rights and dignities inherent in men themselves and which can never be identified with any given constitutional forms, much less with any given system of economy. But the sovereignty of the people is also a *limited* sovereignty because all men stand convicted of pretensions to power and in need of regeneration. It is because constitutional political structures approximate the derived and limited character of the sovereignty of the people under the grace of God that democracy and Calvinism are constructively related.

There is, however, a more important bearing of Calvinism upon democracy. Calvin, in line with the genius of the Protestant Reformation, set new terms for loyalty and responsibility in the common life. No pope or priest, no monarch or merchant, no state or church, can dictate duty and compel conformity. Men are to live—where they are set down—with an eye single to the divine will. And they are to do two things. Starting where they are, men are to be faithful to the necessities that are laid upon them if life is to hold together at all. This means that one cannot retreat from the world nor totalitarianize the world. One can only serve the world in accordance with God's dynamic and fulfilling purpose. But the second thing that men are to do is to move from where they are to where God's purpose has already begun to define new possibilities and new necessities. God's next move is always in the making where the struggle against the deification and the self-justification of power makes conflict bitter and reconciliation indispensable. It is in this sense that the enabling and renewing power of grace can commit men to the kind of organization of technics and politics that will bring true democracy.

On the record, it would seem at least plausible to try to deal with power by the grace of the triune God. On the record, too, it appears that this attempt may be reserved for the generation after this. At all events, we know enough to know that power is a religious as well as a technical phenomenon and that, if we are to overtake the disintegrating dynamic of its technical organization, we shall need to recover the integrating dynamic of a relevant faith.

19

The Church of the Future
and the Homeless Man of Today:
The Vision of Friedrich Naumann*

BY KURT LEESE

Who today recalls the great Christian thinker and social reformer, Friedrich Naumann? So profound are the historical catastrophes which separate us from his era—his life embraces the years 1860–1919—that even professional historians have difficulty in their work of retrospection. In the case of Naumann we are indeed fortunate to have an extensive and particularly vivid monograph by a scholar, also distinguished as a public figure, Theodor Heuss.[1]

The following reflections make no pretense of providing any unpublished material on Naumann's career: if they begin by reviewing his life they do so only in the hope of exploring his great significance for our present concerns.

This unusually gifted, many-sided, influential personality who was to display so marked an aptitude for leadership was a descendant of a family of Saxonian Evangelical Lutheran ministers. He studied theology at the main Lutheran universities of his day, Leipzig and Erlangen. Later at Horn, near Hamburg, at the "Rauhe Haus" he became acquainted with the spirit of Wichern, the so-called "Inner Mission." Becoming a minister in a rural slum district, he had an opportunity to study all the evils which plagued the industrial proletariat. Inspired by his love for the working class, he thus became affiliated with the Christian Socialist movement which had been initiated by the controversial court preacher, Adolf Stoecker. In 1890 Naumann was called to Frankfurt as a pastor of the Inner Mission.

Seven years later he moved to Berlin and gave up his profession as a minister in order to become a free-lance writer and politician. From 1907

* Translated by Anne Liard Jennings.

on he was a member of the Reichstag. With regard to his *political* development it is noteworthy that Naumann adopted the belief that the means of
the Inner Mission, that is, personal charity, and the methods of the Christian
Socialists (the Christian political opposition to Marxism) were powerless
to effect any positive change in the social condition of the needy masses; he
perceived that the only hope lay in the great political struggle of individuals
and parties with respect to social and economic issues. His *religious* development is characterized chiefly by the conviction that (contrary to Naumann's
own original belief) Jesus cannot be looked upon as a "peoples' defender"
engaged in a battle against capital, poverty, deprivation and misery, nor
can he be transplanted into contemporary society as an immediate model
and norm. One must remember, after all, that Jesus belonged to an entirely
precapitalistic age of agricultural cast and could therefore not advocate
"socialism in the modern sense." Original Christianity is historically and
geographically limited in such a way that it can yield no concrete norms
which could lend themselves to the shaping of political and economic relationships in an age of highly developed industrialism and capitalism. A
special "Christian politics" in the social field (such as Stoecker had envisioned) must be rejected. "There is not, and never has been, a 'Christian'
managerial policy, an 'Evangelical' industrial code, a 'religious' method of
price-setting. In spite of all religious enthusiasm, the 'Christianization' of life
must remain something incomplete, something that defies expression in terms
of norms and rules. *The Gospel is no law.*"[2] Naumann was among the first
men to proclaim the controversial theory of the "individual jurisdiction" of
the various areas of human life, such as law, state, politics, and economics.

It is not necessary, for our present purpose, to pursue Naumann's political
or sociopolitical ideas any further. Rather, we shall direct our attention to
certain religious ideas inspired by his ardent interest in defining the relationship between Christianity, the Church, and the school; ideas which he
formulated clearly, concretely and convincingly, and cast before the
guardians of the ecclesiastical tradition as an extremely urgent question.
Naumann does not discuss these ideas in the manner of one theologian
debating with another, but as a layman.

According to the Sermon on the Mount, Jesus said: "Above all, seek ye
the kingdom of God." Here is Naumann's comment:

You want to expand Christianity! Your aim is righteous, but the question
is how you expect to go about it. Do you aspire to build beautiful churches
with mighty arches and colorful windows, churches along the busiest streets,
towers which rise into heaven among smoke stacks? Churches are necessary and

good, but the Kingdom of God does not come with churches alone. Or perhaps you intend to concentrate on the expansion of devotional music, so that Biblical truth may more easily enter into the soul of man in the tones of the noblest masters? Music is good, but it is not the Kingdom of God. Do you seek to bind the faith of the ancestors even today by means of strict preservation of old avowals in which the faith of the fathers was anchored? The avowals are good, but faith does not consist in them alone. Faith is contained in nothing external. The Holy Ghost does not confine itself to altars or certain words. It is the free reign of God in man himself, it is something intimate, which no synods can limit, and no pastor can convey.[2]

How, then, is the Kingdom of God achieved? (By this, Naumann means the coming of God into the soul of man.) Not by means of certain specific words or avowals, not through forms and formulas, nor churches and priests, nor chants and laws, but by means of "free reign" of the Divine Spirit. To be sure, the free reign of the Divine Spirit can be made manifest in words and avowals. But they have no determining power. "The Holy Ghost is not confined to altars and certain words."

Naumann is sitting—a layman among laymen—in the roomy nave of the church. "Under Gothic arches were sitting men and women who had nothing Gothic, nothing Medieval about them. The Church and the church-goers belonged, on the basis of what one could see, to two different ages. Even what we heard was modernized Gothic. The thoughts of the sermon were basically rigid and impenetrable, like the stone walls which swallowed them up, only there was something of modern color, of a new manner of speech, of softened sharpness. The congregation for the most part clung to these external forms, which they understood; the profounder meaning, the structure of the thoughts, was grasped only by a few. It was so difficult, so remote, so old."[3] Imagining himself in the role of the preacher, Naumann attempted to understand his position and do him justice:

Once it is up to him to represent church Christianity, we must give him credit for doing it as gently and adroitly as he can. As an individual, he cannot be expected to have the power of relieving any substantial amount of that pressure which burdens the Church. Of what avail is it if he omits as much as possible of the old traditions? The omissions cannot reinforce that which remains. The minister cannot conjure up a true revival of faith, where new religious ideas are coming to life among the people and rising up with irresistible vigor, seeking to express themselves in new, free, potent forms. He can do nothing more than to say, for himself personally, that which he really believes, experiences, loves and hopes, as honestly and sincerely as possible. He can never give all of Christianity, but he can beware of wearing a coat which does not fit him. That is only a little, and yet it is a great deal. He expresses in words his divine inspiration.[4]

No matter how original, strong and independent his personality, in some way the preacher always remains the servant of his Church. Naumann speaks of the "pressure which burdens the Church," since the Church cannot shake itself loose from an old tradition and embrace freely "new religious ideas."

At the same time, the Church is utterly indispensable for Naumann. What is its indispensability based on? Has it been bestowed upon the world and mankind by God, or the alleged "Lord of the Church," in word and sacrament as an unchangeably holy internal and external form and order? This would indeed be a dubious claim to self-assertion and self-preservation against the attacks of its opponents; it would be a dogmatic-legal claim, lacking in power of conviction. No, it is a different matter, and a simpler one, says Naumann:

That which upholds the Church . . . is a drop of eternal ointment, with which even the worst preacher has been consecrated. Jesus is so indestructible that all popes and consistories could not annihilate him. He lives, and through him live his good and bad servants. In all the world there is hardly a stranger relationship than that between Jesus and the Church. Jesus was against ecclesiasticism, he opposed it with more vehemence than anyone else, and he was crucified by ecclesiasticism. Yet he, he alone became the eternal foundation for the greatest ecclesiasticism of all times, a wellspring which irrigated the fields of the popes, synod-presidents and priests of all zones. Indeed, can Jesus be proclaimed in the whole world without ecclesiasticism? Can molten gold be carried from place to place in anything but crucibles of iron and steel? That is the reason why one can never tear oneself loose from the Church, the only reason—because Jesus is eternal.[5]

To be sure, the Church and its servants are particularly in need of one thing. Sincerity, unconditional sincerity. Insincerity is the death of piety.

The preachers of the Gospel must esteem no tradition, no human institution, no practical consideration, no fearful piety higher than sincerity. They can be mistaken, can make wrong statements, can bring forth shallow and premature thoughts—all this is unavoidable, since all human talk of divine things is only stammering, searching, experimenting. Frequently they themselves will not agree with their earlier teachings at a more advanced age. But there is one thing which must be retained in all searching, experimenting, erring: the unconditional personal sincerity, which makes no pretense of dogmas or sentiments which are not there. It is impossible that a Protestant minister should consider himself to be merely a lifeless instrument of the Church, who, as a person, must recede into the background, and merely surrender himself as a mouthpiece for that which is designated as church dogma. His congregation wants to know whether he personally believes what he says, he as a human being, without his robes, in his study or in his parlor. That which the *man* does not believe, the minister must never say. He does not serve his Lord if he becomes personally insincere in the service of the Church.[6]

It has been said of Naumann: "The dogmatic distinctions of his Christianity were blurred."[7] This is what modern theology will hold against him most of all, and he will be thrown on the scrap heap of the so-called "cultural Protestantism," or "religiosity." With Naumann, the aversion to the "rationalistic methods of dogmaticism," to doctrinal disputes and the warring factions of church politics had deeper roots. *First:* "The socialistic enthusiasm of the first years in the ministry (Jesus and Social Privation) completely overshadowed the awareness of theological problems."[8] *Secondly:* it seemed to him that nothing endangered the inner sincerity as much as the assumption that it would be possible to invalidate the absolute truth by means of a dogmatic formulation, and thereby to lay claim to the rank of a spiritual ruler of souls. "Theories and interpretations of doctrine" can never express "the total and eternal truth." "A portion of it is always human error, and human imperfection is always present. How else could it be explained that even the best representatives of faith could never reach complete agreement among themselves in their teachings?"[9] He maintained that everything which "even remotely resembles the forcing of the various opinions into a mold"[10] must be avoided. It has always been a great detriment to the Church that (in spite of its most outstanding representatives) the average person has conceived of it as "an institution of tutelage and a subduer of liberalistic tendencies."[11] The deepest and most intimate reason for the existence of dogmatic ambiguities in Naumann's religious convictions is revealed in one of the most beautiful, most convincing and profound statements he ever made: "All talk about God was never more than the inarticulate sounds of children—when they are unknowingly moved by some powerful melody, and lack the words to express the mysterious vibration of their souls. God was always the great Unknown—mightier than we and everything that we know."[12]

From this perspective we can understand why Naumann once said: "I feel no obligation to confess, since in my opinion profound thoughts and inner sentiments always seem to defy formulation."[13] And thus he desired to write only for those readers "who are not disposed to contemplate religious questions along established and beaten paths"[14]—namely, for readers who are not willing to give up the freedom and independence of religious, moral and scientific convictions for the sake of yielding to the dogmatic authority and claim of the Church.

Naumann not only held himself aloof from the ideological controversies of the Church of his time, but he also "was lacking in any definite concept of Church at all."[15] He questioned that the concept of Church (on Protestant soil) had any "actual form-shaping power," since the Reformation, in its own course, annihilated the possibility of definite forms of ecclesiasticism through its attack upon the authority of the historical Church. By turning to the Holy Scripture as the sole source of faith, the Reformation prepared the way for a continually recurring devout, but non-church movement. Naumann detects in this turn of events a possibility of directing religious power into new channels outside the Church; the question remains, whether the Church as an institution can at the same time be broad and firm enough to support, or at least endure, such an inner conflict.

Naumann designates the Church's "insistence on the authority of archaic documents" as evidence of "confessionalism" instead of "confession." Naumann was quite able to understand and appreciate confession, especially confession *in statu nascendi*. "At the time when they originated, the 'confessions' were full of a warm glow. At that time words were the waving banners of advancing movements, words which truly expressed the spirit of the brethren. We are also in need of such communal words in the service of the Christianity of our time."[16] Confessionalism is something else. Confessionalism is rigid and narrow-minded, intolerant and fanatical—it is confession which has lost its power of love. Confessionalism "is the way in which free piety was standardized in the majority of the German Protestant churches. Standardized piety, however, is constantly inclined to become impious." And what about orthodoxy, which corresponds to confessionalism? "Almost any kind of orthodoxy is marred by a hidden defect somewhere, but it prefers to cover it up for the sake of preserving its formal legitimacy. This is the irreligious, impious element in the modern form of confessionalism which actually torments truly religious sentiment. In our times, orthodoxy has become the normal and established form of the Church."[17] Also evident is Naumann's conviction that "Protestantism as such cannot possibly possess any Church-forming power," since its vital form is that of the traditional Roman Catholic Church—characterized in its basic structure as a *curative* institution of salvation prescribed by God. Protestantism simply took over and retained this concept of the Church, eliminating everything that seemed to contradict the Scriptures. On this basis we are better able to appreciate Naumann's line of reasoning when he expresses the outcome of his meditations concerning the Church:

The kingdom of God is realized neither in the State nor in the Church, but it is a spiritual movement from man to man; one only asks oneself where and how this movement is to begin. It has need of organs of administration, but it is at a disadvantage as soon as it finds them. It then suffers from the overlordship of state officials, and it suffers, too, when it is forced to set up its own statutes and laws. In one instance the disadvantage prevails because the spiritual movement is cast under the power of an alien, non-spiritual law, while in the other instance the spiritual movement must degrade itself if it is to institute authority and force. No matter how one attacks this problem, the evil results cannot be avoided.

Protestant Church! What does this actually mean? Can something like this exist at all? We know what the Catholic Church is. It is the demilitarized Roman state, in which original Christianity took refuge. This Church does not place upon itself the restriction of having to be in precise accordance with the Scriptures, since it is nourished by an extensive tradition, which, to be sure, began in Bethlehem, but soon found its destination in the Capital of the World. Protestantism, however, by virtue of its intent, is casting aside that tradition for the sake of the immediate return to the New Testament. On the basis of the New Testament, however, no one can establish a Church, because the teachings of the Sermon on the Mount are equally unsuitable for a consistory and for a state council; and the instruction of Jesus to his twelve disciples is radically different from the hiring of a superintendent with a steady income and retirement benefits.

From the Protestant point of view, one can thus turn toward all ecclesiastical questions with far-reaching resignation. One should therefore not set out to identify a pious Protestant by his approval of this or that solution of the practical questions of his faith as relatively the most successful one.[18]

"Far-reaching resignation!" It is perhaps less resignation than the heart-felt lament of a man who once found his home in the German Church of Lutheran denomination and owed to it his best and most profound creative powers. Finally, however, he could find no place within the confines of his beloved denomination; new forces of the modern world, arising in the fields of science, art, literature and politics—avoided and combated by his church—caused him to take upon himself the status of temporary exile and homelessness, a homelessness which he had to accept for the sake of sincerity. "As protestants we are searchers who regard it as a manifestation of God's grace when He crushes some of our endeared possessions."[19]

As Christian, Naumann continued to disturb a church which, having fallen prey to confessionalism, gravely endangered the inner integrity and sincerity of its leading officers and servants. As democrat, he was appalled by the sight of a church which (after the collapse of the monarchistic State

Church during the First World War) was willing to accept the special privileges of an "Institution of Public Law," as well as numerous state subsidies and the state guarantee of collecting church dues—thus practically becoming again a State Church. Owing to these developments, Naumann became a kind of "defense attorney for Church minority groups," of the minority churches, sects and independent religious groups in their organizational struggles for self-determination. "To him they appeared to be more alive and more stimulating than the petrified institution of State Church." His actual ideal, however, was the separation of state and church, after the North American model. This was, he said, "the best way yet discovered to do justice to both parties."[20]

Since the time of Naumann's death there have been many new developments in theology. The "liberal" rubbish was carted away on the trucks of an imposing, new theology. There was a great acclaim. But does the Church exist for the sake of theology and scholars? Or does the Church exist for the sake of those whom we designate, very inadequately, as "laymen"? Are the laymen only the clay to be kneaded by the theological and clerical potters? Or do they also possess ever-valid rights and privileges in a church which boasts of being a church of the "priesthood of everyman"? We could counter Naumann's argument with the objection that the existing Church successfully withstood the crucial test during the Nazi regime. And how else could it have withstood the test than as a "Church of Confession"? This well-deserved glory must not be minimized in the slightest. But the Church's barricades were erected not only by the courage of Christian testimony but also by dogmatism and fanaticism. Dogmatism and fanaticism may be necessary and justified in times of special emergency. But as soon as one is no longer subjected to the rule of totalitarian terror they should be abandoned as unchristian, and one should not insist on seeing in them the eternal salvation of the Church.

That is the reason why Naumann's voice penetrates to our ears through the decades and finds many, very many of us in a situation frightfully similar to his.

In the above we have mentioned the themes of "homelessness" and inner exile into which Naumann was forced. These are not to be equated immediately with what is today referred to as the "man without a home," about whom modern existentialism, as well as Kafka and Rilke, have so much to say, mostly in a negative vein.

The "homelessness" which we have noted is applicable to a much smaller segment of modern man. But does this make it less painful and tragic? When forceful and free minds knock at the door of the Church, then a sullen door-

keeper opens the peephole and demands the certificate of creed. This attitude of the Church has, through the years, served to alienate not only the
intelligentsia but even the "workingman."

It has been necessary to make all these observations in order finally to
take into our hands a faded piece of paper dating from the year 1899. To be
exact, it comes from an 1899 issue of Naumann's periodical, *Die Hilfe (The
Help)*, and the title of the article is "The Church of the Future." Under this
title we read as follows:

In my imagination I walked through the Church of the Future. It was a
building in the middle of a garden, without a steeple, free and open for everyone. I had just come from the subway, and I was weary of the hustle and bustle
of the crowds. My soul was craving for a little peace and quiet, for the feeling
of being at home in surroundings that were not "of this world." The garden
alone, with its familiar old towering trees, was reassuring and refreshing. Old
people and children were sitting here, but there was enough room left for a
silent man inclined to meditation. One could observe men and women stepping
into the house one by one, as well as married couples. One does not need to be a
"steady subscriber" in order to be allowed to enter. The house consisted of one
main hall and numerous additional rooms. Everything was of good modern
construction, without luxury, but in good taste. Nothing was reminiscent of the
old-style churches. There was no trace of the old plague of the Gothic. The
main hall was predominantly built of glass and steel, and it had excellent light
and acoustics. Organ music was played in the afternoon; then the people sat
and filled their daily need of Church music. They were listening to Bach,
Mendelssohn, Pergolese and many other musical masters of devotion, inter-
spersed with simple themes from chorales and liturgies. Several different
preachers were allowed to talk in the hall at different times. Some of them used
the traditional form of the sermon; others preferred to talk in an informal way.
The hall itself was devoted to no particular denomination; it served equally all
groups who wished to gather around the cross, large and impressive with its
image of the crucifixion, which constituted the only decoration of the east wall.
Those, however, who wished to dedicate themselves to devotion in solitude, did
not go into the large hall, but into one of the rooms which were situated to the
right and left of the entrance. One of these rooms was the reading room with
religious periodicals, another room was devoted to religious art, a third to
missions. The Bible, in old and new translations, was to be found on the shelves,
and every room had a selection of books which contained research material even
for the sceptics. On the other side of the spacious hall were rooms for clubs and
instruction. The administration of the whole grounds was supervised by a committee whose sole concern was to supply rooms for religious purposes. The committee left all actual missionary and congregational work in the hands of those
groups who wished to participate in the project.

We are dealing here with a prophetic dream, a vision, which nevertheless lacks any feverish, ecstatic quality, and is confined to the sober realm of possibility. One must also be able to read between the lines. For it is between the lines that Naumann records the experiences which he, as a Christian, had with the Church of his time, and which we have discussed so far.

We must turn our attention to two special points of the vision. It is Naumann's wish that the construction of the church may not "imitate and repeat the style of bygone times in disparate and foolish combinations,"[21] neither the Romanesque, Gothic, nor Renaissance or baroque style of architecture, since none of these styles can correspond to the attitude of modern man. He is, moreover, of the opinion that the architectural style of a church must be capable of expressing that particular, characteristic form principle which is in unity and harmony with a certain epoch. Now Naumann comments (in the year 1896): "With the advancement of industry the leading position of iron and steel is nowhere more pronounced than in architecture. This term 'steel construction' contains possibilities of which earlier times could not even dream. The new style must have a backbone of steel."[22]

His second desired feature also has been put to practice in many places: a daily performance of religious or devotional music without a sermon or the participation of a cleric, thus being limited to religious music alone. But aside from these two particulars, "The Church of the Future" still awaits realization.

Let us now elucidate the essence of the new church, and its purpose as Naumann envisioned it. To begin with, it was not intended to be a clubhouse. Nor is it to be a public recreation center (as one might suppose at first glance), with its stage and kitchen facilities, with special accommodations for men, women and young people, such as can be found in every congregation, or is at least included in the planning stage.

Let there be no confusion: Naumann is referring to an actual *church*, intended for the purpose of divine services, but serving also for lectures and courses of instruction. The church was to have no steeple. Why? Because, in its external appearance, it should avoid any hint of rivalry with the State Church or any official institutions. It was not intended to be a church *among* others; it was not simply to increase the number of churches—nor to keep up with the increasing number of inhabitants, nor to beautify the skyline of the city. This church was to be a decidedly *Christian* church, even though belonging to "no particular denomination." The crucifix on the east wall without an altar was to bear out this intent. Now enter, all ye who seek a place of devotion regardless of denomination! This church is at the disposal of "all groups," as long as they believe in Christ and are willing to gather around the cross. Whatever the form and manner of their devotional services, the Apostle says: "What difference does it make? In either way Christ is being proclaimed, and that fills my heart with joy" (Phil. 1:18). But perhaps only a few of you will seek entrance to this house. You prefer to live in a hidden corner under your own roof.

In the meantime, there is another milling crowd waiting, a vacillating and uncertain crowd, defying sociological analysis. These people are not those who belong to the outskirts of the old traditional Church. They *belong* nowhere, since they have a home nowhere. *They stand on the swaying ground of "in-between."* They are those people who cannot bring themselves to join in the recitation of the "confession of faith" at official church services, since they feel that they would be insincere in feigning a faith which they do not have. They are full of obscure doubts. They are critical in attitude, even impious, since they are not willing to be accepted by the "old faith" nor are they capable of accepting it. The only statement that they can make about themselves is that they are seeking truth, and that they feel "something like a new faith" sprouting in their hearts,[23] a new faith which is still somehow mysteriously connected with Jesus of Nazareth and with what the New Testament calls *agape*. "What is love?" Naumann once asked, and the simplicity and directness of his answer can hardly be equaled.

It is love when someone respects the other as a person, tries to place himself in his position, is familiar with his hopes and wishes, truly serves his best interests, and even endures his weaknesses and sins patiently. It is love when my soul finds time for, and takes pleasure in the soul of another. With mortals, such love is always imperfect, but with God it is perfect, noble and pure.

Love is "working at the loom of eternal goodness."[24] This love is *agape*. You sense that here, if anywhere, lies your bond with Jesus of Nazareth, that which he radiates and which is of the most urgent concern to you. Here you are permitted to live even in an imperfect state of faith, subject to no supervision of faith or creed.

Naumann's vision is more than a liberal gesture. It is a call to penance, which must be heard.

"The Kingdom of God," says Naumann, "hovers over us all as an eternal hope. Our hands try in vain to grasp it. It calls to us enticingly, as does the horizon. As soon as we have wandered to the place where it lies today, we again see it yonder in the distance. This, however, is God's art, that He gives to every place, every generation, every person a proper horizon whose outline can be discerned. He himself, however, sees further than all of us."[25]

20

Theology in the Life of Contemporary American Protestantism

BY WILHELM PAUCK

I

An observer of the American church scene of today can hardly fail to note that theology is not in the center of concern among Protestants. In the main the laity of the churches is unconcerned about theological questions, and few ministers appear compelled to orient their work to clear theological principles.

To be sure, many laymen are preoccupied with the question of the meaning of the Christian faith. They inquire eagerly how the tenets of the Christian gospel can be validated over against the secularist opinions and attitudes that determine the everyday life of Americans. But they are unwilling to think about religion in a disciplined way and are therefore unable really to deepen their understanding of the Christian gospel.

The ministers cannot but be aware of the fact that today Christian truth goes nowhere unchallenged, indeed, that Christianity is actively being opposed by the rival "secular faiths" of scientism, humanism, nationalism, socialism, and even the democratic faith. They therefore know that without an examination of the implications of the Christian gospel (and such an examination is inevitably theological) the gospel's relevance to the human situation of our times cannot be demonstrated. Nevertheless, they do not exhibit a theological responsibility in their professional work. The method and substance of their sermons lead one to suspect that they do not care to think theologically and that they are not interested to find theological criteria of truth. And their other ministerial activities likewise do not appear to be guided by a theological awareness of the specific nature of Christianity.

American Protestantism thus impresses one as being fundamentally untheological. This impression is supported by the fact that theological education, that is, the education which divinity students receive in theological seminaries, is actually not "theological" in the strict sense of the word. Most seminaries and divinity schools interpret their function to be that of training institutes for the ministry and for other professional work of Christian leadership. As such they endeavor to introduce their students to an understanding of the particular traditions of the denominations to which they happen to belong. Their major effort is directed toward a practically effective professional training for the ministry. The theological bases of the ministry are generally taken for granted and are rarely specifically examined. Consequently, the theological disciplines of Biblical exegesis, historical theology, philosophical and systematic theology, do not loom as large in "theological education" as they should. Instead of being considered basic they are regarded as ancillary to practical theology. They are not used in order to furnish the criteria by reference to which the training in practical church work is to be judged and directed but are made subservient to the needs of ecclesiastical or denominational practices.

This condition of theological education correspounds to the situation that actually prevails in the Church. The proof of this can be found in the fact that those few theological schools which endeavor to educate their students primarily in Biblical, historical and constructive theology actually do not exercise a distinctively different theological influence upon the ministry and the churches than do those which emphasize training in the several skills of church leadership. What happens is that as soon as such graduates in theology enter the profession of the ministry they cease to make critical or constructive use of the Biblical, historical and theological ideas or criteria in the understanding of which they were trained. There are very few ministers who in their active careers maintain that competence in distinctly theological studies which they possessed at the time they graduated from theological seminaries. This is not primarily their conscious fault but is the effect of the character of the churches upon them. For the churches of American Protestantism do not encourage a "learned ministry." For this reason the ministers do not understand themselves as theologians.

Now, to be sure, American Protestantism has produced theological leaders; but only a few of them have been as influential as those of Europe. The representative theologians who are now active in contemporary American Protestantism are making contributions to the interpretation of the Christian faith which are as important as those of theological thinkers of other lands—but the significant fact is that their work, though it goes by no means unrecognized and unappreciated, does not significantly shape the life and thought of the churches. Consider, for example, the theological stature of Paul Tillich. He is everywhere recognized as one of the most representative of contemporary theologians. He receives a large hearing all over America. Big audiences come to hear his sermons and public lectures. His books are widely read. But how influential is he actually in the churches? How profoundly have his theological ideas shaped and affected the spirit of American Protestantism? What responsibility for theological thought has he stimulated in the minds of the many hearers and readers who have turned to him during the past twenty years? It is difficult to answer these questions positively, and this very difficulty is symptomatic of the character of American Protestantism. Its life does not move in theological channels.

If this analysis is correct, it raises two fundamental questions: (a) Is it really a weakness of American Protestantism that it does not cultivate theological concerns? (b) Why does not theology determine the life of the American churches in a decisive way?

II

It must be stated first of all that the neglect of theological responsibility by the American Protestant churches is unjustifiable. For theology is an instrument that must be used in order to preserve the distinctiveness of the Christian gospel in differentiation from other religions and religious philosophies of life and in order to interpret the truth of the Christian faith in its relation to the various realms and dimensions of human experience. Theology should therefore never be neglected by the churches.

However, it is not necessary to attribute such a significance to theology that it is placed in the center of the Christian life. Faith and theology are not identical. Theology is a servant of faith, not its master. Theology can deepen and strengthen faith; it can endow it with a sense of relevance by rendering it aware of its special nature and by relating it to the whole of life in its individual, social and cosmic dimensions—but, in the end, it is faith which determines the scope of theology. This is why too exclusive a preoccupation with theology is beset with dangers. The protest against theology in the name of a living faith which has been voiced again and again in the history of Christianity has not been inappropriate, especially at times when religion was identified with assent to doctrines.

It is in this perspective that the fact must be seen that in certain periods and phases of its history the Church has not been determined by theology and that there have been many forms of Christianity which were not shaped decisively by theology. Roman Catholicism, for example, does not attribute primary importance to theology although it has produced significant theological schools and movements in all periods of its history. It is a sacramental-hierarchical institution, a cultic and priestly church. Membership in it has always been practiced without special reference to theological responsibility or competence. Indeed, the Roman Catholic Christian is encouraged to "believe implicitly," that is, to rely on the priestly authority of the Church for an explicit definition of the faith. Moreover, it has often been noted that the classical Roman Catholic theologians, the Scholastics, did not find it necessary to formulate a doctrine of the Church even though priestly orders, sacraments and churchly disciplines were the foremost features of medieval Christianity. An ecclesiology, that is, a specific theological doctrine of the Church, was developed by Roman Catholic theologians only in response to Protestant criticisms of the form and authority of the papal church. Today Roman Catholic ecclesiasticism is therefore much more conscious of itself and also more rigid and vigorous, although the Roman Catholic layman still takes for granted the identification of the Christian religion with a hierarchical sacramentalism, without finding it necessary to cultivate a theological awareness of what he is doing.

In a similar way, Anglicanism has always tended to attribute only secondary importance to theology. The source of its peculiar Christian life is the Book of Common Prayer and not The Thirty-Nine Articles. Participation in the cult, not adherence to the creed, is held to be the chief requirement of Christianity. Theological discipline is therefore not required by Anglicans. Indeed their church allows them wide latitude in all theological matters.

Among the Methodists, of whom we shall have more to say presently, a similar attitude prevails. They are primarily concerned with developing among their members a personal commitment to the gospel and to the life of moral perfection which they see implied in it. They regard Christianity as a social movement which through its organization endeavors to bring about a Christian transformation of the whole of human life. They are not hostile to theology but they relegate theological responsibility to a minor place in the life of both the Church and the individual Christian.

When we note that American Protestantism is on the whole characterized by an absence of theology we, therefore, do not need to see in this fact anything unusual or unique. Nevertheless, we must ask whether Protestantism does not require the discipline of theological work in order to actualize that understanding of the Christian gospel which differentiates it from Roman Catholicism. The answer to this question is plain: Theology must be in the very heart of Protestant Christianity—not, as we have already explained, in the sense that theology is primary to faith itself but in the sense that the Christian faith as the Protestant understands it must express itself by means of theology. If this characterization is true, the untheological character of American Protestantism must be considered as a defect.

Protestantism cannot afford to neglect theology, because the sources of its life are the Bible and personal faith. This statement may seem surprising in view of the fact that theology has often been severely criticized by Protestants (and particularly by those who are represented by several large American denominations) precisely in the name of a "free," doctrinally unbound, Bible and in the name of a "free," dogmatically unbound, faith. Such criticism is valid only in so far as it is directed against the tendency (which, to be sure, has manifested itself in orthodox creedalism and in dogmatic authoritarianism) to set a limit to the spiritual vitality of the Christian faith by means of theological circumscriptions. But it is not valid if it is based on the assumption that the Bible and personal faith are in themselves spiritually sufficient. For both are in need of theological implementation if they are to be understood as the sources of a living Christianity.

To be sure, since the days of the Reformers it has been affirmed again and again by Protestants that the Bible is its own interpreter (*sui ipsius interpres*). But this affirmation means that the meaning of the Christian message (*kerygma*) which the Biblical writers proclaim must not be interpreted by reference to norms that are foreign to the Bible, as is the case in Roman Catholicism. There can be no doubt that, if it is to serve as the objective source of the Christian religion, the Bible requires interpretation. The foremost Protestant means of such an interpretation is the sermon. Its purpose is to render the Biblical meaning relevant to the needs and conditions of man in given times and places. Protestantism is a Biblical religion and as such a preaching religion. It is therefore also a theological religion. For the relationship between the Bible and the sermon must be made subject to theological scrutiny; and the connection between the sermon and the situation of those to whom it is addressed cannot be accomplished except by theological inquiry.

Without a concern for the question of how the Bible is to be interpreted in the sermon, no preacher can exercise his function as the "minister of the Word"; and this concern is actualized in theology. Without a consideration of the question of how the sermon must meet the expectancy of the listening congregation in order to be relevant to concrete human situations, the minister cannot preach effectively; and such a consideration leads to theology. In the latter case, theology is apologetic in character: it must show how the Christian gospel answers the existential questions which arise from the conditions in which men find themselves. In the former case, theology is kerygmatic in character: it must show in detail what the dimensions of the gospel are to which the men of the Bible bear witness.

We come to similar conclusions about the inevitability of theology when we consider the implications of personal faith. Protestants have learned from the Reformers to understand the gospel as a message that must be heard, to consider the Word of God as not really spoken unless it is received by conscientious and responsive listening, to regard the revelation of God in Christ as completed only if it discloses salvation to individual believers. Faith is realized therefore only in the personal commitment of the believer to God. It is a personal experience by which God becomes his God, Jesus his Christ or Saviour, the Biblical word of salvation a word spoken to him and heard by him and responded to by him in the secrecy of his own conscience. Such a faith is not real unless it leads to understanding and issues in action; and both such understanding and such action are theological in character. For faith is not completed in understanding unless the believer is consciously aware of what is implied for his life in the divine light in which he now sees himself; and this is a theological awareness. Moreover, faith is not actualized unless the believer is motivated to act in accordance with what has been disclosed to him concerning the ultimate fountain of life; and the consciousness of this motivation is theological.

This analysis of the Protestant conception of Christianity makes it appear that not only every preacher but also everyone who listens to a sermon must perform a theological task. No one who comes under the sway of the Christian gospel, be he a minister or a layman, can entirely avoid the theological task. It must be performed in individual decision and thought. This explains why there is inevitably such a great variety of theologies.

But because each individual Christian must know himself to be a member of the Church, the preaching of the gospel and faith in it are never merely the concern of individuals but also that of the fellowship of believers. Moreover, because the Bible confronts all believers (regardless of the variety of the situations in which they stand) with the one gospel of the one God who has revealed Himself in the one Christ, the manifold responses to the Bible in preaching and believing become united in relation to the one source from which they are derived and toward which they are directed. This explains why there is inevitably in theology such a great tendency toward unity, all-inclusiveness and ecumenicity.

This tension between the individual variety and the inclusive catholicity of the theological apprehension of the Christian gospel is the source of the dynamic character of theological work. In Roman Catholicism an attempt is made to ignore the reality of this tension: individuality, differentiation, historical variety and relativity are not permitted to be stressed. The theme of theology is only what *semper, ubique, et ab omnibus creditum est*. But this purpose can actually be realized only by means of the arbitrary absolutization of relative historical interpretations of the Christian faith (as it is exemplified in modern Roman Catholicism by the prohibition of any other theological system but that of Thomas Aquinas) and by means of the arbitrary concentration of the exercise of theological authority in the Pope (as it is exemplified in the dogma of papal infallibility with respect to all affairs of faith and morals).

Wherever Protestantism has been faithful to its genius the tension between variety and unity has been given free play and expression. Throughout the history of Protestantism, ever new efforts have been made so to understand the Bible that its message would speak for itself unencumbered by human limitations. Furthermore, though creeds and other sanctions of orthodoxy have often been used to stifle individual theological initiative and to undo the effects of historical differences upon the theological interpretations of the gospel, no Protestant group, church or denomination has ever dared to define its creeds, confessions and theological formulae as if they had an absolute authority in themselves. They have always been held subject to correction by the authority of the Word of God alone.

To be sure, in disregard of this common Protestant definition of authority, Protestant churches or denominations have tried again and again to establish absolute sanctions for an intolerant theological orthodoxy. Whenever this happened, protests soon were voiced against such absolutistic and exclusivistic theological thought in the name of the freedom of the Word of God and the sovereignty of the Holy Spirit speaking through conscience. The result then was either that the static theology was corrected or that in opposition to it and for the sake of a better theology secessions took place. It is in this connection that theology was often condemned as the chief cause of the division of Christendom and that the attempt was made to eliminate theology from Christian life. But the criticism should have been directed against a wrong (namely, an absolutistic and arbitrarily universalized) theology and not against theology as such.

The right use of the Bible and the full understanding of faith lead necessarily to a theological interpretation of their implication for thought and action; failure to develop this interpretation must result in an impoverishing stultification of the Christian religion. We must conclude then that the theological task is an integral part of the Christian religion as Protestantism understands it. In so far as American Protestants do not apply themselves to this task they weaken the spiritual substance of their churches.

III

We must now turn to the question of why it is that theology does not occupy the place it deserves in the life of American Protestantism. The answer is not simple, for it cannot be given apart from a consideration of the rather complex nature of American Protestantism as seen in the light of its historical development. If someone should object to the formulation of the question by observing that it is impossible to speak of American Protestantism as if it were one single entity or movement and that therefore one cannot deal generally with the importance of theology in American Protestant life, he must be given the reply that, though there are profound divisions and differences among American Protestants, they nevertheless have in common certain outstanding traits and precisely such as will illuminate the position of theology.

I call attention to only three characteristics of American Protestantism in order to show why it is on the whole not theologically minded.

The chief difference between American Protestantism and European Protestantism is that the American Protestant churches are preoccupied with the task of evangelization in order to enlarge the membership of the churches, to reach the unchurched, and to extend the influence of Christianity more deeply into the life of American society. The European churches of today find themselves placed in communities where the majority of the people do not actively support organized Christendom, although most of them continue to maintain nominal church membership in accordance with popular traditions shaped by the old state or national churches. Nevertheless, these churches preserve an outlook and a strategy that are determined by the situation which prevailed many years ago when they held a dominant position in public life. With few exceptions, they fail to take into account the fact that the nominal profession of Christianity made by the majority of their members is a fictitious Christianity. Trustworthy statistics concerning the influence of European Protestant churches show that only one out of ten persons actively and responsibly takes part in church life. Nevertheless, the churches do not undertake that kind of evangelistic work which these conditions demand, probably because they have not yet learned how to cope with the fact that they have been losing and are continually losing that influence which they once were wont to exercise.

The American Protestant churches, by contrast, have been evangelistic from the beginning. In a way, they have always known themselves to be a minority movement (a very powerful one, to be sure) in American society. To this day they are accustomed to report increases in church membership instead of losses despite the fact that still more than one-third of the population of the United States participates in no way in the life and work of religious groups. It cannot be denied that the problems of paganism and secularism with which American Protestantism has had to deal from the beginning of its history are today more acute and pressing than they have been in former times (and, in this respect, there exist many parallels between our situation and that of Europe), but nevertheless in this fact American Protestantism faces no new difficulty. The history of the American churches, particularly since the beginning of the so-called national period, has been marked by increasing efforts to gain converts to the Christian cause, to build churches and Christian institutions, to form new congregations of believers, to win influence for the Christian way of life in public affairs. These activities have shaped the character of American Protestantism. Transcending the lines of denominational boundaries, the same spirit of religious enterprise determines the various ecclesiastical groups. Because it has had to perform similar tasks, even the Roman Catholic Church in the United States has developed certain traits (exemplified by localism, concern for home missions, aggressive propaganda and publicity) which closely resemble those of Protestantism. In a word, the American churches have never ceased to be missionary in their outlook. Because, at all times, there have been new fields to conquer they have seldom stopped long enough to assess critically and constructively the measure of their achievements. European observers are wont to note the "activistic" and "dynamistic" nature of American religion (and, by the way, they wrongly seek its origin in Calvinism instead of seeing it in this evangelistic drive which is so noticeable in all denominations from the Episcopalians to the Unitarians). What they intend to suggest when they apply these terms to American Protestantism is that they have found no creative and critical theological activity in it. And who would dare say that this judgment is wrong!

It is a remarkable fact that the missionary enterprise does not engender theological creativity. With the possible exception of the early Church whose theology was decisively shaped by the missionary spirit, no part of Christendom has produced major theological responsibility and creativeness in connection with evangelistic endeavors. This is strange because one should expect that precisely the encounter with other religious claims would cause the missionary to justify and explicate the grounds and reasons for his own faith by means of theological thinking. It seems that theology addresses itself to heretics, schismatics, dissenters and non-conformists rather than to unbelievers, gentiles and pagans. It appears to be relevant to intra-Christian relations rather than to those between Christians and non-Christians. Howsoever this may be, we may explain the largely untheological character of American Protestantism by reference to its preoccupation with evangelistic and missionary tasks.

In this connection we should not fail to observe that the most coherent indigenous theological movement which American Protestantism has produced in the course of its history is the "New England theology," the work of the Congregationalists of the colonial era. It reflects the relative stability of the Puritan church establishment. It is best represented by Jonathan Edwards, who to this day towers over every other theological thinker who has arisen on American soil.

The second feature of American Protestantism which must be specially noted, if its tendency toward theological indefiniteness is to be explained, is the predominance of the non-creedal church groups. These churches have found it possible to relate themselves most effectively to the missionary requirements of the American situation. They certainly have been more effective than the churches which represent the main-line creedal traditions of the older Protestantism of the Reformation. In order to preserve their historic witness and character, these latter denominations have found it necessary to hold to the creedal, liturgical and institutional traditions of their mother churches; they stay bound to the theological norms introduced to the New World from the Old by their founding fathers. This is especially true of the Lutherans and the Reformed. As a result, these denominations tend to cultivate an archaic theology in which are kept alive forms of orthodoxy and traditionalism which in the Old World have long since been shattered by more recent religious and secular forces. The effect of this attitude upon American Protestantism at large is not very positive; the theological interpretations of historic Protestantism kept alive in these churches are not of profound significance in the whole life of American Christianity. The influence of this theological traditionalism remains confined to the internal forums of discussion in the denominations concerned with it.

The American Episcopalians have kept in close touch with the Anglican Church. They differ from the Lutherans and the Reformed in so far as they have opened themselves readily to the modern developments of English theology. But the theological minds also of this denomination are strangely isolated in areas of peculiarly Anglican interests. American Episcopalian theologians have made hardly any decisive contribution to modern Protestant thought.

The Presbyterians, though closely related to Scotland, have shown more independence from their origins. In so far as they are at all theologically conscious of their special traditions they stress the continuity with Calvinist orthodoxy on the basis of the Westminster Confession and Catechism. But just as some of their early American leaders let themselves be guided by the new American Calvinism of Jonathan Edwards and his successors rather than by the teaching of Scottish orthodoxy, modern Presbyterians keep their minds open to ideas and trends peculiar to American religious thought, thus permitting a gradual Americanization of Calvinist traditions.

The most influential (and also the largest) denominations in the United States are the Methodists, the Baptists, and the Disciples of Christ. Their predominance in American Protestantism is important for its character and outlook, because they are non-creedal. To be sure, the Methodists do not belong to the denominational family of the Baptists and the Disciples. Nor are they as professedly non-creedal as the latter groups are. But no denomination has shaped the untheological character of American Protestantism as decisively as the Methodists have done. They were the outstanding missionaries on the frontier. By their hostility to Calvinism and by their emphasis upon practical rather than doctrinal Christianity they developed an outlook which was and has remained essentially untheological. The Christian discipline which they are concerned to develop does not rest on creedally or theologically definable criteria of truth. Methodist piety is marked by an evangelical moralism which is nourished by the Bible and deepened by a remembrance of the classical Protestant teachings on justification and sanctification. The influence of these pietist attitudes upon American Protestantism has been tremendous, especially in so far as they have molded a religious spirit that is unconcerned for the discipline of theological thought and seeks expression in preaching for conversion, in evangelism, and in practices of church fellowship designed to transform social life according to the tenets of an individualistic morality.

Because of their rejection of all forms of creedalism, the Baptists and Disciples have exercised an influence upon American Christianity very similar to that of the Methodists. But by their insistence upon the autonomy of the local church they have fostered an independentism which the Methodists have never permitted to develop in their churches. Moreover, their orientation to the normativeness of the New Testament Church has caused them to become more narrowly Biblicistic than the Methodists ever cared to be. Yet they too practice a moralistic evangelicalism with special emphasis upon personal Christian experience which is very similar to that of the Methodists, especially in so far as it is hostile to the intellectualism of theology.

Methodists, Baptists and Disciples have become the chief representatives of an untheological Protestantism. The size and numerical influence of these denominations have made them determinative of the American Protestant mind. They have caused it to be preoccupied with practical Christianity and have turned it away from the quest for a theological exposition and interpretation of the Christian religion.

This analysis would be incomplete if no recognition were to be given to the fact that these non-creedal and largely anti-theological denominations have actually not been able to disregard doctrine entirely. Despite their hostility to theology they have been forced to become engaged in discussions and debates about the norms and sanctions of their special Christian emphasis. The Baptists' concern for religious freedom and for the autonomy of the local church, the Disciples' yearning for the realization of New Testament Christianity, and the Methodists' preoccupation with the evidences of salvation have produced special theological propensities that have remained characteristic of the special outlook of these denominations.

But the fact is that these basic apprehensions were not developed into theological doctrines and tested by critical theological thought. There was no pressing need to do this because the denominations holding these special points of view could afford to be self-sufficient by keeping aloof from other Christian groups. Thus an awareness of the differences in the tenets of the several denominations and a concern for an understanding of these differences did not produce a full theological responsibility. To be sure, the history of American Protestantism in the nineteenth century is filled with stories of conflicts between Methodists and Presbyterians, Baptists and Disciples, Congregationalists and Presbyterians, and so on, but the debates that attended them were of no lasting importance because American Protestantism learned to get settled in denominationalism.

Here is the third factor under the impact of which American Protestantism has assumed its largely untheological ways. Denominationalism is not only an ecclesiastical condition (made possible by the introduction of freedom of religion into the life of the new American nation) but it is also a state of mind. As such it is the peculiar relation of the members of an individual denomination to themselves and to other denominations. They preserve and cling to the special religious traditions of their own denomination (creeds, if they have any; liturgies; ordinances; polities; ethics; and moral codes) in a stubborn and self-satisfied way as if no other forms of

Christian faith and order existed or had the right to exist—but (and this is the telling feature of denominationalism) they grant the members of other denominations the right to hold and practice the same judgment concerning the traditions and usages which they happen to cherish. Denominationalism is thus a curious combination of intolerance and tolerance. On the one hand, it reflects that exclusiveness which was characteristic of the churches when, in the eras prior to the establishment of religious freedom, they had to conform to the requirement of religious uniformity; on the other hand, it exhibits the freedom of religious profession which was made possible when the modern State assumed a neutral attitude toward the religious faith of its members or citizens. Under the auspices of denominationalism, each church group is enabled to act as if there were no other churches in existence, but in so doing it concedes to the other churches, which do actually exist as its neighbors and rivals, the right to practice the same kind of isolationism. In other words, this attitude engenders a relativistic neutrality of the denominations toward one another, a neutrality which makes it impossible for the members of any denomination to consider seriously the question of whether the diversity of churches is a necessary form of Christianity. It kills a serious concern for the truth of Christianity because it encourages neither self-criticism nor mutual criticism. In short, it stifles theological vitality and fosters theological lethargy.

IV

It is now recognized in all Protestant churches that denominationalism must be overcome. Indeed, no contemporary movement in Protestantism is so strong as that of the aspiration to church unity. All over the Protestant world people respond to the call for the unification of Christendom. During the past decades much has been achieved in furthering co-operation among the churches. Local congregations of different denominations have learned how to work together; interdenominational activities have been undertaken on all levels of church life, from the local to the international scene; reconciliations between separated bodies of individual church families have been effected; several denominations have been united or are actively engaged in exploring possible interchurch unions; the National Council of the Churches of Christ in America has been founded; the World Council of Churches has become a reality.

One must not think that these movements will accomplish complete Protestant church unity in the foreseeable future. But it is already obvious that the divisiveness of Protestant Christianity is gradually being overcome. The historical denominations will maintain themselves and remain independent units for a long time, but they will give up more and more of their isolationist exclusiveness.

In this setting, the people of the churches must develop a theological responsibility. For the greater the demands of interchurch co-operation the greater will be the necessity to inquire by what right the individual denominations can maintain their particular differences. Thus a theological investigation of the religious and Christian adequacy of specific church traditions will become inevitable. Furthermore, as the several churches and denominations learn to co-operate with one another they will be forced to ask themselves how they are related, individually and together, to the one Lord whom they profess to serve. But from such a concern there will necessarily arise interdenominational theological work. This work will be pointed toward an ecumenical theology in the context of which the "theological" traditions of individual churches will have to be compared with one another in the light of the gospel itself.

All this means that, as the interdenominationalism of the present grows in strength, American Protestants will find themselves compelled to turn from their untheological ways. They simply will have to learn how to use the tools of theology. And as they learn this they will probably discover that by the exercise of theological responsibility they can deepen and enrich their Christian faith.

Part VII

Religion and the Encounter
of East and West

21

A Unique Christian Mission:
The Mukyokai ("Non-Church")
Movement in Japan*

BY EMIL BRUNNER

There is in Japan a Christian movement which stands unique in all Christianity. It is called *Mukyokai,* "Non-Church." It is the outcome of the work of the greatest Japanese evangelist, Kaizo Utschimura, whose autobiographical sketch, "How I Became a Christian," was translated into several languages fifty years ago and was read by many of us here in Switzerland. Our attention was drawn to it by Ragaz, whom we students considered a great teacher. However, Utschimura is really among those whose work has only been recognized and become influential posthumously. Recognition of his significance has finally come in two ways: by his writings, comprising twenty volumes, and, above all, through his personal disciples who carried on the work of his life.

Utschimura was a Christian with a boundless urge for freedom. Converted to Christianity by an American missionary, he founded, together with his fellow students, a separate church, which was at the time the only one supported by the Japanese. Later he became a university evangelist, not supported by any church or association but making his living as a freelance Christian teacher. His influence was extraordinary, not so much in the number of his converts as in their outstanding quality and their faithfulness to him and to his cause throughout their lives. A large number of Utschimura's disciples are still living and are now the leaders of the Mukyokai movement. Among them are the following: the president of Tokyo University, Dr. Yanaihara; the former president, Dr. Nambora; and

* Translated by Lydia Leibrecht.

a large number of university or college presidents and professors. There are also men in other important occupations.

Utschimura's impact was caused mainly by the organization of Bible-study groups. The Bible is at the center of this movement—especially the New Testament, with its message of Jesus Christ and the "justification solely through faith." And yet this Bible movement is by no means characterized by a narrow-minded, literalistic fundamentalism; for, if this were true, the movement would certainly not have been able to attract the very cream of the Japanese people. The adherents of the Mukyokai know themselves as decided and radical Protestants in the spirit of the Reformers; like Luther, they derive from the doctrine of "faith alone" that of "the priesthood of all believers." They emphasize the responsibility of every Christian to proclaim the gospel. They train the members of their Bible-study groups to become independent evangelists. This is the real secret of their rapid expansion all over Japan.

For them the printed word is just as important as the spoken one. There are a large number of periodicals published by such laymen. The most important of these periodicals, to which I myself used to contribute an occasional article, has about four to five thousand subscribers. It is published by a lawyer and former diplomat, Tsakanoto; but President Yanaihara, too, publishes his own periodical. A number of these Christian laymen also publish Bible commentaries, Greek synopses and concordances, as well as other writings helpful for Bible study. In so doing, however, they avoid dealing with subtle theological questions. The Bible as it is—and not man's thoughts about it—is, in their intent, to be taken for its value. The total literature produced by the spiritual leaders of this movement already fills a small library. Tsakamoto has been working for years on the translation of the New Testament into colloquial Japanese.

The most important means for evangelizing are the Bible-study groups. There must already be hundreds of them, the total number of members being estimated at about fifty thousand. The individual groups are generally small: the largest are Tsakamoto's, with some three or four hundred members, and Yanaihara's, with about two hundred, mostly students. They meet on Sunday mornings. The leader interprets the Bible in a kind of continuous sermon, and says the prayers. The "congregation" sings and silently prays with him. This is their service. Apart from that, there are smaller groups usually meeting Sunday afternoon for the study of the Greek New Testament; people from various professions have learned Greek just for this purpose!

There are no paid or theologically trained ministers. President Yanaihara, for instance, does all this work in addition to his demanding job as the head of the country's foremost university. He uses part of his summer vacation for setting up Bible-study camps at the foot of Mount Fujiyama. One professor of German literature is traveling around the country to organize new Bible-study groups and visit those already in existence. The same is done by one of Japan's leading economists. There are a few who devote their full time to evangelizing, living on a modest income from their periodicals and from occasional gifts. One of them has given up his position as top executive of a factory in order to devote himself solely to spreading the gospel.

With regard to their relationship with the Church, the members of the Mukyokai, on the whole, keep at a good distance. And yet it would be wrong to call them a sect or a separate church. Apart from their Bible-study groups, they have no organization whatsoever—and on principle. They have no "sacraments"; they avoid all concrete forms pertaining to the establishment of a church or sect. "The word alone will do" is their principle, taken over from Luther and out of the Bible, to which they strictly adhere. No institution, no outward and visible structure, is to hamper the free revelation and action of the Word of God and the Holy Spirit. Therefore, *Mukyokai*—Non-Church.

Their relationship with the Church has been overcast by what amounts to polemics. For that reason I have, from the beginning, endeavored to bring Church and Mukyokai closer to one another. I have succeeded inasmuch as members from both sides recently participated in a service at the biggest church in Tokyo, to which I had invited all the groups of the Mukyokai with which I was familiar. Even some of their leaders were present. A second, similar meeting was planned, and both the largest "United Church of Japan" and a number of the Mukyokai leaders have given their pledges for active participation.

It is by no means the purpose or sense of this common action to lead the Mukyokai into the Church. And only because they are aware of this do the Mukyokai adherents take part. They want to stay out of the Church, and I think they are right. For they must fulfill a special task with their "Non-Churchism." They want to actualize a purely lay Christianity, based on the principle of the priesthood of all believers, which thereby has a special evangelizing power. So many, in Japan, are attracted by the gospel, but not so much by the Church. This does not simply mean "private Christianity" without obligation; the Bible-study groups put great emphasis on the responsibility of their members for the confession of Christ and for evangelizing.

It seems to me that this movement is most promising for the future, and for all Christianity. It is now possible to be a disciple of Christ, to live with Christ, and in fellowship with others to do something in his name—without the necessity of becoming a "church." I am far from suggesting that the churches have come to the end of their mission. They, too, can and shall, in their own way, serve the Lord and his Kingdom; and, due to their set form and organization, they have such possibilities as can hardly exist for a laymen's Bible movement. The very fact that the two exist side by side as long as they do not exist in opposition can only be conducive to the cause of Christ. It is certainly likely that the Non-Church movement may yet undergo developments which are not to be foreseen at this time. As a theologian, I am in a friendly relationship with both the Churches and the Mukyokai and I personally regard this as a great gift bestowed on me. In addition to profound gratitude, I have great hopes for the future, in the light of the vision of new movements in Christendom which I have seen in Japan.

22

Buddhism and Existentialism: The Dialogue between Oriental and Occidental Thought

BY YOSHINORI TAKEUCHI*

I. CURRENT OUTLOOKS AND HISTORIC TRADITIONS

The problem of encounter between being and non-being has recently given rise to much discussion among Western existentialists in both philosophy and theology. We Japanese philosophers have had more than a passing interest in this development from the start. This should occasion no surprise to students of the history of culture. Eastern philosophy, especially Buddhism, has been concerned with this problem for two and a half millennia, inded, since its origin.

The current situation is one of great promise for all men of good will. Our several ways of philosophical thinking appear to be converging more than they have for many centuries. It does not seem too sanguine to hope that the concentrated attack on this problem may, for the first time in world history, yield a real basis of mutual understanding between East and West. At the present juncture the destiny of mankind depends more than most men know on the visions and revisions of philosophers. Of course, where there is an enhanced possibility of mutual appreciation there is also the increased risk of misunderstanding.

The future of Christianity and Buddhism will, I hope, see more intimate spiritual exchange, at least in the realm of philosophy of religion and

* I should like to express my heartfelt gratitude to Professor Tetsutaro Ariga, of Kyoto University, who so freely and willingly gave of his time to read my whole text, and to make many helpful suggestions and corrections without which this study would not have been possible. I also express my profound gratitude to Dr. Galen Eugene Sargent, who translated parts of this text from Japanese into English, and made many suggestions for the correction of my English in its other sections.

theology. Both faiths must fight hand in hand to save men's minds from the dehumanization threatened by the new technological world. The mutuality of the two religions becomes especially urgent now that East and West are in process of becoming one world. In this situation one may hope that Western philosophers and theologians will develop much more interest in and sympathy for the spiritual problems of the other side of the world. Perhaps they will even come to withhold some of their final opinions about Buddhism, which in the past have more often tended to be dogmatic than informed.

In the present situation, contributions to the philosophy of religion and theology must be appraised chiefly in terms of their potential for promoting the spiritual life of the future. In this regard Professor Paul Tillich is surely one of the most interesting figures among Christian theologians. His ideas are very suggestive even for us Buddhists. In the following pages I shall offer some reflections on Buddhist views concerning a complex of terms which are admirably developed by Professor Tillich in his *Systematic Theology* and other recent works. I refer to the problem of "being, non-being, and being itself."

Whenever discussion arises concerning the problem of encounter between being and non-being, Western philosophers and theologians, with hardly an exception, will be found to align themselves on the side of being. This is no wonder. The idea of "being" is the Archimedean point of Western thought. Not only philosophy and theology but the whole tradition of Western civilization have turned around this pivot.

All is different in Eastern thought and Buddhism. The central notion from which Oriental religious intuition and belief as well as philosophical thought have been developed is the idea of "nothingness." To avoid serious confusion, however, it must be noted that East and West understand non-being or nothingness in entirely different ways. Absolute nothingness or non-being—"*mu*" in Japanese—is not the "*me on*" of Platonism. Neither is it by any means limited to the meaning of the so-called "annihilating nothingness" of existentialism. It includes, of course, this negative meaning, but by means of a thoroughgoing negativity the very negation turns itself into the most positive activity. The closest approximation which Western thought offers to our Oriental view is, I believe, the Hegelian notion of "absolute negativity" or "negation of negation." In Hegel, however, due to the primacy of the universal and objective side of his *Begriff*, the dialectic of absolute negativity does not express its genuine character as the action of the subject, and so it is bereft of "the passion of inwardness." Such a "passion of inwardness" should be regarded as prerequisite for the dynamic activity of his dialectic logic.

The principal point of my following argument is the relation between non-being as the *first* negative (that is, annihilating nothingness) and absolute negativity as the *second* negative. In this respect there is a striking parallel between the two relations, that is, the relation of non-being and absolute negativity, on the one hand, and that of being and being-itself, on the other. The question then arises: How are being-itself and absolute negativity related in God or in the Absolute?

In human consciousness the finitude of one's being is experienced as the threat of non-being to his being. All mortal beings are condemned to be finite. But the awareness of the finitude of his being, as well as of everything else in the world, is solely limited to the human being. As it happens, this awareness is his first step toward religious awakening. All this is due to the fundamental and ontological structure of his being.

Here Eastern and Western thought converge. Buddhism renders this view with a distinctive accent. Man's consciousness of the transience of life is, according to Buddhism, fundamental for his religious experience. Only by reflecting on this thought with all his mind and heart is he able to comprehend the full meaning of Buddha's words: (a) "All created things are impermanent," (b) "All created things are suffering," and (c) "All beings are Non-Self." These brief sentences convey the quintessence of Buddhist teaching. It will be shown presently that they represent three successive stages of religious awakening, respectively, (a) anxiety, (b) suffering, and (c) absolute negativity.

I shall endeavor to use the *phenomenological* method in beginning my description of the states of religious consciousness or awakening. My approach will be not that of a Buddhist theologian, who presupposes certain dogmatic creeds as absolute, but rather that of a student of the philosophy of religion, who is anxious to be fair to all forms of religious truth. Thus by confronting my interpretation with Buddhist doctrine, on the one hand and with that of Western existentialists, on the other, I hope to be able to find in the labyrinth of non-being a thread that will lead us to the solution of our principal problem. The contribution to this end of two key Buddhist ideas, the theory of *pratītya-samutpāda* (chain of causation) and the doctrine of *karman-saṃsāra* ("eternal return") will be elucidated in the closing section (III) of this essay.

II. THE STAGES OF RELIGIOUS AWAKENING

A. *The Encounter of Being and Non-Being*

(1) Religious awakening occurs, in general, when something extraordinary happens in the midst of our daily, ordinary life. Here the designation "ordinary life" has been chosen deliberately. It embraces our individual as well as our social life. The common ontological structure of our daily life, whether social or individual, is the object of our investigation. When the extraordinary suddenly seizes the taken-for-granted structure of our daily life and shakes it to its very foundations, our religious consciousness is aroused. In a primitive society, for instance, wars, calamities, epidemics, play this role of awakening the religious consciousness. For the individual, death, sickness, or other crucial events have similar effects. Now the question is: How is such a movement of consciousness possible?

In order to obtain a right answer, it must be remembered (a) that the very structure of ordinary life, simply because it is ordinary life, does not permit religious consciousness to function in a concrete way, that is, except as abstract knowledge. It is solely through *the shock caused by the extraordinary* that we can realize the basic structure of our daily life. It is a life that has many orders. But the order that is tested by the probe of the shock is the fundamental one. All other orders of life and their qualities may be neglected in the face of this one. It is the order where life's routine is being performed. In ordinary life, today is much like yesterday, nor will tomorrow be different from today. For a human being who starts his daily routine every morning there is no reason to be startled by the fact that a polar bear in a cage is able to bear the repetition of his monotonous pacing. For it is only through the shock caused by the extraordinary that the tediousness (ennui) of ordinary life begins to wound our heart; only then is our knowledge a true learning.

To interpret religious experience we must further remember that (b) these stereotyped repetitions in ordinary life are not only repetitions in time, such as hours, days, months, years, generations, centuries, they also impinge upon the spatial dimension of life. Viewed closely, the spatial aspect appears to be more important because it connects so inextricably with what is peculiarly human. The space in which I live represents my ordinary life. My house is in order, that is to say, it is arranged to match the order of every day's repetitions. The arranged tools and articles in my room—all furniture is fixture in this sense—have their own periodicity. Whenever they are worn out they must be refurnished, repeatedly. In short, like the many cogs inside a watch, every part of space turns its wheel when its tooth is touched by that of another. Thus they are all in contact with each other so that one monotonous repetition of ordinary life, like the movement of a watch hand, is derived from all the respective parts.

The first step toward ontological analysis of ordinary life has not yet brought us to the innermost core of the matter. What is here revealed is rather the *ontic structure of everyday existence*. This is preliminary to an existential analysis of boredom (*Langweile*). Of course, in this preliminary stage, the deep meaning of the "eternal return" (Nietzsche) or of *karman* and *saṃsāra* cannot yet be understood. But at any rate the wheel of life and the world expresses itself clearly in ordinary affairs.

(2) The extraordinary occurs suddenly. It unsettles the round of ordinary life, disturbing its routines. But a disorder within ordinary life does not necessarily point to the extraordinary. There is in the occurrence of the extraordinary something else which is more than a mere disorder. The extraordinary implies the negation of life itself. Life being threatened with its negation feels fear and dread toward the extraordinary. Therefore, fear and dread in this situation will reflect the inner relation between the extraordinary and the ordinary life.

(a) If the impact of the extraordinary upon the ordinary were immediate, it would mean a complete destruction of meaning, without allowing any time for the awakening of religious consciousness. Actually there is some distance between the extraordinary and the ordinary life, so that the latter may while waiting take some attitude toward the visitation of the former. The extraordinary, which is in the midst of ordinary life and yet maintains a distance from it, becomes a problem to the person. Fear and dread characterize consciousness of this threat to life.

(b) Extraordinary and ordinary life have order and disorder as their intermediates. The extraordinary in its attack upon ordinary life sends a disorder as its vanguard. Immediately, ordinary life begins to defend itself against it within the fortress of daily order. Therefore, the life problem is to stave off the forces of disorder and to evade in some way the decisive battle within the fort. But is there any prospect of being successful with such a strategy of life? Ordered life supposes it has a chance, because the extraordinary is *extra*-ordinary; the ordinary life believes that the extraordinary lies outside its fort and comes only rarely to attack upon it. There is some plausibility for this belief. As we have seen, the order of daily life is consolidated in its many parts. Our habits and customs are not *disjecta membra*. They work always as an organized whole and resist with all their power any attack made on one of their parts. This is the reason why it is so difficult to change our customs, and, in the present case, why the attack of the extraordinary seems so rare and unusual.

But how is it, if with all our efforts and strategies our life ends in death? What shall we gain if the extraordinary is not *extra* to our life? For the structure of our finitude, non-being is essential as well as being.

(3) The qualitative difference between the feeling of anxiety and that of fear and dread is well known today. Religious awakening is due to anxiety and not to fear or dread. While the latter is always attached to its object (that is, the extraordinary) and is obsessed with the thought of doing away with the extraordinary as the cause of the threat, anxiety is detached from the object and with infinite resignation transcends it—I should prefer to say transdescends it—and returns into its own depth. In fear and dread, our feeling is distracted; but in anxiety it is concentrated on its own inwardness and, all perplexity and confusion having been cleansed away, is transformed into transparency. In short, anxiety is fear and dread metamorphosed into a pure crystal. Now, what is reflected in the center of this clarified feeling? Western existentialists answer, "It is nothing, or non-being."

(a) Anxiety is the awareness of *the shock of non-being.* From this feeling there arises the question of being. This ontological problem is phrased by Heidegger in his typical way as follows: "Why is there any being at all— why not rather nothing?"[1] Although this question provokes us to ask with astonishment about the problem of being and non-being, such a formulation of the problem gives us the impression that it is looked at chiefly from the viewpoint of philosophy. From a religious point of view, the formulation of the problem should rather be the converse: "Why is there any nothing and why not rather being?"[2] And with this question we come nearer to the meaning of Buddha's teaching: "All created things are impermanent."

In our anxious awareness of "being-unto-death," it is not only *our* finitude but being-as-such in its finitude that slips into the abyss of non-being. For our awareness, non-being is not a matter of the future; it already appears in our human present as death, which swallows all being and life. The idea of *saṃsāra,* the wheel of life and death, is a radical expression of this "being-unto-death." The acceptance of this view of life does not mean that man has to withdraw from the creative activities of the world. On the contrary, as in the case of the atheistic existentialists—Nietzsche and Sartre, for example— such a view of life may perhaps form a necessary presupposition for man's sense of freedom and creative activities. Thus, although the view of "the ring of life and death" does not allow us to take a naïve affirmative atti- tude toward life, it is by no means mere negativism or simple despair. The despair in this case ought to be defined as "the despair of despair." Of course, the creative activities in this despair of despair may be compared to our efforts to clean the window glass of a ship when she is sinking with us; yet we can take this attitude deliberately.

(b) The unconscious assumption of the taken-for-granted order is the unconscious acceptance of being and meaning in their immediate identity. When the shock of the extraordinary seizes upon the ordinary life, a disorder ensues; and the disorder awakens the anxiety of "being" threatened by "non-being." With this threat it is not only the power of being but also the meaning of being which is now at stake. In the stages previous to anxiety, only the power of being is brought into crisis, and therefore life tries somehow to save it from its danger. This is why a pre-anxiety feeling is attached to its object. But in anxiety the crisis of the power of being is followed by that of the meaning of being.

In the face of the fundamental problem of life—"Why nothing and not being?"—the life which has been till the last moment so interesting and colorful suddenly begins to fade and to become wearisome and bleak. Now, it is not only our life but also the entirety of being as such whose meaning is exposed to uncanny doubt. Thus to the anxiety of death and fate is added the anxiety of meaninglessness and emptiness. From the typological point of view, these two types of anxiety must be clearly distinguished. The distinction becomes manifest to us when the extraordinary retreats. For, while the anxiety of death and fate now disappears, that of meaninglessness still remains. But then, conversely, the anxiety of meaninglessness and emptiness of life presses our being to decide the question whether "to be or not to be." So the anxiety of meaninglessness in its turn may cause that of death. But, strictly speaking, this decision itself is meaningless, for all beings, including ourselves and therefore our decisions, are meaningless. This is what I have called the "despair of despair." Therefore, in this "sickness unto death" (Kierkegaard) our being suffers a twofold despair. Attacked on two sides by non-being, our finitude itself, which is limited by birth and death, is symbolic of this despair of despair.

Therefore, this awareness of our finitude not only gives an occasion for transcending it, in the sense that it directs our mind to the experience of our own potentiality, that is, cultural and spiritual creativity,[3] but further it also drives us to *transdescend* from this transcendence and fall into the abyss of non-being.

B. *Suffering, Sin, and the Kantian Doctrine of Radical Evil*

The thoroughgoing awareness of interdependence between the two types of anxiety, that is, between death and meaninglessness, leads our religious consciousness to the higher stage. This is the consciousness of suffering and sin. Although it may *seem* at first rather strange to combine suffering and sin, since each represents a different stage of religious awakening,[4] yet the necessity of such a combination will, I hope, become clearer in the following analysis. Suffering enters our consciousness as the despair of despair. Therefore, in the suffering which is the result of the interdependence between the two anxieties, the meaning and power of being return to their quasi-unity (polar relation) again, now not as existence in the immediate identity of the daily order, but rather as maintenance of an ever-changing balance between death and the meaning moment.

It requires some concentration of mind to realize that this suffering is an inwardness of our self. In the ordinary sense, for instance when we say "I suffer from such and such a thing," the "I" as the subject of suffering is presupposed as a being. But here in the despair of despair suffering is presupposed as the whole of our being and as the complete form of our self-consciousness. For all other self-reflection and self-realization—in our theorizing and practical activities—except that in our religious awakening, is not so thoroughgoing as suffering. From the viewpoint of suffering, our infinite self-transcendence toward unlimited potentialities, whether theoretical or practical, brings nothing but the tortures of tantalization.

The despair of despair, as we have seen, is devoid of decision, for it is now meaningless to be earnest about the problem of decision in the suffering of despair. But this does not mean that we now can come back to the easy-goingness of ordinary life. On the contrary, the decision devoid of conviction is the very suffering of the fate of Sisyphus.

Sin is the third type of religious anxiety. It brings us the awareness of guilt and condemnation.[5] But in this anxiety an ethical feeling of earnestness is predominant, which does not simply stare at or peep into the threatening non-being. Rather, it concerns the problem of the self as being. Sin is therefore the anxious earnestness of my self threatened by non-being. Furthermore, in the awareness of sin, this threatening non-being is itself a consequence of the nature of myself, the self I have inherited and—as predisposed thereby—the self I now am. So death is called in Christianity "the wages of sin" and Buddhism teaches that our *saṃsāra* is due to our *karman*. In short, sin is the awareness of *the shock of non-self*.

The fundamental structure of suffering and sin as the despair of despair is best revealed in the relation of freedom and destiny in this situation. Perhaps the key to this problem is furnished by Kant's[6] conception of radical evil in his philosophy of religion. Although he classifies two sorts of propensity (*Hang*), namely, physical and moral propensity, it is clear from the context that the latter is expressed in the metaphor of the former. But what is the intention of this metaphor? Kant gives the following apt example: a savage who knows nothing about alcoholic liquors has no desire to get intoxicated, but once he has a taste for it his inborn propensity is awakened and with an irresistible power conquers his future life.

The intention of the metaphor is clear. Moral evil comes from our individual free act, but with this act our inborn propensity to evil, which has made our doing bad inevitable, becomes suddenly clear to our mind. This presupposes, so to speak, the experience of the crystallization in our mind of the propensity. In an early winter morning the water of a pond may be ice-cold, but it does not necessarily follow that the water is at that moment in process of freezing. But a leaf fluttering in the wind happens to fall into the pond, and the whole surface of the water begins to freeze simultaneously. So it is with the crystallization of the propensity in our mind. Although our consciousness is bad from the first, one fatal evil which is due to our free act makes us realize the propensity to evil in our heart once for all.

This means that the awareness of original sin (the "propensity to evil") has the characteristic of a counter-conversion to evil. We do not intend to discuss here Kant's concept of sin in detail. It must only be noted that there are three stages of religious consciousness in his philosophy: (1) the ethico-religious belief which is explained in his ethical works, (2) the counter-conversion from this belief to the radical evil, and (3) the authentic conversion from this evil—as it is called by him, "revolution in the heart." Psychologically speaking, counter-conversion shares the same general character as conversion; we may therefore conclude from what he said about the latter what he was thinking about the former. Influenced by the doctrine of conversion commonly accepted in the pietistic tradition of his time, he thought of conversion as coming decisively and once for all in one's life. So it is with the counter-conversion to original sin: it is decisive and no more to be eradicated, because man has now realized in experience what before was only a propensity to evil. The counter-conversion is made once for all; it freezes his heart, which will not begin to melt till the coming of spring (that is, the authentic conversion).

In the second place, according to Kant, this propensity to evil manifests itself in three stages: *fragilitas, impuritas,* and *vitiositas.*[7] Discussing the first state, Kant discloses his own personal experience regarding this matter. It is the Pauline cry, he explains—"To will is present with me; but how to perform . . . I find not"—that characterizes the frailty of heart. And here, at the same time, we see that the aforementioned problem of our awareness of finitude is now brought into the sphere of the ethical. In this experience of a breakdown in our ethical earnestness our action and decision of transcendence turns out to be that of *transdescendence*.

In Buddhism the term *duḥkha* (suffering), especially in combination with *duḥkha-samudaya* (the cause and origin of suffering), denotes this *transdescendence*. Originally *duḥkha* expressed pain. But in the *Agamuas* (the early Buddhist scriptures), the feeling of pleasure and the feeling of pain as well as indifferent feeling are all called suffering. It is clear that suffering is not meant in its ordinary sense, but rather in its metaphysical sense. Dr. Hakuju Ui explains this suffering as infinite religious endeavor to attain the ideal. But, as the *duḥkha* is also our feeling of failure, so its meaning, especially when used in the combination *duḥkha-samudaya,* is directed toward our experience of *transdescendence*. Thus, in the Pali commentaries, suffering is always portrayed by enumerating "the boundary situations": death, old age, struggle, and the like.

Our question is therefore: How does our act of transcendence lead us to awareness of transdescendence? But as these states of our ethical and religious consciousness have already been investigated by Professor Tillich with wider scope in his essay "The Trans-Moral Conscience,"[8] I shall not explore here the points I would otherwise address.

As our happiness is conditioned by our virtue (Kant), so our suffering *must be* the result of our sin. The first part of this proposition is concerned with our ideal and is thus a matter of hope, while the latter part is based on the recognition of reality. But it does not mean that, with this recognition and ensuing resignation, the significance of the first part is entirely lost. On the contrary, our suffering in consequence of our radical sin reflects upon itself the original glory, now lost, of our being. "All these same miseries prove one's greatness. They are the misery of a great lord, of a deposed king," says Pascal. The very depth of the Fall suggests the height where once we stood. To say the same thing from the standpoint of Kantian ethics, the height of the ideal corresponds to the depth of propensity. Thus the *transdescendence* reflects upon itself the transcendence. So our suffering is a to-and-fro movement. If it were not so, we would indeed be in misery but would have no consciousness of it. Therefore, suffering is the awareness of our whole being's oscillation between misery and greatness. Otherwise Nietzsche's protest against the combination of suffering and sin (punishment) would be legitimate. But the nature of suffering as a prelude to all symphonies of religious sentiments should not be misunderstood. The idea of suffering is predominant in Greek tragedies.[9] It plays an important role in Biblical religion and it is also the principal doctrine of early Buddhism.

In our present technological age, when the spirit of resentment (Nietzsche), hand in hand with the dehumanized mechanical relationship between man and nature and between man and man, is raging all over the world, it is an urgent necessity that we should be cured of this fatal disease of revengefulness.[10] But it is also worthy of note that, owing to our too-great attachment to the complacencies of everyday life, we are all rapidly forgetting what suffering properly means, indeed, so rapidly and thoroughly that today it is difficult to represent to our mind what Nietzsche meant when he attacked the traditional doctrine of suffering.

With a penetrating insight Pascal held all the antinomies of the reason to be based on this to-and-fro movement between the misery and the greatness of human nature. In this respect he was truly a precursor of Kant's doctrine of transcendental dialectics. By comparing Pascal and Kant in regard to this problem we may be able to realize why its solution should be sought through the practical and not through the theoretical reason and, furthermore, why it is insufficient to search for a clue to the solution of these difficulties solely in the ethico-religious belief as the first stage of conversion. Rather, it is by authentic conversion as repentance from radical sin that one can find a true solution of the antinomies of the reason.

C. *"Neither/Nor"—Beyond the Antinomies of Reason*

Dr. Hajime Tanabe (1885–   ) has recently introduced a "philosophy of *metanoetics*." According to his view, so far as I understand it, the only true way to transcend noetics (that is, metaphysics as speculative philosophy in the realm of subject-object relationship) is to go through a complete *metanoia* in the "death and resurrection" experience of conversion. Therefore, the true dialectic is neither the "as well as" of the speculative synthesis of Hegel nor the "either/or" of the ethical earnestness of Kierkegaard. It is "neither/nor": a thoroughgoing negativity of our immediacy (the repentance of one's radical sin) by the mercy of the Absolute, who also negates Himself for the sake of Love and Mercy. Our repentance of sin means the forgiveness and negation of it by the grace of the Absolute. For the very reason that God or Buddha is the Absolute Nothingness, He is the power and mercy of absolute self-surrender. Here, it seems to me, Dr. Tanabe has been successful in bringing into unity, according to his unique way of thinking rooted in his own experience, the innermost cores of Christianity and Buddhism.

In early Buddhism, as we shall shortly see, the antinomies of the metaphysical problem are explained with a method strikingly similar to that of Kant.[11] But the Buddhist solution is quite different from the European. In

Buddhism the problems are always answered by a "neither/nor" with regard to each pair of contrary assertions, while both Pascal and Kant give
their answers from a supposedly higher standpoint—whether that of faith
or that of the practical reason—bringing about the restoration of the
original theses. As a logical reaction against such a method of solution,
there has appeared, it seems to me, the present atheistic existentialism.
Even an existentialist theologian like Professor Tillich precludes such problems as the natural immortality of the soul and the existence of God.

In this spiritual situation, I hope that the idea of regarding the Absolute
as Absolute Nothingness is not so strange for European scholars as it once
was. For instance, Heidegger's interpretation of Nietzsche's words "God is
dead"[12] and his recent thoughts on the relation between *Sein* and *Nichts*[13];
Professor Tillich's demand to transcend the God of theism[14]; and Bergson's
deep insight into the religious experience of "the dark night of the soul"[15]—
these can be regarded as three directions, followed respectively by the existentialist philosopher, the theologian, and the philosopher of life, which will converge into a focus on God as Absolute Nothingness. God is at once Being-itself
and Absolute Nothingness. As Being-itself infinitely transcends every finite
being, so Absolute Nothingness transcends mere non-being. And "on the
other hand, as everything finite participates in being-itself,"[16] so the mere
negative participates in Absolute Negativity. For God in His very nature is
com-passionate to the suffering of all being. In the case of Absolute Negativity the significance of transcendence and participation is of course different
from that in the case of Being-itself. But for those who can endure the suffering of the neither/nor unto the end, the analogical structure of Being-itself
and Absolute Nothingness is quite clear. God is at once Being-itself and
Absolute Nothingness. It is understandable that I prefer the latter designation, because Absolute Nothingness as Absolute Negativity (that is, the
negation of negation) at the same time implies the former, the affirmative.[17]

(1) Let us recapitulate the development of the awareness of our suffering
from another standpoint. In ordinary life, we reflect everything in the
mirrors of the past and the future. (To have the representation of a thing
is to reflect it in either mirror.) Thus we are always running after the past
(*atītaṃ anvāgameti*) or searching for the future (*anāgataṃ paṭikankhati*).
So we always indulge ourselves in the images of being—subject-object relationship—in order to evade the fatal encounter between the real I and the
real other. For instance, we are accustomed to say "tomorrow, tomorrow"
because we unconsciously know that our present is suffering. On this point
Buddha and Pascal are the same.

Hence the first step to religious awakening is to come back to one's present (that is, one's real presence). But with the awareness of our suffering, our object is now presence itself. In this case, we neglect all the outward things, and only reflect ourselves in both mirrors. It is as if we set ourselves between two parallel mirrors. If I hold up my right hand I see my images in the infinite series produced by reflection between the two mirrors holding up their left hands against my will. Our old self, our propensity to evil, is nothing but this infinite series of images. Suffering is the surrender of the lonely present self to this infinite array of the old self. We find our present will and decision are preoccupied by our old selves. And further, since this is not a mere objective judgment, we must have true realization of this miserable state of ours by trying at all times to act up to the level of good resolution. So the eternal return of the same things, or *karman* and *saṃsāra,* is the structure of our being as will and decision which is realized by the awareness of suffering.

Suffering is, therefore, the feeling and self-consciousness of suffering defeat. It is an eternal circular motion starting from the old self to the present self and returning from the latter to the former. But this eternal circular motion is in fact a spiral one, and so it has a conical direction and also has its end in itself, namely, the apex of the cone. For the drive of the suffering is the neither/nor: it is a double-edged blade thrust deep into our sick soul to find and cut off the afflicted part. In this sense suffering is the evidence that the surgical operation is going on in our innermost heart. "Suffering (*Qual*) is not only the center of I (*Ichheit*), but it is also the source (*Quelle*) of all being," because it is the fundamental structure of the world.[18] Furthermore, suffering is at once our way to come to the center of "I" and God's compassionate way to come down to "I" as the source of the world.

(2) Heidegger points out that the inner working principle in both Hegel's *Logic* and his *Phenomenology of Mind* is the idea of suffering as the work of Absolute Negativity.[19] According to Heidegger, suffering in Greek is *algos,* and there may be an etymological kinship between *algos* and *logos.* Whether this is true or not, I do not know. But at any rate it is clear that suffering as the religious parallelism to the philosophical *logos* means the concentration of our mind into innermost inwardness, where the peak of personal individuation is at the same time its complete participation in the whole being. Suffering, or self-concentrated suffering, is the pivot of the absolute negativity (the negation of negation), where the negative is converted to the affirmative and vice versa.

It is well known that the way of Hegel's *Phenomenology* is that of our suffering and despair. Hegel asserts, against the idea of God of Schlegel and

Novalis: "The life of God and intelligence, then, can, if we like, be spoken of as love disporting with itself; but this idea falls into edification, and even sinks into insipidity, if it lacks the seriousness, the suffering, the patience, and the labour of the negative."[20] God is not only *aseity;* He is suffering, the subject of infinite self-estrangement. God as Being-itself is the ground of all finite beings, but the ground of this ground is His foreground (that is, this real world). Therefore God must come to this world every time as an action of revelation of His entirety of Being-itself. God is at once *An-sich-sein* and *Für-sich-sein.*

Although I cannot agree with Hegel's teleological methodology in the treatment of dialectical development as *An sich, Für sich* and *An und für sich,* I understand his idea of the trinity of the personal God at the heart of his dialectics; and I think it must not be neglected when we are reflecting on our religious experience—on the condition of having intercourse with the living God. If we were to transcend the personal God (trinity of God), it would not be toward Being-itself, but rather toward Absolute Nothingness. The concept of Godhead or Being-itself as standing behind the trinity of God arises, according to my view, from misunderstanding the personal God as the God of deism.

III. THE BUDDHIST ANSWER

Self-concentrated suffering is in Buddhistic terminology *duḥkha-samudaya.* This is the cause and origin of all sufferings. Our spiral way of suffering leads us, by the accumulation of our acts of self-negation, toward the vantage point where we can get the whole view of our situation. Although the compassionate Absolute is always with us so long as we are suffering, yet it is only here that we are struck by the lightning of grace. This is the divine-human encounter. This is our authentic conversion. As it is through conversion that we can realize what the *duḥkha-samudaya* was, so the realization of the *duḥkha-samudaya* and its annihilation (*duḥkha-nirodha*) must be at the same instant.

But the problem is: How does the conversion really dispose of the suffering? Another Greek word meaning "to suffer" is *pathein.* It is the authentic passion (*pathos*) of wonder (*thaumazein*) that is the beginning and the principle (*arche*) of all philosophical thinking. Heidegger discusses the meaning of this passion in one of his most recent works.[21] In the passion of wonder we are made to retreat from our attitude to represented things (our subject-object relationship) and remain in our inwardness. But simultaneously we are tied up with our whole being to the realm of relation between *Sein* and *Seiendes.* From this deep feeling of our belonging to this realm, and with our wonder that *Sein* appears in *Seiendes,* the philosophical question arises: Why is there any being at all—why not rather nothing? Therefore, the deep feeling of philosophical wonder emancipates us from the subject-object relationship, in which always (though we are unconscious of it) lurks the spirit of revenge. This is the philosophical way of existential awakening. Religiously speaking, our way of existential awakening through suffering is fairly different from the philosophical one. In Christianity suffering (*pathein:* to suffer) is the Passion, and our suffering is to follow in the wake of Jesus Christ. In Buddhism the similarity and difference between the philosophical way and the religious way is especially clear. According to Heidegger, Nietzsche's two enigmatic thoughts—the enternal return of the same things and the superman—are essentially correlated in the ideal of "emancipation from the spirit of revenge." So are correlated in early Buddhism both *karman-saṃsāra* and Buddha or Tathāgata in the ideal of the annihilation of *duḥkha-samudaya* (that is, emancipation from our conscious and subconscious attachment to the represented "I" and the objective world).

A. Suffering and Repentance in Buddhism

Let us now fix our attention on the Buddhistic idea of suffering, and consider how the origin of suffering (*duḥkha-samudaya*) is annihilated, and further how the suffering of man is related to the *com-passion* of Buddha. This will show, I hope, in concrete terms how the religious way is related to and at the same time different from the philosophical one, even in the learning of existential truth.

(1) First we must introduce two ideas: (a) *pratītya-samutpāda* and (b) *karman-saṃsāra.*

(a) The doctrine of *pratītya-samutpāda* is usually translated by European scholars as "the chain of causation." In one of the sutras the motive for this way of thinking is clearly expressed:

Before my enlightenment, monks, when I was unenlightened and still a *bodhisattva,* I thought: "Into wretchedness, alas, has this world fallen, it is born, grows old, dies, passes away, and is reborn. But from this pain it knows no escape, from old age and death. When indeed from this pain shall an escape be known, from old age and death?"

Then, monks, I thought, "Now when what exists do old age and death exist, and what is the cause of old age and death?" And as I duly reflected, there came the comprehension of full knowledge: it is when there is rebirth that there is old age and death. Old age and death have rebirth as cause.

Then, monks, I thought, "Now when what exists does rebirth exist, and what is the cause of rebirth?"[22]

Thus, in the first place, *pratītya-samutpāda* theory seeks the cause of our misery (birth, old age, death) and traces successively the conditioned to its condition till it reaches the final one. Usually the series of these conditions is mentioned as twelve. (1) old age and death (*jarā-maraṇa*), (2) rebirth (*jāti*), (3) will to be (*bhava*), (4) grasping (*upādāna*), (5) craving and love (*tṛṣṇā*), (6) feeling (*vedanā*), (7) contact (*sparśa*), (8) six sense organs (*ṣaḍ-āyatana*), (9) mind-and-body or the world into which our being is projected (*nāma-rūpa*), (10) consciousness and self (*vijñāna*), (11) aggregates (*saṃskāra*), (12) ignorance (*avidyā*).

Then, in the second place, it explains how the destruction of the final cause (ignorance, *avidyā*) leads us to conditioning in reverse order, back to the first term (old age and death, *jarā-maraṇa*).

European scholars tend to suppose that *pratītya-samutpāda* theory aims to explore the physical and psychological cause of our human misery, and to explain objectively how it happened that we are all destined to suffer such fullness of misery, as the Abhidharma Schools in India had already asserted. But even from the above-quoted sutra, which, defaced by the long oral traditions, gives only the stereotyped expression of the original experience, it is manifest that the drive which solicits this sort of meditation on our misery arises from the impact of death and rebirth experienced in the existential boundary situation. Therefore, the present author is convinced that although there are, between the conditioned and the condition, some cases of artificial combination, yet generally speaking the series of these conditions (twelve links) must be understood as that of existential categories, and further that the principle of their relation is the dialectical movement of *"zu-Grunde-gehen"*—thus the recognition of the cause is, at the same instant, its annihilation. *Pratītya-samutpāda* is the theory of conversion, or of the awakening to the Absolute Truth. *It is the spiral of stages followed step by step by religious hearts.*

On this spiral path toward the cause and origin of suffering (*duḥkha samudaya*) the predominant feeling is the anxiety of ethical earnestness. With penitent heart he who is suffering concentrates his mind on the problem of his propensity to evil, which is also common to the human mind in general. And then with gratitude and rejoicing he understands how this thoroughgoing negativity (*non-self*), which is now in his innermost self, turns out to be affirmative (*Non-Self*) by means of the grace and compassion of Buddha. So, contrary to philosophical thinking, religious thinking is chiefly concerned with the relation of the negativity and Absolute Negativity. *Pratītya-samutpāda* theory leads in this way to *nirvāna*. But since this religious idea is more simply expressed in the context of *karman* and *samsāra* by means of myths and symbols, I should like to proceed along this line, using such a method.

(b) *Karman* and *samsāra* is the *duḥkha-samudaya* intuitively expressed. One might ask: What is the relation between our suffering and Buddha's compassion? What is actually meant when he says: all beings are Non-Self? How are Being-itself and Absolute Nothingness correlated, as well as non-self and Non-Self, and being and non-being? The Buddhist replies to these questions will be clarified in the following description. As the matter is symbolic, so our way of thinking must be pictorial and parabolic in order to get a glimpse of the glory of the Absolute. But let us start with some preliminary remarks on the subject of *karman* and *samsāra*.

(2) *Karman* and *samsāra* come to us from pre-Buddhist Indian belief. *Karman* explains why we are under the heavy burdens of suffering in this world. Originally *karman* meant action which was valued as good, bad, or indifferent. But from earliest time *karman* was commonly taken to be the result of bad deeds. *Karman* in this sense is our habitual disposition binding our future action necessarily to one direction (that is, toward a bad action). Moreover, according to this belief, our beings themselves are the result of the past *karman*, because we are always responsible for our deeds. Therefore, death means going to our account, and thus our birth, our being in this world, is considered as the result of the past deeds. (Hence, palingenesis.) *Karman* and *samsāra* (transmigration) denote the same thing. The world as the correlate of our being is also the result of the same *karman* and *samsāra*. In Buddhism there are six possible worlds (literally, six possible walks or paths) through which mortal beings must transmigrate according to the measures of their sins. The wicked must go to hell and the good can enjoy the life of heaven after their death. But even the highest world is estranged from the realm of salvation. Because in none of them can man escape his destiny of death, and thus in the last analysis all these worlds mean suffering.

The idea of transmigration, it is said, belongs to the belief of primitive religion and even the Buddhist conception of *karman* and *samsāra* is quite mythological. Nevertheless, it cannot be denied, as we shall explain shortly, that there are some truths of religious intuition hidden under the mythological garb. Therefore, in the developed stage of Mahāyāna Buddhism, all philosophical thinking on the correlation between the self and the world and all religious reflection on the meaning of suffering, sin and salvation gravitate around the core of this basic myth.

B. *The True Significance of Karman-Saṃsāra*

When a mother says to her child who is crying in a nightmare, "It is just a dream, dear," it is a simple matter of waking up the child. In the same way, the concept of transmigration (*karman* and *saṃsāra*) is not predicable as an objective judgment on the fact of being. The proposition that all mortals are subject to transmigration likewise simply calls for an awakening; for those who accept this call, this proposition is an unconditional imperative. Unfortunately, however, the doctrine of *karman-saṃsāra* is not ordinarily understood in this way. Looked at merely objectively, the doctrine may seem to emphasize a fatalistic and deterministic view of life. *Looked at subjectively and existentially, which I believe is the proper way of understanding the doctrine, it is conducive to liberty and salvation.* When something throws a dark shadow in bright sunshine, its contour becomes clearly distinct, making the bright side look brighter in the sunshine. So the shadow of *karman* and *saṃsāra* suggestes another aspect of the picture, radiating the effulgence of the joy of emancipation and deliverance from this world. The theory of *karman-saṃsāra* in this sense is a springboard: our religious existence first takes a firm stand on this, in the assurance that, leaping from it, we may plunge into the bliss of salvation and emancipation.

In pre-Buddhist Indian thought the theory of *karman-saṃsāra* had already been dressed in a coherent form: we find Yājñavalkya, the philosopher of the Upanishads presenting the essence of this concept, the internal spark hidden in it. The reader of the Upanishads is made to feel that somehow from the gloomy stream of predestination (*karman* and *saṃsāra*), the light of salvation sometimes suddenly shines forth. That is to say, the idea of *karman-saṃsāra* illustrates the bleakness of human existence, which we can perceive only by witnessing this transcendent light. The fatalistic correlation, implied by the doctrine, between the self and the world may be compared to that between flint and steel: when they meet in a collision, they awaken in us the fundamental awareness of destiny-time. The inner spark of spiritual fire is thus kindled. To apprehend the meaning of transmigration, therefore, one ought to look upon it as if man were "a serpent who beholds the skin he has shed." Hence the *karman* doctrine of this philosopher is esoteric; it is a theme of conversation between just two persons, you and myself in close communion: "My dear, take my hand! We two alone shall know of this (*karman*); let this question of ours not be discussed in public," as Yājñavalkya says to his disciple.[23] Thus, only those who dare to climb the cliff up to the summit of being-itself (*sat eva*) have courage enough to peep into the abyss of non-being (*asat*). Otherwise they would be seized with faintness at the awesome sight of the abyss, only to fall into its unfathomable depths. This is the reason why the *karman* doctrine should be kept within the select circle.

But this esoteric doctrine soon became exoteric. It was immediately after the rapid spread and popularization of this belief that Buddha appeared on the philosophical and religious stage in India and gave his new message to the people. By this time the esoteric core of the *karman* theory had fairly well disintegrated and the whole theory, on that account, had deteriorated. It became something superficial, no more than a by-product of folklore. Nevertheless, or for this reason, the theory aroused an intriguing interest on the part of the majority during Buddha's time. The six masters of the heterodox schools, all contemporaries of Buddha, formulated their own opinions upon this matter. Whether they affirmed the *karman* theory or denied it, at least they paid attention to the problem. A scathing attack on the critics betrays the deep interest shown by the opposite party.

The Buddha himself was not indifferent. But his attitude toward this problem was far different from that of the other thinkers. For his answer was at once affirmative and negative; or rather it was *neither* yes *nor* no. For instance, when one disciple, named Sāti, voiced the opinion: there is a soul (*vijñāna*) which maintains self-identity in all changes of transmigration, as if this were the true meaning of his master's teaching on this matter, the Buddha rebuked him. But, on the other hand, the Buddha protested more sharply against those who contended that there was absolutely no *karman* at all in the world, because, according to him, this idea would lead to immoral conduct on the part of those who entertained such a theory.

There is some similarity, it seems to me, between the Buddha's attitude toward the *karman* theory and that of Jesus toward apocalyptic eschatology. Taken in their historical forms, both *karman* theory and eschatology were parts of the popular views of the world and life shared by the masses of their respective countries. Behind the mythological expressions, nonetheless, there are discernible religious intuitions in both cases, awakened by the very finitude of our being which is always threatened by non-being. Moreover, in both cases the religious intuitions are expressed in terms of time, suggesting the inner relationship between being and temporality. Of course, the standard of time reckoning is not the same: in the East, it is fatalistic and individualistic, while in the West it is historical and social. And yet it was precisely these mythological elements that formed the cradles in which the world religions grew up. They may well be likened to a wadi in a dry season. Now there is seen no water, but as soon as the storm ends the drought, a powerful stream will begin to flow down to the ocean. So when the weather of world history changes and "time is filled," through mythological wadies the streams of religion begin flowing and pour into the seas of world religions. With the appearance of Buddha and Jesus, the old vein began to pulsate. Or, we might say that both kindled the inner spark hidden in the petrified forms, that is, the popularized *karman* theory, accepted with pessimistic resignation, and the eschatology calculated by apocalyptic speculation. They brought a new spiritual fire to their peoples which spread out into the world beyond national boundaries.

In Indian mythology, *karman* theory, once it had been objectified and popularized, lost its original power as an appeal to the true Self. The true nature of the *karman* theory, on account of its enigmatic double meaning above mentioned, ought by means of the very myth to be able to stir up the feeling of freedom in the depth of man's mind. But now, since it fails to function as an appeal, it withers him with its double-edged logic. For the objectified *karman* theory, whether it be affirmed or denied, leads to the conclusion that man is a mere victim of fate.

And this was exactly the case with Brahmans and other heterodox teachers of Buddha's time. For while those who repudiate the *karman* theory (materialists, hedonists, blind occasionalists among them) represent one form of despair with regard to salvation, even the most earnest belief on the affirmative side, with its meditations and austerities to escape the miseries of life and world, turns out to be only another form of despair, the prospect of salvation being put off till an infinitely distant future. These two forms of despair are called by Buddha the two extremities.[24]

Thus with respect to the affirmation or denial of this *karman* doctrine, the Buddha opens in a sense the third dimension of "salvation by awakening to the New Self or New Being," which is at the same time determined as Non-Self or Absolute Nothingness and establishes the so-called "Middle Path" that rises above the two extremities. In any case, the thirst and hunger for salvation which is so manifest in early Buddhism cannot be considered without regard to the doctrine of *karman* and *saṃsāra* as its background.[25] And that earnest aspiration is now satisfied by Buddha. The Buddha, aware that "the release of my mind is unshakable, this is my last existence, now there is no rebirth,"[26] arrived at a genuine salvation, and he invited his disciples, saying, "Come and see!" The story of Yasa will explain the meaning of this invitation: "Then Yasa not far from the Blessed One (the Buddha) breathed forth the cry 'O what wretchedness, O what affliction!' And the Blessed One spoke thus to Yasa: 'Here is no wretchedness, Yasa; Here is no affliction. *Come,* Yasa, *sit; I will show thee the Law'* (*dharma*)."[27] Indeed, placing ourselves in the viewpoint of the Buddha as Yasa did, we can know clearly what the world of *karman* really is, what meaning it has in the facts of human existence. And this is what the Buddha recommends as his Law.[28]

For only he who wakes up from sleeping (this is the etymological meaning of "Buddha") knows what sleeping means, and therefore he can awaken another who is asleep. Therefore, paradoxical though it may sound, we are justified in saying that only he who is awake can participate with others in their sleeping as well as awakening. Thus the true understanding of his own *karman* is the source of his compassion upon the *karman* of all mortal beings. Just as the philosopher in Plato's *Republic* who has succeeded in escaping the cave of blindness comes back again to the cave to emancipate others, so he who has already transcended the *karman* can and must go to others still bound by the *karman,* in order to liberate them from that bond to the end that they may rejoice together that they have attained the transcendence. At the same time they suffer together for the fact that there are in the world still many miserable beings who are blind and sunk in the *karman.*

The following words, spoken by the Buddha to his disciples, when, in an early period of his preaching, he was sending them forth to convey his message to the world, will inevitably remind us of the scene of Jesus sending forth the Twelve on their mission (Mark 6:7 f.):

"I have been liberated, mendicant brothers, from all the snares, whether of spirits or of men; and ye also, mendicant brothers, have been liberated from all the snares, whether of spirits or of men. Go forth, mendicant brothers, upon journeys for the help of the many, for the well-being of the many, out of compassion for the world, for the sake of, for the help of, for the well-being of spirits and men. Let not two go the same way. Make known, mendicant brothers, the Law, good in the beginning, good in the middle, good in the end, in the meaning and in the letter; make clear the complete and pure holy-life. There are beings whose natures are scarcely tainted; through not hearing of the Law they are lost. They will comprehend the Law."[29]

C. *The Law of Love in Christ and Buddha*

Therefore, the awareness of *karman* and *saṃsāra* brings into existence an openness of the world, where the religious existential communication through this mutual appealing to the Self becomes possible. In natural and ordinary relations between man and man the exchange of love can be expressed in various ways. But with regard to any natural tie of love and friendship, however noble and refined, a sting of selfness remains hidden in the unconscious until the last. Both in our love of truth, goodness and beauty and in our sincere self-sacrifice for others, there is something of the arrogance of egoism which overvalues its self-righteousness. Thus in truth it is one's own

self-seeking interest that is satisfied by one's self-surrender. So far as this
blind ego is not awakened and is not penitent, is not denied and conquered,
then even in what seems at first sight to be an act of pure love a kind of
dangerous poison is concealed which renders everything worthless. Worthless
because man is alone in the face of the ultimate boundary situation; he
must perceive that when the *karman* leads him down to "underground,"
Dostoevski's, where the whole of the naked self is ruthlessly exposed, there
can be no recourse to his self-reliance.

Yet in this awareness of the *karman* the fundamental ground of all life is
revealed, and the courage to expose himself here on this ground brings to
him true blessedness by converting his *Dasein* into *Existenz*. Out of this conversion and opening of one's eyes a stream of compassion gushes forth which
will not stop until all beings are awakened. This is the so-called "vow
(*praṇidhāna*) to save all beings even into infinity." Man in his conversion
(awareness and penitence of sin) confesses the "solidarity" of his guilt,
namely, the oneness or jointness with the guilts of the infinite number of
others. Recognizing his own guilt, he pardons the sins of others. By being
compassionate with regard to the common guilt of mortals, and by being
taken up into the charitable sphere of grace, he now takes a charitable attitude toward the remorse of others as well as himself. And thus the magnificent compassion and charity (*mahākaruṇāmaitrī*) appears, ushering
himself and others into the realm of emancipation. It is from this standpoint
of compassion that I can deny completely my arrogance and self-love and so
cause others to do the same. Strictly speaking, this standpoint of compassion
must be in its very nature devoid of any standpoint. For truly compassionate
is our heart, only when it is entirely absorbed into the suffering of others.
It may be likened to a cool refreshing wind blowing over the scorching world
of *karman*. Compassion perceives a voice of cosmological signification in all
being. All existence and all living are bound to the same life. "All being is
my mother and father, my brothers and sisters in this life and the next; everything . . . when I become a Buddha, must be saved." This citation from
Shinran, the great reformer of Japanese Buddhism, and also the sentiment of
the ancient song

> *I think of my father and mother*
> *in the next life*
> *Even in the call of the copper pheasant*

conveys the tone of such a cosmic love which is echoed in the openness of
the world.

All living beings blown by this cool breeze will recover their breath. When words of love and compassion are carried along on this wind, there is for the first time a touching of souls between you and me. The world of *karman* is the real world in which the ultimate boundary condition of human existence is shown. Thus the unexpected circumstances of the fatalistic encounter between you and me, which occurs only once, appear on this existential stage. What Yājñavalkya said on taking leave from his wife—"My meeting with you is not limited to this life"—has a deep meaning to a wife who is also seeking salvation. The idea of *karman* and *saṃsāra* in this kind of expression shows the deep emotion of our minds stirred up by the awareness of the single encounter between you and me.

For one whose heart is deeply moved by the transcience of life, even a short, casual, and once-for-all meeting between you and me here in this world is a wonder and a mystery. How much more impressive the scene will be in a religiously apprehended communication, evoking a profound emotion which is elevated from grief to joy! Because it has happened once for all, so argues an awakened religious mind, it must have been repeated in the past and will surely be repeated in the future as well. In this sense, the rings of *saṃsāra,* or "eternal return of the same," are nothing but a paradoxical exaggeration of "the instant" of time in contact with eternity. The following illustrations will clarify in vivid pictures the meaning of the instant and of the relation between the relative and the absolute.

(1) A lovely pond in the heart of the mountains, branches spreading over the surface of the pond; neither a white cloud nor a flying bird in the sky is reflected there. Then, a small bird comes to bathe in the pond; it alights on the surface of the water; from the point where the bird is bathing, ripples spread out as from a center one by one to the bank. To me, gazing from the bank, the waves that come to the shore originating from that point are understood as having been caused by the small bird taking a bath.

However, suppose I were not there, and if the visit of a small bird were known only to the small bird itself and the surface of the water, what would happen? Since a small bird is a sensitive creature, it would approach the water only when nobody is standing in its neighborhood. In such a case what marks the visit of a bird to the water will be nothing but so many concentric circles of ripples spreading over the surface from the point where the bird touched the water. If the water were to recognize the bird's visit, the only way would be for it to trace the ripples from the periphery back to the center, on which point the bird had alighted vertically from above. Thus the thought would have to move in the reverse direction of the ripples. But in reality the movement on the surface of the water proceeds only from the center to the periphery, diffusing over the whole surface of the water the melodious vibrations of rejoicing at the visit of the bird.

This, I hope, will explain the rings of *saṃsāra*. Starting from the periphery and going back ripple by ripple to the center, we see the waves as the rings of *saṃsāra;* we come to realize that our being is besieged by the rings of fate and destiny. Yet in the reverse direction, when we start from the center and entrust ourselves to the natural stream of spreading waves, we recognize the same waves, but they are now the waves of freedom and emancipation. It is the glad tidings communicated between you and me (ripple and ripple) about the fact that in the center there arose once for all a revelation from the absolute to the relative.

In the above metaphor the small bird is a messenger from the unlimited void where its mate soars; the water surface represents the lower dimensional world that is contained in this limitless, profound void. We thus truly become aware that the encounter of the transcendent absolute otherness and the world (the meeting of the absolute and the relative) is meaningful.

Now, we may learn a further lesson from this metaphor. First, the absolute otherness which comes directly from above to this relative world, in spite of its transcendent character, does not decline to be the *Umgreifendes* that envelops the relative—the correlation of the world and the self—within it. The divine is a container that contains the lower dimensions within it. There is found the same relation as that between "being" and "being-itself," so clearly brought out by Professor Tillich. If it were not so, the encounter of the opposites, that is, the absolute and the relative, would require a third party, which would provide a place for the encounter. It may be called an *intermedium* coming into force at the same time with the two opposites. But such a third term (in the above metaphor, the "I" looking from the outside upon the encounter of the bird and the water) should have no room in our discussion. This sort of encounter is a secret affair between the two parties concerned. The concept of *intermedium,* however, has always been a favorite of philosophers. For when they reflect upon the relation between the absolute and the relative, they frequently disregard the fact of experience that there is actually no third party present at the encounter of two persons. So they elaborate in their thoughts and logic the function of the intermediary. However, contrary to their anticipation, such a logic and way of thinking, being a product of "discriminatory intelligence," in its effort to have a system draws unconsciously a blasphemous picture of the meeting of the absolute and the relative. But the fact of revelation is quite the reverse. The very absolute, while stressing its own absolute otherness against the relative, reveals itself within this partial and relative world, and that at just one point of this partial world, not in a generality conceived in the mind of a philosopher. Thus the unlimited void reveals itself as the small bird alighting on the point of the water surface, the eternity touching just one moment of time. As the place of divine-human encounter such a part, though only a part of parts, is in truth the whole of wholes. This is exactly the point that will provide a key for the understanding of the paradoxical structure of the encounter or revelation.

Second, it will not be unreasonable to think that the point of divine-human encounter is located in the *hic et nunc* of religious awakening. Our existence in the world is just a point within the vast ocean of infinite time and space. It does not matter where it is located in the commonly accepted time reckoning. It may be located in the past or the present or the future.

As a happening of the past, it becomes a historical revelation (Christianity); as that of the present, it is the "eternal now" (Christian mysticism and Zen Buddhism); as that of the future, it elicits eschatological expectations (Christianity and Amida Buddhism). In any case, this point of awakening is selected, in front of the absolute, with basic contingency, from the infinite series of temporal-spatial points. Why is it I and not you? Why is it here and not there? Why now and not tomorrow or yesterday? or the reverse? These questions man cannot answer. Notwithstanding this, the visit to the one point of the water surface, in the repetition of the same ripple activity, is transmitted to the whole surface of the water; sooner or later all the points of the surface are affected by the activity originating from the center point of motion. Caused by the violent shock in one point of time, the wave activity is transmitted to the whole of time past and future.

(2) There once lived a man of faith, Shichisaburō by name, in the town of Shiozawa in the province of Mikawa. To the man who had stolen trees from his mountain, he was thankful; those who saw and heard of this asked him why. He replied, "It must have been retribution for the fact that I in my past existence had stolen something from that person. And I didn't know the way to return the stolen things. As I think that he came to take back what I had robbed, there is due to him nothing but thanks."

There are numerous similar anecdotes told about this sort of *myōkōnin,* a humble lay saint. In such stories we find the same conduct often repeated and imitated, which fact gives them a scent of hypocrisy. Even in the above-quoted story it may not be impossible to take the man's motive in a bad sense. Yet we need not be so suspicious. Accepting the story just as it is, we may grasp there the nature of genuinely religious feeling in its simplicity. Above all, it shows clearly to us the essence of religious love. I do not deny that there is a basic difference between the compassion of Buddhism and the love (*agape*) of Christianity, which cannot be completely identified. Even within Buddhism "there is a sharp distinction in the idea of compassion between the way of 'Self-Power' and that of 'Other-Power' (that is, grace, as Shinran pointed out)." But common to all is the great law of love as it is voiced by Jesus in his commandment, "Love your neighbor and even your enemies." Still more, its outstanding characteristic is the manifestation of the pure religious heart overflowing as a stream of spontaneous sentiments that contains within itself and transforms into the indicative the moral imperative: "Thou shalt love."

This description of love applies to Buddhism and Christianity alike. For instance, in Christianity this love is best illustrated by Stephen's praying for his persecutors as he was being stoned (Acts 8:54 f.) In the case of Shichisaburō, is not such an extraordinary, spectacular scene. It is nearer to our daily affairs; yet it is no less meaningful and certainly more practicable because it comes closer to our personal lives. If we observe his act carefully, we shall find that his compassionate heart takes the idea of *karman* and *saṃsāra* as an excuse for his conduct of love. We should not, therefore, blame him for his idea of transmigration as though it were an absurd view, separating it from his conduct of love. Shichisaburō himself might have been caught by a fit of anger when he saw that someone had cut and stolen the trees from his forest. Perhaps such an anger was quite natural to him in such a case: for he found that he had lost things valuable to him, and it must have been difficult for him to resist his feeling of justice in order to vindicate his violated rights and to be revenged on the thief.

But for such a passion of anger there is no room in Buddhist ethics because anger, as well as other passions, is due to one's attachment to one's own possessions, and passions in their turn increases one's sense of attachment. Influenced by the teachings of the Buddha, he could, we may well suppose, suppress his passion of anger so completely that it appeared in his mind only for a moment, or no sooner did it appear than it quickly disappeared, so quickly that he himself was not aware of it. At any rate, even though unconsciously, such a sentiment must have crept into his mind as we may gather from the context of the story. In other versions of the story, a *myōkōnin* is represented as confessing that he actually replied with a fit of anger. For convenience sake, I shall call this sentiment the "first sentiment."

Then, as the second step, comes the awareness which denies the first sentiment as not congruous to the spirit of a Buddhist. By dint of this awareness Shichisaburō has now a mind of non-attachment and compassion. Thus the moral law that a religious person should love his enemy governs completely and imperatively the mind of Shichisaburō. However, love cannot remain a simple ethical imperative; the ethical needs to be fulfilled in the religious, and thus there is evoked as the third step another awareness from which overflows a spontaneous love of compassion. Shichisaburō, as a devotee of the Shin Sect ("True Doctrine of the Pure Land"), founded by Shinran, although a layman without much education, has well mastered the quintessence of the *karman-saṃsāra* doctrine, which made it possible for him to comprehend the unextinguishable root of arrogance and self-love, which no human power but only the compassion and mercy of Buddha can remove. In his deep repentance, his mind heartily rejoices in the Buddha's gracious mercy; his foremost desire is now (a) to be compassionate for the sins of others, (b) to pray the Buddha to forgive and save others as himself, and (c) still more, learning Buddha's great charity to the best of his ability, to forgive and save even his own enemies. Thus the compassion, which is a reflection of the Buddha's great compassion upon him, cannot but radiate from him.

The unconditional imperative, "Love your enemy," if restated in full, should be: "As your sins are forgiven you by God, so forgive you the sins of your enemy." When this oughtness of love is perfectly obeyed, there gushes forth a stream of spontaneous love. It is a command (the oughtness as the Buddha's voice), but in my response to it my whole person becomes love. The second-step awareness is obeyed at first as a command, but before long obedience becomes my spontaneous action. The third-step awareness, the kindled heart of love, is thus what deepens the second-step awareness. It is a synthesis of the two types of awareness. But we have noted that here is presupposed the sense of solidarity of sin and that all human beings alike participate in death and sin. This is where the ground of all beings is to be found. But this common ground of sin and death can be recognized as such only in what we call "the compassion of Buddha"; when such an insight comes into our mind, it is conceivable only as a reflection of Buddha's great light. Therefore the ground of all being (death and sin) is and is not. For it is precisely on this ground that the communication of redemptive love cuts its way through.

Now, Shichisaburō, considering himself as a former thief, wishes to pardon the injustice done him by the wood robber. Full of compassionate feeling, he identifies himself subjectively, that is in his innermost heart, with the robber's sin, and forgives him willingly and lovingly. But as he has not actually experienced the perpetration of that crime, the question arises: How is it possible that he take that crime on himself? The answer is sought in the idea of previous existence. Along with this thought, the first sentiment is evoked in him and Shichisaburō feels himself accused. The thief now appears as a claimant demanding the restoration of what had earlier been stolen from him. We find here that the first sentiment reappears in a different form, for although both the first sentiment and the second sentiment are lifted up and sublimated into the third sentiment, they are not entirely lost but only transformed in the third sentiment.

Man in his compassion pardoning his enemy's sin should not be indifferent to the judgment of right and wrong, even in his act of pardoning. Religious love is not a simple case of non-resistance; sometimes the aspects of judgment and conflict may come clearly to the fore. All our attitudes are religious in so far as they are within love and compassion. Thus, when a religious person judges his fellow man he judges himself through this judgment; there further arises within himself an intention to judge himself rather than any other person. Both the first and second judgments are religious in so far as they proceed from the third judgment. In the awareness and repentance of sin and sin's solidarity, the Buddha and I, my fellow beings and I, are revived in my consciousness, all enwrapped in great Compassion. Thus we all are thankful and grateful toward each other and all toward the Buddha.

~~~~~~ Part VIII
Religion and World Order

The Demand for Freedom and Justice in the Contemporary World Revolution

BY JOHN C. BENNETT

I. CHRISTIAN CONSCIENCE AND THE CONTEMPORARY CRISIS

It is commonplace to say that there is a rising of the peoples, a vast revolutionary upheaval, on most continents. Great segments of mankind which in the past have been neglected or exploited and which have never before known the possibility of social changes favorable to them now have gained a voice and make claims which are everywhere heard. In many places their leaders have won power, power to command attention, power to threaten, to dismiss, or to overthrow those who have controlled them in the past.

The industrial workers in the West were the first to make their claims heard. In many countries, including the United States which is reputed to be economically conservative, there has been a transformation of economic life in the interests of the great majority of the people. This transformation has been made possible in large part by political movements based upon the industrial workers.

We have seen the colonial peoples in Asia succeed in winning political independence and we see them beginning to work for new social and economic institutions and a higher standard of living. Similar stirrings have begun in Africa.

We see the colored peoples everywhere claiming equal rights and opportunities; we see them winning their way and putting the white race on the defensive morally even where it continues to hold the dominant power.

It would be satisfying if one could report that these changes have come in large measure because the Christian Churches early realized that God is no respecter of persons and that the special advantages held so generally by white, middle- and upper-class Christians in the West were an affront to Him. It would be satisfying if we could say that the Christian conscience had directly taken the lead in these changes. Unfortunately we cannot say that. Churchmen in recent years have frankly recognized that the Churches have often been on the wrong side in these struggles and that they have had to be pushed by secular movements, sometimes by movements controlled by an atheistic ideology.

In 1948 the Amsterdam Assembly of the World Council of Churches, in the report of its third section, stated the situation with great candor:

Christians should recognize with contrition that many churches are involved in the forms of economic injustice and racial discrimination which have created the conditions favourable to the growth of Communism, and that the atheism and the anti-religious teaching of Communism are in part a reaction to the chequered career of a professedly Christian society. It is one of the most fateful facts of modern history that often the working classes, including tenant farmers, came to believe that the churches were against them or indifferent to their plight.

The same year the Bishops of the Anglican Communion, meeting in Lambeth, made a remarkable confession concerning the backwardness of the churches in dealing with the problems raised by modern industrialism. They said:

We have to admit that the Christian Church throughout the formative decades of the industrial era showed little insight into what was befalling human society. It was still thinking in terms of feudalism. The Church of England was identified almost completely with the ruling classes, as were the Churches in Central and Eastern Europe. Its own economy had the marks of a dying feudalism or latterly of a bourgeois society. Apart from provision for the education of the poor and the work of some Churchmen for the emancipation of slaves and of children in the factories, it was slow to take the initiative in the desperate fight for social justice. A Churchman here or there, a Christian group here or there, wholeheartedly upheld the cause of the oppressed, but only in more recent times has the Church begun to make a radical critique of western society, and to provide a climate that is not hostile to revolutionary spirits.[1]

I do not quote this statement in order to call attention to any special weakness of the Anglican Communion in these matters. What the Bishops —who would not be captious critics—say of their own church is generally true of the great churches of Christendom.

To be sure, the Christian conscience was in some countries an important factor in movements for emancipation, and elsewhere it was often indirectly related to them, since Christ's mediation of God's love for the poor and the disadvantaged has never been confined to officially ecclesiastical channels or to explicitly Christian channels. Many people have been prepared by Christian sensitivity to participate in secular or even anti-Christian movements for social justice. Today the Christian mind has been widely transformed, even though it is true that the transformation is partly the result of social pressures from outside the Churches.

The very fact of radical social change has broken the connection between commonly held conservative conceptions of divine providence and the social *status quo*. It is no longer plausible to identify the Will of God with traditional patterns of domination and superiority which have either been destroyed or are already morally discredited.

Let me give two illustrations from American experience which show how changes in patterns of life create situations in which the convictions of learned and orthodox theologians no longer even make sense.

In the middle of the nineteenth century in the United States there were reputable theologians in the South who taught that slavery was ordained by God as a providential discipline and that it was supported by Biblical teaching. At the same time there were reputable theologians in the North who taught that the laws of laissez-faire economics were laws of God and that it was wrong to interfere with the free market in the establishing of wage rates. Cannot we say that in both cases the ideas of providence, of God's working in history, were so clearly false that they do not even have to be refuted?

Professor Ben Marais of South Africa has done a great service in his book, *Colour, the Unsolved Problem of the West*. He has published in that book the results of a questionnaire addressed to many of the leading Protestant (mostly Calvinistic) theologians of Europe, asking them if there was any sound Biblical or theological basis for racial segregation in the Church and the community or even for the Church's opposing intermarriage between races. He received a unanimous reply, often stated with great emphasis, that there is no Biblical or theological basis for such forms of racial segregation.

Are we here merely saying that contemporary theologians or the most recent thinking in the churches must be corrected? No, as is usually the case when the Christian conscience moves forward, we discover that what is true in the new is also consistent with the spirit of the Biblical understanding of God's will for man. It has been necessary for the minds and the eyes of Christians to be opened by the social upheaval of our times in order to be freed from the bias that has so often accompanied privilege and power. Our Christian traditions came to be the traditions of the more comfortable white Christians in the Western world. Today may we not say that the radicalism that has always been implicit in the gospel has been released? Jesus often turned upside down the usual human ways of arranging people so that with him the first became last. In the context of the life of the Church in the first century, this reversal had no direct political implications. But if we see the people and the institutions of our day with the same radicalism we must translate it into political terms, for it overturns the pretensions and the defenses which surround the privileges and power of every human elite.

Seldom has this essential radicalism of the gospel, with its political implications, been put more powerfully than by Karl Barth. In his postwar essay, *Christengemeinde und Bürgemeinde,* there is this wonderful passage:

> The Church is witness of the fact that the Son of man came to seek and to save the lost. And this implies that—casting all false impartiality aside—the Church must concentrate first on the lower and lowest levels of human society. The poor, the socially and economically weak and threatened, will always be the object of its primary and particular concern, and it will always insist on the State's special responsibility for these weaker members of society. That it will bestow its love on them—within the framework of its own task (as part of its service)—is one thing and the most important thing; but it must not concentrate on this and neglect the other thing to which it is committed by its political responsibility; the effort to achieve such a fashioning of the law as will make it impossible for "equality before the law" to become a cloak under which strong and weak, independent and dependent, rich and poor, employers and employees, in fact receive different treatment at its hands: the weak being unduly restricted, the strong unduly protected. The Church must stand for social justice in the political sphere.[2]

The ecumenical Christian community can greatly help us to see the world as it appears to the people who are or have been disadvantaged, because within the Church itself they now have strong voices. The Christians who represent the continents of Asia and Africa are usually small minorities in their own countries but they speak for the needs and aspirations of their peoples. Indeed they must often make the same protest within the life of the Church against paternalistic forms of domination from the West that they and their fellow countrymen have had to make against Western political domination.

Now I shall speak of two concepts which have been transformed by the experience of recent generations: the concepts of *justice* and *freedom*.

II. JUSTICE—AND LOVE

We cannot relate Christian love for the neighbor to the large-scale problems of society without making use of the concept of justice. Justice is the
standard which should control immediately the institutions of society. In
its basic meaning it is the corrective for arbitrariness. It means that each
person and each group should be treated fairly, should receive its due
according to principles which are accepted in the community. There are
procedural principles of justice which are deeply embedded in the legal
tradition of the West, and these provide precious protections of the rights
of men when those rights are themselves recognized in the culture. But
justice as a legal norm is no self-sufficient standard of social morality. Its
application differs with differing conceptions of the rights of various segments of humanity.

What do we believe to be the *due* of the white race in comparison with
that of the colored races? What do we believe to be the *due* of the children
of the poor in comparison with that of the children of the rich? What is the
due of women? What is the due of industrial workers or of working farmers? Even when we consider that aspect of justice which deals with the
protection of society against crime there is no ready-made answer in terms
of justice as to what forms of punishment are morally acceptable.

In relation to the institutions of justice, two questions especially are
raised by the gospel:

1. What does God's love for people whose due is set low by society mean
for our institutions, for our conception of what is just?

2. What does the judgment of God concerning the pride and the self-
serving minds and hearts of men mean for the ways in which we defend—
often ardently—the conviction that much more is due to us than to most
of our neighbors?

Justice criticized and lifted by love is dynamic; it is informed by imagination; it seeks to raise the neglected and exploited people. This does not
mean that we can be guided by love in preference to justice or that we can
dispense with justice because it is not self-sufficient. Those who stress only
love are tempted to take their own false short cuts, to assume that the
structures created in the name of justice to distribute and balance power
are not necessary. No, for those who are tempted to assume that love is
all-sufficient, justice is needed for the defense of others against their tendency to assume that their love will always keep them from misusing power.
Justice preserves a balance which helps to keep us all from assuming that
in our love or in our wisdom we know all of what is best for others—

whether those others be members of another class or race or nation or generation.

The concept of justice must always be kept very close to the concept of equality. Men are not equal in gifts, character, in spiritual insight, or in the contribution which they can make to society. They are equal basically in two respects: as objects of God's concern and therefore in their claim upon the concern of all men who seek to be open to God's will for them; and as sinful creatures in need of mercy. Equality in neither of those senses can prescribe the pattern of social institutions. But equality does provide a basis for judgment upon all such patterns. It continuously explodes the pretensions of all who are so sure that they should be the unequal beneficiaries of providence or of social arrangements. These basic forms of human equality constantly press the question upon us: why is it that these and these and these persons, loved of God, are so much neglected or exploited by man? This question always has also this more personal form: why is it that I convince myself that so much more is due to me than to them?

III. FREEDOM—AND FREEDOMS

The Biblical understanding of freedom seems far removed from modern notions of political freedom and of civil liberties. In the New Testament we read chiefly of freedom from sin, of freedom to obey God, of the freedom that is slavery to Christ.

There is one connection between Christian freedom in this sense and the external forms of freedom which are our concern here: it is the fact that Christians, when they seek to obey God rather than men, do take freedom to act in relation to the powers of the world. Responsibility to preach the gospel in its fullness leads men to take freedom for themselves as far as this is possible—and in doing so they often open the door for the freedom of other men, even for freedom in the political sphere. And yet this road from Christian freedom to civil freedom has often been blocked by Christians themselves when they concentrated only upon their freedom of witness or action. For they have often taken this freedom and then have denied a comparable freedom to others, when they have had the power to do so. We may be thankful that they no longer have the power to do so in many places, so that Christian freedom does now usually favor the civil freedom of men as men.

I doubt, however, if we can understand the relation of Christian faith to civil freedom by thinking only of Christian freedom and its wider implications. There are two other aspects of the faith which are also essential: the implications of Christian love and of Christian teaching concerning men's sinful natures.

We can understand the implications of Christian love in this context only when we take seriously the needs of persons as they grow in mind and spirit. God in His own dealings with men has avoided the overwhelming of their minds and consciences by His power, even in the interests of His truth or of their salvation. The risks of freedom, of the freedom to be wrong, the importance of enabling persons to come to see the truth for themselves, from their own insight—these belong to God's way of dealing with men. And we know that when men coerce the minds of other men through false inducements or through playing upon fears they sin against love, for they tempt their neighbors to be hypocrites. If there is any one atrocity that is worse than any other among all the horrors of our time it is the tendency for those in power to use terror against their opponents to induce them to betray their own consciences. Security from this kind of threat is one of the rights of men for which those who seek civil freedom are today most concerned, and they are concerned when they find subtler forms of pressure in the interests of conformity in societies which are proud of their freedom.

Martin Luther was one of the great Christians of the past who had a sensitive understanding of this problem of freedom though in his own experience events at times seemed to obscure it for him. He wrote:

For the proverb is true, "thoughts are free." Why then would they constrain people to believe from the heart, when they see that it is impossible? In this way they compel weak consciences to lie, to deny, and to say what they do not believe in their hearts, and they load themselves down with dreadful alien sins. For all lies and false confessions which such weak consciences utter fall back upon him who compels them. It were far better, if their subjects erred, simply to let them err, than that they should constrain them to lie and to say what is not in their hearts.[3]

Much of the best thought in the Church has been given to the problems of religious liberty, but is it not clear that the institutions of religious liberty cannot survive without other forms of civil liberty and that these other forms of civil liberty cannot survive without religious liberty? A society that tried to have the one without the other would find that religious heretics would be persecuted as political dissidents or that those suspected of political dissidence would be smeared as religious heretics.

I have referred to the sinful nature of man as forming a basis for Christian emphasis upon political and civil forms of freedom. There is no group so wise or so good that the members should determine the fate of other men without being subject to criticism and to restraint. Abraham Lincoln once said, in speaking of slavery, that "no man is good enough to govern another without that other's consent." In saying that, Lincoln proved himself to be a sounder theologian than many of his more orthodox contemporaries. When governments or any other human agencies use political or economic power to control men, those who control are inclined to do so for the sake of the interests which are most vivid to them, usually their own rather narrow interests. Forms of control should provide the opportunity for those who are controlled to share in the process, to criticize its results and, eventually, to displace those in power by orderly procedures.

IV. FREEDOM—ORDER—JUSTICE

Neither justice nor freedom can stand alone. The freedom of men in a society that lacks common loyalties, that knows no divine judgment, that has no principle of order may easily lead to anarchy and thus destroy itself. "Responsible emancipation," a phrase used in recent ecumenical literature to describe the desired goal for nations which are now seeking to establish their freedom, involves the disciplines that make for order and justice as well as freedom. Freedom without order would soon disappear but, if the order does not involve a strong trend toward economic justice, freedom itself becomes largely formal for the majority of men. Without the external forms of freedom which I have emphasized any system of order is likely to become unjust because it lacks the continuous criticism and correction from those whose lives are most affected by it. Indeed no order without freedom can be just because, as we understand the need that persons have for freedom if they are to grow as persons, justice itself calls for wide access to freedom.

There are those in countries which are committed to free enterprise in economic life who conceive of freedom with great narrowness, as chiefly the economic freedom of the businessman, and exhibit no interest in a direct approach to order or justice because they, optimistically, assume a natural order which freedom does not threaten, and they assume that as much economic justice as is good for society can be expected as a by-product of freedom. Such persons fail to see that they are usually defending the freedom of only a small segment of the population and that the substantial freedom of the great majority depends in part upon the function of government to defend the interests of the weak, to preserve the stability of the economy, to plan for the general welfare—a function which the adherents of this philosophy of economic freedom deny. I speak of them not because they are today very numerous or because they have much political or intellectual influence in any country but because they often try to claim that the Christian emphasis upon the freedom of the person supports their own narrow conception of economic freedom and thus they cause some confusion in the Church. There is an element of truth in their preference for many private centers of economic power rather than the union of both political and economic power in the state. Only the most consistent theorists who hold this view really keep economic and political power separate, for most often this is the ideology of those who seek every opportunity to use the state in support of private economic interests.

V. COMMUNISM, CHRISTIANITY, AND ANTI-COMMUNISM

I began this essay by speaking about the revolutionary upheaval that has come in our time and it is in that context that I have dealt with the concepts of justice and freedom. The central impulse behind this contemporary struggle for political freedom and economic justice and a status of human dignity for all equal to that of the now most favored races and classes is a sign of the working of God's providence. We should, and most of us do, welcome it with gratitude and say that on the deepest level what is happening has been long overdue. But I should leave a false impression if I did not say anything about the new problems which revolution creates and especially about the perversions of the revolution which have already taken place.

There is a great tragedy in the fact that those who proved to be best prepared to stimulate and to lead revolution in many places were the Communists. We must always distinguish, as the Bangkok Conference of 1949 emphasized, between the revolution in itself and the Communist form which it has taken in some countries and which it may take in others in the future unless other forms for the revolution become available.

The Communist movement has succeeded in capturing the loyalty of millions of effective and willing workers, has given them a goal for living, a structure for their thought, and a closely-knit community to which they may belong. It has broadcast to the world an explanation of history and of the conditions which many nations face which seems to make sense to them and which gives them direction and hope for the future. It has appealed successfully to every conceivable grievance in many regions, especially to the vast grievance of the colonial peoples against the white West. As is usually the case with political propaganda, it has played upon exaggerations of this grievance.

The Communist movement has been successful to an astonishing degree because those who might have provided a better channel for the revolution failed to understand the need of revolution, or because they opposed it as against their own interests. Even after decades of Communist challenge and competition it is difficult to arouse comfortable countries to any such imaginative understanding of the world revolution. They become concerned, by fits and starts, because of their own fears of communism and not because they understand or care about the human problems for which communism seems to so many to provide solutions.

Communism has been able to take advantage of the revolutionary struggle that it did not create and has deeply distorted it. The distortion does not come from communism as an economic system but from the fact that it has sought to impose upon nations an absolute system, a program based upon an ideology which is believed to provide the true social science and the true philosophy. This absolute system has become a substitute for religion, an atheistic faith which denies the Christian revelation and which deprives society of any transcendent judgment. The political rulers are economic planners and are also the teachers of what is believed to be the true philosophy. When absolute rulers become absolute teachers little room remains for the free growth of the human spirit. The tendency has been for communism to be a vast international system with its center in the Soviet Union which denies the substance of political independence as well as spiritual freedom to other Communist nations. This monolithic system appears to be breaking down and there may be hope here. The world has much less to fear from the existence of several Communist countries, each of which has its own independent experiments, each of which has its own independent relations with non-Communist countries.

If there is one miscalculation that is more fateful than others in the Communist system, it is the assumption that if Communists are successful by any methods in establishing their system, if by political terror they bring their revolution to its goal, an ideal society will develop, a society which has no need of a coercive state. This belief about the future means in practice that they can concentrate on the revolution—on conspiracy, dictatorship and terror, and, if they are successful, the result will be a society that is both just and free. In other words, freedom will come as a by-product of a successful tyranny. The root of this error is the Communist belief that the only important source of evil in human life is in the economic system, and that when capitalism or feudalism is fully overcome, this source of evil will disappear. There is no realization of the truth in the Christian teaching that men in their pride and self-centeredness will continue to distort new economic and political systems and that improvement in society depends in part upon awareness of the new temptations which come with new social patterns and upon specific provisions to counteract them.

I do not want to emphasize this well-worn subject of communism but to call attention to the general fact that revolutions can easily be perverted, that this perversion may not be the work of wicked men but of idealists and the advocates of rationalistic schemes who are sure that their program will cure the ills of humanity and who, with devotion that turns into fanaticism, seek to indoctrinate whole nations with their illusions.

One effect of communism has been to create great disillusionment about revolution in non-Communist countries and often in the Christian Church. We see today a re-enactment of the revulsion against the French Revolution in many circles. Fanatical anti-communism can pervert the Christian response to revolution as much as communism can pervert the revolution itself. Such anti-communism blinds many people to the possibility of real changes in Communist countries and so they advocate policies based upon the vividly remembered past rather than on the present. It also so dominates their minds that in their fear of Communist subversion they are willing to sacrifice the liberties which make free societies worth defending against communism.

VI. TOWARD THE FUTURE

Quite apart from this blind anti-communism, there are sober second thoughts about aspects of the revolution in our time which come in part from disillusionment concerning communism but which have deeper sources and cannot be ignored even by those of us who believe that the present rising of the peoples is overdue. I can only summarize briefly the warning that comes to us from those who reflect upon the dangers that usually follow social revolution.

The deepest and most pervasive danger is that the majority itself even under democratic form may become a most oppressive tyrant. The process of leveling down both ancient privileges and traditional institutions and of subjecting all things to the will of the contemporary majority may become a threat to human freedom that is more destructive than the old order. If all the traditional centers of power, some of them based upon private ownership of property, are removed, nothing stands between the individual and the State or between the individual and the majority. Alexis de Tocqueville, more than a century ago, saw this danger partly as a result of his own experience of the results of the French Revolution and partly as a result of his observations in the United States. He wrote in his *Democracy in America*:

The authority of a king is physical and controls the actions of men without subduing their will. But the majority possesses a power that is physical and moral at the same time, which acts upon the will as much as upon the actions and represses not only all contest but all controversy.

If we emphasize equality without also emphasizing freedom of persons and of private institutions, freedom indeed to become unequal, we may produce a mass society which stifles personal life, which discourages differences of quality. Equality is an important basis for criticism upon unjust social patterns, but if it is sought consistently as an end in itself it is likely to result in regimentation by social pressure, if not by governmental coercion, in the interests of a poor common denominator of human life.

If we heed this warning we must emphasize constitutional protections for minorities, for the individual's right to be true to his own convictions, even more than we emphasize the idea of the people's sovereignty. We must encourage not only formal legal protections but also the social strength of many nonpolitical associations, as different as the family and the university, which have norms that are independent of the State and of the contemporary majority. Above all we must emphasize the freedom of the Church to be true to its own foundation in God's revelation in Christ, to be independent of control by the State and of domination by the national culture. Wherever there is a Church that is true to its essential nature it brings to the community a message which is no mere echo of the mind of the community. The struggle of the Church to be the Church in this sense is a struggle for human freedom; it is a struggle against the domination of the minds of men by any contemporary wills that control the means of livelihood or the mass media; it is a struggle against the threat of what is often called "totalitarian democracy."

One aspect of this warning is the emphasis upon the danger of the union of both political and economic power under the State, a subject that was considerably illumined by both the Amsterdam and Evanston Assemblies. It is a mistake to develop a universal dogma about the right relations of state control and private economic initiative. The advocates of unhindered private enterprise need to be convinced of the State's responsibility for the general welfare. They need to learn about the truth in the statement in the Evanston report that, "while the state is sometimes the enemy of freedom, under many circumstances the state is the only instrument which can make freedom possible for large sectors of the population." Those who have no hesitation about the continuous extension of the functions of government should learn about the truth in the statement in the Amsterdam report that "centers of initiative in economic life must be so encouraged as to avoid placing too great a burden upon centralized judgment and decision."

Socialism and capitalism are slogans and stereotypes; both are smear words in different circles. In the United States any move to enable the State to act for the economic welfare of the people is often called "creeping socialism," and so condemned; in other countries the word "capitalism" suggests only exploitation or imperialism. We shall see things more clearly when Americans come to admit that their own economy now has strong socialistic elements which have come to stay and when they also admit that other countries may be right in their circumstances when they choose more extensively socialized economies for themselves. But it is also important for those who use the word "capitalism" as a smear to realize that it stands for a division between political and economic power and for the distribution of economic power. When capitalistic institutions became so centralized that such distribution of power has little substance, the capitalistic factor in an economy has no moral claim to exist.

This acceptance of the need for "mixed economy" means that the old slogans of both right and left have lost their point. Christians who have derived their social thinking from the socialistic tradition must find new concepts and, if they have borrowed much of their social enthusiasm from the spirit of socialistic movements, they will have to look again at their foundations. I have already indicated the bankruptcy of Christian capitalistic ideologies. Sometimes the words "Christian pragmatism" have been used to describe this Christian freedom from doctrinaire social theories, but it is a confusing term and, in so far as it suggests relativism, it points to the fact that the goals of freedom, justice and productivity are all indispensable but that the exact pattern of their relationship does depend upon the special needs of each situation.

This warning from those who call themselves "the New Conservatives" and who draw their inspiration from such thinkers as Edmund Burke, de Tocqueville, and Jakob Burckhardt needs to be heard but it should not be allowed to take the place of the revolutionary impulse. The warning against the leveling effects of equality should not take the place of the passion for social justice that is under the criticism of equality. Those who speak today from the point of view of an enlightened conservatism rather than a callous or predatory reactionary spirit must presuppose the overcoming of the great inequalities which have humiliated and burdened most of humanity. Their warnings are needed to correct but not to prevent the basic revolution. For their own social philosophies would never have provided the dynamic that has been necessary and that remains necessary in the overcoming of the inequalities.

Comfortable people can afford to wait for a more balanced social policy, but those who bear the burden of social wrong can be expected to press for earlier, more decisive, and even more one-sided action. Our hope should be that in the Church neither of these groups may allow its social goals to be frozen by social dogmas or ideological illusions.

The ecumenical Christian community includes those who live in all varieties of social situations demanding different priorities and emphases in policy and action. Together they live under the guidance and judgment of God's Kingdom as known in Christ, which transcends and corrects every purpose which men have for their societies. To some extent they can be helped by one another in this correction out of their contrasting experiences, helped to see the necessity of revolution for the sake of more equal justice, helped to see that revolution can be greatly distorted if it develops its own fanaticisms and idolatries. The distortions that stem from equality can be counteracted only if there remains a devotion to truly human freedom, freedom from both political tyranny and economic oppression and from the pressure upon men's minds of majority opinion.

Freedom in society can best be preserved when, in the minds and hearts of Christian citizens, it is the freedom which is obedience to God.

∿∿∿∿∿∿∿∿∿∿∿∿∿∿∿∿∿∿∿∿∿∿∿∿∿∿ *24*

Christians and the Prevention of War in an Atomic Age

BY HELMUT THIELICKE

The atomic age confronts the Christian with some familiar questions concerning war, but also with some entirely new ones.

Inasmuch as atomic energy is only a technical extension of the human arm, some of the questions are the same. The new energy increases man's creative power to "subdue the earth" but, on the other hand, it also increases the influence and scope of the forces of destruction which arise from sin. The duality of fallen man is thereby intensified. All the old problems of human existence stand out more clearly. The basic problem of the atomic age is not technical but anthropological, and the Church's competence to consider atomic questions is, of course, confined to this aspect. Clearly, what people fear today (and this applies equally to Christians and to non-Christians) is fundamentally not the atomic bomb but the fact that atomic power is now at the disposal of man. It is not the weapon that they fear, but the hand that controls it.

At the same time, the Christian in the atomic age is faced by *new* problems: nuclear and supernuclear weapons not only extend the scope of future wars to an incalculable extent, they alter the whole *nature* of the war. Any future war between opponents with more or less equal atomic potential at their disposal will lead not only to the destruction of the enemy but also to self-destruction. This is the type of change seen in Karl Marx's dictum (taken from Hegel): that quantity (that is, the increased importance of the powers of destruction) changes into quality. The social process becomes different in nature; in this case war is transformed into a form of self-destruction. War is no longer restricted to killing others; from now on it involves destroying oneself also.

This change in the quality, and not merely in the outreach, of war can mean only one thing: there must not be any nuclear wars and consequently there can be no discussion about the rightness of a *justum bellum*. For the concept of the *justum bellum,* which is usually identical with that of the defensive war, is significant only as long as defense is possible and as long as there is some chance of survival. But if attack and defense with atomic weapons are identical with self-destruction, these distinctions are no longer valid and the concept of the *justum bellum* loses all significance.

The whole new shift in the realities of war raises the question: What should the Church's attitude be in this situation? In my opinion it would be unrealistic for Christians to urge the abolition of atomic weapons, suicidal as these armaments are; such an attitude would be touting a mere phrase which would discredit the Church's message. By "unrealistic" here I do not mean primarily in the political, but in the theological sense. I mean that a demand of this kind does not reckon with human nature *after the Fall.* Human life is determined by fear and mistrust, because we live in a world that is filled with incalculable people and incalculable forces. The story of the Tower of Babel (Gen. 11:1 ff.) describes this world of people who have become incalculable for one another, who are afraid of one another, and who are therefore centrifugally separated from one another.

This is the theological aspect of a human situation which takes the following form: Owing to fear that the enemy might secretly produce atomic weapons, or that their disarmament might not synchronize exactly with our own, or that they might set off a nuclear attack a moment sooner than ourselves, we will not relinquish the relative security of a balance of atomic power. When a world has lost its uniting Center, the fellowship which originally existed is bound to break up into mutually suspicious factions. This fact must form the first tenet of any Christian theology of history. When peace is gone, men try to substitute security for it. If two parties both feel the need for security, and both feel suspicious of one another, then each feels an urge to increase his own strength. That is why it would be unrealistic in the theological sense to urge the abolition of atomic weapons.

Although the Christian cannot agree with Jacob Burckhardt's saying that power is evil in itself—because it is not permissible to mythologize in this way about the nature of power, as if it were personally responsible for a role—he may agree that Burckhardt's words are nevertheless true, if they are de-mythologized. In this form the phrase would read: "the strong man" is dangerous in himself, because man is evil. For his power produces the seductive urge to Hybris, to become like God. Hence the art of democracy consists in dividing power, controlling it and preventing it from accumulating in *one* place. This policy is derived not so much from mistrust of *power* itself as from mistrust of *the man who exercises power*. This mistrust expresses (without necessarily realizing it) a reckoning with the factor of the Fall: it implies that man, by his very nature, cannot support either a monopoly of power or a high degree of power.

This kind of reflection casts fresh light on the unrealistic nature of the demand to abolish atomic weapons. The other nation is never sure to fulfill the abolition demand, and we must therefore reckon with a secret accumulation of power in *one place*. This is undoubtedly dangerous. But the division of the nuclear energy available in the world means at least that it is neutralized to a certain extent and provides a certain guarantee that peace will be maintained.

The peace which is the aim, and perhaps also the achievement, of a non-abolition policy will be characterized by two factors:

It will be peace based on fear. Apart from the Christian message, the world knows nothing of the redeemed peace that springs from God's good will to men (*eudokia*, Luke 2:14); the world only knows the unredeemed peace of this world (John 14:27)—that respite from fear and that order which is merely a balance of the elements of disorder. *Dilectio filialis* has been replaced by *timor servilis*.

This condition can be interpreted theologically only by referring to God's covenant with Noah (Gen. 9). This covenant repeats the commandments and promises made by God at the Creation, but with some characteristic nuances. The commandment "Be fruitful and multiply!" is linked up with the prophecy "and the fear of you . . . shall be upon every beast of the earth." The sanctity of the life created by God is protected by the warning that "Whoso sheddeth man's blood, by man shall his blood be shed." The order of creation is replaced by the emergency-order of the fallen world. "From the beginning (*ap'archês*) it was not so" (Matt. 19:8). This present emergency-order is characterized by the fact that God protects the fallen world from itself by its own methods and at the same time treats it homeopathically (*similia similibus*): the force of human pride which breaks out in the fallen world is directed against itself, by being divided into criminal force and penal power. Power is not exclusively in the hands of *malum* but is also held by the authorities (the State, the law, the police), who carry on the *arcere malum*. Similarly fear is limited by fear; fear of the other, which leads to the shedding of human blood, is held in check by the fear of revenge, punishment and expiation. Theological ethics must learn to apply the old doctrine of the *providentia Dei* (which speaks of the *causae secundae* established in the world) also to the concept of emergency-order in the fallen world; paradoxically, God maintains this fallen world through the help of the powers of destruction and rebellion immanent in it. These powers therefore have the rank of *causae secundae*. They become signs of God's mercy, because God turns even what were originally signs of rebellion against Him to the good of mankind, and makes them into tokens of His patience and agents of His promises. In this sense peace based on fear is (or, at any rate, may be) a special form of that law of life which was guaranteed to the fallen world through God's covenant with Noah.

The second characteristic of this peace based on fear is that it is very *relative*. It is not a real peace, but merely a respite. The neutralization of the forces of self-destruction is only a superficial cure for the symptoms of humanity's sickness; but it cannot heal the organism itself. To quote Goethe, while humanity makes technical progress (and this progress is not without influence on the outbreak of wars), man himself remains the same. But as the secret cause of war lies in the bellicose nature of man himself—just as power is dangerous because of the man who exercises it—war is not eradicated and abolished; it only changes its form. In the epoch of nuclear weapons war will shift from the military sphere (at any rate, from the nuclear military sphere) to the plane of economic, social and ideological warfare. To formulate this in a slogan: the wars of the future will be distinguished from those of the past by their temperature; they will no longer be hot but cold wars.

This raises a new question for Christians. For quite apart from the fact that the sparks of that "cold fire" are bound to keep coming very close to the nuclear powder magazine, and that mankind is therefore constantly exposed to the very worst possibilities, Christians are challenged to say something about "the bellicose nature of man."

What Christians have to say can take only two forms: what they "preach" and what they "counsel."

What will Christians preach? What I have said above already shows that the cause of war (both cold and hot war) is to be sought in the inmost soul of fallen man. Today the Church is in a promising position to show where the healing forces are to be found, not primarily by giving advice as an institution but by really showing the greatness, the misery and the vocation of man. Christians are concerned with the center, and therefore must not wander about on the periphery by giving advice on the cure of mere symptoms—or, at any rate, must have such advice only as a secondary concern. This is true not only of the problem of war but also of all the essential questions that concern theology today. Consider, for instance, the question of how people should spend their leisure in the age of automatization. In this case also the Church's message must not consist merely of advice on how to fill leisure time; it must go to the heart of the problem, which is the "ful-fillment" of man's existence. For what matters is not what people do with their leisure but what they do with *themselves* and whether they find them-selves. This is a theological problem. If man seeks to "full-fill" himself and his vocation, everything will be "added unto him," including the fulfillment of his leisure (Matt. 6:33).

The Church's preaching therefore has the task of showing that the prob-lem of war, or rather of the desire to make war, is a macrocosmic reflection of the microcosmic attitude of the human heart to God.

In addition to *preaching*, the Church must give *counsel*. It has this task also, because what it knows about the ultimate origin of disorder applies to a society which consists of both Christians and non-Christians. This is a society (as every conception of the Church implies, however it may be formulated) which is never completely synonymous with the congregation which hears the preaching. If the Church's counsel does not relate to putting its preaching into practice and therefore does not apply to the congregation to which that preaching was addressed, and if it is really a substitute for preaching *extra muros ecclesiae*, then the counsel can deal with only one question. That question is, what can be done to prevent the spirit of war—if it cannot be eradicated by legal methods—from developing beyond the incubation stage and becoming virulent? In contrast to its preaching, there-fore, the Church's counsel can only be directed toward curing the symptoms. But this counsel will try to do more than merely cure the symptoms, in-asmuch as it does not rest content with the external limitation of the growth of power by dividing and balancing it, but will endeavor to control the spirit of war, thus penetrating deep into the human heart. The measures to be advised by the Church are essentially the following:

(1) Combating the glorification of any collective ideologies, such as the worship of class, race, nation or interests.

(2) Education in tolerance and readiness to understand others in the visible spheres of every day. This includes a new attitude toward compro-mise in every sphere of interest and of judgment. It is only through respect for compromises that the tendency to solve problems by force can be weakened.

(3) Education in the ability to distinguish between people and things and not to think in rigid terms of "groups" and opposing ideologies, but to perceive the living person apart from his group. (The commandment in the New Testament to love our enemies is based on this ability to distinguish between people and things.) A practical way of strengthening this faculty is for opponents to be brought together so that they have to live together.

Institutions must be created in which such contacts can take place, in order to reduce the tensions which exist. An example of an experiment of this kind is the Evangelical Academies in Germany, whose most important achievement probably consists less in any practical solutions and helpful advice which they can give than in creating places where people with opposing opinions can meet and get to know each other on a level which transcends the causes they defend.

The edge must be taken off bitter antagonisms by combating ideological prejudices early in children and by paying homage to sober fact and reason in our ethical thought.

(4) Kierkegaard defined the nature of sin in the following formula: sin makes people adopt an absolute attitude toward what is relative. One form of this tendency is the ideological exaggeration of standpoints which should be based solely on practical arguments. Arguments in themselves do not destroy communication—even when people disagree—because they are always connected with the *tertium comparationis* of objectivity in that argument (which is built up on thesis and antithesis) always seeks the opposing view. But if people's attitudes are exaggerated by ideologies, they become mutually exclusive and withdraw into hostile doctrinal camps which refuse to be reconciled.

The definition of sin as something which makes people behave absolutely toward what is relative again discloses war as the projection of man's attitude onto his environment. For this definition shows that, if man's vertical relationship with God is disturbed, this causes disorder in his horizontal relationships (Rom. 1:18 ff.) and leads to hostility between people who ought to live in fellowship. It also shows that true peace between people and forces can only be the peace of God if He heals that disorder. Everything else— including what the Church may "advise" in addition to its preaching—is a defense against unrest, but is not peace.

The "peace of this world" is at the best merely coexistence, but not *pax*. That is why the aim of "preaching" can never be too high—because it manifests the eschatological sovereignty of God. And that is why the aims "counseled" can never be sufficiently modest. If we confuse these two things (which seems to happen quite often in Christian statements) we make the Christian message untrustworthy and harden people's hearts. We "preach" plans for reform instead of God's message; or we "counsel" policies which are too otherworldly because they belong to a sphere which is no longer dominated by pain and shouting, where the tumult of war is silent and where death—the last enemy—has been overcome.

The Spiritual Significance of the United Nations

BY CHARLES MALIK

The United Nations is a political organization. Political considerations on the whole permeate all its activity. It arose at the close of the Second World War mainly for the purpose of "maintaining international peace and security." It is composed of eighty-one members, all of which are independent, sovereign states. It operates through six separate though interrelated organs: the General Assembly of which every member is a member and ordinary decisions are taken by simple majorities while important decisions require a majority of two-thirds; the Security Council composed of eleven states, five of which—the so-called big five—are permanent, with a special voting system where the so-called veto comes into play; the Economic and Social Council, the Trusteeship Council, the International Court of Justice, and the Secretariat, each with a special mode of election and voting, and with precisely defined functions. The Charter of the United Nations is the fundamental statute of the Organization, determining the structure, purpose and function of its various organs.

The members of the Secretariat and of the International Court of Justice are, in the nature of the case, supposed to be above politics; and in general a high degree of integrity and detachment is manifested by the membership and operation of these two organs. But the other four organs of the United Nations—what might be termed the substantive organs, for the sake of which in the last analysis the other two organs exist—whatever their intention may be in theory, in practice are charged—one might almost say supercharged—with politics. Here I use the term "politics" in the highest sense. These eighty-one nations have each its own fundamental national policy, and its representatives on any of these organs simply put forward and carry out that national policy insofar as it bears upon the activity of that organ. There is no other way in which sovereign entities can act or

341

can come together, and until they are prepared—for whatever reason and under whatever compulsion—to subordinate much more of their sovereignty than they have been willing so far to do under the Charter, the national interests of the individual sovereign states must remain the fundamental spring of action of the United Nations. This is a necessary and good thing, for the United Nations is not a club of armchair idealists, but an organization conceived and constituted by the responsible governments of the world. Unless this essential political character of the United Nations is understood, we cannot appreciate the spiritual significance or lack of significance of the United Nations.

Thus the first question that we must ask is how much international politics admits of spirituality. By spirituality I necessarily mean the recognition of objective, existing norms which judge our action, of which our mind can be absolutely certain, and to which therefore we voluntarily endeavor to conform. Apart then from the existence of a real objective truth common and accessible to us all, and apart from the unrebellious willingness to respect and submit to such a truth, we cannot speak of spirituality, whatever else we may speak of. The spiritual is the realm of free self-conformation to something—a concrete norm, law, standard, principle, essence— absolutely real, but at the same time quite above our immediate interests. The constraint of the spirit is the free vision of a truth that is more or less wonderful for which one then strenuously craves. The concrete reality of the norm, the transcendence of the norm, our recognition of the norm, and the freedom whereby we joyously seek to conform to the norm—where these things are, there abides the spirit.

I am not here raising the all-absorbing question of the mode of existence of the norm, whether it is a self-subsisting Platonic idea or whether it is further somehow grounded in God. I am only saying that genuine spiritual phenomena arise only when men recognize something higher—higher, I mean, than anything human—something to which they are properly related by fear, not indeed the negative fear of avoiding and running away from that thing, but precisely the positive fear that if they did not seek the fearful thing all would not go well with them. The fear of the Lord, whether the Lord is the living God or a principle, is certainly the beginning of all wisdom.

The question then becomes: do we find such freedom, such objectivity, such transcendence, such humble recognition, in United Nations politics? The answer is almost wholly, but not quite, in the negative. I must now proceed to explain how there is a bare trace of the spirit in the United Nations and why for the most part the spirit is absent from it.

To say that there is some free submission to some objective transcendent norm is, in one sense, to say that there is some agreement among the nations. For when they agree there is something, no matter how modest or formal, that brings them together.

They have agreed to set up the United Nations, and they continue to attach great importance to it, as is evidenced by the facts (a) that the Organization has not broken up despite many setbacks and many discouragements, (b) that some members have received searing defeats in it and yet they would never dream of withdrawing from it, (c) that responsible leaders in the United States, in the United Kingdom, in India, and in the Soviet Union have repeatedly proclaimed support of the United Nations as a cornerstone in their national policy, (d) that some of these leaders have criticized certain policies precisely because they were not conceived and carried out within the United Nations, (e) that the United Nations has been time and again chosen, as for instance by President Eisenhower in August, 1958, as an appropriate platform for the enunciation of fundamental policy, and (f) that evidently such great store is set by membership in the United Nations that one of the great international issues of the present moment turns precisely around whether Communist China should or should not be admitted to the United Nations.

They have agreed that the permanent headquarters of the United Nations should be in New York, a very important decision so far as the interpenetration of the United States and the world is concerned. They have agreed on the Charter of the United Nations, one of the basic international documents of this age, with its aims of maintaining international peace and security, of developing friendly relations among nations, of respecting the equal rights and self-determination of peoples, of seeking international cooperation in economic, social, cultural and humanitarian realms, of promoting human rights and fundamental freedoms, of having all members pledge themselves to settle their disputes by peaceful means and to refrain in their international dealings from the threat or use of force, and of giving to the big nations with mighty military resources primary responsibility for the maintenance in unison of international peace and security. The fact that in practice these ideals and engagements of the Charter were not fully honored certainly expresses and reflects upon the political realities of the world, but does not detract from the theoretical recognition by the nations of these ideals as norms worthy of elucidation and respect; and it is this recognition that confers some unity, some sort of spiritual aegis, some underlying frame of reference, upon the activity of the United Nations. They have agreed on rules of procedure, on certain proprieties and amenities, for the mere conduct of business, rules and proprieties derived for the most part from the experience of deliberative national bodies, but adapted for the necessarily greater freedom that representatives of sovereign states must enjoy. They have agreed on certain expressions of hope that the big nations redouble their efforts to explore by all possible means how they might promote peaceful understandings among themselves. They have agreed on setting up machinery and making sizable contributions for extending to the less-developed regions of the world some technical assistance that might help them in developing themselves. They have agreed on a Declaration of Human Rights setting forth what is believed to belong to the essential dignity of man, a Declaration that will certainly go down as among the fundamental creations of this epoch. They have agreed on many other resolutions of varying degrees of importance or efficacy, though of course this measure of agreement, whether because of the issues involved or because of the development of factors entirely outside the pale of the Organization, has not been able by itself to arrest the steady deterioration of the world situation. Where agreement was not general, distinct blocs formed within the United Nations, such, for instance, as the Soviet bloc, the Latin American bloc, the Arab bloc, the Asian-African bloc, the British bloc, the Western European bloc, the Atlantic bloc, the colonial bloc, the anti-colonial bloc, the industrial bloc, the bloc of the underdeveloped, the bloc of the free world; blocs whose principle of formation was either political or economic or regional or racial and cultural, but in every case a real objective principle of solidarity bringing nations together and calling forth their spiritual loyalty to something beyond themselves. The action of the United Nations, such as it has been, expresses in effect the interlacing, interaction, interpenetration of this bewildering profusion of blocs.

The spiritual comes into play whenever men seek in freedom something real beyond themselves. To be sure, the grade of spirituality is measured by the object sought, but regardless of this fundamental question of depth and order, wherever men agree in freedom, there is a common bond among them which expresses and engenders spiritual energy. There are these diverse ways in which the nations have agreed either partially or wholly, and to that extent the United Nations reflects something spiritual. The element of freedom is ensured by the principle of "sovereign equality," for there is in principle complete equality in freedom among the member nations, and no nation is compelled, *under the Charter*, to adopt any policy it has not already freely and willingly accepted under the Charter when it became a member of the Organization. For the student of the spirit, then, it is significant that there is so much real, though to be sure modest, community of mind among the nations. At least this irreducible residue of spiritual unity will remain: that in this age, when the world has miraculously shrunk into a neighborhood, when international war, by reason of the current technological revolution, entails universal risks of unprecedented kind and magnitude, the nations, no matter how much they might disagree on every issue, no matter how exasperating and disgusting and frustrating every conference turns out to be, must have a place where and a mechanism through which they can physically meet and confer. *In an age of total danger, the norm of conference of the nations is the one abiding spiritual bond among them.* It follows that if the United Nations is scrapped today, another world instrument will arise tomorrow. In an age of indispensable world organization nothing is more necessary or has a more assured future than the United Nations or whatever world system might succeed it tomorrow.

Of the diverse activities of the United Nations, none is more pregnant with spiritual significance than the work on human rights. Whoever studies the proceedings on this question with a searching and critical mind will come out with a depth of vision concerning the great issues of this age which he can perhaps acquire in no other way. For the central theme of this undertaking is to determine the proper nature of man, and to seek ways and means for ensuring that nature against any violation. Since, however, it can be shown that the tragic conflicts of our times are all rooted in man's division over his own interpretation of himself—of his origin, his essence, his destiny, his place in the universe—it is evident that in the human rights enterprise these conflicts come to the sharpest focus, and that not between armchair philosophers or well-meaning idealists, but among the responsible representatives of the governments and effective cultures of the whole world.

The structure of the vision that this concern over the last nine years discloses in the sharpest and concretest form includes: (a) the conviction that the Second World War was caused at least in part by a brutal assault upon human rights by the doctrine and practice of the Nazis and Fascists; (b) the decisive part played by the churches and the non-governmental organizations in general in incorporating in the Charter the present significant undertakings with respect to human rights and fundamental freedoms; (c) the fact that the doctrine of the Charter places concern for human rights as second only to concern for peace and security and establishes a sort of casual connection between the two; (d) the way in which diverse cultures, outlooks, traditions, legal systems, schools of thought, individual thinkers, contributed to the formation of the Universal Declaration of Human Rights; (e) the relationship, both positive and negative, of this Declaration to its great historical predecessors, such as the English Magna Carta, the French Declaration of the Rights of Man and of the Citizen, the American Bill of Rights, and the Atlantic Charter; (f) the amazing manner in which this Declaration has energized during the last six years in courts of law, in new national constitutions, in the platforms of political parties, in the debates and resolutions of the United Nations, in international treaties, in the statements of American leaders, and in the consciences of men; (g) the question of materialism, debated concretely again and again at length, namely, which is more fundamental, man's material and economic rights and needs, or man's political, personal and intellectual rights; (h) the question of socialism, debated concretely again and again at length, namely, the question as to the place of the individual human person in modern society, whether, namely, man is free vis-à-vis his social group or whether he is completely and absolutely determined by it; (i) the question of totalitarianism, debated concretely again and again at length, namely, which is for the sake of the other, the individual human person or the state; (j) the question of order and articulation and hierarchy of human rights; (k) the question as to whether there is an irreducible core of essential rights from which there can be no derogation whatsoever under any circumstances; (1) the question of the place of the intermediate institutions, such as the family, the school, the church, the circle of friends, in the nurture of our fundamental freedoms; (m) the question of the origin and status of these rights, namely, whether they are conferred upon me by society or the government or the United Nations, or whether they originally constitute my natural dignity as a human being; (n) the question of how human rights may be implemented—by international conventions, by the setting up of an international organ precisely for this purpose, or by the gradual process of education and internal legislation; (o) the question of whether and how petitions and complaints are to be received and acted upon by some international agent; and (p) the strange phenomenon of the absence of vigorous moral leadership in this field among the nations, thus demonstrating how in this age of universal fear and distrust political calculation overwhelms any sense of universal spiritual mission.

These are among the most important issues of this age, and nowhere have they received as dramatic, as authoritative, as exhaustive, as responsible a discussion as they have in the United Nations. The tragic concrete dialectic between the political and the spiritual is best revealed in the living clash of thought and the tangled problematic of the human right debates in the United Nations during the last nine years. And when the Western world, perhaps after much suffering still, wakes up one day to the necessity of taking the current war of ideas infinitely more seriously than it has, and when it then plans to make a vigorous ideological counteroffensive, I dare predict it will find in the Universal Declaration of Human Rights a potent weapon for that purpose.

Whether or not the decisions of the various bodies of the United Nations have been implemented, some of the debates of this Organization are of the greatest importance. There is an almost infinite wealth of spiritual significance in the clash of opinion, idea, aspiration, national policy, individuality, which is our daily experience at the United Nations. After one of these debates—say the debate on the Essentials of Peace in 1949—one feels he has undergone a profound spiritual *catharsis*. If you want to know the history-fashioning movements in the world today, movements like Communism, nationalism, anti-colonialism, national liberation, the development of the underdeveloped, the urge at peace and disarmament, the fellowship of the Asian countries; if you want to see and enjoy the turn of thought and humor and expression with which the representatives of these movements articulate themselves; if you want to observe how these movements clash and coalesce in a practically infinite variety of forms; if you want to appreciate the legalism of the French, the empiricism of the British, the economism of the Americans, the profuse imagery of the Russians, the humane oratory of the Latin Americans, the impulse at self-assertion of Asia and Africa; if you desire to be educated in these matters, you can certainly read about them in books, but what a pale and distant reflection books reveal by comparison with responsible participation in the living enactment of these things in actual contest. And the objective arena of this contest is none other than the United Nations. If you watch and take part in this contest, both behind the scenes and on the stage, day after day and year after year, you will soon acquire a few priceless persuasions about human nature and about the real effective forces in the world today. You may then see that pride, dignity, fear, freedom, security, comfort, self-seeking a certain irreducible belief in one's own national and cultural values, actuate men and nations everywhere; that the West really faces three formidable challenges, the challenge of Communism, the challenge of the rising East, and the challenge of freedom—namely, of the West's own internal problems, above all, the political, moral and spiritual problems; that when you are dealing with mass fears and aspirations the norms of conduct of individuals do not strictly apply; that although you may be sure of your votes, it is most important also that your friends believe in your integrity, honesty and devotion to truth; that the one great failing of the West is in the power of articulation and conviction; that nothing therefore is more needful than belief in reason, argument, fundamental ideas; that you are not really dealing with eighty-one separate units indifferently and equally related to one another, but with half a dozen cultural groupings acting each for the most part as a whole; that the cold war, the critical state of tension between the Communist and Western worlds, enters into and qualifies every international endeavor; that nothing is more important for peace and understanding than the opportunity which the United Nations affords for the Soviets to be everlastingly confronted and challenged, on every level, by the West, and for the West to be everlastingly confronted and challenged, on every level, by the Soviets; that only through this unceasing mutuality of challenge can these two world forces break through the abstract constructions of their own imaginations under which they have been living as in a fool's paradise, and face what each is really up against; that Marx and his followers constitute a radical rebellion against some of the most important spiritual values of the East and West alike; and that unless Marx and his movement are adequately answered and arrested on every level—militarily, politically, economically, and above all, theoretically and spiritually—the best intentions in the United Nations will always be vitiated. I suppose an organization that helps elucidate these issues in concrete debate is not without spiritual significance.

One great value of the United Nations has been to serve as a training ground for the emerging nations. A score of independent nations have arisen in recent years, and their participation in the United Nations has afforded them an excellent opportunity of flexing the muscles of their responsibility. The meaning of both the United States and the Soviet Union is to liberate dependent territories, though of course in different senses and with different ends in view. This formal agreement between these two power giants has made possible the enjoyment of "sovereign equality" within the United Nations even by the small countries. The United Nations is thus conceived as the one fellowship to which all belong, in which all national points of view may be represented, all political forces brought into play. Because the small nations are not as politically engaged as the big ones, in many an issue of principle they could perhaps speak with greater moral clarity. But this so-called "moral leadership" of the small and middle nations should not be exaggerated, and that for two reasons: it may give them a sense of false security altogether out of proportion to what the United Nations really provides, and in power relations authority, even moral authority, is a direct function of responsibility. There is no blinking the fact that the weakness, the brokeness, the humility, the joy, the certainty of the spirit hardly has a chance to assert itself in the United Nations.

Thus we must not exaggerate the positive spiritual significance of the

United Nations. Considering the infinite dimensions of the spirit, considering the desperate spiritual needs of the moment, and considering by comparison the concrete meagre spiritual output of the United Nations, it were far more correct to say, I suggest, that if you were seeking real spiritual phenomena, you would not find them in the United Nations. In the first place, although there is agreement on the text of the Charter and of many resolutions, the nations often give conflicting interpretations of these texts. Terms like "peace," "justice," "progress," "science," "free elections," "freely expressed wishes of the people," "self-determination of peoples," "government," "law," "democracy," "arbitrary action," "human rights and fundamental freedoms," "human dignity," "independence," "sovereignty," "aggression," "fascism," "warmongering," these and suchlike terms are, mathematically speaking, variables whose real value is variously assigned by different nations. When certain texts are adopted, we all know not only that they admit of varying interpretations but precisely where and how these interpretations are likely to turn up. Thus we all enter into a sort of tacit conspiracy to employ the felicitously ambiguous phrase, under the obvious conviction that, at least for the present, it is far better to agree on what is essentially ambiguous and variable than to disagree on what is unambiguous and constant. The effect is a perpetual postponement of a showdown on meaning, for the nations do not seem yet to be prepared to face all the consequences of a possible showdown. But it is obvious such a day cannot be indefinitely put off, for the spirit of man requires some identity of meaning if it is to live. If there is only the prospect of verbal and formal agreement, and even that in relatively unimportant realms, and no prospect of agreement as to meaning and intention and concrete content, not even in these superficial realms, let alone in the deeper realms of life, then the peoples of the world will soon despair of all international organization. A showdown is sooner or later inevitable with regard to the possibility of real, significant, spiritual agreement.

Again, compare the questions on which there was agreement with those on which there was no agreement, and you will find that the latter are by far the more important. There was a significant split in the ranks of the United Nations with regard to Korea, to disarmament, to the control and regulation of atomic weapons, to many colonial issues, to fundamental matters in the later stages of the development of the human rights program, to mention only a few such important areas. All other agreement would go up in smoke if there should be a mishap with respect to the central aim of the Organization—the maintenance and strengthening of international peace and security. To be sure, the lack of agreement here is not the fault of the

United Nations, but whatever its cause, its effect is to depress considerably the spiritual significance of the United Nations.

Moreover, the blocs to which I referred before formed themselves for the most part independently of the United Nations, and the Councils and Committees of this Organization served for the most part only as occasions or platforms in which these blocs manifested decisions they had severally already arrived at outside and independently of the United Nations. This circumstance lends a theatrical quality to the United Nations: we seem only to have a stage on which acts prepared and rehearsed outside are enacted. There is no escape from the inevitable fact that the United Nations is but a derivative reality of which the original is the chancelleries of the nations in their decisions both individually and in the groupings to which they belong apart from the United Nations. But these groupings have interests and aims quite at variance with one another, and when they all get together with a view to achieving some world decision, the currents, cross-currents and undercurrents are so varied and opposite that the net result is either zero or something eminently approaching that posture. The spirit is undermined at its source when it faces futility after futility.

The two most important features so far as the effectiveness of the United Nations is concerned are, first, the fact that General Assembly decisions have only the force of recommendations and, second, that the veto operates in the Security Council. Whoever studies what really happened at Dumbarton Oaks and San Francisco will realize that without these two conditions the United Nations would never have been set up. In security matters the big powers—and this meant the planning and inviting powers—were unitedly adamant that they must reserve for themselves the right of veto in the Security Council, while in general matters they would allow "sovereign equality" in the General Assembly—i.e., practically the right of every nation, be it Luxembourg or the United States of America, to cast but one vote of equal value—only on condition that the resolutions of this body have the legal force of a recommendation. Considering the power realities of the world, these two conditions were unavoidable. But the records of the General Assembly and the Councils which operate along its lines are cluttered with resolutions which, despite the attenuation resulting from the process of compromise among viewpoints so varied and so conflicting, remain for the most part a dead letter; and the Security Council is virtually paralyzed on account of the veto, whether this is cast positively, or negatively in the form of the necessary number of abstentions. The result is the settling of a pall of unreality and irrelevance upon the United Nations. In such an atmosphere the spirit suffers and seeks salvation elsewhere.

There has been a steady decline in seriousness and responsibility so far as some of the non-political functions of the United Nations are concerned. The discussion at times bears no relation whatever either to the home conditions of some of the members or to what is really possible under the circumstances. Attitudes are often developed either from rhetorical or from emotional or from spiteful motives. There is thus an element of individual caprice, and in some cases representatives really represent only themselves, with only the most tenuous possible relationship to the policy or will of their governments. It would seem that in those bodies their governments do not really care what transpires. When one harangues on, say, the subject of human rights in some other country towards which for one reason or another one harbors some grievance, without humble reflection on the state of human rights in one's own land; or when one urges a text that, even if adopted, you know and he knows and everybody knows his country will not bind itself by; when these things happen, there is obviously a tragicomic divorce from reality which can only be described as a sin against the truth. If in the organs where the spirit is supposed to act under its own autonomous laws in relative freedom from the operations of power and pride, the spirit nonetheless sinks to such levels, need we wonder at the deterioration in the political functionings of the United Nations whose constituent principles are precisely pride and power?

The source of all evil is the absolutization of politics. Nations and cultures do not fear God: on the contrary, they set themselves up as a sort of god, with nothing above them. The supreme need therefore is for the recognition of some transcendent norm to which we willingly and freely submit.

Since desire, whether of power or of material goods, has no limits, and since the field of power and of matter is quite limited, it is obvious, conflict and clash are inevitable. The answer therefore is the self-curbing of desire. But this can come about either negatively, when one is physically restrained from without, or positively, when one recognizes a larger loyalty with which one freely identifies oneself. Negative obstruction is never stable: it is mechanical and external. The only answer therefore is inner self-restraint under a genuine community of ideas. This is the way of freedom.

The promotion of larger ideals, more universal norms, elaborated, not arbitrarily, but according to the nature of things—I mean norms concerning justice and truth, concerning man and his dignity, concerning the place of material goods in human life, concerning the source of political power, concerning freedom of thought and conscience, concerning intercultural interaction and respect, concerning how to meet aggression, whether it comes by external invasion or by internal subversion effectively directed from without—the promotion of some binding understanding among the nations upon these fundamental things is the only hope for peace in the world.

But faith in such promotion means necessarily faith in the unity of mankind in the truth; namely, faith that there is an objective common good for all men, that it is not something arbitrary but belongs to the nature of things, that we are not therefore the subjects of some cosmic trick, but that we can, by effort and inquiry and discourse and reason and love, discover this common good and completely fling ourselves upon it. Let men believe, absolutely believe, honestly and genuinely believe, in the existence and accessibility of a real common good, and they will forthwith stop fighting; instead they will seek this good with all their heart.

It is despair of the objectively given common good that is at the base of all evil in the world. One does not mind difference of opinion, of outlook, of interest, of temperament, even of culture, provided there is fundamentally no despair of the truth. We will bear then all our differences, no matter how radical, because of the prize of the great common good above us all, a good that we may not now clearly glimpse but which is nonetheless certainly there beckoning us all the time.

Peace is promised to men of good will, namely, in my judgment, to the men who allow for the possibility of a rational common good; but even angels, if faced with men who absolutely reject such a possibility, who teach instead that the good is not determined by reason and love but by force—no matter how ingenious their dialectical interpretations of this force might be—even angels, I say, facing such a breed of men must take up arms and fight.

War arises either from hatred or from fear or from greed, and all three are fundamental sins against reason. For hatred at bottom wills the elimination of the other fellow, because it is blind to the possibility that there is a truth, a community of the spirit, that can bracket you both, provided both of you are humbly and practically exposed to it. Fear, on the other hand, fears precisely that the other fellow rejects such a possibility, and therefore moves to strike first. Greed does not recognize the truth of objective justice, namely, that infinite desire is the source of all evil, because while there may be enough and plenty for all our need, as a matter of fact there is not enough for all our greed.

The spirit flourishes and peace supervenes when men believe in the possibility of a real, common, natural good.

Overshadowing everything is the terrible chasm between Communism and the rest of the world. In all fundamental issues the two power blocs eye each other all the time, and whatever posture they take, it is in function of the cold war that they take it. But the rest of us are thus offended twice: first, because we are not taken into account except as incidents in the requirements of the cold war and, second, because we see no progress whatever made by the Soviet Union and the Western world in the settlement of their disputes. We would gladly forgive our personal affront if only the giants showed some progress in their war. Nothing therefore is more certain than that until a fundamental settlement is arrived at between Communism and the rest of the world, the spirit in the United Nations will continue laboring under profound tribulation.

Considering soberly the actualities and potentialities of power in the world, and affirming faith in the traditional view of man and his spirit, it would seem that this settlement must include (a) the effective independence of China, (b) the effective independence of Eastern Europe so as to restore fundamental unity to European culture, (c) the radical giving up by the followers of Marx of their revolutionary teaching and technique, (d) a much greater freedom of movement between the Soviet Union and the rest of the world with respect to goods, men and ideals, (e) adequate security assurances for the Soviet Union, and (f) a satisfactory agreement about the use of weapons of mass destruction. It is difficult to imagine, I defy anybody to imagine, how, if any of these six conditions were lacking, there would be a sense of confidence anywhere in the world.

The ultimate spiritual significance perhaps of the United Nations so far as the Western world is concerned is to compel this world, faced constantly as it is by the challenge of Communism and the challenge of the East, to fall back upon its own spiritual resources. There must be an original conviction and regeneration of the spirit expressing itself in the policies of governments and in the attitude and tone of their representatives. Because of its derivative character, the United Nations cannot provide this spiritual regeneration.

Am I to be told that the world which at its best has assigned infinite worth to the individual human soul; which has not fundamentally repudiated reason and the possibility of objective truth; which has a wonderful living deposit in the theory and practice of the arts; which has not broken away from its continuous, cumulative history; in which the university and the church are free each to obey its own principle; in which the transcendent is still worshipped not as a distant ideal but as a living God; and whose deepest vision is faith, hope and love: am I to be told that a world so burdened and so determined cannot yet awaken in order to develop the necessary universal material, social, intellectual and spiritual message which will enable it to save both itself and the rest of the world? I believe no such thing.

$$\approx\!\!\approx\!\!\approx\!\!\approx\!\!\approx\!\!\approx\!\!\approx\!\!\approx\!\!\approx\!\!\approx$$ *Notes*

1. THE LIFE AND MIND OF PAUL TILLICH

[1] Those who are likely to misunderstand this should remember that Tillich subjects his whole thought to the modern scientific principle.

[2] There is this difference between Tillich and Sartre. Tillich remains within the circle of the philosophy of identity; he interprets existence as both the actualization of and the estrangement from essence. Sartre speaks only of existence cutting out essence. Tillich's statement that God is being itself is rejected by Heidegger, Bultmann, Barth and Niebuhr, all of whom reject classical metaphysics unreservedly.

[3] Tillich's continued use of the analogy of being, which Barth fights vehemently, and Tillich's combination of the Christian doctrine of reconciliation and the idealist concept of identity show how far he and Barth are separated in the fundamentals of their thought. Since Barth has recently introduced the idea of analogy of relation (between man and the true man in Jesus Christ), there have been remarkable similarities between the two thinkers, particularly in their Christologies.

[4] In fact Kierkegaard, a true romantic himself, emphasized the conflict of man's existence in "the unhappy conscience" before God to such an extent that the Christian doctrine of Redemption came to play a secondary role in his thought. The existential conflict was never fully overcome by the love of God. Modern theology has inherited this tendency from Kierkegaard.

[5] *The Interpretation of History* (New York, 1936) p. 76.

[6] *Ibid.*, p. 32.

[7] Bultmann, following Barth and Heidegger, has no such ontology as Tillich's. He reduces being to a mode of existence and, consequently dissolves the historical into the existential, making the cross and the resurrection of Christ into mere expressions of man's existence. But Tillich is concerned with being. Although he shows the correspondence of history and the understanding self in any act of interpretation, he never dissolves the truly concrete historical character of the appearance, the factum of the New Being.

[8] *The Protestant Era* (Chicago, 1948), p. 30.

[9] Theology is for Tillich the interpretation of the symbols of man's ultimate concern. Not the creation but the interpretation of symbols is the task of theology. Symbols cannot be made, they "grow and die"; they participate in the reality which they symbolize. Symbols are for Tillich the bearers of revelation, which is the self-manifestation of the ultimate. Ultimate reality is expressed through symbols in ecstatic experiences. The principle of the interpretation of the symbol is the *Logos;* the New Being is the universal *Logos* of creation. Thus Tillich's understanding of myth and symbol is quite different from that of Bultmann, where these become the expression of man's existential attitudes and no longer expressions, as for Tillich, of a real relation to the ultimate which can only be expressed through symbols.

[10] By transporting the element of "serious otherness" into being itself, into the divine ground, Tillich revives a mystical tradition. Some of his thoughts remind one of Duns Scotus' and Martin Luther's concept of the hidden and revealed God. The struggle of being versus non-being as such is seen by Tillich in the ground of being itself, where the divine *no* is overcome eternally by the divine *yes*. It is the overcoming of non-being in Himself which makes God the "living God." (This definition, used by Tillich, means,

however, something quite different from the statement "the Living God" in the Bible. Does Tillich not "eternalize" the continuous rhythm of life and death, of *"Stirb und Werde,"* by projecting it into the ground of being, the ultimate?)

2. THE LIMITATIONS AND DANGERS OF PSYCHOLOGY

[1] Isaac Babel, *The Collected Stories* (New York, 1955).

[2] In children we often see this path to knowledge quite overtly, and as a part of the normal desire of the child to orient himself in a world of physical reality. The child takes something apart and breaks it up in order to know it; or it takes an animal apart; cruelly tears off the wings of a butterfly in order to know it, to force its secret. The apparent cruelty itself is motivated by something deeper: the wish to know the secret of things and of life.

5. WOLFGANG AMADEUS MOZART

[1] This address was given on the occasion of the Anniversary in the Music Hall at Basel, January 29, 1956.

[2] The Festival was opened and ended with the Serenade in C Minor, KV 388.

6. CHRISTIAN PRESUPPOSITIONS FOR A CREATIVE CULTURE

[1] Discussion of these themes will be found in the author's *Faith and Reason* (*New York*, 1946), and subsequent writings.

[2] An attempt is made to deal with this aspect of evil in the author's *Evil and the Christian Faith* (New York, 1947).

7. THE MODERN DIOGENES: A KIERKEGAARDIAN CROTCHET

[1] Robert Browning, *The Pied Piper of Hamelin.*

[2] Sören Kierkegaard, "He Was Believed On in the World" from "Thoughts Which Wound from Behind—For Edification," *Christian Discourses;* tr. by Walter Lowrie (New York, 1939), p. 248.

[3] Sören Kierkegaard, *Concluding Unscientific Postscript;* tr. by David F. Swenson (Princeton, 1941), pp. 339, 338.

[4] *Ibid.,* p. 332n.

[5] Sören Kierkegaard, *Philosophical Fragments,* tr. by David F. Swenson (Princeton, 1936), pp. 29–31.

[6] *Christian Discourses,* p. 249.

[7] *Ibid.,* italics mine.

[8] *Ibid.,* p. 248.

[9] *Ibid.,* pp. 248–249, italics mine, cf. Pascal: "Fear not, provided you fear; but if you fear not, then fear." *Pensées,* No. 775.

[10] *Ibid.,* p. 249.

[11] W. H. Auden, "For the Time Being," *The Collected Poetry of W. H. Auden* (New York, 1945), p. 446. Used by permission of Random House.

[12] *Pensées,* No. 552, ed. by Brunschvicg (Paris, 1925), p. 216.

[13] *Portraits of the Seventeenth Century,* tr. by Katherine P. Wormeley (New York, 1904), Part II, p. 184.

[14] "Heimkunft, An die Verwandten"; cf. the author's essay "On the Naming of the Gods in Hölderlin and Rilke" in *Christianity and the Existentialists,* ed. by Carl Michalson (New York, 1956), for a fuller treatment of this problem in Hölderlin.

[15] *Edifying Discourses,* Vol. IV, tr. by David F. and Lillian Marvin Swenson (Minneapolis, 1946), pp. 7 ff.; *Thoughts on Crucial Situations in Human Life,* tr. by David F. Swenson (Minneapolis, 1941), pp. 1 ff.

[16] *Edifying Discourses,* IV, p. 31.

[17] Matthew Arnold, "Dover Beach."

[18] Kierkegaard, *Edifying Discourses,* p. 31.

[19] *Ibid.,* p. 31, 32.

[20] *Ibid.,* p. 43, italics mine.

[21] *Thoughts on Crucial Situations in Human Life,* p. 13.

[22] *City of God,* Bk. XXII, Ch. 24.

[23] Christopher Fry, *The Lady's Not for Burning* (New York, 1950), p. 55. Used by permission of Oxford University Press.

[24] *Crucial Situations,* p. 14.

[25] *Ibid.,* p. 16.

[26] *Ibid.,* p. 21.

[27] *Ibid.,* p. 19.

[28] *Ibid.,* p. 19.

[29] *Philosophical Fragments,* p. 5.

[30] *Ibid.,* p. 12.

[31] *Ibid.,* p. 11.

[32] *The Stromata,* Bk. V, Ch. iii, iv; *The Ante-Nicene Fathers,* Vol. II, ed. by Roberts and Donaldson (Buffalo, 1887), pp. 448–449.

[33] *Ibid.,* V, iii, p. 448.

[34] T. S. Eliot, "East Coker," III, *The Four Quartets* (New York, 1943), pp. 14–15. Used by permission of Harcourt, Brace & Co.

[35] Quoted in Ralph Harper's *The Sleeping Beauty* (New York, n.d.), p. 77.

[36] *Waiting for Godot,* the title of a tragicomedy in two acts by Samuel Beckett (New York, 1956).

[37] Clement, *op. cit.,* V, xii, "God Cannot Be Embraced in Words or by the Mind."

[38] *Ibid.*

[39] *Ibid.*

[40] *Ibid.,* V, iii.

[41] *The Journals of Sören Kierkegaard,* ed. and tr. by Alexander Dru (New York, 1938), No. 633.

[42] *Ibid.,* No. 22.

[43] *Ibid.,* No. 620.

[44] *Crucial Situations,* p. 25.

[45] See note No. 2 above.

[46] *Crucial Situations,* p. 21, italics mine.

[47] Rainer Maria Rilke, *Duino Elegies,* viii; tr. by J. B. Leishman and Stephen Spender (New York, 1939), p. 71. Used by permission of W. W. Norton and Co., Inc.

[48] T. S. Eliot, "The Hollow Men," from *Collected Poems, 1909–1935* (New York, 1936). Used by permission of Harcourt, Brace & Co.

[49] *Ibid.*

[50] John LaFarge, "The Future of Religious Symbolism—*A Catholic View,*" in *Religious Symbolism,* ed. by F. Ernest Johnson (New York, 1955), p. 220.

[51] Wallace Fowlie, *Age of Surrealism* (New York, 1950), p. 163.

[52] Jacques Maritain, *Rouault,* Pocket Library of Great Art (New York, 1953), preceding color plate No. 45.

[53] Karl Barth, *The Doctrine of the Word of God* (New York, 2nd ed., 1949), pp. 350 ff.

[54] Charles De Coster, *Tyl Ulenspiegl,* (New York, 1943), p. 211.

[55] *Journals,* p. 144.

[56] See *Journals,* No. 552, "The Dialectic of Beginning."

[57] Sören Kierkegaard, *The Sickness Unto Death* (Princeton, 1941), p. 19.

[58] *Religiöse Verwirklichung,* 2nd ed., 1930, p. 20; quoted in Barth, *op. cit.,* p. 83.

[59] *Ibid.*

[60] Gabriel Marcel, *Homo Viator,* "Introduction to a Metaphysic of Hope"; tr. by Emma Craufurd (Chicago, 1951), p. 126.

[61] e. e. cummings, from χαιρε (New York, 1944–1950).

[62] *Crucial Situations,* p. 14.

[63] Maritain, *op. cit.,* opposite color plate No. 45.

[64] Ira Progoff, *The Death and Rebirth of Psychology* (New York, 1956), p. 251.

[65] *The Confessions of St. Augustine,* tr. by J. G. Pilkington (New York), Bk. X, Ch. xvii, 26; xviii, 27; xx, 29; xxvii, 38.

[66] Thomas Mann, *Joseph and His Brothers,* Prelude (New York, 1934), p. 3.

[67] Halévy, *Charles Péguy and Les Cahiers de la Quinzaine*, p. 183; quoted in Amos Wilder, *Modern Poetry and the Christian Tradition* (New York, 1952), p. 265.

[68] W. H. Auden, from "Vespers" in *The Shield of Achilles* (New York, 1955), p. 79.

[69] *The Notebooks of Malte Laurids Brigge*, tr. by M. D. Herter Norton (New York, 1949), p. 209.

[70] Franz Kafka, "On Parables," in *The Great Wall of China* (New York, 1946). Used by permission of Schocken Books.

[71] Nietzsche, *Menschliches, Allzumenschliches*, II, 7.

[72] "On the Free Will," tr. by Richard McKeon, Bk. II, Ch. xi, 32; Ch. xvi, 41.

[73] *Ibid.*, Ch. xvi, 43.

8. CHRISTIAN ROOT-TERMS

[1] Tillich, *Die religionsgeschichtliche Konstruktion in Schelling's positiver Philosophie* (Breslau, 1910), and *Mystik und Schuldbewusstsein in Schelling's philosophischer Entwicklung* (Gütersloh, 1912).

[2] Cf. *Kairos*, I (Darmstadt, 1926), and *Kairos*, II (Darmstadt, 1929). Cf. also the author's analysis of Tillich's philosophy of religion: *Humanitas* (Nürnberg, 1952).

[3] Cf. my *Christentum gemaess Johannes* (Nürnberg, 1943), pp. 229 ff.

[4] Cf. "Religionsphilosophie" in Max Dessoir, ed., *Lehrbuch der Philosophie* (Berlin, 1925), and *Das Daemonische* (Tübingen, 1926).

[5] Compare with the program of the "Evangelischen Michaelsbrudershaft": *Credo Ecclesiam* (Kassel, 1954).

[6] W. Otto, *Die Gestalt und das Sein* (Duesseldorf, 1955).

[7] *Ibid.*, pp. 80, 86.

[8] Paul Tillich, *Rechtfertigung und Zweifel* (Giessen, 1924), p. 28.

[9] See Max Dessoir, ed., *op. cit.*, p. 804.

[10] *Ibid.*, p. 808.

[11] Cf. my books: *Alter and Neuer Bund* (Vienna, 1956) and *Gespräch Zwischen den Kirchen* (Nürnberg, 1957).

9. MYTH, SYMBOL AND ANALOGY

[1] (1) 2:19–20. (2) 3:3–4. (3) 4:10–11. (4) 4:32–33. (5) 6:51–52. (6) 7:33–35. (7) 8:18–19. (8) 8:56–57. (9) 11:11–12. (10) 12:32–34. (11) 13:8–9. (12) 13:36–38. (13) 14:3–5. (14) 14:7–8. (15) 18:33–37. (16) 21:22–23.

[2] *Quaestio quodlibetalis VII*, q. 6, art. 15. corp.

[3] *Epistula contra Vincentium Donatistam*, Ep. 93, c. 8, n. 24. PL. xxxiii, 384.

"Is it not the height of impudence to interpret an allegorical locus to one's own advantage unless the obscurity of the allegory is removed in the light of testimonies whose meaning is clear?"

[4] *Summa theologica*, I, 1, 10, and 1.

[5] Reinhold Niebuhr, "Reply to Interpretation and Criticism," in *Reinhold Niebuhr, His Religious, Social and Political Thought*, C. W. Kegley and R. W. Bretall, eds., The Library of Living Theology, Vol. III (New York, 1956), p. 446.

[6] Two newer studies are well worth mentioning: E. C. Blackman, "The Task of Exegesis," *The Background of the New Testament and Its Eschatology, In Honour of Charles Harold Dodd*, W. D. Davies and D. Daube, eds. (Cambridge, 1956), pp. 3–26, and in the same volume, H. Riesenfeld, "The Mythical Background of New Testament Christology," pp. 81–95.

[7] This point is well illustrated in an article by Heinrich Schlier, "Das neue Testament und der Mythus," *Hochland*, 48, Heft 3 (February, 1956), 201–212.

[8] In appendix to G. Weigel's "The Theological Significance of Paul Tillich," *Gregorianum*, 37, 1 (January, 1956), 34–54 at p. 54.

[9] *Loc. cit. supra*.

[10] Cf. Avery Dulles, S.J., "Paul Tillich and the Bible," *Theological Studies*, 17, no. 3 (September, 1956), 345–367.

[11] A pertinent study of gnosticism and the New Testament is given by R. P. Casey, "Gnosis, Gnosticism and the New Testament," pp. 52–80 in the memorial volume to C. H. Dodd mentioned in note 6 above.

12 William F. Albright, "Toynbee's Book on Religion Reviewed," *Evening Sun*, Baltimore, Sept. 11, 1956; second last paragraph, p. 20, col. 7.

13 Ben F. Kimpel, *Religious Faith, Language, and Knowledge. A philosophical preface to theology* (New York, 1952), p. 72.

14 *Loc. cit.* in note 8.

15 Cf. Joseph Owens, C.Ss.R., *The Doctrine of Being in the Aristotelian Metaphysics* (Toronto, 1951), pp. 49 ff.

16 A Protestant theologian, Hampus Lyttkens, has made a diligent study of Thomistic analogy, bringing forth a wealth of material: *The Analogy between God and the World. An Investigation of its Background and Interpretation of its Use by Thomas of Aquino* (Uppsala, 1952). The older work of the Brazilian, Maurilio Texeira-Leite Penido, *Le Rôle de l'analogie en théologie dogmatique* (Bibliothèque Thomiste, XV; Paris, 1931), is highly esteemed in Catholic circles, though Lyttkens has found shortcomings in it.

17 This is admirably brought out by J. V. Langmead Casserly in "Event-Symbols and Myth-Symbols," *Anglican Theological Review*, 38, nos. 2 and 3 (April and July, 1956), 127–137, 242–248.

10. FAITH AND REASON IN THE THOUGHT OF ERASMUS AND LUTHER

1 *Enchiridion militis christiani*, ed. by H. and A. Holborn, (London, 1905) p. 46.

2 *Ibid.*, p. 52.

3 October 19, 1516. *Correspondence* (Weimar ed., 1910), II, 70 ff.

4 March 1, 1517. *Ibid.*, I, 90.

5 *De libero arbitrio*, ed. Joh. von Walter (Leipzig, 1936) p. 3.

6 *Ibid.*, p. 4.

7 *De amabili ecclesiae concordia* (the customary, abbreviated title) In *E. Conloquiis Familiaribus* (Boston, 1896).

8 Introduction to a work of Antonius Corvinus, opposing Erasmus' book. Weimar ed., 38, pp. 273 ff.

9 *Table Talk* (Weimar ed.), I, No. 1160.

10 *Institutio principis christiani* (1516). Cf. an earlier work, *Enchiridion* (London, 1905) p. 105.

11. THE PREDICAMENT OF THE CHRISTIAN HISTORIAN

1 Marc Bloch, *Apologie pour l'Histoire, ou Metier d'Historien*, "Cahiers des Annales," 3 (Paris, 1949); English translation, *The Historian's Craft* (New York, 1953), p. 4.

2 Gerhard Kittel, "The Jesus of History," in *Mysterium Christi*, ed. by G. K. A. Bell and Adolf Deissman (Longmans, 1930), pp. 31 ff.

3 F. M. Powicke, *Modern Historians and the Study of History* (London, 1955), pp. 227–228.

4 H. E. Manning, *The Temporal Mission of the Holy Ghost: or Reason and Revelation* (New York, 1866), pp. 227 ff.

5 An interesting discussion of this issue took place at the Anglo-American Conference of Historians, July, 1926; three addresses given at the conference by C. H. McIlwain, A. Meyendorff, and J. L. Morison are published under the general title, "Bias in historical writing," in *History*, XI (October, 1926), 193–203.

6 M. Bloch, pp. 64–65.

7 See the penetrating analysis of experimental method by Claude Bernard, in his classical essay, *Introduction à l'étude de la médecine experimentale* (Paris, 1865). Bergson compares this book with the *Discours sur la methode* of Descartes: "The Philosophy of Claude Bernard," in *The Creative Mind* (New York, 1946), pp. 238 ff.

8 See the caustic remarks of R. G. Collingwood, *The Idea of History* (New York, 1946), pp. 257 ff.

9 Benedetto Croce, *La Storia come Pensiero e come Azione*, 4th ed., (Bari, 1943); English translation, *History as the Story of Liberty* (London, 1949), pp. 85 ff.

10 Benedetto Croce, *Teoria e Storia della Storiografia*, 6th ed. (Bari, 1948), p. 11.

11 Collingwood, p. 214.

[12] Leopold von Ranke, *Weltgeschichte*, Theil I, 3 Aufl. (Leipzig, 1883), "Vorrede," s. VI.

[13] Henri-Irenée Marrou, *De la connaissance historique* (Paris, 1954), p. 83.

[14] Collingwood, *op. cit.*, pp. 218–219.

[15] Collingwood, *An Autobiography* (New York, 1949), p. 31.

[16] Croce, *Teoria e Storia*, pp. 29 ff.; cf. Collingwood, *The Idea*, pp. 214 ff.

[17] Fr. Ad. Trendelenburg, *Logische Untersuchungen*, Bd. II. 2, s. 408.

[18] G. Spet, "Istorija kak predmet logiki" ("History as the Matter of Logic"), in *Nauchnyja Izvestija*, coll. 2 (Moscow, 1922), pp. 15–16.

[19] Marrou, *op. cit.*, p. 120.

[20] Marrou, *op. cit.*, p. 101.

[21] Collingwood, *Autobiography*, pp. 127–128.

[22] For the whole section 2 of this article see my essay, "O tipakh istoricheskago istolkovanija" ("The types of historical interpretation"), in *Sbornik v chest' na Vasil N. Zlatarski* (Sofia, 1925), pp. 523–541 (in Russian). It is gratifying for the author to discover that this conception is now widely shared by many historians and philosophers, although his Russian article was hardly likely to have been read by many. In addition to the studies by Croce, Collingwood, and Marrou, already quoted, one should mention: Raymon Aron, *Introduction à la Philosophie de l'Histoire, Essai sur les limites de l'objectivité historique* (Paris, 1948); *La Philosophie critique de l'Histoire, Essai sur une théorie allemande de l'histoire* (Paris, 1950). Of earlier writers one should mention Wilhelm Dilthey; on him see H. A. Hodges, *Wilhelm Dilthey, An Introduction* (London, 1944); *The Philosophy of Wilhelm Dilthey* (London, 1952). On Benedetto Croce see A. Robert Caponigri, *History and Liberty: The Historical Writings of Benedetto Croce* (London, 1955). For other points of view see, e.g., Patrick Gardiner, *The Nature of Historical Explanation* (New York, 1952); S. G. F. Brandon, *Time and Mankind* (London, 1951); G. N. Renier, *History, Its purpose and method* (Boston, 1950).

[23] V. V. Bolotov, *Lekzii po istorii drevnej cerkvi* ("Lectures on the History of the Early Church") (St. Petersburg, 1907), I, 6–7.

[24] Ranke, "Geschichte der Romanischen und Germanischen Völker von 1494 bis 1514," in *Vorrede zur ersten Ausgabe* (October, 1824), *Samtliche Werke*, 3 Aufl., Bd. 33 (Leipzig, 1885), s. VII.

[25] See von Laue, *Leopold Ranke, The Formative Years* (Princeton, 1950), and especially H. Liebeschutz, *Ranke* (Historical Association, G 26, 1954); cf. Eberhard Kessel, "Rankes Idee der Universalhistorie," in *Historische Zeitschrift*, Bd. 178.2, ss. 269–308 (with new texts of Ranke).

[26] Collingwood, *The Idea*, pp. 282 ff.

[27] *Ibid.*, p. 233.

[28] Cf. H. Gouhier, "Vision retrospective et intention historique," in *La Philosophie de l'Histoire de la Philosophie* (Rome–Paris, 1956), pp. 133–141.

[29] Marrou, *op. cit.*, p. 47.

[30] Collingwood, *The Idea*, pp. 42 ff.

[31] See Isaiah Berlin, *Historical Inevitability* (New York, 1954), and Pieter Geyl's remarks in *Debates with Historians* (London, 1955), pp. 236–241.

[32] See my earlier articles: "Evolution und Epigenesis, Zur Problematik der Geschichte," in *Der Russische Gedanke*, Jh. I, Nr. 3 (Bonn, 1930), ss. 240–252; "Die Krise des deutschen Idealismus," in *Orient und Occident*, Hf. 11 & 12, 1932.

[33] Robert Flint, *History of the Philosophy of History* (Edinburgh and London, 1893), p. 62.

[34] Lucretius, *De rerum natura*, III, 945.

[35] Werner Jaeger, *Aristoteles. Grundlegung einer Geschichte seiner Entwicklung* (Berlin, 1923); English translation: *Aristotle, Fundamentals of the History of His Development*, translated with the author's corrections and additions by Richard Robinson (2nd ed.; Oxford, 1948), p. 389. (italics mine) Cf. O. Hamelin, *Le Système d'Aristote* (2nd ed.; Paris, 1931), pp. 336 ss.; J. Chevalier, *La Notion du Nécessaire chez Aristote et chez ses prédécesseurs, particulièrement chez Platon* (Paris, 1915), pp. 160 ss.; R. Mugnier, *La Théorie du Premier Moteur et l'Evolution de la Pensée Aristotelienne* (Paris, 1930), pp. 24 ss.; J. Baudry, *Le Problème de l'origine et de l'éternité du Monde dans la philosophie*

grecque de Platon à l'ère chrétienne (Paris, 1931), especially chapters on Aristotle (pp. 99–206) and conclusion (pp. 299 ss.).

[36] B. A. van Groningen, "In the Grip of the Past, Essay on an Aspect of Greek Thought," in *Philosophia Antiqua*, ed. by W. J. Verdenius and J. H. Waszink (Leiden, 1953), vol. VI; Pierre Duhème, *Le Système du Monde, Histoire des Doctrines Cosmologiques de Platon à Copernic* (Paris, 1913), t. I; (Paris, 1914), t. II; Hans Meyer, "Zur Lehre von der Ewigen Wiederkunft aller Dinge," in *Festgabe A. Ehrhard* (Bonn, 1922), ss. 359 ff.; Jean Guitton, *Le Temps et l'Eternité chez Plotin et St. Augustin* (Paris, 1933); John F. Callahan, *Four Views of Time in Ancient Philosophy* (Cambridge, Mass., 1948); Victor Goldschmidt, *Le système stoicien et l'Idée de temps* (Paris, 1953); Mircea Eliade, *Der Mythos der Ewigen Wiederkehr* (Duesseldorf, 1953); Henri-Charles Puech, "Temps, Histoire et Mythe dans le Christianisme des premiers siècles," in the *Proceedings of the 7th Congress for the History of Religions, Amsterdam, 4th–9th September 1950* (Amsterdam, 1951), pp. 33 ff.; "La Gnose et le Temps," in *Eranos*, Bd. XX, *Mensch und Zeit* (Zurich, 1952), pp. 57 ss. An attempt of Wilhelm Nestle to prove that there existed a certain "philosophy of history" in ancient Greece was unsuccessful; see his "Griechische Geschichtsphilosophie," in *Archiv fur die Geschichte der Philosophie*, Bd. XLI (1932), ss. 80–114. Nor are the remarks of Paul Schubert convincing; see his chapter, "The Twentieth-Century West and the Ancient Near East," in *The Idea of History in the Ancient Near East*, ed. by Robert C. Dentan, American Oriental Series (New Haven, 1955), vol. 38, pp. 332 ff.

[37] See, *e. g.*, C. H. Dodd, *History and the Gospel* (London, 1938); cf. "Eschatology and History," an Appendix in *The Apostolic Preaching and Its Developments* (New York, 1936 [new ed. in 1944]).

[38] Rudolf Bultmann, *History and Eschatology*, The Gifford Lectures, 1955 (Edinburgh, 1955).

[39] Karl Loewith, *Meaning in History: The Theological Implications of the Philosophy of History* (Chicago, 1949), pp. 196–197; cf. also his articles: "Skepsis und Glaube in der Geschichte," in *Die Welt als Geschichte*, Jh. X. 3 (1950); "Christentum und Geschichte," in *Christentum und Geschichte, Vortraege der Tragung in Bochum vom 5. bis 8. October 1954* (Duesseldorf, 1955).

[40] Cyril C. Richardson, "Church History Past and Present," in *Union Seminary Quarterly Review* (November, 1949) p. 9.

[41] For a further elaboration of this topic see my Dudleian Lecture, *The Christian Dilemma*, delivered at Harvard University on April 30, 1958, in press.

[42] The problem of "Christian history" (in the double meaning of the word: "actual history" and "historiography") has been extensively discussed in recent years, and literature is enormous. There are several competent surveys: G. Thils, "Bibliographie sur la theologie de l'histoire," in *Ephemerides Theologicae Lovanienses*, 26 (1950), pp. 87–95; F. Olgiati, "Rapporti fra storia, metafisica e religione," in *Rivista di filosofia neoscholastica* (1950), pp. 49–84; P. Henry, "The Christian Philosophy of History," in *Theological Studies*, XIII (1952), 419–433; see also R. L. Shinn, *Christianity and the Problem of History* (New York, 1953); M. C. Smit, *De Veroudingvan Christendom en Historie in der huidige Roms-Katholicke geschicolbeschouwing* (Kampen, 1950) [with a French résumé]).

The following publications also should be especially mentioned in the context of the present article: Oscar Cullmann, *Christus und die Zeit* (Zurich, 1945); English translation, *Christ and Time* (London, 1951); Karl Barth, *Kirchliche Dogmatik*, Bd. III. 2 (Zollikon-Zurich, 1948), ss. 524–780; John Marsh, *The Fulness of Time* (London, 1952); Jean Danielou, *Essai sur le Mystère de l'Histoire* (Paris, 1953); *Le Mystère de l'Avent* (Paris, 1948); *Papers of the Ecumenical Institute*, 5: "On the Meaning of History," in *Oikoumene* (Geneva, 1950); Erich Frank, *Philosophical Understanding and Religious Truth* (New York, 1945); "The Role of History in Christian Thought," in *The Duke Divinity School Bulletin*, XIV, No. 3 (November, 1949), pp. 66–77; H. Butterfield, *Christianity and History* (New York, 1950); E. C. Rust, *The Christian Understanding of History* (London, 1947); Reinhold Niebuhr, *Faith and History* (New York, 1949); Pietro Chichetta, *Teolgia della storia* (Rome, 1953); John McIntyre, *The Christian Doctrine of History* (Edinburgh, 1957); Christopher Dawson, *Dynamics of*

362 Religion and Culture

World History, ed. by John J. Mulloy (New York, 1957); Jacques Maritain, *On the Philosophy of History,* ed. by Joseph W. Evans (New York, 1957).

12. A PHILOSOPHER'S ASSESSMENT OF CHRISTIANITY

[1] See A. Campbell Garnett, *Religion and the Moral Life* (New York, 1955), Ch. 2.
[2] Mark 12:30; Deut. 6:5. I am, of course, following Tillich in making this text the key to thought about the divine.
[3] See the Epilogue in my *Man's Vision of God* (New York, 1941).

13. CHRISTIAN FAITH AND THE GROWING POWER OF SECULARISM

[1] Fritz Mauthner, *Der Atheismus und seine Geschichte* (Stuttgart and Berlin, 1920–23).
[2] Johann Kepler, *Harmonices mundi liber V* (Lincii Austriae, 1619).
[3] Ludwig Klages, *Der Geist als Widersacher der Seele* (Leipzig, 1929–32).
[4] Rudolf Diesel, *Theory and Construction of a Rational Heatmotor* (New York, 1894).

14. KNOWLEDGE AND FAITH

[1] Cf. the author's *Heidegger, Denker in dürftiger Zeit* (Frankfurt, 1953), pp. 93 ff.
[2] Cf. L. Strauss, *Die Religionskritik Spinozas* (Leipzig, 1930), pp. 87 ff.
[3] Cf. Fustel de Coulanges, *La Cité Antique;* H. Maine, *Ancient Law;* G. Sorel, *Le Procés de Socrate* (Paris, 1889).
[4] Cf. A. Harnack, *"Der Vorwurf des Atheismus in den ersten drei Jahrhunderten,"* *Texte und Untersuchungen zur Geschichte der altchristlichen Literatur,* N.F. Vol. XIII, No. 4 (1905).
[5] Cicero, *De natura deorum,* II, 2, 5, 7, 8, 11 ff., 17, 37; III, 8.
[6] Cf. Karl Barth, *Anselms Beweis der Existenz Gottes* (Munich, 1931).
[7] The discussion which follows refers to *"De utilitate Credendi"* and *"De fide rerum quae non videntur."*
[8] Cf. Augustinus, *Epist.,* 120:2, *Opera omnia* (Paris, 1841).
[9] Cf. G. Krüger, *"Das Problem der Authorität,"* in the *Festschrift "Offener Horizont"* for Karl Jaspers (Munich, 1953).
[10] Cf. Immanuel Kant, *Critique of Pure Reason, Transcendental Methodology,* II, 3.
[11] Cf. Augustinus, The tract on the Gospel of John, 29:6. *Opera omnia* (Paris, 1841).
[12] Cf. G. F. Hegel, *Theologische Jugendschriften* (Stuttgart, 1907), pp. 230 ff., 297 ff.
[13] Cf. F. v. Baader, *Werke* (Leipzig, 1851), I, 357 ff., 321 ff.
[14] Cf. the author's *Von Hegel zu Nietzsche,* pp. 350 ff.
[15] Cf. K. Jaspers, *Der Philosophische Glaube* (Zurich, 1948), tr. 1949.
[16] Cf. Martin Heidegger, *"Uber den Humanismus,"* (Frankfurt, 1949) p. 42, *Holzwege,* (Frankfurt, 1950) p. 325, *Vorträge und Aufsätze,* (Pfullingen, 1954) p. 44.
[17] G. F. Hegel, *The Phenomenology of Mind* (tr. London, 1910), preface.
[18] Heidegger, *Sein und Zeit,* (Halle, 1935) 32.
[19] Cf. Kierkegaard, *Journals* (London, 1938); *Die Tagebücher,* ed. H. Uhlrich (1930), pp. 128 ff. and 463 ff.
[20] Cf. Plato, *Phaedo, The Dialogues of Plato* (London, 1851).

16. RUDOLF SOHM'S THEOLOGY OF LAW AND THE SPIRIT

[1] Karl Barth's bibliography of contemporary writings on Sohm (Kirchliche Dogmatik, IV/2, 4, p. 766) could be extended considerably.
[2] *Law and Constitution of the Church* (Eng. trans.; London, 1910), p. 176.
[3] *Luther im Spiegel der Deutschen Geistesgeschichte* (Heidelberg, 1955), p. 50.
[4] *The Divine Imperative* (Eng. trans.; New York, 1947), p. 716.
[5] Within the brief compass of this essay it is not possible to give the cumbersome documentation for the formulations drawn from his various writings on law and rendered here in summary fashion.
[6] In Sohm's description of this whole process one may discern an anticipation of Max Weber's typology of authority: charismatic, legal, and traditional.
[7] *Kirchenrecht,* I, 162–163. Trans. by J. L. Adams.
[8] *Outlines of Church History,* pp. 34–35.

[9] *Kirchenrecht,* II, 130–139. Trans. by D. B. Young.

[10] *Kirchenrecht,* II, 133–134. Trans. by J. O. Evjen.

[11] Cf. Bo Reicke, "The Constitution of the Primitive Church in the Light of Jewish Documents," in Krister Stendahl, ed., *The Scrolls and the New Testament* (New York, 1957), pp. 143–156.

[12] Cf. Dieter Stoodt, "Religionsgeschichtliche Erwägungen über den Ursprung des Kirchenrechts," *Zeitschrift für evangelischen Kirchenrecht,* VI (1957), 61–65.

18. RELIGION, POWER, AND CHRISTIAN FAITH

[1] Paul Tillich, *The Protestant Era* (Chicago, 1948), p. xv.

[2] This cultic distortion of the method and aim of analytic philosophy must not, however, be allowed to obscure its constructive significance for theological analysis. The relevance of language analysis for Christian theology has been suggestively explored in two recently published discussions. One is by D. M. Mackinnon, "Philosophy and Christianity," in T. H. L. Parker, *Essays in Christianity* (London, 1956). The other is by W. H. Poteat, "The Incarnate Word and the Language of Culture," in *The Christian Scholar,* XXXIX, No. 2 (June, 1956).

[3] G. F. Moore, *The History of Religions* (New York, 1929), I, 255.

[4] The critical relation of religion to power emerges in all religions. The protest focuses upon the theory and practice of sacred energy. The Upanishads make this protest against the Vedas; Buddhism makes it against Brahmanism; Mohammed takes it up against the polytheism and ceremonialism of the Bedouin, and against the greed and ceremonialism of the Byzantine Empire. But in the case of the Upanishads and Buddhism, the protest ends in pantheism; in the case of Islam, the protest ends in politics. Pantheism undertakes to rescue the true office of religion from the power monopoly by abandoning the world and severing the power of religion from the dynamic energies of existence. Islam undertakes to rescue the true office of religion from the power monopoly by conforming the world to the arbitrary mystery of the divine decree. There are, of course, exceptions. The militant character of Islam has, in modern times, been greatly modified. The philosophical schools of the post-Upanishadic period divide over the positive evaluation of the world. Even Buddhism has entered into a debate over whether Nirvana is pure negation. But these exceptions do not change the significance of the lack in all religious traditions, except the prophetic-Christian one, of an effective and meaningful integration of the dynamic and the delimiting aspects of reality.

[5] Cf. Charles Cochrane, *Christianity and Classical Culture* (Oxford, 1940).

[6] Not least among the perils to which this lack of wisdom and virtue exposed the Pax Augusta was the tendency to gauge the needs and opportunities for the growth of an entire community by the limited capacities of a single man, however competent, and even devout, he may from time to time have proved himself to be.

19. THE CHURCH OF THE FUTURE AND THE HOMELESS MAN OF TODAY

[1] Theodor Heuss, *Friedrich Naumann: Der Mann, das Werk und die Zeit* (Stuttgart, 1937).

[2] Friedrich Naumann, *Briefe über Religion* (1903) (Berlin, 1916), pp. 104 f.

[3] Friedrich Naumann, *Gotteshilfe. Gesamtausgabe der Andachten aus den Jahren 1895–1902 sachlich geordnet* (Göttingen, 1926), pp. 530 f.

[4] *Ibid.,* p. 566.

[5] *Ibid.,* p. 567.

[6] *Ibid.,* pp. 571 f.

[7] Heuss, *Friedrich Naumann,* p. 266.

[8] *Ibid.,* pp. 181 f., 356 f.

[9] Naumann, *Gotteshilfe,* p. 538.

[10] *Ibid.,* p. 536.

[11] Naumann, *Geist und Glaube* (Berlin-Schöneberg, 1911), p. 41.

[12] Naumann, *Briefe,* p. 33.

[13] Heuss, *op. cit.,* p. 356.

[14] Naumann, *Briefe,* p. 3.

[15] Heuss, *op. cit.*, p. 182.
[16] Naumann, *Gotteshilfe*, p. 539.
[17] Naumann, *Geist und Glaube*, pp. 181 f.
[18] *Ibid.*, p. 258.
[19] Heuss, *op. cit.*, p. 184.
[20] Naumann, *Geist und Glaube*, p. 263.
[21] Heuss, *op. cit.*
[22] *Ibid.*, pp. 290 ff.
[23] Naumann, *Geist und Glaube*, p. 86.
[24] Naumann, *Gotteshilfe*, p. 289.
[25] *Ibid.*, p. 559.

22. BUDDHISM AND EXISTENTIALISM

[1] Heidegger, *Was ist Metaphysik?* (Frankfurt A.M., 1949) 38.

[2] Hence Heidegger's recent effort to interpret his problem once again. If I am not mistaken, he is endeavoring to follow his thought back to one source, where the philosophical and the religious questions are one and the same. If we read the last half of his question —"why not rather nothing?" ("*—und nicht vielmehr Nichts?*")—in the light of his recent suggestion, then it follows necessarily that the first part will also change in meaning (*Zur Seinsfrage* [Frankfurt A.M., 1956] pp. 39 ff.). The result is that the philosophical question approaches the religious.

Though I do not believe the religious question is so antagonistic to the philosophical that God will destroy the wisdom of philosophy, yet there is a clear-cut distinction between them. For instance, Heidegger's "ontological difference between *Sein* and *Seiendes*" is of a philosophical nature, and, on the other hand, Kierkegaard's "absolute distinction between absolute *telos* and relative *telos*" (cf. *Concluding Unscientific Postscript* [Princeton, 1941], pp. 347 ff.) is of a religious nature; notwithstanding, both are the expression of authentic existential passion (*pathos*).

The religious question does not demand articulation. It suffices that it be existentially pathetic. But if it should be expressed, in the present-day spiritual situation the religious question would be just the opposite of the philosophical formulation mentioned above.

[3] Tillich, *Systematic Theology* (Chicago, 1951), I, 180.

[4] Kierkegaard, *Concluding Unscientific Postscript*, p. 386.

[5] Cf. Tillich, *The Courage to Be* (New Haven, 1952), pp. 38, 48 ff.

[6] Cf. Kant, *Gesammelte Werke*, ed. by B. Cassirer (Berlin, 1923) Bk. 6, p. 167.

[7] *Ibid.*, p. 168.

[8] Tillich, *The Protestant Era* (Chicago, 1948), pp. 136 ff.

[9] Cf. Hegel, *The Phenomenology of Mind*, trans. by J. Baillie (London, 1931) pp. 484–499, esp. his interpretation of the words of Antigone, p. 491.

[10] In the following description I have always in mind what Heidegger has developed in his treatise: "Who is Nietzsche's Zarathustra?" *Vorträge und Aufsätze* (Pfullingen, 1954) pp. 101 ff.

[11] H. Beckh, *Buddhismus* (Berlin, 1922) Bk. I, pp. 119 f.

[12] Heidegger, *Holzwege* (Frankfurt A.M., 1950) pp. 193 f.

[13] Heidegger, *Zur Seinsfrage*, p. 38.

[14] Tillich, *The Courage to Be*, p. 172.

[15] Bergson, *The Two Sources of Morality and Religion* (London, 1935) pp. 197 ff.

[16] Cf. Tillich, *Systematic Theology*, I, 237.

[17] The Absolute Nothingness in early Buddhistic terminology is Non-Self (*anātman*). It is the demand to transcend the God of Brahmātman mysticism. In Upanishadic mysticism by means of mystical union our finite being participates in Being-itself; in the ultimate fact of our being, our finite self is identical with the Self of Universe. From the Buddhist point of view, this *ātman* doctrine is the attachment of our heart, in the subtlest abstraction, to metaphysical theses. When this last barrier is removed by means of "neither/nor," or through thoroughgoing negativity of anxieties—anxiety of non-being, meaninglessness, and sin—non-self (in a negative sense) converts to Non-Self. Therefore, Non-Self is the perfect form of detachment of our heart; so far as it is one's beloved, what belongs to one's self (*ātmīya*) should be entirely rejected, even to this last sublime form of Being-

itself. It is characteristic of Buddhism that this detachment is regarded as the purest form and the efflorescence of religious love.

[18] Hegel, *Gesammelte Werke,* ed. Glockner (Stuttgart, 1928) Bk. 19, pp. 306 ff.; Bk. 10, p. 370.

[19] *Zur Seinsfrage,* p. 38.

[20] Hegel, *The Phenomenology of Mind,* p. 81.

[21] Heidegger, *Was ist das—die Philosophie?* (Pfullingen, 1956) pp. 36 ff.

[22] E. J. Thomas, *Early Buddhist Scripture* (London, 1935) p. 119.

[23] *Bṛhad-āraṇyaka Upaniṣad,* III, 2, 13.

[24] They are sometimes mentioned as sensuous pleasure and self-mortification; but sometimes they are referred to as the assertion of being, and that of non-being (nihilism). In most cases, however, they are called a belief in the self-identity of the soul, and the negation of the same. All these contradictory views of life, according to his teaching, must be superseded by his new doctrine of *pratītya-samutpāda.*

[25] But unfortunately this is not the authorized opinion of contemporary Japanese scholars on this matter, for they are all making strong efforts to exclude the *karman* doctrine from the genuine teachings of the Buddha. These de-mythologizing efforts on the side of Buddhists are, according to my view, based on a misunderstanding of the nature of the *karman* theory.

[26] *Vinaya-Piṭaka. Mahāvagga,* I, 6, 29.

[27] *Mahāvagga,* I, 7, 4.

[28] The gist of the Law is the Four Noble Truths, that is to say, suffering, the cause of suffering (that is, *karman*), the annihilation of suffering (that is, absolute negativity), and the way that leads to this end (that is, the Middle Path). Or to speak of its more developed formula, this Law is nothing but the theory of *pratītya-samutpāda,* which we have already discussed.

[29] *Mahāvagga,* I. 9, 1. English translation by J. G. Jennigs in his *The Vedantic Buddhism of the Buddha* (London, 1948) p. 63.

23. THE DEMAND FOR FREEDOM AND JUSTICE IN THE CONTEMPORARY WORLD REVOLUTION

[1] *Report of the Lambeth Conference, 1948.* From the *Committee Report on the Church and the Modern World,* section on "Communism."

[2] Published in English in *Against the Stream* (New York, 1954), p. 36.

[3] Luther, *Secular Authority,* Part II, *Works of Martin Luther,* Vol. VIII (Philadelphia, 1915).

[4] De Tocqueville, *Democracy in America,* ch. 15 (Cambridge, Mass., 1862).

A Bibliography of Paul Tillich

(COMPILED BY PETER H. JOHN)

PREFATORY NOTE

This bibliography covers all the published writings from 1910 to 1958 which I have been able to locate. It contains a first section on "Books and Articles" (pp. 367–92) and a second on "Literary Critiques, Reviews, Prefaces" (pp. 392–96). In each section the items are arranged chronologically, although within a given year the listing of individual books and contributions to symposia generally precedes articles in periodicals. In a few of the references to early writings I have been unable to obtain the original material and have relied on secondary sources.

Included also are all the known translations to date, as well as references to reprints in other publications. Explanatory sub-titles and notes usually appear only where such information accompanies the item involved.

P. H. J.

BOOKS AND ARTICLES

1910

Die religionsgeschichtliche Konstruktion in Schellings positiver Philosophie, ihre Voraussetzungen und Prinzipien. Inaugural-Dissertation zur Erlangung der philosophischen Doktorwürde der hohen philosophischen Fakultät der Kgl. Universität Breslau. Breslau: H. Fleischmann, 1910. Pp. vi + 143.

1912

Mystik und Schuldbewusstsein in Schellings philosophischer Entwicklung. Inaugural-Dissertation zur Erlangung der Lizentiatenwürde der hochwürdigen theologischen Fakultät Halle-Wittenberg. *Beiträge zur Förderung christlicher Theologie,* XVI, No. 1. Gütersloh: C. Bertelsmann, 1912. Pp. 135. ("Selbstanzeigen." *Kant-Studien* [Berlin], XVII, No. 3 (1912), 306–307.)

1915

Der Begriff des Übernatürlichen, sein dialektischer Charakter und das Princip der Identität, dargestellt an der supranaturalistischen Theologie vor Schleiermacher. Habilitationsschrift gedruckt mit Genehmigung der hochwürdigen theologischen Fakultät der Universität Halle-Wittenberg. Königsberg Nm.: H. Madrasch, 1915. Pp. vii + 58.

"Predigt, gehalten nach den Kämpfen bei Tahure am 30. und 31. Oktober 1915." Text: 2. Kor. 4, 17 u. 18. (*Privately printed.*)

1919

Der Sozialismus als Kirchenfrage. Leitsätze von Paul Tillich und Carl Richard Wegener. Berlin: Gracht, 1919. Pp. 18.

"Über die Idee einer Theologie der Kultur." (Vortrag, gehalten in der Berliner Abteilung der Kant-Gesellschaft am 16. April 1919.) *Religionsphilosophie der Kultur.* Zwei Entwürfe von Gustav Radbruch und Paul Tillich. ("Philosophische Vorträge der Kant-Gesellschaft," No. 24.) Berlin: Reuther & Reichard, 1919, pp. 5, 28–51. Second edition, 1921.

"Christentum und Sozialismus." *Das neue Deutschland* (Gotha), VIII, No. 6 (Dec. 15, 1919), 106–110. Reprinted in *Die freideutsche Jugend* (Hamburg), VI, No. 5/6 (May–June, 1920), 167–170.

1920

"Die Jugend und die Religion." *Die freideutsche Jugendbewegung;* Ursprung und Zukunft. Eds. Adolf Grabowsky and Walther Koch. (Drittes Ergänzungsheft der Halbmonatsschrift, *Das neue Deutschland.*) Gotha: F. A. Perthes, 1920, pp. 8–13. Second edition, 1921.

"Masse und Persönlichkeit." *Die Verhandlungen des 27. und 28. Evangelisch-Sozialen Kongresses,* abgehalten in Leipzig, am 15. und 16. Oktober 1918 und in Berlin, am 23. und 24. Juni 1920. Ed. W. Schneemelcher. Göttingen: Vandenhoeck & Ruprecht, 1920, pp. 76–96. (Included in *Masse und Geist,* pp. 5–23).

1921

"Masse und Religion." *Blätter für Religiösen Sozialismus* (Berlin), II, Nos. 1, 2, 3, (1921), 1–3, 5–7, 9–12. (Included in *Masse und Geist.*)

"Die Theologie als Wissenschaft." *Vossische Zeitung* (Berlin), No. 512 (Oct. 30, 1921), 2–3.

1922

Masse und Geist. Studien zur Philosophie der Masse. (Masse und Persönlichkeit; Masse und Bildung; Masse und Religion.) Die Schriftenreihe "Volk und Geist," No. 1. Berlin/Frankfurt a.M.: Verlag der Arbeitsgemeinschaft, 1922. Pp. 55.

"Albrecht Ritschl. Zu seinem hundertsten Geburtstag." *Theologische Blätter* (Leipzig), I, No. 3 (March, 1922), 49–54.

"Anthroposophie und Theologie. Das theologische Ergebnis des Berliner anthroposophischen Hochschulkursus." *Ibid.,* No. 4 (April, 1922), 86–88.

"Religiöse Krisis." *Vivos voco* (Leipzig), II, No. 11 (April–May, 1922), 616–621.

"Kairos." *Die Tat* (Jena), XIV, No. 5 (August, 1922), 330–350. Translated in *The Protestant Era,* pp. 32–51, with additional note on the term "unconditional," p. 32.

"Die Überwindung des Religionsbegriffs in der Religionsphilosophie." (Vortrag, gehalten in der Berliner Abteilung der Kant-Gesellschaft am 25. Januar 1922.) *Kant-Studien* [Festschrift zu Hans Vaihingers 70. Geburtstag] (Berlin), XXVII, No. 3/4 (1922), 446–469.

"Gotteslästerung." (Anlässlich des Prozesses gegen Karl Einstein.) *Vossische Zeitung* (Berlin), No. 485 (Oct. 13, 1922), 1–2.

"Renaissance und Reformation. Zur Einführung in die Bibliothek Warburg." *Theologische Blätter* (Leipzig), I, No. 12 (December, 1922), 265–267.

"Zur Klärung der religiösen Grundhaltung." *Blätter für Religiösen Sozialismus* (Berlin), III, No. 12 (December, 1922), 46–48.

1923

Das System der Wissenschaften nach Gegenständen und Methoden. Ein Entwurf.

Göttingen: Vandenhoeck & Ruprecht, 1923. Pp. viii + 167. English translation by Werner Rode, with a new Foreword by the author. New York: Meridian Books, 1959; cloth and paperback editions. (In preparation.)

"Die Kategorie des 'Heiligen' bei Rudolf Otto." *Theologische Blätter* (Leipzig), II, No. 1 (January, 1923), 11–12.

"Ernst Troeltsch." *Vossische Zeitung* (Berlin), No. 58 (Feb. 3, 1923), 2–3.

"Grundlinien des religiösen Sozialismus. Ein systematischer Entwurf." *Blätter für Religiösen Sozialismus* (Berlin), IV, No. 8/10 (1923), 1–24 (Sonderheft).

"Kritisches und positives Paradox. Eine Auseinandersetzung mit Karl Barth und Friedrich Gogarten." *Theologische Blätter* (Leipzig), II, No. 11 (November, 1923), 263–269.

"Antwort" [auf Karl Barth, "Von der Paradoxie des 'positiven Paradoxes': Antworten und Fragen an Paul Tillich." *Theologische Blätter*, II, No. 12 (December, 1923), 287–296]. *Ibid.*, No. 12 (December, 1923), 296–299.

1924

Kirche und Kultur. (Vortrag, gehalten vor dem Tübinger Jugendring im Juli 1924.) ("Sammlung gemeinverständlicher Vorträge und Schriften aus dem Gebiet der Theologie und Religionsgeschichte," No. 111.) Tübingen: J. C. B. Mohr, 1924. Pp. 22. Translated as "Church and Culture" in *The Interpretation of History* (1936), pp. 219–241.

"Rechtfertigung und Zweifel." *Vorträge der theologischen Konferenz zu Giessen*, 39. Folge. Giessen: Alfred Töpelmann, 1924, pp. 19–32.

"Erwiderung" [zu dem Artikel "Nationale Erneuerung" in der Januarnummer der Wingolfsblätter von Dr. jur. Heppe, Gütersloh.] *Wingolfs-Blätter* (Mühlhausen), LIII, No. 2 (Feb. 21, 1924), 27.

"Jugendbewegung und Religion." *Werkland* [Neue Folge von *Vivos Voco*], (Leipzig), IV, No. 1 (April, 1924), 61–64.

"Antwort" [auf Mennicke, "Zu Tillichs Systematik"]. *Blätter für Religiösen Sozialismus* (Berlin), V, No. 5/6 (1924), 18–22.

"Die religiöse und philosophische Weiterbildung des Sozialismus." *Ibid.*, 26–30.

"Ernst Troeltsch. Versuch einer geistesgeschichtlichen Würdigung." *Kant-Studien* (Berlin), XXIX, No. 3/4 (1924), 351–358.

1925

"Religionsphilosophie." *Lehrbuch der Philosophie*, ed. Max Dessoir. Vol. II: *Die Philosophie in ihren Einzelgebieten.* Berlin: Ullstein, 1925, pp. 765–835.

Die religiöse Lage der Gegenwart. Berlin: Ullstein, 1925. Pp. 153. ("Wege zum Wissen," Vol. 60.)

"Die religiöse Lage der bürgerlichen Gesellschaft im 19. Jahrhundert," from the Introduction, is reprinted in *Neuwerk* (Schlüchtern), VII, No. 10 (January, 1926), 407–412.—Italian translation, and with a preface (pp. 9–13), by Antonio Banfi: *Lo spirito borghese e il Kairos.* ("XIII Volume della Collezione di Storia, Religione, Filosofia.") Rome: Doxa, 1929. Pp. 168.—English translation, and with a preface (pp. vii–xxii), by H. Richard Niebuhr: *The Religious Situation.* New York: Henry Holt, 1932. Pp. xxv + 182. Reprinted: New York: Meridian Books (Living Age Books, No. 6), 1956. Pp. 219. London: Thames & Hudson (cloth edition).—Japanese translation by Enkichi Kan and Makoto Goto: *Gendai no Shūkyōteki Jōkyō.* Tokyo: Nippon Kirisutokyō Seinenkai Dōmei (YMCA Press), 1950. Pp. 187.

"Die Staatslehre Augustins nach *De civitate Dei.*" (Vortrag, gehalten vor der Marburger Studentenschaft im Dezember 1924.) *Theologische Blätter* (Leipzig), IV, No. 4 (April, 1925), 77–86. (Included in *Religiöse Verwirklichung* (1929), pp. 233–252.)

"Denker der Zeit: Der Religionsphilosoph Rudolf Otto." *Vossische Zeitung* (Berlin), No. 308, July 2, 1925.

1926

Das Dämonische. Ein Beitrag zur Sinndeutung der Geschichte. ("Sammlung gemeinverständlicher Vorträge und Schriften aus dem Gebiet der Theologie und Religionsgeschichte," No. 119.) Tübingen: J. C. B. Mohr, 1926. Pp. 44. Excerpts printed in *Philosophie und Leben* (Leipzig), III, No. 9 (September, 1927), 260–264. Translated as "The Demonic" in *The Interpretation of History*, pp. 77–122. Japanese translation, 1944.

Kairos: Zur Geisteslage und Geisteswendung. Ed. Paul Tillich. (Erstes Buch des Kairos-Kreises.) Darmstadt: Otto Reichl, 1926. Pp. xi + 483.
Contents: "Einführung des Herausgebers," pp. ix–xi. Paul Tillich, "Kairos: Ideen zur Geisteslage der Gegenwart," pp. 1–21. *Ibid.*, "Kairos und Logos: Eine Untersuchung zur Metaphysik der Erkenntnis," pp. 23–75. Wilhelm Loew, "Idealität und Realität." Theodor Siegfried, "Phänomenologie und Geschichte." Walter Riezler, "Die Baukunst am Scheidewege. Ein Versuch." Eduard Heimann: "Sozialismus und Sozialpolitik." Karl Mennicke, "Das sozialpädagogische Problem in der gegenwärtigen Gesellschaft." Heinrich Frick, "Der katholisch-protestantische Zwiespalt als religionsgeschichtliches Urphänomen." Nikolaus Berdjajew, "Die russische religiöse Idee." Christian Herrmann, "Bücherschau."
Pages 23–75 are translated as "Kairos and Logos: A Study in the Metaphysics of Knowledge" in *The Interpretation of History* (1936), pp. 123–175. Japanese translation, 1944.

"Die geistige Welt in Jahre 1926." *Reichls Bücherbuch.* Siebzehntes Jahr, 1926. Darmstadt: Otto Reichl, 1926, pp. 6–14; photo, p. 72.

Das Berneuchener Buch. Vom Anspruch des Evangeliums auf die Kirchen der Reformation. (Herausgegeben von der Berneuchener Konferenz.) Hamburg: Hanseatische Verlagsanstalt, 1926. Pp. 182. Later edition, Schwerin: F. Bahn, 1929. (A work in which Tillich collaborated.)

"Denker der Zeit: Karl Barth." *Vossische Zeitung* (Berlin) No. 32 ("Das Unterhaltungsblatt," No. 16) (Jan. 20, 1926).

"Der Begriff des Dämonischen und seine Bedeutung für die systematische Theologie." *Theologische Blätter* (Leipzig), V, No. 2 (February, 1926), 32–35.

"Zum Problem der evangelischen Sozialethik." (Critiques by Paul Tillich and Carl Mennicke of an article by Wilhelm Loew in *Zwischen den Zeiten* [Munich], IV, No. 1 [1926], 60–75.) *Blätter für Religiösen Sozialismus* (Berlin), VII (July–August, 1926), 73–79, 79–87. (Pp. 73–79 included in *Religiöse Verwirklichung*, pp. 307–312.)

1927

"Predigt zum Semesterschluss vor der Theologenschaft der Universität Marburg" (Juli 1925). Text: Mark 1:16–20. *Neuwerk* (Schlüchtern), VIII, No. 11 (February, 1927), 469–472. (Included in *Von der Heiligung des Lebens.* 20 religiöse Reden von bekannten deutschen und ausländischen Kanzelrednern. Ed. Hans Hartmann. Leipzig: J. C. Hinrichs, 1928, pp. 13–16.)

"Die Überwindung des Persönlichkeitsideals." (Vortrag, gehalten auf der Augustusburg, Pfingsten 1926.) *Logos* (Tübingen), XVI, No. 1 (March, 1927), 68–85. (Included in *Religiöse Verwirklichung*, pp. 168–189; annotations added, pp. 295–298. Reprinted, in part, in *Sächsische Schulzeitung* [Dresden], XCIV, No. 9 [1927], 149–151.) Translated as "The Idea and the Ideal of Personality" in *The Protestant Era*, pp. 115–135.

"Ostern." *Hannoverscher Kurier* (Hannover), LXXIX, No. 179 (April 17, 1927), 1.

"Gläubiger Realismus." (Vortrag auf der Älterentagung des Bundes deutscher Jugendvereine in Hannoversch-Münden am 9. Juli 1927.) *Theologenrundbrief für den Bund deutscher Jugendvereine e. V.* (Göttingen), II (July–August, 1927), 3–13. Reprinted (with Theodor Siegfried: "Zum Problem des religiösen Sozialismus"), Göttingen: H. Kloppenburg, 1927. Pp. 22.

"Logos und Mythos der Technik." (Vortrag, gehalten bei der Feier des 99. Gründungstages der Technischen Hochschule Dresden.) *Logos* (Tübingen), XVI, No. 3 (November, 1927), 356–365.

"Die Idee der Offenbarung." (Antrittsvorlesung in Leipzig, gehalten Juni 1927.) *Zeitschrift für Theologie und Kirche* (Tübingen), N.F., VIII, No. 6 (1927), 403–412.

"Eschatologie und Geschichte." (Vortrag im Bund für Gegenwartchristentum, Meissen, 5. Oktober 1927.) *Die Christliche Welt* (Gotha), XLI, No. 22 (Nov. 17, 1927), 1034–1042. (Included in *Religiöse Verwirklichung*, pp. 128–141; additional notes, pp. 290–293.) Translated as "Eschatology and History" in *The Interpretation of History* (1936), pp. 266–284.

1928

"Der soziale Pfarrer." Diskussionsrede, *Die Verhandlungen des 35. Evangelisch-Sozialen Kongresses in Dresden am 29.–31. Mai 1928.* Ed. Johannes Herz. Göttingen: Vandenhoeck & Ruprecht, 1928, pp. 74–77.

"Das religiöse Symbol." (Symposium: "Das Symbolische.") *Blätter für deutsche Philosophie* (Berlin), I, No. 4 (January, 1928), 277–291. (Included in *Religiöse Verwirklichung*, pp. 88–109; additional notes, pp. 284–286.) Translated and revised in *The Journal of Liberal Religion* (Chicago), II, No. 1 (Summer, 1940), 13–33. Reply to criticism, *ibid.*, No. 4 (Spring, 1941), 202–206.

"Das Christentum und die Moderne." *Schule und Wissenschaft* (Berlin/Hamburg), II, No. 4 (1928), 121–131; Fortsetzung, *ibid.*, No. 5 (1928), 170–177.

"Die technische Stadt als Symbol." (Geschrieben anlässlich der Eröffnung der Dresdener Ausstellung "die technische Stadt," zugleich zur Hundertjahrfeier der technischen Hochschule in Dresden.) *Dresdner Neueste Nachrichten*, No. 115 ("Die technische Stadt") (May 17, 1928), 5. Reprinted in *Aus deutscher Geistesarbeit* (Reval), IV, No. 17 (Sept. 14, 1928), 258–262.

"Ueber gläubigen Realismus." (Vortrag, gehalten vor der Theologenschaft der Universitäten Marburg, Tübingen und Halle 1927.) *Theologische Blätter* (Leipzig), VII, No. 5 (May, 1928), 109–118. (Included in *Religiöse Verwirklichung*, pp. 65–87; additional notes, pp. 279–284.) Translated as "Realism and Faith" in *The Protestant Era*, pp. 66–82; notes omitted.

"Die Bedeutung der Gesellschaftslage für das Geistesleben." (Vortrag, gehalten auf der Abschlussfeier des zweiten Studienganges der Verwaltungsakademie Dresden im Juni 1927.) *Philosophie und Leben* (Leipzig), IV, No. 6 (June, 1928), 153–158.

"Das Christentum und die moderne Gesellschaft." *Student World* (Geneva), XXI, No. 3 (July, 1928), 282–290; summary, in English, 290–292.

"Zum 'theologischen Nachwort zu den Davoser internationalen Hochschulkursen.'" (Reply to G. Kuhlmann.) *Theologische Blätter* (Leipzig), VII, No. 7 (July, 1928), 176–177.

"Der Geistige und der Sport." (Symposium.) Zweite Beilage zur *Vossische Zeitung* (Berlin), No. 608 (Dec. 25, 1928), 2.

1929

Protestantismus als Kritik und Gestaltung. Ed. Paul Tillich. (Zweites Buch des Kairos-Kreises.) Darmstadt: Otto Reichl, 1929. Pp. xi + 407.

Contents: "Vorwort des Herausgebers," pp. ix–xi. Paul Tillich, Einleitung: "Der

Protestantismus als kritisches und gestaltendes Prinzip," pp. 3–37. *Part I:* Das protestantische Problem im Aufbau der evangelischen Kirchen. Ernst Lohmeyer, "Kritische und gestaltende Prinzipien im Neuen Testament." Theodor Siegfried, "Das gewissen bei Luther und Kant." Heinrich Frick, "Die gestaltenden Kräfte des westlichen Protestantismus und die protestantische Einheit." Alfred Dedo Müller, "Die Möglichkeit einer protestantischen Kirche." Adolf Allwohn, "Der Protestantismus als Abbau und Aufbau des Kultus." Eugen Rosenstock, "Protestantismus und Seelenführung." *Part II:* Das protestantische Problem ausserhalb der evangelischen Kirchen. Von einem katholischen Theologen, "Kritik und Gestaltung oder das Geistprinzip im Katholizismus." Simon Frank, "Gestalt und Freiheit in der griechischen Orthodoxie." Max Wiener, "Tradition und Kritik im Judentum."

Religiöse Verwirklichung. Berlin: Furche, 1929. Second edition, 1930. Pp. 312.

Collected Essays: *A. Grundsätzliches zur religiösen Verwirklichung.* (1) Das Religiöse als kritisches Prinzip: "Die protestantische Verkündigung und der Mensch der Gegenwart." (Vortrag, gehalten auf der Aarauer Studentenkonferenz im März 1928.) (2) Das Religiöse als gestaltendes Prinzip: "Protestantische Gestaltung." (Vortrag, gehalten vor der Theologenschaft in Münster i. W., Januar 1929.) (3) Wirklichkeit und religiöse Verwirklichung: "Über gläubigen Realismus," 1927. *B. Innerreligiöse Verwirklichung des Religiösen.* (4) Zur Gotteserkenntnis: "Das religiöse Symbol," 1928. (5) Zur Christologie: "Christologie und Geschichtsdeutung." (Aufsatz, geschrieben im Anschluss an die Vorlesungen über "religiöse Geschichtsdeutung" im Wintersemester 1928/29 in Dresden und Leipzig.) (6) Zur Eschatologie: "Eschatologie und Geschichte," 1927. (7) Zum Sakrament: "Natur und Sakrament." (Vortrag, gehalten auf der Berneuchener Konferenz, September 1928.) *C. Ausserreligiöse Verwirklichung des Religiösen.* (8) Zur Ethik: "Die Überwindung des Persönlichkeitsideals," 1927. (9) Zum Sozialen: "Klassenkampf und religiöser Sozialismus." (Vortrag, gehalten vor der sozialistischen Studentenschaft in Marburg 1928 und Frankfurt 1929.) (10) Zur Politik: "Der Staat als Erwartung und Forderung." (Nach einem in Dresden 1928 gehaltenen Vortrag.) *D. Historische Parallelen.* (11) Zur Politik und Sozialethik: "Die Staatslehre Augustins nach *De civitate Dei,*" 1925. (12) Zur evangelischen Profanität: "Lessing und die Idee einer Erziehung des Menschengeschlechtes." (Vortrag, gehalten vor der Dresdener Lehrerschaft zum Lessing-Jubiläum 1929.) *E. Anmerkungen und Beilage.* (1) Anmerkungen zu Vortrag 1–12. (2) "Zum Problem der evangelischen Sozialethik," 1926.

Translations of Chapters 1, 2, 3, 7, and 8 appear, respectively, as XIII, XIV, V, VII, and VIII in *The Protestant Era* (1948). Chapters 5 and 6 are translated in *The Interpretation of History.* Chapter 4 appeared in English in 1940. Chapter 2 and "Das transmoralische Gewissen," from the German translation of *The Protestant Era,* are reprinted in *Glaube und Handeln. Grundprobleme evangelischer Ethik.* (Texte aus der evangelischen Ethik der Gegenwart ausgewählt von Heinz-Horst Schrey mit einer Einleitung von Helmut Thielicke.) Bremen: Carl Schünemann, 1956, pp. 198–222, 269–286.

Except for Chapter 4, the extensive annotations are omitted in the English translations.

"Aussprache." (Discussion of "Die Begründung des Sozialismus," addresses by Hendrik de Man and Eduard Heimann.) (With Martin Buber, Alfred Meusel, Franz Grosse, Hans Hartmann, Karl Mennicke, Elisabeth Busse-Wilson, Leonhard Ragaz, Reinhold Sputh and Adolf Löwe; cf. also de Man, pp. 141–147.) *Sozialismus aus dem Glauben.* Verhandlungen der sozialistischen Tagung in Heppenheim a. B., Pfingstwoche 1928. Zürich/Leipzig: Rotapfel, 1929, pp. 101–104.

"Nichtkirchliche Religionen." (Vortrag, gehalten in der Deutschen Vereinigung für Staatswissenschaftliche Fortbildung auf dem Herbstlehrgang 1928 vom 26. August bis zum 15. September in Bad Reichenhall in Oberbayern.) *Volk und Reich der Deutschen.* (Vorlesungen gehalten in der Deutschen Vereinigung für Staatswissenschaftliche Fortbildung.) Ed. Bernhard Harms. Vol. I. Berlin: R. Hobbing, 1929, pp. 456–475. (Cf. references, Vol. III, p. 660.)

"Religiöse Verantwortung." (Symposium: "Verantwortung: Worte an die Jugend," by Martin Buber, Adolf von Hatzfeld, F. Siegmund-Schultze, Paul Tillich and Leo Weismantel.) *Berliner Tageblatt*, LVIII, No. 1 (Supplement 5) (Jan. 1, 1929), 2.

"Gegenwart und Religion." (Vortrag, gehalten in Kassel im Dezember 1928.) *Neuwerk* (Kassel), XI, No. 1 (April, 1929), 2–11.

"Philosophie und Schicksal." (Akademische Antrittsvorlesung, gehalten in Frankfurt a. M., Juni 1929.) *Kant-Studien* (Berlin), XXXIV, No. 3/4 (1929), 300–311. Translated as "Philosophy and Fate" in *The Protestant Era*, pp. 3–15. Japanese translation, 1944.

1930

"Mythus, begrifflich und religionspsychologisch." *Die Religion in Geschichte und Gegenwart.* Handwörterbuch für Theologie und Religionswissenschaft. Eds. Hermann Gunkel and Leopold Zscharnak. Second edition. Tübingen: J. C. B. Mohr, 1927–1932. Vol. IV (1930), 363–370. (Volume I [A–C] of the third edition, ed. Kurt Galling, appeared in 1957.)

"Offenbarung: Religionsphilosophisch." *Ibid.*, 664–669.

"Philosophie: Begriff und Wesen." *Ibid.*, 1198–1204.

"Philosophie und Religion, grundsätzlich." *Ibid.*, 1227–1233.

"Sozialismus." *Neue Blätter für den Sozialismus* (Potsdam), I, No. 1 (January, 1930), 1–12.

"Religiöser Sozialismus." (Ein Rundfunkvortrag, gehalten im Juli 1930.) *Ibid.*, I, No. 9 (September, 1930), 396–403.

"Neue Formen christlicher Verwirklichung. Eine Betrachtung über Sinn und Grenzen evangelischer Katholizität." *Reclams Universum* (Leipzig), XLVII, No. 10 (Dec. 4, 1930), 194–195; illus.

"Kult und Form." (Vortrag, gehalten bei der Eröffnung der Ausstellung des Kunst-Dienstes in Berlin am 10. November 1930.) *Die Form* (Berlin), V, No. 23/24 (Dec. 15, 1930), 578–583; illus. Reprinted in *Kunst und Kirche* (Berlin), VIII, No. 1 (1931), 3–6; illus. Also in *Deutsche Goldschmiedezeitung* (Leipzig), XXXV, No. 43 (1932), 419–421; abridged in *Das Werk* (Zürich), XX, No. 9 (1933), 273–274. (Als Sonderheft, *Kult und Form*, Berlin, 1930.)

1931

Protestantisches Prinzip und proletarische Situation. Bonn: F. Cohen, 1931. Pp. 33. Translated as "The Protestant Principle and the Proletarian Situation" in *The Protestant Era*, pp. 161–181.

"Religiöser Sozialismus." *Die Religion in Geschichte und Gegenwart.* Second edition. Tübingen: J. C. B. Mohr, 1931. Vol. V, coll. 637–648.

"Theonomie." *Ibid.*, 1128–1129.

"Wissenschaft." *Ibid.*, 1985–1987.

"Das Wasser." *Das Gottesjahr 1932.* (Jahrbuch des Berneuchener Kreises. Vol. XII: "Natur und Glaube.") Ed. Wilhelm Stählin. Kassel: Bärenreiter, 1931, pp. 65–68.

"Mensch und Staat." (A weekly column in *Der Staat seid Ihr.* Zeitschrift für deutsche Politik [Berlin].) "Mensch und Staat," I, No. 1 (March 2, 1931), 11. "Blut gegen Geist," I, No. 2 (March 9, 1931), 26. "Kunstpolitik," I, No. 3 (March 16, 1931), 43. "Die Einheit des Widerspruchs," I, No. 4 (March 23, 1931), 56. "Dämonen," I, No. 6 (April 6, 1931), 91. "Neue Schöpfung," I, No. 7 (April 13, 1931), 107. "Utopie,"

I, No. 8 (April 20, 1931), 124. "Drei Stadien," I, No. 9 (April 27, 1931), 139. "Menschliche Möglichkeiten," I, No. 10 (May 4, 1931), 155. "Das Fragen," I, No. 11 (May 11, 1931), 171. "Menschheit," I, No. 12 (May 18, 1931), 187–188.

"Goethe und die Idee der Klassik." (Gedenkrede, gehalten am Sonntag, den 20. März 1932 zur Goethefeier des Nationaltheaters.) *Bühnen-Blätter* (Nationaltheater Mannheim), No. 17 (1931/32), 193–207; illus. (Included in *Hegel und Goethe*, 1932.)

"Das Problem der Macht. Versuch einer philosophischen Grundlegung." *Neue Blätter für den Sozialismus* (Potsdam), II, No. 4 (April, 1931), 157–170. Translated as "The Problem of Power: Attempt at a Philosophical Interpretation" in *The Interpretation of History*, pp. 179–202.

"Kirche und humanistische Gesellschaft." (Vortrag, gehalten auf der Berneuchener Arbeitskonferenz in Pätzig, am 5. Oktober 1930.) *Neuwerk* (Kassel), XIII, No. 1 (April–May, 1931), 4–18.

"Zum Problem des evangelischen Religionsunterrichts." *Zeitschrift für den evangelischen Religionsunterricht an höheren Lehranstalten* (Berlin/Frankfurt), XLII, No. 6 (1931), 289–291.

"Zum Fall [Pfarrer] Eckert." *Neue Blätter für den Sozialismus* (Potsdam), II, No. 8 (August, 1931), 408–409.

"Die Doppelgestalt der Kirche." (Reply to criticisms of "Kirche und humanistische Gesellschaft.") *Neuwerk* (Kassel), XIII, No. 4 (October–November, 1931), 239–243.

"Gibt es noch eine Universität?" (Fachhochschulen und Universität). *Frankfurter Zeitung*, LXXVI, No. 869–871 (Nov. 22, 1931), 11. (Discussions by Emil Lederer, Erich Przywara, S.J., Theodor Haecker, Ernst Bloch, Eugen Rosenstock, Georg Swarzenski, Ernst Krenek, Eduard Spranger, Karl Jaspers, Erwin Madelung, Ludwig Waldecker, Hans Fehr, Richard Koch, and others, in succeeding issues: Dec. 6, 14, and 20, 1931; Jan. 3, 17, etc., 1932.)

1932

Hegel und Goethe. Zwei Gedenkreden. ("Sammlung gemeinverständlicher Vorträge und Schriften aus dem Gebiet der Theologie und Religionsgeschichte," No. 158.) Tübingen: J. C. B. Mohr, 1932. Pp. 48. (I. "Der junge Hegel und das Schicksal Deutschlands," pp. 1–32. [Akademische Rede zum 18. Januar 1932.] II. "Goethe und die Idee der Klassik," pp. 33–48.)

"Zehn Thesen." *Die Kirche und das Dritte Reich*. Fragen und Forderungen deutscher Theologen. (First Series.) Ed. Leopold Klotz. Gotha: Klotz, 1932, pp. 126–128.

"Der Sozialismus und die geistige Lage der Gegenwart." *Neue Blätter für den Sozialismus* (Potsdam), III, No. 1 (January, 1932), 14–16. (Discussion, with Hendrik de Man, of a broadcast talk by Gustav Radbruch.)

"Protestantismus und politische Romantik." *Ibid.*, III, No. 8 (August, 1932), 413–422.

1933

Die sozialistische Entscheidung. Potsdam: Alfred Protte, 1933. Pp. 201. ("Die sozialistische Aktion," Heft 2. Schriftenreihe der *Neuen Blätter für den Sozialismus*.)

"Selbstanzeigen." *Neue Blätter für den Sozialismus* (Potsdam), III, No. 12 (December, 1932), 667–668. Reprinted in the series "Schriften zur Zeit," ed. August Rathmann. Offenbach a. M.: Bollwerk, 1948. Pp. 131. The Introduction, "Die beiden Wurzeln des politischen Denkens" is translated as "The Two Roots of Political Thinking" in *The Interpretation of History*, pp. 203–215.

"Das Wohnen, der Raum und die Zeit." (Rede, gehalten zur Einweihung des Hauses auf dem Küssel in Potsdam.) *Die Form* (Berlin), VIII, No. 1 (January, 1933), 11–12; illus. Cf. also *Das ideale Heim* (Winterthur, Switzerland), VII, No. 5 (May, 1933), 176–180.

1934

"The Religious Situation in Germany To-day." *Religion in Life* (New York) III, No. 2 (Spring, 1934), 163–173.

"Die Theologie des Kairos und die gegenwärtige geistige Lage. Offener Brief an Emanuel Hirsch." *Theologische Blätter* (Leipzig), XIII, No. 11 (November, 1934), 305–328.

"The Totalitarian State and the Claims of the Church." *Social Research* (New York), I, No. 4 (November, 1934), 405–433.

1935

"What Is Wrong with the 'Dialectic' Theology?" *Journal of Religion* (Chicago), XV, No. 2 (April, 1935), 127–145. Translated as "Was ist falsch in der 'dialektischen' Theologie?" in *Die Christliche Welt* (Gotha), L, No. 8 (April 25, 1936), 353–364.

"Um was es geht. Antwort an Emanuel Hirsch." *Theologische Blätter* (Leipzig), XIV, No. 5 (May, 1935), 117–120.

"Marx and the Prophetic Tradition." *Radical Religion* (New York), I, No. 4 (Autumn, 1935), 21–29. Translated by Alida C. Bohn.

"Natural and Revealed Religion." (The Dudleian Lecture, delivered at Andover Chapel, Harvard University, April 30, 1935.) *Christendom* (Chicago), I, No. 1 (Autumn, 1935), 159–170. Excerpts in *Contemporary Religious Thought: An Anthology,* comp. T. S. Kepler. New York/Nashville: Abingdon Press, 1941, pp. 64–68.

1936

The Interpretation of History. Translated by N. A. Rasetzki (Part One) and Elsa L. Talmey (Parts Two, Three and Four). New York/London: Charles Scribner's Sons, 1936. Pp. xii + 284.

Part One: "On the Boundary: An Autobiographical Sketch" (1936), pp. 3–73. Part Two: Philosophical Categories of the Interpretation of History: "The Demonic: A Contribution to the Interpretation of History" (1926); "Kairos and Logos: A Study in the Metaphysics of Knowledge" (1926). Part Three: Political Categories . . . : "The Problem of Power" (1931); "The Two Roots of Political Thinking" (1933). Part Four: Theological Categories . . . : "Church and Culture" (1924); "The Interpretation of History and the Idea of Christ" (1929); "Eschatology and History" (1927). Pp. 77–284.

"The Social Functions of the Churches in Europe and America." *Social Research* (New York), III, No. 1 (February, 1936), 90–104.

"Christianity and Emigration." (Address delivered on behalf of the American Committee for German Christian Refugees, Riverside Church, New York, Oct. 6, 1936.) *Presbyterian Tribune* (New York), LII, No. 3 (Oct. 29, 1936), 13, 16.

"An Historical Diagnosis: Impressions of a European Trip" (April–September, 1936). *Radical Religion* (New York), II, No. 1 (Winter, 1936), 11–17.

1937

"Brief" an die Redaktion des "Aufbau." (Von Prof. Dr. Tillich, Obmann der "Selbsthilfe deutscher Ausgewanderter.") *Aufbau/Reconstruction* (New York), III, No. 3 (Feb. 1, 1937), 6.

"The End of the Protestant Era." *Student World* (Geneva), XXX, No. 1 (First Quarter, 1937), 49–57.

"The Church and Communism." *Religion in Life* (New York), VI, No. 3 (Summer, 1937), 347–357.

"Mind and Migration." (Address delivered in a series of discussions under the auspices of the Graduate Faculty of the New School for Social Research, in celebration of its Fourth Anniversary, April 13, 1937, New York.) *Social Research* (New York), IV, No. 3 (September, 1937), 295–305. Reprinted as "Migrations Breed New Cultures" in *Protestant Digest* (New York), III, No. 2 (February, 1940), 10–19.

"Protestantism in the Present World-Situation." (Address given at Chicago Theological Seminary, Feb. 27, 1936.) *American Journal of Sociology* (Chicago), XLIII, No. 2 (September, 1937), 236–248. Reprinted as "The End of the Protestant Era?" in *The Protestant Era* (1948), pp. 222–233.

1938

"The Kingdom of God and History." (Address delivered before the World Conference on Church, Community and State, Oxford, England, July, 1937.) *The Kingdom of God and History,* by H. G. Wood, C. H. Dodd, Edwyn Bevan, Eugene Lyman, Paul Tillich, H. D. Wendland, and Christopher Dawson. ("The Official Oxford Conference Books," Vol. III.) Chicago/New York: Willett, Clark, 1938, pp. 107–141. London: George Allen & Unwin. Excerpt (pp. 119–127) reprinted as "Christ as the Center of History" in *Contemporary Thinking about Jesus: An Anthology,* comp. T. S. Kepler. New York/Nashville: Abingdon-Cokesbury, 1944, pp. 217–222.

"The Meaning of Our Present Historical Existence." *The Hazen Conferences on Student Guidance and Counseling.* Haddam, Conn.: Edward W. Hazen Foundation, Inc., 1938, pp. 19–29.

"The Significance of the Historical Jesus for the Christian Faith." (Lectures and discussion by Ernest F. Scott and Paul Tillich.) *Monday Forum Talks* (Union Theological Seminary, New York), No. 5, Feb. 28, 1938. Pp. 6 (mimeographed).

"The Attack of Dialectical Materialism on Christianity." *Student World* (Geneva), XXXI, No. 2 (Second Quarter, 1938), 115–125. Reprinted in *World's Youth* (Geneva), XIV, No. 2 (Spring, 1938), 147–157.

"Nicholas Berdyaev." *Religion in Life* (New York), VII, No. 3 (Summer, 1938), 407–415.

"The Gospel and the State." (Address to the Annual Pastors' Conference, Crozer Theological Seminary, April 25–27, 1938.) *Crozer Quarterly* (Chester, Pa.), XV, No. 4 (October, 1938), 251–261.

"German-Americans Take Stand for Democracy, Against Nazis. Speech Given November 21, 1938, in Madison Square Garden, New York, by Prof. Paul Tillich, formerly of the University of Frankfurt, now of Union Theological Seminary." (Address delivered at a meeting in protest of Hitler's persecution of the Jews.) Headlines in *Deutsches Volksecho/German People's Echo* (New York), II, No. 48 (Nov. 26, 1938), 1–2. Reprinted as "Germany Is Still Alive" in *Protestant Digest* (New York), I, No. 3 (February, 1939), 45–46. Spanish translation, "Alemania Vive Aún," in *La Nueva Democracia* (New York), XX, No. 9 (September, 1939), 12; abridged. Revised and expanded as "The Meaning of Anti-Semitism" in *Radical Religion* (New York), IV, No. 1 (Winter, 1938), 34–36.

1939

"History as *the* Problem of Our Period." *Review of Religion* (New York), III, No. 3 (March, 1939), 255–264.

"The Conception of Man in Existential Philosophy." (Address in a symposium, with Edwin E. Aubrey, at a meeting of the National Council on Religion in Higher Education.) *Journal of Religion* (Chicago), XIX, No. 3 (July, 1939), 201–215. Reprinted as "The Nature of Man" in *The Examined Life: An Introduction to Philosophy,* ed. Troy Wilson Organ. Boston: Houghton Mifflin, 1956, pp. 339–346.

"De situatie van Europa: religie en christendom." *Het Kouter* (Arnhem), IV, No. 9–10 (September–October, 1939), 325–337.

"Und die Kirche?" *Press Service of the German-American Writers Association* (New York), No. 5 (1939), 1–2.

"The European War and the Christian Churches." *Direction* (Darien, Conn.), II, No. 8 (December, 1939), 10–11; photo. Reprinted as "The War and the Christian Churches" in *Protestant Digest* (New York), III, No. 1 (January, 1940), 15–20.

1940

"Freedom in the Period of Transformation." *Freedom: Its Meaning,* ed. Ruth Nanda Anshen. (Vol. I: "Science of Culture Series.") New York: Harcourt, Brace, 1940, pp. 123–144.

"Has Higher Education an Obligation to Work for Democracy?" (Address delivered to the Teachers' Union of New York University.) *Radical Religion* (New York), V, No. 1 (Winter, 1940), 12–15.

"The Meaning of the Triumph of Nazism." *Christianity and Society* (New York), V, No. 4 (1940), 45–46. (Résumé of an address.)

"The Idea of the Personal God." (Reply to an address by Albert Einstein: "Science and Religion.") *Union Review* (New York), II, No. 1 (November, 1940), 8–10.

1941

"Ethics in a Changing World." (Address delivered at the Bicentennial Conference of the University of Pennsylvania.) *Religion and the Modern World,* by Jacques Maritain and others. Philadelphia: University of Pennsylvania Press, 1941, pp. 51–61. (Included in *The Protestant Era,* pp. 150–160.)

"Philosophy and Theology." (Inaugural address delivered on becoming Professor of Philosophical Theology in Union Theological Seminary, New York, Sept. 25, 1940.) *Religion in Life* (New York), X, No. 1 (Winter, 1941), 21–30. Reprinted in *Theology* (London), XLIV, No. 261 (March, 1942), 133–143. (Included in *The Protestant Era,* pp. 83–93.)

"The Permanent Significance of the Catholic Church for Protestantism." *Protestant Digest* (New York), III, No. 10 (February–March, 1941), 23–31.

"Our Disintegrating World." *Anglican Theological Review* (Evanston), XXIII, No. 2 (April, 1941), 134–146. (Church Congress Syllabus No. 6: "Drift or Mastery in a Changing World?")

"Religion and Education." *Protestant Digest* (New York), III, No. 11 (April–May, 1941), 58–61.

"Symbol and Knowledge." *Journal of Liberal Religion* (Chicago), II, No. 4 (Spring, 1941), 202–206. A response to criticism by W. M. Urban and E. E. Aubrey of "The Religious Symbol" (1928), translated by James Luther Adams, *ibid.,* No. 1 (Summer, 1940), 13–33.

"I Am an American." Editorial, *Protestant Digest* (New York), III, No. 12 (June–July, 1941), 24–26. Spanish translation, "Yo Soy Americano," in *La Nueva Democracia* (New York), XXIII, No. 2 (February, 1942), 6.

"Why War Aims?" ("War Aims—I.") *Protestant Digest* (New York), III, No. 12 (June–July, 1941), 33–38.

"What War Aims?" ("War Aims—II.") *Ibid.,* IV, No. 1 (August–September, 1941), 13–18. Spanish translation, "La Unión Federal de Europa," in *La Nueva Democracia* (New York), XXII, No. 12 (December, 1941), 6–8.

"Whose War Aims?" ("War Aims—III.") *The Protestant* (New York), IV, No. 2 (October–November, 1941), 24–29. (The articles also appeared as a brochure, *War Aims,* published by *The Protestant.* Pp. 22.)

"Dr. Richard Kroner." *Alumni Bulletin of the Union Theological Seminary* (New York), XVII, No. 1 (November, 1941), 3–4.

1942

"Love's 'Strange Work.'" *The Protestant* (New York), IV, No. 3 (December–January, 1942), 70–75.

"Challenge to Protestantism." (Speech given at a dinner in Dr. Tillich's honor by friends of *The Protestant,* Feb. 9, 1942.) *Ibid.,* IV, No. 4 (February–March, 1942), 1–4.

"Marxism and Christian Socialism." (Symposium with Eduard Heimann: "Marxism and Christianity.") *Christianity and Society* (New York), VII, No. 2 (Spring, 1942), 13–18. (Included in *The Protestant Era,* pp. 253–260.)

"Protestant Principles." (A basic policy for *The Protestant:* a statement of the Executive Council, Paul Tillich, chairman.) *The Protestant* (New York), IV, No. 5 (April–May, 1942), 17–19.

"The Word of Religion to the People of This Time." *Ibid.,* 43–48. Reprinted as "The Word of Religion" in *The Protestant Era,* pp. 185–191.)

"Läuterndes Feuer." (Rede auf dem "Goethe-Tag 1942" im Hunter College von New York [original title: "Verbranntes Buch—Unzerstörbare Kultur"], veranstaltet von der *Tribüne für freie deutsche Literatur und Kunst in Amerika,* May 18, 1942.) *Aufbau/Reconstruction* (New York), VIII, No. 22 (May 29, 1942), 10.

"Was soll mit Deutschland geschehen?" (Gegen Emil Ludwigs neueste Rede.) *Ibid.,* No. 29 (July 17, 1942), 6.

"Es geht um die Methode." (Antwort . . . an die Kritiker im "Aufbau." *Ibid.,* No. 32 (Aug. 7, 1942), 7–8.

"Spiritual Problems of Post-war Reconstruction." *Christianity and Crisis* (New York), II, No. 14 (Aug. 10, 1942), 2–6. (Included in *The Protestant Era,* pp. 261–269.) Spanish translation, "La Reconstrucción Espiritual de Postguerra," in *La Nueva Democracia* (New York), XXIII, No. 11 (November, 1942), 3–6, 32. Reprinted in *Flor de Traslaciones: Ensayos de Tiempo de Angustia,* translated by Alberto Rembao. Buenos Aires: La Aurora, 1947, pp. 47–58.

"Our Protestant Principles." (Editorial in explication of "Protestant Principles," above.) *The Protestant* (New York), IV, No. 7 (August–September, 1942), 8–14.

"'Faith' in the Jewish-Christian Tradition." *Christendom* (New York), VII, No. 4 (Autumn, 1942), 518–526; photo, xiv.

"Kierkegaard in English." *American-Scandinavian Review* (New York), XXX, No. 3 (September, 1942), 254–257.

"Kierkegaard as Existential Thinker." *Union Review* (New York), IV, No. 1 (December, 1942), 5–7.

1943

"Storms of Our Times." (Address delivered before the Fiftieth Church Congress of the Protestant Episcopal Church, Indianapolis, May 6, 1942.) *Anglican Theological Review* (Evanston), XXV, No. 1/2 (January–April, 1943), 15–32; discussion (43–44, 47–53) with Frederick C. Grant, Angus Dun, Joseph F. Fletcher, George F. Thomas. (Included in *The Protestant Era,* pp. 237–252; discussion omitted.)

"Flight to Atheism." *The Protestant* (New York), IV, No. 10 (February–March, 1943), 43–48. Reprinted as "The Escape from God" in *The Shaking of the Foundations,* pp. 38–51. (Included in *Best Sermons, 1949–1950,* ed. G. Paul Butler.) New York: Harper & Brothers, 1949, pp. 138–146. Spanish translation, "La Huída al Ateísmo," in *La Nueva Democracia* (New York), XXIV, No. 6 (June, 1943), 3–6;

reprinted in *Flor de Traslaciones: Ensayos de Tiempo de Angustia,* 1947, pp. 121–131.

"Comment" on the report of "The Commission on a Just and Durable Peace." *The Witness* (New York), XXVI, No. 45 (April 8, 1943), 4; photo, 3.

"What Is Divine Revelation?" *Ibid.,* No. 46 (April 15, 1943), 8–9.

"Immigrants' Conference." (With Henry I. Selver, in Symposium: "Warum 'Immigrants' Victory Council'?") *Aufbau/Reconstruction* (New York), IX, No. 27 (July 2, 1943), 3.

"Man and Society in Religious Socialism." (Paper presented in the Philosophy Group at the "Week of Work," National Council on Religion in Higher Education.) *Christianity and Society* (New York), VIII, No. 4 (Fall, 1943), 10–21.

1944

"Critiques" of articles by F. S. C. Northrop ("Philosophy and World Peace") and John A. Ryan ("Religious Foundations for an Enduring Peace"). *Approaches to World Peace.* Fourth Symposium of the Conference on Science, Philosophy and Religion in their Relation to the Democratic Way of Life, Inc. Eds. L. Bryson, L. Finkelstein, R. M. MacIver. New York: Harper & Brothers, 1944, pp. 684–685, 816–817.

"Trends in Religious Thought that Affect Social Outlook." (Lecture in the "Religion and Civilization Series" for the academic year 1942–43, The Jewish Theological Seminary of America, New York.) *Religion and the World Order,* ed. F. Ernest Johnson. New York: Institute for Religious and Social Studies, Harper & Brothers, 1944, pp. 17–28. (Included in *Outside Readings in Sociology,* ed. E. A. Schuler and others. New York: T. Y. Crowell, 1952, pp. 420–430.)

Kairosu to Rogosu: Rekishi Kaishaku no Mondai. (Translations of "Kairos und Logos," "Das Dämonische," and "Philosophie und Schicksal," by Enkichi Kan.) Tokyo: Kyōbunkan, 1944. Pp. 206.

"Existential Philosophy." *Journal of the History of Ideas* (New York), V, No. 1 (January, 1944), 44–70.

"Russia's Church and the Soviet Order." *Think* (New York), X, No. 1 (January, 1944), 22–23; illus. Reprinted in *The Cathedral Age* (Washington, D.C.), XIX, No. 1 (Easter, 1944), 14–15, 31–32.

"The God of History." *Christianity and Crisis* (New York), IV, No. 7 (May 1, 1944), 5–6. Reprinted as "The Two Servants of Jahweh" in *The Shaking of the Foundations,* pp. 29–33.

"A Program for a Democratic Germany." (A statement by members of The Council for a Democratic Germany, Paul Tillich, chairman.) *Christianity and Crisis* (New York), IV, No. 8 (May 15, 1944), 3–5. Reprinted in a symposium in the St. Louis *Star-Times,* May 18, 1944, p. 15; photo.

"Depth." *Christendom* (New York), IX, No. 3 (Summer, 1944), 317–325. Reprinted as "The Depth of Existence" in *The Shaking of the Foundations,* pp. 52–63.

"A Statement." *Bulletin of the Council for a Democratic Germany* (New York), I, No. 1 (Sept. 1, 1944), 1, 4. (Five issues published from September, 1944, to May, 1945; minor articles *passim.*)

"Estrangement and Reconciliation in Modern Thought." (Presidential address to the American Theological Society, April 14, 1944.) *Review of Religion* (New York), IX, No. 1 (November, 1944), 5–19. Translated by Nina Baring and Renate Albrecht as "Entfremdung und Versöhnung im modernen Denken" in *Eckart* (Berlin), XXVI, No. 2 (April–June 1957), 99–109.

"'Now Concerning Spiritual Gifts. . . '." *Union Review* (New York), VI, No. 1 (December, 1944), 15–17. Reprinted as "The Theologian," Part I, in *The Shaking of the Foundations,* pp. 118–121.

1945

"Critiques" of articles by Robert J. Havighurst ("Education for Intergroup Co-operation"), Rudolf Allers ("Some Remarks on the Problems of Group Tensions"), A. Campbell Garnett ("Group Tensions in the Modern World"), and Amos N. Wilder ("Theology and Cultural Incoherence"). *Approaches to National Unity.* Fifth Symposium of the Conference on Science, Philosophy and Religion. Eds. Bryson, Finkelstein, MacIver. New York: Harper & Brothers, 1945, pp. 407–408, 522–523, 537, 923.

"The World Situation." *The Christian Answer,* ed. Henry P. Van Dusen. New York: Charles Scribner' Sons, 1945, pp. 1–44; illus. London: Nisbet, 1946, pp. 19–71. Excerpt translated as "Christentum, Wirtschaft und Demokratie" in *Neue Auslese aus dem Schrifttum der Gegenwart* (Munich/Vienna), I, No. 7 (July, 1946), 2–6.

"All Things to All Men." *Union Review* (New York), VI, No. 3 (May, 1945), 3–4. Revised as "The Theologian," Part II, in *The Shaking of the Foundations,* pp. 122–125.

"Nietzsche and the Bourgeois Spirit." (Comments on the Symposium on Nietzsche's Centenary.) *Journal of the History of Ideas* (New York), VI, No. 3 (June, 1945), 307–309.

"The Christian Churches and the Emerging Social Order in Europe." (The Kingsbury Lecture, Berkeley Divinity School, New Haven.) *Religion in Life* (New York), XIV, No. 3 (Summer, 1945), 329–339.

"The Redemption of Nature." *Christendom* (New York), X, No. 3 (Summer, 1945), 299–305; prayer, 306; photo, ix. Reprinted (omitting "prayer") as "Nature, Also, Mourns for a Lost Good" in *The Shaking of the Foundations,* pp. 76–86.

"Conscience in Western Thought and the Idea of a Transmoral Conscience." *Crozer Quarterly* (Chester, Pa.), XXII, No. 4 (October, 1945), 289–300. Reprinted as "The Transmoral Conscience" in *The Protestant Era,* pp. 136–149; German translation "Das transmoralische Gewissen," reprinted in *Glaube und Handeln,* comp. Heinz-Horst Schrey. Bremen: C. Schünemann, 1956, pp. 269–286.

1946

"The Meaning of the German Church Struggle for Christian Missions." *Christian World Mission,* ed. William K. Anderson. Nashville: Commission on Ministerial Training, The Methodist Church, 1946, pp. 130–136.

"Vertical and Horizontal Thinking." (Symposium, with Raphael Demos and Sidney Hook, in the American Scholar *Forum:* "The Future of Religion.") *American Scholar* (New York), XV, No. 1 (Winter, 1945–46), 102–105; reply, 110–112. Translated as "Die Zukunft der Religion. Vertikales und horizontales Denken" in *Zeitwende* (Hamburg), XXIII, No. 2 (Oct. 1, 1951), 245–249.

"Religion and Secular Culture." (Lecture given at the University of Chicago, January, 1946, on the Hiram W. Thomas Foundation.) *Journal of Religion* (Chicago), XXVI, No. 2 (April, 1946), 79–86. (Included in *The Protestant Era,* pp. 55–65.)

"The Relation of Religion and Health: Historical Considerations and Theoretical Questions." (A paper contributed to the "University Seminar" on Religion and Its Human Relations, Columbia University, Spring, 1945.) *Review of Religion* (New York), X, No. 4 (May, 1946), 348–384. Selections (pp. 356–359, 360, 362–365, 365–366, 379–383) reprinted as "The Relation of Religion and Health" in *Pastoral Psychology* (Great Neck, N.Y.), V, No. 44 (May, 1954), 41–42, 44–52; references omitted. Reprinted also in *Healing: Human and Divine,* ed. Simon Doniger. ("Pastoral Psychology Series.") New York: Association Press, 1957, pp. 185–205. Slightly abridged in *Religion and Health,* ed. Doniger. New York: Association Press "Reflection Book," 1958, pp. 13–31.

"The Two Types of Philosophy of Religion." *Union Seminary Quarterly Review* (New York), I, No. 4 (May, 1946), 3–13. Author's translation, "Zwei Wege der Religionsphilosophie," in *Natur und Geist.* (Festschrift für Fritz Medicus zum siebzigsten Geburtstag.) Eds. H. Barth and W. Rüegg. Erlenbach/Zürich: Eugen Rentsch, 1946, pp. 210–229.

"Redemption in Cosmic and Social History." *Journal of Religious Thought* (Washington, D.C.), III, No. 1 (Autumn–Winter, 1946), 17–27.

"The Nature of Man." (Abstract of a paper read at the Forty-third Annual Meeting of the Eastern Division of the American Philosophical Association, Yale University, December, 1946.) *Journal of Philosophy* (New York), XLIII, No. 25 (Dec. 5, 1946), 675–677.

1947

"The Problem of Theological Method." (Symposium with E. A. Burtt at the American Theological Society, New York, Spring, 1946.) *Journal of Religion* (Chicago), XXVII, No. 1 (January, 1947), 16–26. Selections (pp. 17–19, 22–23) reprinted as "The Method of Theology" in *Varieties of Experience: An Introduction to Philosophy,* ed. Albert William Levi. New York: The Ronald Press, 1957, pp. 514–518. (Included unabridged in *Four Existentialist Theologians.* A Reader from the Works of Jacques Maritain, Nicolas Berdyaev, Martin Buber, and Paul Tillich. Selected and with an Introduction and Biographical Notes by Will Herberg. Garden City, N.Y.: Doubleday Anchor Books, No. 141, 1958, pp. 238–255. Cloth edition, pp. 263–282.)

" 'Behold, I Am Doing a New Thing.' " *Union Seminary Quarterly Review* (New York), II, No. 4 (May, 1947), 3–9. (Included in *The Shaking of the Foundations,* pp. 173–186.) Excerpts reprinted in *The Intercollegian* (New York), LXXIV, No. 8 (April, 1957), 3.

1948

The Protestant Era. Translated and with a Concluding Essay by James Luther Adams. Chicago: University of Chicago Press, 1948. Pp. xxix + 323.

Contents: "Author's Introduction." I. *Religion and History:* (1) "Philosophy and Fate" (1929). (2) "Historical and Nonhistorical Interpretations of History: A Comparison" (1948). (3) "Kairos" (1922). II. *Religion and Culture:* (4) "Religion and Secular Culture" (1946). (5) "Realism and Faith" (1928). (6) "Philosophy and Theology" (1941). (7) "Nature and Sacrament" (1929). III. *Religion and Ethics:* (8) "The Idea and the Ideal of Personality" (1927). (9) "The Transmoral Conscience" (1945). (10) "Ethics in a Changing World" (1941). (11) "The Protestant Principle and the Proletarian Situation" (1931). IV. *Protestantism:* (12) "The Word of Religion" (1942). (13) "The Protestant Message and the Man of Today" (1929). (14) "The Formative Power of Protestantism" (1929). (15) "The End of the Protestant Era?" (1937). V. *The Present Crisis:* (16) "Storms of Our Times" (1943). (17) "Marxism and Christian Socialism" (1942). (18) "Spiritual Problems of Postwar Reconstruction" (1942). *Tillich's Concept of the Protestant Era* (Concluding Essay by James Luther Adams). Several of the essays have been altered for publication in this volume.

Abridged edition, comprising Chapters 1–15: "Phoenix Books" (University of Chicago Press), 1957. Pp. xxvi + 242. "Note for the Abridged Edition," pp. xxv–xxvi; section V omitted.—British edition, London: Nisbet, 1951. Pp. xlvi + 305. "Introduction" by R. H. Daubney; concluding essay omitted.—German edition, *Der Protestantismus. Prinzip und Wirklichkeit,* translated by R. Albrecht, N. Baring, G. Siemsen, F. Steinrath; ed. W. Braune ("Schriften zur Zeit," New Series, ed. August Rathmann.) Stuttgart: Steingrüben, 1950. Pp. 324; concluding essay and index omitted. The extensive annotations to Chapters 5, 7, 8, 13, and 14 which originally appeared in *Religiöse Verwirklichung* are absent from the editions in German and English.

The Shaking of the Foundations. New York: Charles Scribner's Sons, 1948. Pp. 186. Contents: (1) "The Shaking of the Foundations." (2) "We Live in Two Orders." (3) "The Paradox of the Beatitudes." (4) "The Two Servants of Jahweh." (5) "Meditation: The Mystery of Time." (6) "The Escape from God." (7) "The Depth of Existence." (8) "On the Transitoriness of Life." (9) " 'Nature, Also, Mourns for a Lost Good.' " (10) "The Experience of the Holy." (11) "The Yoke of Religion." (12) "The Meaning of Providence." (13) "Knowledge Through Love." (14) "Doing the Truth." (15) "The Theologian" (Parts I, II, III). (16) "The Witness of the Spirit to the Spirit." (17) "He Who Is the Christ." (18) "Waiting." (19) "You Are Accepted." (20) "Born in the Grave." (21) "The Destruction of Death." (22) " 'Behold, I Am Doing a New Thing.' "

London: SCM Press, 1949. Pp. 200.—Japanese translation by Makoto Gotō: *Chi no Motoi Furuiugoku.* Tokyo: Shinkyō Shuppansha, 1951. Pp. 286.—German translation by R. Albrecht, E. Seeberger, G. Stöber; A. Rathmann, ed.: *In der Tiefe ist Wahrheit.* (Religiöse Reden.) Stuttgart: Evangelisches Verlagswerk, 1952. Pp. 204.—(Korean translation in preparation.)

Chapters 4, 6, 7, 9, 15, and 22 appeared in 1944, 1943, 1944, 1945, 1944–45, and 1947, respectively. Excerpts from Chapter 19 appear in *Alone in the Crowd* (National Student Council of the YMCA and YWCA, New York), June 1954, pp. 20–25.

From the German edition, Chapters 1, 5, 7, 18, 20, and 21 ("Die Erde erbebt," "Das Mysterium der Zeit," "Von der Tiefe," "Vom Warten," "Im Grabe geboren," and "Der Tod ist tot") are reprinted, respectively, in: *Reformatio* (Bern), I, No. 11–12 (November–December, 1952), 622–628; *Evangelischer Kulturbund* (Düsseldorf), No. 41 (July, 1952), 1; *Universitas* (Stuttgart), VII, No. 9 (September, 1952), 963–968 (abridged); *Der Weg zur Seele* (Göttingen), V, No. 12 (December, 1953), 367–368 (excerpts); *Einkehr* (Bremer Kirchenzeitung), X, No. 9 (April 10, 1955), 1; *Christ und Sozialist* (Frankfurt a. M.), No. 11–12 (1955), 2–3.

"The Disintegration of Society in Christian Countries." *The Church's Witness to God's Design.* An Ecumenical Study Prepared under the Auspices of the World Council of Churches, Amsterdam, August 22—September 4, 1948.) (Vol. II, "The Amsterdam Assembly Series.") New York: Harper & Brothers, 1948, pp. 53–64; Toronto: Macmillan; London: SCM Press. Four volumes appear in one-volume edition: *Man's Disorder and God's Design.* New York: Harper & Brothers, 1949.

Translations: "La désintégration de la société dans les pays chrétiens." *Le dessein de Dieu et le témoignage de l'Église.* Etudes oecuméniques préparées sous les auspices du Conseil oecuménique des Eglises. (Vol. II, Documents de l'Assemblée d'Amsterdam en 5 volumes sous le titre: *Désordre de l'homme et dessein de Dieu.*) Neuchâtel/Paris: Delachaux & Niestlé, 1949, pp. 77–94.

"Die gesellschaftliche Auflösung in christlichen Ländern." *Die Kirche bezeugt Gottes Heilsplan.* (Vol. II, Beiträge zum Amsterdamer ökumenischen Gespräch 1948: *Die Unordnung der Welt und Gottes Heilsplan.*) Stuttgart: Evangelisches Verlagswerk; Tübingen: Furche-Verlag; 1948, pp. 58–71.

"Die philosophisch-geistige Lage und der Protestantismus." *Philosophische Vorträge und Diskussionen.* (Bericht über den Mainzer Philosophen-Kongress 1948.) Ed. Georgi Schischkoff. Sonderheft 1 der *Zeitschrift für philosophische Forschung.* Wurzach/Württ.: Pan Verlag, 1948, pp. 119–124; discussion, pp. 124–126.

"Martin Buber and Christian Thought: His Threefold Contribution to Protestantism." *Commentary* (New York), V, No. 6 (June, 1948), 515–521.

"Das geistige Vakuum." (Vortrag, gehalten an der Technischen Universität Berlin im Juli 1948 unter dem Titel "Die geistige Weltlage.") *Das sozialistische Jahrhundert* (Berlin), II, No. 20 (Sept. 15, 1948), 303–305.

"How Much Truth Is In Karl Marx?" *Christian Century* (Chicago) LXV, No. 36 (Sept. 8, 1948), 906–908. Translated as "Wieviel Wahrheit finden wir bei Karl Marx?" in *Christ und Welt* (Stuttgart), I, No. 23 (Nov. 5, 1948), 12.

"Visit to Germany." *Christianity and Crisis* (New York), VIII, No. 19 (Nov. 15, 1948), 147–149.

1949

"A Reinterpretation of the Doctrine of the Incarnation." *Church Quarterly Review* (London), CXLVII, No. 294 (January–March, 1949), 133–148.

"Psychotherapy and a Christian Interpretation of Human Nature." (A paper contributed to the "University Seminar" on Religion and Health, Columbia University.) *Review of Religion* (New York), XIII, No. 3 (March, 1949), 264–268. Translated as "Psychotherapie und eine christliche Deutung der menschlichen Natur" in *Der Weg zur Seele* (Göttingen), II, No. 1 (January, 1950), 24–28; translated by R. Albrecht and G. Stöber in *Psyche* (Stuttgart), V, No. 7 (1951), 473–477.

"Creative Love in Education." *World Christian Education* (New York), IV, No. 2 (Second Quarter, 1949), 27, 34.

"Das Ja zum Kreuze." (Eine Rundfunkrede über "Die Stimme Amerikas.") *Monatsschrift für Pastoraltheologie* (Göttingen), XXXVIII, No. 6 (June, 1949), 287–289.

"The Present Theological Situation in the Light of the Continental European Development." *Theology Today* (Princeton), VI, No. 3 (October, 1949), 299–310. Slightly revised and translated as "Zur theologischen Lage" in *Die Zeichen der Zeit* (Berlin), V, No. 10 (1951), 361–368. Also translated (pp. 304–310) by Fritz Buri as "Das Problem von Diastase und Synthese in der heutigen theologischen Situation" in *Schweizerische theologische Umschau* (Bern), XX, No. 1–2 (February, 1950), 36–41. Also translated as "Die kontinentaleuropäische Theologie" in *Universitas* (Stuttgart), V, No. 6 (June, 1950), 649–654.

"Beyond Religious Socialism." *Christian Century* (Chicago), LXVI, No. 24 (June 15, 1949), 732–733.

"Existentialism and Religious Socialism." (In Symposium: "The Meaning of Existentialism.") *Christianity and Society* (New York), XV, No. 1 (Winter, 1949–50), 8–11.

1950

"Anxiety-Reducing Agencies in Our Culture." (Address delivered before the American Psychopathological Association, New York, June 3, 1949.) *Anxiety.* Eds. Paul H. Hoch and Joseph Zubin. New York: Grune and Stratton, 1950, pp. 17–26.

"The Concept of God." (Reply to W. T. Stace.) *Perspective* (Princeton), II, No. 3 (January, 1950), 12.

"The Protestant Vision." *Chicago Theological Seminary Register,* XL, No. 2 (March, 1950), 8–12. (Cf. expanded version, *Protestantische Vision,* 1951).

"Religion and the Intellectuals." *Partisan Review* (New York), XVII, No. 3 (March, 1950), 254–256. Reprinted in *Religion and the Intellectuals.* A Symposium. *Partisan Review Series,* No. 3, 1950, pp. 136–139.

"Reply" to Gustave Weigel, S.J., "Contemporaneous Protestantism and Paul Tillich." *Theological Studies* (Baltimore, Md.), XI, No. 2 (June, 1950), 177–201; "reply," 201–202.

"The New Being." *Religion in Life* (New York), XIX, No. 4 (Autumn, 1950), 511–517. (Included in *The New Being,* pp. 15–24.)

The Recovery of the Prophetic Tradition in the Reformation. (Three lectures delivered at the Washington Cathedral Library, November–December, 1950.) "Christianity and Modern Man Publications." Washington, D.C.: Henderson Services, 1950. Pp. 30; mimeographed. (Contents: I. "The Divinity of the Divine." II. "The Human Predicament." III. "The New Community.")

The Christian Conscience and Weapons of Mass Destruction. (Report of a Special Commission appointed by the Federal Council of the Churches of Christ in America.) New York: The Department of International Justice and Goodwill, December, 1950. Pp. 23. (Dr. Tillich served as a member of the Commission.)

1951

Systematic Theology. (Vol. I: "Introduction," "Reason and Revelation," "Being and God.") Chicago: University of Chicago Press, 1951. Pp. xi + 300. London: Nisbet, 1953. Pp. xiv + 330.

German translation, *Systematische Theologie,* Bd. I, by R. Albrecht and others. Stuttgart: Evangelisches Verlagswerk, 1955. Pp. 349. Second edition, revised, 1956. Pp. 352. Japanese translation of "Introduction" and "Reason and Revelation" by Mitsutake Suzuki: *Soshiki Shingaku.* Tokyo: Shinkyō Shuppansha, 1955. Pp. 222.

Excerpts (pp. 238–240, 235–237, 204–210) reprinted in *The Universal God:* An Interfaith Anthology of Man's Eternal Search for God. Ed. Carl Hermann Voss. Cleveland/New York: World Publishing Co., 1953, pp. 34–36, 61–63, 91–93. Excerpt (pp. 235–252) included in *Four Existentialist Theologians.* A Reader from the Works of Jacques Maritain, Nicolas Berdyaev, Martin Buber, and Paul Tillich. Ed. Will Herberg. Garden City, N.Y.: Doubleday Anchor Books, No. 141, 1958, pp. 256–276. Cloth edition, pp. 283–305.

Christianity and the Problem of Existence. (Three lectures delivered in Andrew Rankin Chapel, Howard University, April 24, 1951.) Washington, D.C.: Henderson Services, 1951. Pp. 33; mimeographed. (Contents: I. "Naturalism Transcended." II. "The Existentialist Movement." III. "Is There a Christian Answer?")

Politische Bedeutung der Utopie im Leben der Völker. (Vier Vorträge, gehalten an der Deutschen Hochschule für Politik Berlin, Frühsommer 1951.) "Schriftenreihe der Deutschen Hochschule für Politik Berlin." Berlin: Gebrüder Weiss, 1951. Pp. 65.

Protestantische Vision. Katholische Substanz, Protestantisches Prinzip, Sozialistische Entscheidung. (Vortrag, gehalten am 8. Juli 1951 im Robert-Schumann-Saal zu Düsseldorf.) Düsseldorf: "Schriftenreihe des Evangelischen Arbeitsausschusses Düsseldorf," No. 3, 1951. Pp. 15. Reprinted, 1954, in *Der Mensch im Christentum und im Marxismus.* . . .

1952

The Courage to Be. (The Dwight Harrington Terry Foundation Lectures on Religion in the Light of Science and Philosophy, 27th series, delivered at Yale University, Oct. 30–Nov. 2, 1950.) New Haven: Yale University Press, 1952. Pp. ix + 197. London: Nisbet. Pp. xii + 185.

German translation by Gertie Siemsen: *Der Mut zum Sein.* Stuttgart: Steingrüben, 1953. Pp. 142 (3rd ed., 1958.)—Japanese translation by Michio Taniguchi: *Sonzai e no Yūki.* Tokyo: Shinkyō Shuppansha, 1954. Pp. 230.—Dutch translation by C. B. Burger: *De Moed om te Zijn.* Over de Redding der Menselijke Persoonlijkheid. Utrecht: E. J. Bijleveld, 1955. Pp. 168. (Korean translation in preparation.)

Excerpt (pp. 64–78) reprinted as "Anxiety, Religion and Medicine" in *Pastoral Psychology* (Great Neck, N.Y.) III, No. 29 (December, 1952), 11–17.

"Autobiographical Reflections." *The Theology of Paul Tillich.* ("The Library of Living Theology," Vol. I.) Eds. Charles W. Kegley & Robert W. Bretall. New York:

The Macmillan Co., 1952, pp. 3–21. (Cf. also "Author's Introduction" to *The Protestant Era*, pp. ix–xxix; "On the Boundary: An Autobiographical Sketch," in *The Interpretation of History*, pp. 3–73; and the "Lebenslauf" in the Dissertations of 1910 and 1912.)

"Answer." (Reply to Interpretation and Criticism in *The Theology of Paul Tillich*. Eds. Kegley & Bretall. New York: The Macmillan Co., 1952, pp. 329–349.

"Being and Love." *Moral Principles of Action*. Ed. Ruth Nanda Anshen. (Vol. VI: "Science of Culture Series.") New York: Harper & Brothers, 1952, pp. 661–672. (Included in *Four Existentialist Theologians*. A Reader from the Works of Jacques Maritain, Nicolas Berdyaev, Martin Buber, and Paul Tillich. Ed. Will Herberg. Garden City, N.Y.: Doubleday Anchor Books, No. 141, 1958, pp. 300–312.) Cloth edition, pp. 332–346.

"Victory in Defeat: The Meaning of History in the Light of Christian Prophetism." *Interpretation* (Richmond), VI, No. 1 (January, 1952), 17–26.

"Jewish Influences on Contemporary Christian Theology." (The Milton Steinberg Lecture in Jewish Theology, delivered at the Park Avenue Synagogue, New York.) *Cross Currents* (New York), II, No. 3 (Spring, 1952), 35–42.

"Is There a Judeo-Christian Tradition?" *Judaism* (New York), I, No. 2 (April, 1952), 106–109.

"Authority and Revelation." (The Dudleian Lecture, Harvard University, delivered in Andover Chapel, April 10, 1951.) *Official Register of Harvard University: Harvard Divinity School* (Cambridge), XLIX, No. 8 (April 7, 1952), 27–36.

"Communicating the Gospel." (Address to the First Annual Mid-Winter Minister's Conference and Workshop, Union Theological Seminary, Jan. 15, 1952.) *Union Seminary Quarterly Review* (New York), VII, No. 4 (June, 1952), 3–11. (Ensuing discussion with Henry P. Van Dusen, David E. Roberts, John C. Bennett, and Paul Scherer, unpublished.) Reprinted in *Pastoral Psychology* (Great Neck, N.Y.) VII, No. 65 (June, 1956), 10–16. Abridged in *The Evangel* (New York), LXX, No. 4 (May–June, 1957), 10–14. (Available also on tape and long-playing record from the Audio-Visual Department, Union Theological Seminary, New York.)

"Human Nature Can Change." (Symposium with Harold Kelman, Frederick A. Weiss, and Karen Horney.) *American Journal of Psychoanalysis* (New York), XII, No. 1 (1952), 65–67.

"Christian Criteria for Our Culture." (Address to the Yale Christian Association, Dwight Hall, Yale University, Oct. 19, 1952.) *criterion* (New Haven), I, No. 1 (October, 1952), 1, 3–4. French translation by Laurence Bellême, "Critère chretien de notre culture," in *Comprendre* (Revue de politique de la culture) (Venice), No. 19 (1958), 202–209.

"Love, Power and Justice." (A broadcast talk on the BBC's Third Programme, based on the Firth Lectures delivered in Nottingham.) *The Listener* (London), XLVIII, No. 1231 (Oct. 2, 1952), 544–545.

"The Four Levels of the Relationship between Religion and Art." (Brief notes to "An Exhibition of Contemporary Religious Art and Architecture" presented by the Religious Art Committee of the Student Body, Dec. 1–16, 1952, Union Theological Seminary.) *Contemporary Religious Art*. New York: Union Theological Seminary, 1952. (Brochure listing the exhibit.)

1953

"The Conquest of Theological Provincialism." *The Cultural Migration: The European Scholar in America*, by Franz L. Neumann, Henri Peyre, Erwin Panofsky, Wolfgang Köhler and Paul Tillich. Ed. W. Rex Crawford. (The Benjamin Franklin

Lectures of the University of Pennsylvania. Fifth Series, Spring, 1952.) Pennsylvania: University of Pennsylvania Press, 1953, pp. 138–156.

Der Mensch im Christentum und im Marxismus. (Vortrag, gehalten am 29. Juli im Robert-Schumann-Saal zu Düsseldorf.) Düsseldorf: "Schriftenreihe des Evangelischen Arbeitsausschusses Düsseldorf," No. 5, 1953. Pp. 20. Reprinted in 1954.

Die Judenfrage, ein christliches und ein deutsches Problem. (Vier Vorträge, gehalten an der Deutschen Hochschule für Politik Berlin.) "Schriftenreihe der Deutschen Hochschule für Politik Berlin." Berlin: Gebrüder Weiss, 1953. Pp. 48. Excerpt (pp. 38–42) translated as "Nation of Time, Nation of Space" by Marion Hausner, in *Land Reborn* (New York), VIII, No. 1 (April–May, 1957), 4–5.

"The Person in a Technical Society." *Christian Faith and Social Action.* A Symposium. Ed. John A. Hutchison. New York/London: Charles Scribner's Sons, 1953, pp. 137–153.

Reprinted in *Perspectives USA* (New York), Number 8 (Summer, 1954), 115–131. Also published in British, French, German and Italian editions (Intercultural Publications, Inc., N.Y.): "La personne dans une société technique." *Profils* (Paris), Numéro 8 (Été 1954), 72–91 (transl. Jean-Paul de Dadelsen). "Der Mensch in der technisierten Gesellschaft." *Perspektiven* (Frankfurt am Main), Heft 8 (Sommer 1954), 129–145 (transl. Gertie Siemsen). "L'individuo nella società industriale." *Prospetti* (Florence), Ottavo Numero (Estate 1954), 122–137 (transl. Marcello Pagnini).

"The Truth Will Make You Free." *Pulpit Digest* (Great Neck, N.Y.), XXXIII, No. 180 (April, 1953), 17–23; cover photo. Reprinted in *Campus Lutheran* (Chicago), V, No. 1 (November, 1953), 10–15; "prayer," 17. Reprinted as " 'What Is Truth?' " in *Canadian Journal of Theology* (Toronto), I, No. 2 (July, 1955), 117–122; "prayer" omitted. (Included in *The New Being,* pp. 63–74.)

"Karen Horney" (Sept. 16, 1885—Dec. 4, 1952). (A funeral address given in New York, Dec. 6, 1952.) *Pastoral Psychology* (Great Neck, N.Y.) IV, No. 34 (May, 1953), 11–13, 66.

"The Nature of Authority." *Pulpit Digest* (Great Neck, N.Y.), XXXIV, No. 186 (October, 1953), 25–27, 30–32, 34. Reprinted as " 'By What Authority?' " in *The New Being,* pp. 79–91.

"Hermann Schafft zum 70. Geburtstag." *Evangelische Welt* (Bethel b. Bielefeld), VII, No. 23 (1953), 703.

"Zur Frage christlicher Grundbegriffe. Ein Beitrag in Form eines Briefes." *Das Evangelische Düsseldorf,* No. 58 (December, 1953).

1954

Love, Power, and Justice. Ontological Analyses and Ethical Applications. (Given as Firth Lectures in Nottingham, England, and as Sprunt Lectures in Richmond, Va.) New York/London: Oxford University Press, 1954. Pp. viii + 127.

German translation by Gertie Siemsen and Gertraut Stöber: *Liebe, Macht, Gerechtigkeit.* Tübingen: J. C. B. Mohr, 1955. Pp. viii + 134.—Japanese translation by Michio Taniguchi: *Ai, Chikara, Seigi.* Tokyo: Shinkyō Shuppansha, 1957. Pp. 163. Dutch translation by H. A. C. Snethlage: *Liefde, Macht en Recht.* Ontologische Analyses en Ethische Toepassing. Delft: W. Gaade, 1956. Pp. 147.

Excerpts (pp. 101–106, 122–124) reprinted as "Can Uniting Love Never Unite Mankind?" in *New Republic* (Washington, D.C.), CXXX, No. 13 (March 29, 1954), 17–18. Excerpt (pp. 24–34) reprinted as "Being and Love" in *Pastoral Psychology* (Great Neck, N.Y.), V, No. 43 (April, 1954), 43–46, 48.

(1) *Der Mensch im Christentum und im Marxismus.* (2) *Protestantische Vision:* Katholische Substanz, Protestantisches Prinzip, Sozialistische Entscheidung. (Zwei

Vorträge, gehalten am 29. Juli 1952 und am 8. Juli 1951 in Düsseldorf.) Stuttgart/ Düsseldorf: Ring, 1954. Pp. 20 + 18.

"Religion in Two Societies." (Lecture in a Symposium on *The Contemporary Scene*, held at the Metropolitan Museum of Art, March 28–30, 1952.) New York: Metropolitan Museum of Art, 1954, pp. 41–48.

"Authentic Religious Art." Preface (with Theodore M. Greene) to *Masterpieces of Religious Art*. (Exhibition held in connection with the Second Assembly of the World Council of Churches, July 15 through Aug. 31, 1954.) Chicago: Art Institute of Chicago, 1954, pp. 8–9. Reprinted as "The Nature of Religious Art" in *Symbols and Society*. Ed. Lyman Bryson and others. New York: Harper & Brothers, 1955, pp. 282–284.

"Ansprache zum Semesterbeginn." (Address to students and faculty of Union Theological Seminary.) *Freies Christentum* (Frankfurt a.M.), VI, No. 5 (May 1, 1954), 54–57. Translated by Erhard Seeberger.

"The Hydrogen Cobalt Bomb." Symposium in a Special Issue of *Pulpit Digest* (Great Neck, N.Y.), XXXIV, No. 194 (June, 1954), 32, 34.

"The Meaning and Sources of Courage." (Address delivered before the Annual Conference of the Child Study Association of America, New York, March 1, 1954.) *Child Study* (New York), XXXI, No. 3 (Summer, 1954), 7–11.

"The Theology of Missions." (Revision of a lecture in Systematic Theology, Union Theological Seminary.) *Occasional Bulletin of the Missionary Research Library* (New York), V, No. 10, Aug. 10, 1954. Pp. 6. Reprinted in *Christianity and Crisis* (New York), XV, No. 5 (April 4, 1955), 35–38; condensed as "Reading History as Christians" in *New Christian Advocate* (Chicago), I, No. 1 (October, 1956), 44–49.— Spanish translation, "Teología de las Misiones," in *La Nueva Democracia* (New York), XXXV, No. 1 (January, 1955), 64–72.

1955

Biblical Religion and the Search for Ultimate Reality. (The James W. Richard Lectures in the Christian Religion, University of Virginia, 1951–52.) Chicago: University of Chicago Press, 1955. Pp. x + 85. London: Nisbet, 1956.

Chapter VIII reprinted in *Four Existentialist Theologians*. A Reader from the Works of Jacques Maritain, Nicolas Berdyaev, Martin Buber, and Paul Tillich. Ed. Will Herberg. Garden City, N.Y.: Doubleday Anchor Books, No. 141, 1958, pp. 292–299. Cloth edition, pp. 323–331.—German translation by Nina Baring: *Biblische Religion und die Frage nach dem Sein*. Stuttgart: Evangelisches Verlagswerk, 1956. Pp. 80.—French translation of pp. 1–20, 58–85, by Marie-Claire Frommel, "Religion biblique et recherche de la réalité dernière," *Revue de Théologie et de Philosophie* (Lausanne), Third Series, V, No. 2 (1955), 82–103.

The New Being. New York: Charles Scribner's Sons, 1955. Pp. 179. London: SCM Press, 1956. German translation by Maria Rhine and Gertraut Stöber: *Das Neue Sein*. Religiöse Reden, 2. Folge. Stuttgart: Evangelisches Verlagswerk, 1957. Pp. 160.

Contents: (1) " 'To Whom Much is Forgiven . . .' " (2) "The New Being." (3) "The Power of Love." (4) "The Golden Rule." (5) "On Healing" (Parts I and II). (6) "Holy Waste." (7) "Principalities and Powers." (8) " 'What Is Truth?' " (9) "Faith and Uncertainty." (10) " 'By What Authority?' " (11) "Has the Messiah Come?" (12) " 'He Who Believes in Me . . .' " (13) "Yes and No." (14) " 'Who Are My Mother and Brothers . . . ?' " (15) " 'All Is Yours.' " (16) " 'Is There Any Word from the Lord?' " (17) "Seeing and Hearing." (18) "The Paradox of Prayer." (19) "The Meaning of Joy." (20) "Our Ultimate Concern." (21) "The Right Time." (22) "Love Is Stronger Than Death." (23) "Universal Salvation."

Chapter 1 is included in *Best Sermons, 1955 Edition*, ed. G. Paul Butler. New York:

McGraw-Hill, pp. 172–181. Also in *Sermons from an Ecumenical Pulpit,* ed. Max F. Daskam. Boston: Starr King Press, 1956, pp. 27–36. Abridged as "The Source of Forgiveness and Love" in *The Intercollegian* (New York), LXXIII, No. 6 (February, 1956), 6–8. Chapter 2 appeared in 1950. Chapter 5 (Part I) appears also in *Pastoral Psychology* (Great Neck, N.Y.), VI, No. 55 (June, 1955), 25–28, 30. Chapter 8 was published in *Pulpit Digest* (Great Neck, N.Y.) XXXIII, No. 180 (April, 1953), 17–22 ("prayer," 22–23); Chapter 10, *ibid.,* XXXIV, No. 186 (October, 1953), 25–27, 30–32, 34. Chapter 18 is reprinted in *Pulpit Digest,* XXXV, No. 206 (June, 1955), 23–25. Chapter 19 is reprinted in *The Spirit of Man:* Great Stories and Experiences of Spiritual Crisis, Inspiration and the Joy of Life by Forty Famous Contemporaries. Ed. Whit Burnett. New York: Hawthorn Press, 1958, pp. 257–265.

From *Das Neue Sein,* Chapter 6, "Heilige Verschwendung" appears in *Freies Christentum* (Frankfurt a. M.), VIII, No. 8 (Aug. 1, 1956), 93–94. Chapters 1 and 15, "'Ihr ist viel vergeben . . .'" and "'Alles ist euer,'" appear in *Radius* (Stuttgart), No. 2 (June, 1957), 16–20.

"Moralisms and Morality from the Point of View of the Ethicist." (Address to the Second Conference on Ministry and Medicine in Human Relations, New York Academy of Medicine. Arden House, Harriman, N.Y., April 18, 1952.) *Ministry and Medicine in Human Relations,* ed. Iago Galdston. New York: International Universities Press, 1955, pp. 125–140.

"Das Neue Sein als Zentralbegriff einer christlichen Theologie." *Eranos-Jahrbuch XXIII* ("Mensch und Wandlung"). Zürich: Rhein, 1955, pp. 251–274.

"Theology and Symbolism." *Religious Symbolism,* ed. F. Ernest Johnson. (Lectures under the auspices of the Institute for Religious and Social Studies of the Jewish Theological Seminary of America, Winter 1952–53.) "Religion and Civilization Series." New York: Institute for Religious and Social Studies—Harper & Brothers, 1955, pp. 107–116.

"Participation and Knowledge: Problems of an Ontology of Cognition." *Sociologica.* Aufsätze, Max Horkheimer zum sechzigsten Geburtstag gewidmet. (Vol. I: "Frankfurter Beiträge zur Soziologie," eds. Theodor W. Adorno and Walter Dirks.) Frankfurt a. M.: Europäische Verlagsanstalt, 1955, pp. 201–209.

"Religion." (A broadcast talk, Nov. 28, 1954: "Religion as an Aspect of the Human Spirit.") *Man's Right to Knowledge.* Second Series: "Present Knowledge and New Directions." New York: Herbert Muschel, Box 800, Grand Central, 1955, pp. 78–83. (A series of lectures in an international symposium on "Tradition and Change," presented by the Columbia Broadcasting System over its radio network in honor of the Bicentennial of Columbia University, 1754–1954.)

Reprinted in *Perspectives USA* (N.Y.), Number 15 (Spring 1956), 43–48. Also appears in British, French, German and Italian editions (Intercultural Publications, Inc., N.Y.): "La religion et l'esprit humain." *Profits* (Paris), Numéro 15 (Printemps 1956), 5–11 (transl. Blaise Allan). "Religion als ein Aspekt des menschlichen Geistes." *Perspektiven* (Frankfurt am Main), Heft 15 (Frühjahr 1956), 45–50 (transl. Gertie Siemsen). "Religione." (Un aspetto dello spirito umano.) *Prospetti* (Florence), Quindicesimo numero (Primavero 1956), 46–51 (transl. Giacomo Vertova).

Reprinted in *The Gadfly* (Great Books Foundation, Chicago), VIII, No. 1 (July–August, 1956), 2–4. Translated as "Der religiöse Aspekt des menschlichen Geistes" in *Wege zum Menschen* (Göttingen), VIII, No. 8 (August, 1956), 232–236.

"Religion and Its Intellectual Critics." (Address in the series of January Lectures for Women, Union Theological Seminary, Jan. 25, 1954.) Abridged in *Christianity and Crisis* (New York), XV, No. 3 (March 7, 1955), 19–22.

Reprinted in *Motive* (Nashville), XV, No. 8 (May, 1955), 28–31. Also in *What the Christian Hopes for in Society.* Cultural Perspectives from Christianity and Crisis. Ed.

Wayne H. Cowan. New York: Association Press "Reflection Books," 1957, pp. 51–65. Excerpts in *The Pulpit* (Chicago), XXVI, No. 5 (May, 1955), 26. Spanish translation, "La Religión y sus Críticos Intelectuales," in *La Nueva Democracia* (New York), XXXVI, No. 1 (January, 1956), 64–73.

"Schelling und die Anfänge des existentialistischen Protestes." (Gedächtsnisfeier zum 100. Todestag von Friedrich Wilhelm Joseph von Schelling am 26. September 1954.) *Zeitschrift für philosophische Forschung* (Meisenheim/Glan), IX, No. 2 (1955), 197–208.

"Psychoanalysis, Existentialism and Theology." (The William Ellery Channing Lecture, Chicago, May 18, 1954.) *Faith and Freedom* (Oxford), IX, Part I, No. 25 (Autumn, 1955), 1–11. Reprinted in *Christian Register* (Boston), CXXXV, No. 3 (March, 1956), 16–17, 34–36. Also in *Pastoral Psychology* (Great Neck, N.Y.), IX, No. 87 (October 1958).

"Das christliche Menschenbild im 20. Jahrhundert." (Vortrag, gehalten bei der Rias-Universität Berlin, 1955.) *Universitas* (Stuttgart), X, No. 9 (September, 1955), 917–920.

"Religious Symbols and Our Knowledge of God." (Address at Shimer College, Mt. Carroll, Ill., and the Northern Illinois Philosophical Club.) *Christian Scholar* (New York), XXXVIII, No. 3 (September, 1955), 189–197.

"Beyond the Dilemma of Our Period." i.e., *The Cambridge Review* (Cambridge, Mass.), No. 4 (November, 1955), 209–215.

"Heal the Sick; Cast Out Demons." (Commencement address to the graduating class of Union Theological Seminary, New York; at Riverside Church, May 24, 1955.) *Union Seminary Quarterly Review* (New York), XI, No. 1 (November, 1955), 3–8. Reprinted in *Religious Education* (New York), L, No. 6 (November–December, 1955), 379–382; and in *A History of Christian Thought,* second edition, 1956, pp. 271–274.

Translated, with "The Eternal Now," by Renate Albrecht: *Das ewige Jetzt. Heilt die Kranken, treibt die Dämonen aus.* Zwei Predigten. Düsseldorf: "Schriftenreihe des Evangelischen Arbeitsausschusses Düsseldorf," No. 8, 1956. Pp. 23. First published in *Das Evangelische Düsseldorf,* No. 84 (February, 1956), 1–3; and No. 85 (March, 1956), 1–3, respectively.

"Theology and Architecture." ("Forum": Round Table on Protestant church architecture.) *Architectural Forum* (New York), CIII, No. 6 (December, 1955), 131–134; discussion, 135–136; photos, 105, 135; illus. Reprinted as "Theology, Architecture and Art" in *Church Management* (Cleveland), XXXIII, No. 1 (October, 1956), 7, 55–56; discussion omitted.

"Comment" on criticisms of Nels F. S. Ferré. *Presbyterian Outlook* (Richmond), CXXXVII, No. 50 (Dec. 26, 1955), 6.

1956

A History of Christian Thought. (Thirty-seven lectures delivered in the Spring Semester, Union Theological Seminary, 1953.) Recorded and edited by Peter H. John. Providence, R.I.: multigraphed by the editor, 87 Prairie Ave. Second edition, 1956. Pp. 309. (Circulation restricted.)

Die Philosophie der Macht. (Zwei Vorträge, gehalten im Juni 1953 an der Deutschen Hochschule für Politik Berlin.) "Schriftenreihe der Deutschen Hochschule für Politik Berlin." Berlin: Colloquium, 1956. Pp. 35.

"Existential Analyses and Religious Symbols." *Contemporary Problems in Religion,* ed. Harold A. Basilius. Detroit: Wayne University Press, 1956, pp. 35–55. (Included in *Four Existentialist Theologians.* A Reader From the Works of Jacques Maritain, Nicolas Berdyaev, Martin Buber, and Paul Tillich. Ed. Will Herberg. Garden City,

N.Y.: Doubleday Anchor Books, No. 141, 1958, pp. 277–291. Cloth edition, pp. 306–322.)

"Existentialist Aspects of Modern Art." *Christianity and the Existentialists*, ed. Carl Michalson. New York: Charles Scribner's Sons, 1956, pp. 128–147; illus. (Section on "Levels of Relation between Religion and Art," pp. 132–144, translated as "Religion und bildende Kunst" in *Quatember* (Kassel), XX, No. 4 (Michaelis, 1956), 198–203. Reprinted in *Reformatio* (Bern), VI, No. 5/6 (May–June, 1957), 264–271.)

Japanese translation by Antei Hiyane: "Kindai Bijutsu no Jitsuzonshugiteki Tokushoku," in *Kirisutokyō to Jitsuzonshugishatachi*. Tokyo: Nippon Kirisutokyōdan Shuppanbu, 1957, pp. 160–182.

"Reinhold Niebuhr's Doctrine of Knowledge." *Reinhold Niebuhr: His Religious, Social, and Political Thought*. ("The Library of Living Theology," Vol. II.) Eds. Charles W. Kegley & Robert W. Bretall. New York: The Macmillan Co., 1956, pp. 36–43.

"Reply" to Nels F. S. Ferré:" Where Do We Go from Here in Theology?" *Religion in Life* (New York), XXV, No. 1 (Winter, 1955–56), 19–21.

"Theology and Counseling." (Lecture delivered at the Fourth Annual Workshop sponsored by the Boston University School of Theology and the Pastoral Counseling Service, Marsh Chapel, Boston University, Nov. 14, 1955.) *Journal of Pastoral Care* (Washington, D.C.), X, No. 4 (Winter, 1956), 193–200.

"Reply" to Gustave Weigel, S.J., "The Theological Significance of Paul Tillich": *Gregorianum* (Rome), XXXVII, No. 1 (1956), 34–53; "reply," 53–54. Reprinted in *Cross Currents* (New York), VI, No. 2 (Spring, 1956), 141–155.

"Reply" to William Rickel, "Is Psychotherapy a Religious Process?" *Pastoral Psychology* (Great Neck, N.Y.), VII, No. 62 (March, 1956), 39–40.

"Letter" to Reinhold Niebuhr on Picasso's "Guernica" and its Protestant significance. *Christianity and Crisis* (New York), XVI, No. 3 (March 5, 1956), 24.

"The Church and Contemporary Culture." (Address to the General Board of the National Council of the Churches of Christ, U.S.A., June 8, 1955.) *World Christian Education* (New York), XI, No. 2 (Second Quarter, 1956), 41–43. Excerpts in *Information Service* (New York), XXXIV, No. 35 (Oct. 29, 1955), 3–4.

"The Christian Consummation: A Conversation." (With Albert T. Mollegen and Nels F. S. Ferré.) *The Chaplain* (Washington, D.C.), XIII, No. 2 (April, 1956), 10–13, 18–19; photo, 11.

"The Beginning of Wisdom." *Pulpit Digest* (Great Neck, N.Y.), XXXVI, No. 218 (June, 1956), 27–31.

"Relation of Metaphysics and Theology." (Address to the Metaphysical Society of America, Fordham University, March 23, 1956.) *Review of Metaphysics* (New Haven), X, No. 1 (September, 1956), 57–63.

"The Nature and the Significance of Existentialist Thought." (Symposium with George Boas and George A. Schrader, Jr.: "Existentialist Thought and Contemporary Philosophy in the West.") *Journal of Philosophy* (New York), LIII, No. 23 (Nov. 8, 1956), 739–748.

1957

Systematic Theology. (Vol. II: "Existence and the Christ.") (The Gifford Lectures, University of Aberdeen, Scotland, 1953.) Chicago: University of Chicago Press, 1957. Pp. xi + 187. London: Nisbet. Pp. xii + 216.

Dynamics of Faith. ("World Perspectives" Series, Vol. X, ed. Ruth Nanda Anshen.) New York: Harper & Brothers, 1957. Pp. xxi + 127. London: George Allen & Unwin. Reprinted, 1958, Harper "Torchbooks," TB 42. Pp. x + 134.)

Selections from Chapter 6 appear as "Faith and the Integration of Personality," in

Pastoral Psychology (Great Neck, N.Y.), VIII, No. 72 (March, 1957), 11–14; "personal message," 13.

"Theology of Education." *The Church School in Our Time.* (Symposium, Oct. 13–14, 1956, in celebration of the One Hundredth Anniversary of St. Paul's School, Concord, N.H.). Concord: St. Paul's School, 1957, pp. 3–14; photos, 79, 80, 81, 85.

"The Word of God." *Language: An Enquiry Into its Meaning and Function,* ed. Ruth Nanda Anshen. (Vol. VIII: "Science of Culture Series.") New York: Harper & Brothers, 1957, pp. 122–133.

"Loneliness and Solitude." *Divinity School News* (University of Chicago), XXIV, No. 2 (May 1, 1957), 1–7. Revised as "Let Us Dare to Have Solitude" in *Union Seminary Quarterly Review* (New York), XII, No. 4 (May, 1957), 9–15.

"Environment and the Individual." (Address delivered before the Centennial Convention of the American Institute of Architects, May 14, 1957.) *Journal of the American Institute of Architects* (Washington, D.C.), XXVIII, No. 2 (June, 1957), 90–92; photo, 90.

"The Dance." (Symposium: "The Dance: What It Means to Me.") *Dance Magazine* (New York), XXXI, No. 6 (June, 1957), 20.

"Discussion" of "The Immortality of Man" by Margaret Mead, in *Pastoral Psychology* (Great Neck, N.Y.), VIII, No. 75 (June, 1957), 17–22; "discussion," 22–24.

"Conformity." (Address delivered at the Commencement Exercises of the New School for Social Research, New York, June 11, 1957.) *Social Research* (New York), XXIV, No. 3 (Autumn, 1957), 354–360.

"Protestantism and the Contemporary Style in the Visual Arts." *Christian Scholar* (New York), XL, No. 4 (December, 1957), 307–311.

1958

"Conversation with Werner Rode." (One of the "Wisdom" series, televised Jan. 1, 1956, as part of NBC Television Special Projects.) *Wisdom.* Conversations with the Elder Wise Men of Our Day. Edited and with an introduction by James Nelson. New York: W. W. Norton & Co., 1958, pp. 163–171.

"The Theology of Pastoral Care." (Address delivered at the National Conference of Clinical Pastoral Education, Atlantic City, Nov 9, 1956.) *Clinical Education for the Pastoral Ministry.* Proceedings of the Fifth National Conference on Clinical Pastoral Education. Eds. Ernest E. Bruder and Marian L. Barb. Washington, D.C.: Advisory Committee on Clinical Pastoral Education (Chap. Ernest E. Bruder, St. Elizabeth's Hospital), 1958, pp. 1–6. (Discussion by James M. Gustafson (pp. 6–8), Earl A. Loomis (pp. 8–11), William B. Oglesby (pp. 12–15.)

"Kairos." *A Handbook of Christian Theology.* Definition Essays on Concepts and Movements of Thought in Contemporary Protestantism. Eds. Marvin Halverson and Arthur A. Cohen. New York: Meridian Books (Living Age Books, No. 18), 1958, pp. 193–197. (Also clothbound.)

"Humanität und Religion." *Hansischer Goethe-Preis 1958.* Gedenkschrift zur Verleihung des Hansischen Goethe-Preis 1958 der gemeinnützigen Stiftung F.V.S. zur Hamburg an Professor D. Dr. Paul Tillich. Hamburg: Stiftung F.V.S., 1958, pp. 25–35; photos, pp. 2, 6, 10, 17, 20, 24.

"Do Not Be Conformed." *Pulpit Digest* (Great Neck, N.Y.), XXXVIII, No. 237 (January, 1958), 19–24. Revised in *A History of Christian Thought,* second edition, 1956, pp. 255–259. Abridged and translated as "Seid keine Konformisten!" in *Aufbau/Reconstruction* (New York), XXII, No. 13, "Der Zeitgeist" No. 39 (March 30, 1956), 15–16.

"God's Pursuit of Man." *Alumni Bulletin of Bangor Theological Seminary* (Bangor, Maine), XXXIII, No. 2 (April, 1958), 21–25.

"The Riddle of Inequality." *Union Seminary Quarterly Review* (New York), XIII, No. 4 (May, 1958), 3–9.

"Beyond the Usual Alternatives." (Third in a series on "Prospects and Portents.") *Christian Century* (Chicago), LXXV, No. 19 (May 7, 1958), 553–555. (German translation in *Zeitwende* (Hamburg), XXIX, No. 9 (September, 1958), 617–620. Slightly abridged.)

"Freedom and the Ultimate Concern." (Lecture delivered in the Seminar on Religion and the Free Society, May 9, 1958, World Affairs Center, New York; sponsored by the Fund for the Republic.) *Religion in America:* Original Essays on Religion in a Free Society. Ed. John Cogley. Meridian Books (M60), 1958, pp. 272–286. (Cloth and paperback editions.)

"The Lost Dimension in Religion." (Sixth in a series on "Adventures of the Mind.") *Saturday Evening Post* (Philadelphia), 230, No. 50 (June 14, 1958), 29, 76, 78–79; photo, 28.

Contribution to "Theologians and the Moon," *Christianity Today*, III, No. 1 (Oct. 13, 1958), 31.

1959

"Is a Science of Human Values Possible?" (Address to the Research Society for Creative Altruism, Oct. 5, 1957, Massachusetts Institute of Technology.) *New Knowledge in Human Values,* ed. Abraham H. Maslow. New York: Harper & Brothers, 1958, pp. 189–96.

Theology and Culture. Essays by Paul Tillich. Ed. Robert C. Kimball. New York: Oxford University Press. In preparation.

Contents: I. *Basic Considerations.* 1. "Religion as a Dimension in Man's Spiritual Life" (1955). 2. "The Two Types of Philosophy of Religion" (1946). 3. "The Struggle of Time and Space" (heretofore unpublished). 4. "Aspects of a Religious Analysis of Culture" (1956). II. *Concrete Applications.* (5) "The Nature of Religious Language" (1955). 6. "Protestantism and Artistic Style" (1957). 7. "Existential Philosophy: Its Historical Meaning" (1944). 8. "The Theological Significance of Existentialism and Psychoanalysis" (1955). 9. "Science and Theology: A Discussion with Einstein" (1940). 10. "Moralisms and Morality: Theonomous Ethics" (1955). 11. "A Theology of Education" (1957). III. *Cultural Comparisons.* 12. "The Conquest of Intellectual Provincialism: Europe and America" (1953). 13. "Religion in Two Societies: America and Russia" (1954). 14. "An Evaluation of Martin Buber: Protestant and Jewish Thought" (1948). IV. *Conclusion.* 15. "Communicating the Christian Message: A Question to Christian Ministers and Teachers" (1952).

"The Marxist View of History: A Study in the History of the Philosophy of History." *Culture and History: Essays Presented to Paul Radin.* Ed. Stanley Diamond. New York: Columbia University Press. (In preparation, title tentative.)

LITERARY CRITIQUES, REVIEWS, PREFACES

"Revolution und Kirche." (Critique of *Revolution und Kirche;* Zur Neuordnung des Kirchenwesens im deutschen Volksstaat, by Friedrich W. K. Thimme and Ernst Rolffs.) *Das neue Deutschland* (Gotha), VII, No. 20 (July 15, 1919), 394–397.

"Religiöser Stil und religiöser Stoff in der bildenden Kunst." (Critique of *Die deutsche expressionistische Kultur und Malerei,* by Eckart von Sydow, and *Kunst und Religion;* Ein Versuch über die Möglichkeit neuer religiöser Kunst, by G. F. Hartlaub.) *Ibid.,* IX, No. 9/12 (February–March, 1921), 151–158.

Emanuel Hirsch: *Die Reich-Gottes-Begriffe des neueren europäischen Denkens.* Ein Versuch zur Geschichte der Staats- und Gesellschafts-Philosophie. *Theologische Blätter* (Leipzig), I, No. 2 (February, 1922), 42–43.

Ludwig Bendix: *Die Neuordnung des Strafverfahrens. Kant-Studien* (Berlin), XXVII, No. 1–2 (1922), 203–205.

Emanuel Hirsch: *Der Sinn des Gebets. Theologische Blätter* (Leipzig), I, No. 6 (June, 1922), 137–138.

Theodor Birt: *Von Homer bis Sokrates.* Ein Buch über die alten Griechen. *Theologische Literaturzeitung* (Leipzig), XLVII, No. 15 (July 29, 1922), 349.

Helmut Hatzfeld: *Dante. Seine Weltanschauung.* Joseph Mausbach: *Der Geist Dantes und seine Kulturausgaben.* Ernst Troeltsch: *Der Berg der Läuterung.* (Rede zur Erinnerung an den 600. jährigen Todestag Dantes, gehalten im Auftrage d. Ausschusses für eine deutsche Dantefeier am 3. Juli 1921 i. d. Staatsoper z. Berlin.) *Ibid.,* 350.

"Holls Lutherbuch." (Karl Holl: *Gesammelte Aufsätze zur Kirchengeschichte.* Bd. I. Luther.) *Vossische Zeitung* (Berlin), No. 381, "Literarische Umschau" No. 33 (Aug. 13, 1922), 1.

Joseph Geyser: *Neue und alte Wege der Philosophie.* Eine Erörterung der Grundlagen der Erkenntnis im Hinblick auf Edmund Husserls Versuch ihrer Neubegründung. *Theologische Literaturzeitung* (Leipzig), XLVII, No. 16–17 (Aug. 26, 1922), 380–381.

Paul Feldkeller: *Graf Keyserlings Bekenntnisweg zum Übersinnlichen.* Die Erkenntnisgrundlagen des Reisetagebuchs eines Philosophen. *Theologische Blätter* (Leipzig), I, No. 9 (September, 1922), 210–211.

Eduard Spranger: *Der gegenwärtige Stand der Geisteswissenschaften und die Schule. Ibid.,* No. 10 (October, 1922), 235.

Rudolf Stammler: *Lehrbuch der Rechtsphilosophie. Theologische Literaturzeitung* (Leipzig), XLVII, No. 20 (Oct. 7, 1922), 417–420.

Werner Leopold: *Die religiöse Wurzel von Carlyles literarischer Wirksamkeit.* (Dargestellt an seinem Aufsatz "State of German Literature.") *Ibid.,* 433.

A. v. Gleichen-Russwurm: *Philosophische Profile.* Erinnerungen und Wertungen. *Ibid.,* No. 22 (Nov. 4, 1922), 478.

Heinrich Eildermann: *Urkommunismus und Urreligion,* geschichtsmaterialistisch beleuchtet. *Archiv für Sozialwissenschaft und Sozialpolitik* (Tübingen), L, No. 1 (1923), 247–248.

Ernst Lohmeyer: *Soziale Fragen im Urchristentum. Ibid.,* 250.

Emil Walter Mayer: *Ethik (Christliche Sittenlehre). Theologische Blätter* (Leipzig), II, No. 1 (January, 1923), 16–17.

Kurt Leese: *Die Geschichtsphilosophie Hegels* auf Grund der neuerschlossenen Quellen untersucht und dargestellt. *Ibid.,* No. 3 (March, 1923), 72–73.

Hermann Schwarz: *Das Ungegebene.* Eine Religions- und Wertphilosophie. *Ibid.,* 73–74.

Ditlef Nielsen: *Der dreieinige Gott in religionsgeschichtlicher Beleuchtung.* (Vol. I: Die drei göttlichen Personen.) *Vossische Zeitung* (Berlin), No. 201, "Literarische Umschau" No. 17 (April 29, 1923), 1.

Ernst Horneffer: *Der junge Platon.* Erster Teil: Sokrates und die Apologie. *Kant-Studien* (Berlin), XXVIII, No. 3/4 (1923), 437.

Ernst Troeltsch: *Der Historismus und seine Probleme.* (Vol. I: Das logische Problem der Geschichtsphilosophie.) *Theologische Literaturzeitung* (Leipzig), XLIX, No. 2 (Jan. 26, 1924), 25–30.

"Probleme des Mythos." (Ernst Cassirer: "Die Begriffsform im mythischen Denken," in *Studien der Bibliothek Warburg.* Artur Liebert: "Mythos und Kultur," in *Kant-Studien* (Berlin), XVII, No. 3/4, 1922.) *Ibid.,* No. 6 (March 22, 1924), 115–117.

Ernst Troeltsch: *Der Historismus und seine Überwindung. Ibid.,* No. 11 (May 31, 1924), 234–235.

Günther Dehn: *Ich bin der Herr dein Gott!* (Zwölf "religiös-soziale" Reden.)

Theologe und Christ. Erinnerungen und Bekenntnisse von Martin Kähler. Ed. Anna Kähler. Berlin: Furche-Verlag, 1926, p. 384.

"Religiöse Gestalten." (Gerhard Ritter: *Martin Luther. Gestalt und Symbol.* Martin Lamm: *Swedenborg. Eine Studie über seine Entwicklung zum Mystiker und Geisterseher.* Swedenborg: *Himmel und Hölle,* beschrieben nach Gehörtem und Gesehenem von Emmanuel Swedenborg. Karl Müller, ed.: *Der Weg des Mathäus Stach.* Ein Lebensbild des ersten Grönlandmissionars der Brüdergemeinde. Eugen Jäckh: *Blumhardt Vater und Sohn* und ihre Botschaft. R. Lejeune, ed.: *Christof Blumhardt, Predigten und Andachten.* Christof Blumhardt, Hausandachten für alle Tage des Jahres, 2nd ed. Anna Kähler, ed.: *Theologe und Christ. Erinnerungen und Bekenntnisse von Martin Kähler.* Erich Stange, ed.: *Die Religionswissenschaft der Gegenwart.* Hans Prager: *Die Weltanschauung Dostojewskis.)* *Vossische Zeitung* (Berlin), No. 52, "Literarische Umschau" No. 4 (Jan. 31, 1926).

Wilhelm Diltheys gesammelte Schriften. (Vol. 5–6: *Die geistige Welt.* Einleitung in die Philosophie des Lebens. Erste Hälfte: Abhandlungen zur Grundlegung des Geisteswissenschaften. Zweite Hälfte: Abhandlungen zur Poetik, Ethik und Pädagogik.) *Theologische Literaturzeitung* (Leipzig), LI, No. 6 (March 20, 1926), 148–150.

"Das religiöse Erlebnis. Neue religionsphilosophische Schriften." (Paul Hoffmann: *Das religiöse Erlebnis, seine Struktur, seine Typen und sein Wahrheitsanspruch.* Johann Peter Steffes: *Religionsphilosophie.* Emil Mattiesen: *Der jenseitige Mensch.* Eine Einführung in die Metapsychologie der mystischen Erfahrung. E. Baerwald, ed.: *Zeitschrift für kritischen Okkultismus und Grenzfragen des Seelenleben.)* *Vossische Zeitung* (Berlin), No. 324, "Literarische Umschau" No. 27 (July 11, 1926), 1–2.

"Die religiöse Lage der Gegenwart. Um die Idee des Christentums." (Adolf Faut: *Romantik oder Reformation.* Eine Wertung der religiösen Kräfte der Gegenwart. Willy Lüttge: *Das Christentum in unserer Kultur.* A. F. Stolzenburg: *Anthroposophie und Christentum.* Heinrich Hermelink: *Katholizismus und Protestantismus in der Gegenwart.* Gertrud Bäumer: *Die seelische Krisis.* Nicolas Arseniew: *Ostkirche und Mystik.* W. Heinsius: *Krisen katholischer Frömmigkeit und Konversionen zum Protestantismus.* Charles S. Macfarland: *Die internationalen christlichen Bewegungen,* amerikanisch gesehen.) *Vossische Zeitung,* No. 480, "Literarische Umschau" No. 40 (Oct. 10, 1926), 2.

"Christentum und Idealismus. Zum Verständnis der Diskussionslage." (Critical study of Friedrich Brunstäd, *Die Idee der Religion;* Emil Brunner, *Philosophie und Offenbarung;* Wilhelm Lütgert, *Die Religion des deutschen Idealismus und ihr Ende;* and Emanuel Hirsch, *Die idealistische Philosophie und das Christentum.)* *Theologische Blätter* (Leipzig), VI, No. 2 (February, 1927), 29–40.

"Kirchengeschichte und Neues Testament." (Paul Wernle: *Der schweizerische Protestantismus im 18. Jahrhundert.* F. X. Kiefl: *Leibniz und die religiöse Wiedervereinigung Deutschlands.* E. Buchner: *Religion und Kirche.* Kulturhistorisch interessante Dokumente. J. Schlosser: *Vom inneren Licht. Die Quäker.* O. Holtzmann, trans.: *Das Neue Testament.* G. Brandes: *Die Jesus-Sage.* Bauer-Bertholet-Ködderitz-Krohn: *Der Christus.)* *Vossische Zeitung* (Berlin), No. 274, "Literarische Umschau" No. 24 (June 12, 1927).

"Noch einmal: Christentum und Idealismus." (Helmut Groos: *Der deutsche Idealismus und das Christentum.* Versuch einer vergleichenden Phänomenologie.) *Theologische Blätter* (Leipzig), VI, No. 7 (July, 1927), 196–198.

Hans Wilhelm Schmidt: *Zeit und Ewigkeit.* Die letzten Voraussetzungen der dialektischen Theologie. *Ibid.,* No. 8 (August, 1927), 234–235.

"Hendrik de Man: Zur Psychologie des Sozialismus." *Blätter für Religiösen Sozialismus* (Leipzig), VIII, No. 5/6 (October, 1927), 21–25.

Gerhard Heinzelmann: *Glaube und Mystik. Theologische Literaturzeitung* (Leipzig), LII, No. 25–26 (Dec. 17, 1927), 597–598.

"Kritisches zum Christentum." (Georg Brandes: *Urchristentum.* Ernst Barnikol: *Das entdeckte Christentum im Vormärz.* Bruno Bauers Kampf gegen Religion und Christentum und Erstausgabe seiner Kampfschrift.) *Vossische Zeitung* (Berlin), No. 97, "Literarische Umschau" No. 9 (Feb. 26, 1928), 1–2.

"Mythos und Geschichte." (Emil Ludwigs *"Menschensohn." Vossische Zeitung,* No. 219, "Das Unterhaltungsblatt" No. 109 (May 10, 1928), 1–2.

Eugen Rosenstock and Josef Wittig: *Das Alter der Kirche. Vossische Zeitung,* No. 259, "Literarische Umschau" No. 23, June 3, 1928.

"Kritisches zum Christentum." (Kaevels: *Expressionismus und Religion.* H. Frick: *Wissenschaftliches und pneumatisches Verständnis der Bibel.* K. Müller: *Die Forderung der Ehelosigkeit für alle Getauften in der alten Kirche.* L. Köhler: *Das formgeschichtliche Problem des Neuen Testaments.*) *Vossische Zeitung,* No. 343, "Literarische Umschau" No. 30, (July 22, 1928).

"Die Selbstverwirklichung. Das neue Buch von Richard Kroner." *Dresdner neueste Nachrichten,* No. 171 (July 24, 1928), 2. Cf. also Richard Kroner: *Die Selbstverwirklichung des Geistes.* Prolegomena zur Kulturphilosophie. *Vossische Zeitung,* No. 46, "Literarische Umschau" No. 5, (Jan. 27, 1929).

"Zur Geschichte des Christentums." (L. Feiler: *Die Entstehung des Christentums aus dem Geiste des magischen Denkens.* W. Michaelis: *Täufer Jesus Urgemeinde.* K. Völker: *Mysterium und Agape.* K. Holl: *Gesammelte Aufsätze zur Kirchengeschichte II.*) *Vossische Zeitung,* No. 376, "Literarische Umschau" No. 32 (Aug. 5, 1928).

"Zur Geschichte des Christentums. Von Savonarola bis Luther." (Robert Jelke: *Das Erbe Martin Luthers und die gegenwärtige theologische Forschung.* Josef Schnitzer: *Hieronymus Savonarola. Auswahl aus seinen Schriften und Predigten.* Franz Strunz: *Johannes Hus. Sein Leben und sein Werk.* Friedrich Gogarten: *Martin Luthers Predigten.* Theologische Studien und Kritiken: *Lutherana V. Fünftes Lutherheft.* Hartmann Grisar, S.J.: *Martin Luthers Leben und sein Werk.* Zusammenfassend dargestellt.) *Vossische Zeitung,* No. 427, "Literarische Umschau" No. 37 (Sept. 9, 1928), 2–3.

"Zur neuen Religionsgeschichte." (Fritz Blanke: *J. G. Hamann als Theologe.* Hans R. G. Günther: *Jung-Stilling.* Ein Beitrag zur Psychologie des deutschen Pietismus. Arnold Gilg: *Sören Kierkegaard.* Christian Schrempf: *Sören Kierkegaard. Eine Biographie.* G. Schenkel: *Die Freimaurerei im Lichte der Religions- und Kirchengeschichte.* Will-Erich Peuckert: *Die Rosenkreuzer.* Zur Geschichte einer Reformation.) *Vossische Zeitung,* No. 499, "Literarische Umschau" No. 43 (Oct. 21, 1928), 3.

Walter von Molo: *Mensch Luther. Vossische Zeitung,* No. 535, "Literarische Umschau" No. 46 (Nov. 11, 1928), 2.

"Ideologie und Utopie." (Critique of Karl Mannheim: *Ideologie und Utopie.*) *Die Gesellschaft* (Berlin), VI, No. 10 (October, 1929), 348–355.

Theodor Wiesengrund-Adorno: *Kierkegaard. Konstruktion des Ästhetischen. Journal of Philosophy* (New York), XXXI, No. 23 (Nov. 8, 1934), 640.

Emil Brunner: *The Mediator.* A Study of the Central Doctrine of the Christian Faith. *Christian Century* (Chicago), LI, No. 49 (Dec. 5, 1934), 1554–1556. Translated by A. C. McGiffert, Jr.

Fedor Stepun: *The Russian Soul and Revolution. Christendom* (New York), I, No. 2 (Winter, 1936), 366–367.

Henry Nelson Wieman and Walter Marshall Horton: *The Growth of Religion. Journal of Religion* (Chicago), XX, No. 1 (January, 1940), 69–72.

Johannes Hessen: *Platonismus und Prophetismus. Anglican Theological Review* (Evanston), XXIII, No. 1 (January, 1941), 82–83.

Reinhold Niebuhr: *The Nature and Destiny of Man.* (Vol. I: Human Nature.) *Christianity and Society* (New York), VI, No. 2 (Spring, 1941), 34–37.

"Existential Thinking in American Theology." (Critique of H. Richard Niebuhr: *The Meaning of Revelation.*) *Religion in Life* (New York), X, No. 3 (Summer, 1941), 452–455.

Herbert Marcuse: *Reason and Revolution.* Hegel and the Rise of Social Theory. *Studies in Philosophy and Social Science* (New York), IX, No. 3 (1941–42), 476–478.

Raymond B. Blakney: *Meister Eckhart: A Modern Translation. Religion in Life* (New York), XI, No. 4 (Autumn, 1942), 625–626.

Jacques Maritain: *The Rights of Man and Natural Law. Religion in Life,* XIII, No. 3 (Summer, 1944), 465–466.

Nicolas Berdyaev: *Slavery and Freedom. Theology Today* (Princeton), II, No. 1 (April, 1945), 130–132.

"Christianity without Paul." (George Santayana: *The Idea of Christ in the Gospels or God in Man.* A Critical Essay.) *The Nation* (New York), CLXIII, No. 15 (Oct. 12, 1946), 412–413.

Emil Brunner: *Revelation and Reason. Westminster Bookman* (Philadelphia), VI, No. 3 (January–February, 1947), 5–7.

Arthur Koestler: *The Yogi and the Commissar. Journal of Religion* (Chicago), XXVII, No. 2 (April, 1947), 135–136.

John C. Bennett: *Christianity and Communism. Union Seminary Quarterly Review* (New York), IV, No. 2 (January, 1949), 41–42.

David E. Roberts: *Psychotherapy and a Christian View of Man. Pastoral Psychology* (Great Neck, N.Y.), I, No. 8 (November, 1950), 61–64. Abridged, *ibid.,* II, No. 18 (November, 1951), 60–62.

Erich Fromm: *Psychoanalysis and Religion. Pastoral Psychology,* II, No. 15 (June, 1951), 62–66.

Helmut Thielicke: *Theologische Ethik.* (I: Dogmatische, philosophische, und kontroverstheologische Grundlegung.) *Anglican Theological Review* (Evanston), XXXV, No. 1 (January, 1953), 64–65.

"Foreword" to John Dillenberger: *God Hidden and Revealed.* Philadelphia: Muhlenberg Press, 1953, pp. vii–viii.

"Introduction" to David E. Roberts: *The Grandeur and Misery of Man.* New York: Oxford University Press, 1955, pp. v–viii. Reprinted in *Union Seminary Quarterly Review* (New York), XI, No. 1 (November, 1955), 51, 53; *Christianity and Crisis* (New York), XV, No. 19 (Nov. 14, 1955), 149; *Pastoral Psychology* (Great Neck, N.Y.), VI, No. 59 (December, 1955), 12–13.

"Erich Fromm's *The Sane Society.*" *Pastoral Psychology,* VI, No. 56 (September, 1955), 13, 16.

"Preface" to John Joseph Stoudt: *Sunrise to Eternity. A Study in Jacob Boehme's Life and Thought.* Philadelphia: University of Pennsylvania Press, 1957, pp. 7–8.

James Luther Adams, Professor of Christian Ethics, Harvard Divinity School, Cambridge, Mass.
Publications: *Taking Time Seriously,* "The Law of Nature in Greco-Roman Thought," "The Political Responsibility of the Man of Culture," "Authority and Freedom," "The Meaning of Love."

Karl Barth, Professor of Theology, University of Basel, Basel, Switzerland.
Publications: *The Epistle to the Romans, The Resurrection of the Dead, Die Theologie und die Kirche, Credo, The Church and the War, Against the Stream, Church and State, Church Dogmatics I–IV* (vols. I and II being translated into English), *Come, Holy Spirit, Dogmatics in Outline, The Holy Ghost and the Christian Life, The Word of God and the Word of Man.*

John C. Bennett, Professor of Christian Ethics, Union Theological Seminary, New York, N.Y.
Publications: *Christianity and our World, Christianity and Communism, Christian Values and Economic Life, Christian Realism, The Christian as Citizen, Christian Ethics and Social Policy, The Crisis in Human Affairs.*

Heinrich Bornkamm, Professor of Church History, University of Heidelberg, Heidelberg, Germany.
Publications: *Luthers geistige Welt, Luther und das Alte Testament, Luther und Boehme, Luther im Spiegel der Deutschen Geistesgeschichte, Imago Dei, Beiträge zur Theologischen Anthropologie.*

Emil Brunner, Professor of Theology, University of Zurich, Zurich, Switzerland.
Publications: *Revelation and Reason, Gerechtigkeit, Man in Revolt, Christianity and Civilization, The Divine-Human Encounter, The Divine Imperative, Dogmatics I–II, Eternal Hope, The Mediator, Faith, Hope and Love, God and Man, The Great Invitation, Justice and the Social Order, Die Kirche Zwischen Ost und West, The Misunderstanding of the Church, Die Mystik und das Wort, Natur und Gnade, Our Faith, The Philosophy of Religion, The Scandal of Christianity, Der Staat als Problem der Kirche, The Theology of Crisis, Vom Werk des Heiligen Geistes, Das Wort Gottes und der moderne Mensch.*

Rudolf Bultmann, Professor of New Testament, University of Marburg, Marburg, Germany.
Publications: *Die Erforschung der synoptischen Evangelien, Das Evangelium des Johannes, Glaube und Verstehen, History and Eschatology, Jesus, Kerygma and Myth, Primitive Christianity in its Contemporary Setting, Theology of the New Testament I–II, Essays: Philosophical and Theological, Gnosis, Jesus and the Word.*

Nels F. S. Ferré, Professor of Theology, Andover Newton Theological School, Newton, Mass.
Publications: *Swedish Contributions to Modern Theology, Faith and Reason, Evil and*

397

*the Christian Faith, Christian Faith and Higher Education, Christ and
the Christian, The Christian Faith, an Inquiry into its Adequacy as Men's
Ultimate Religion, the Christian Fellowship, The Christian Understanding of God, Christianity and Society, Making Religion Real, Reason and
the Christian Faith I–II, Return to Christianity.*

Georges Florovsky, Professor of Eastern Orthodox Church History, Harvard Divinity
School, Cambridge Mass.
Publications: *Eastern Fathers of the Fourth Century, Byzantine Fathers of the Fifth–
Eighth Centuries, The Ways of Russian Theology,* "The Challenge of
Disunity," "Faith and Culture."

Erich Fromm, Professor of Psychology, University of Mexico, Mexico City, Mexico.
Publications: *Escape from Freedom, Man for Himself, Psychoanalysis and Religion,
The Sane Society, The Art of Loving, The Forgotten Language.*

Charles Hartshorne, Professor of Philosophy, Emory University, Atlanta, Georgia.
Publications: *The Philosophy and Psychology of Sensation, Beyond Humanism, Man's
Vision of God, Reality as Social Process, Philosophers Speak of God*
(coauthor), *The Divine Relativity.*

Karl Heim, Professor of Theology, University of Tübingen, Tübingen, Germany.
Publications: *Die Christliche Ethik, Die Gemeinde des Auferstandenen, Glaube und
Denken, Christian Faith and Natural Science, The New Divine Order,
The Power of God, The Transformation of the Scientific World View,
The Church of Christ and the Problems of the Day, Glaubensgewissheit,
Das Wesen des Evangelischen Christentums, Weltschöpfung und Wel-
tende.*

Stanley Romaine Hopper, Professor of Christian Philosophy and Letters and Dean of
the Graduate School, Drew University, Madison, New Jersey.
Publications: *The Crisis of Faith, Spiritual Problems in Contemporary Literature* (ed.),
*Exposition of the Book of Jeremiah, The Christian Faith and the Tragic
Vision* (ed.).

Karl Jaspers, Professor of Philosophy, University of Basel, Basel, Switzerland.
Publications: *Allgemeine Psychopathologie, Psychologie der Weltanschauung, Philosophie I–III, Nietzsche, Von der Wahrheit, The European Spirit, Existentialism and Humanism, The Origin and Goal of History, Reason and
Existenz, Die Frage der Entmythologisierung, Die geistige Situation der
Zeit, Man in the Modern Age, The Perennial Scope of Philosophy, Der
philosophische Glaube.*

Kurt Leese, Professor of the Philosophy of Religion, University of Hamburg, Hamburg, Germany.
Publications: *Die Religion des protestantischen Menschen, Recht und Grenze der
natürlichen Religion, Ethische und religiöse Grundfragen im Denken der
Gegenwart, Geistesmächte und Seinsgewalten, Die Krisis und Wende des
christlichen Geistes, Moderne Theosophie, Die Religionskrisis des Abend-
landes und die religiöse Lage der Gegenwart.*

Paul L. Lehmann, Professor of Theology, Harvard Divinity School, Cambridge, Mass.
Publications: *Forgiveness,* "The Antipelagian Writings," "The Christology of Reinhold
Niebuhr," "The Changing Course of a Corrective Theology."

Walter Leibrecht, Director of the Evanston Institute of Ecumenical Studies, Evanston, Illinois
Publications: *Gott und Mensch bei Johann Georg Hamann,* "Philologia Crucis."

Karl Loewith, Professor of Philosophy, University of Heidelberg; formerly at the University of California
Publications: *Kierkegaard und Nietzsche, Von Hegel bis Nietzsche, Meaning in History.*

Charles Malik, President of the United Nations' General Assembly; Professor of Philosophy, University of Beirut
Publications: *War and Peace, The Problem of Asia.*

Gabriel Marcel, French philosopher and writer, Paris, France.
Publications: *The Metaphysical Journal, Being and Having, Homo Viator, The Decline of Wisdom, Men against Humanity, The Mystery of Being I–II, The Philosophy of Existence.*

Reinhold Niebuhr, Graduate Professor of Ethics and Theology; Vice-President, Union Theological Seminary, New York, N.Y.; Institute of Advanced Study, Princeton, 1958.
Publications: *The Nature and Destiny of Man I–II, Beyond Tragedy, Faith and History, Moral Man and Immoral Society, The Irony of American History, The Self and the Dramas of History, The Children of Light and the Children of Darkness, Christian Realism and Political Problems, Christianity and Power Politics, Discerning the Signs of the Times, Does Civilization Need Religion?, An Interpretation of Christian Ethics, Leaves from the Notebook of a Tamed Cynic, Love and Justice, Reflections on the End of an Era.*

Wilhelm Pauck, Professor of Church History, Union Theological Seminary: Adjunct Professor, Department of Religion, Columbia University, New York, N.Y.
Publications: *Karl Barth—Prophet of a New Christianity, The Church against the World, The Heritage of the Reformation, Das Reich Gottes auf Erden.*

Erich Przywara, S.J., Professor of Theology, University of Munich, Munich, Germany.
Publications: *Augustinus, Gott; Fünf Vorträge über das religionsphilosophische Problem, Alter und neuer Bund, Polarity, An Augustine Synthesis, Gott geheimnis der Welt, Humanitas; der Mensch gestern und morgen, Ringen der Gegenwart I–II.*

Yoshinori Takeuchi, Professor of Philosophy, University of Kyoto, Kyoto, Japan.
Publications: Books and articles in Japanese on the philosophical interpretation of Buddhism.

Helmut Thielicke, Professor of Theology, University of Hamburg
Publications: *Fragen des Christentums an die moderne Welt, Der Glaube der Christenheit, Die Lebensangst und ihre Überwindung, Der Nihilismus, Theologische Ethik I–II, Christliche Verantwortung im Atomzeitalter, Offenbarung, Vernunft und Existenz, Theologie der Anfechtung, Tod und Leben, Zwischen Gott und Satan.*

Gustave Weigel, S.J., Professor of Theology, Woodstock College, Woodstock, Md.
Publications: *Faustus of Riez, Psicologia de la Religion, A Survey of Protestant Theology in our Time, Contemporaneous Protestantism and Paul Tillich,* "The Theological Significance of Paul Tillich."